ROUTLEDGE LIBRARY EDITIONS: ETHNOSCAPES

Volume 1

ENVIRONMENTAL PERSPECTIVES

ENVIRONMENTAL PERSPECTIVES

Edited by
DAVID CANTER,
MARTIN KRAMPEN
AND
DAVID STEA

Routledge
Taylor & Francis Group

LONDON AND NEW YORK

First published in 1988 by Avebury (Gower Publishing Co. Ltd)

This edition first published in 2025
by Routledge
4 Park Square, Milton Park, Abingdon, Oxon OX14 4RN

and by Routledge
605 Third Avenue, New York, NY 10158

Routledge is an imprint of the Taylor & Francis Group, an informa business

British Library Cataloguing in Publication Data
A catalogue record for this book is available from the British Library

ISBN: 978-1-032-86590-4 (Set)
ISBN: 978-1-032-81616-6 (Volume 1) (hbk)
ISBN: 978-1-032-81622-7 (Volume 1) (pbk)
ISBN: 978-1-003-50058-2 (Volume 1) (ebk)

DOI: 10.4324/9781003500582

Publisher's Note
The publisher has gone to great lengths to ensure the quality of this reprint but points out that some imperfections in the original copies may be apparent.

Disclaimer
The publisher has made every effort to trace copyright holders and would welcome correspondence from those they have been unable to trace.

New Series Introduction to
RLE: Ethnoscapes

The neologism *Ethnoscapes*[1] was created by David Canter and David Stea in 1987 when they happened both to be in Yogjakarta at the same time. They wanted a term to cover the rapidly emerging multidisciplinary field of research into many aspects of how individuals, groups and cultures interact and transact with their surroundings. It was derived as follows:

Ethno (combining form) indicating race, people or culture.

Scape (suffix-forming nouns) indicating a scene or view of something.

Ethnoscapes (plural noun) Scholarly and/or scientific explorations of the relationships people and their activities, have with the places they create and/or inhabit; historical, psychological, anthropological, sociological, and related disciplines that study the experiences of places, attitudes towards them, or the processes of shaping, managing, or designing them. The term was subsequently used to provide an umbrella for a series of books. These cover topics that are so multidisciplinary that they do not sit comfortably in any of the constrained silos of academic and scholarly research. As indicated on the opening page of the first book in the series, many disciplines "have developed marauding sub-groups who move freely across each others' borders, carrying ideas almost like contraband, without declaring that they have crossed any disciplinary boundaries."

They include domains labelled as Behavioural or Perceptual Geography, Environmental/Architectural Psychology, Urban History, Social Ecology, Behavioural Archaeology, Urban Planning, Behavioural Architecture, and Landscape Architecture. There are also many other areas of research and practice that, whilst not being overtly psychological, social, or cultural, do explore and act on the built and natural environment in a way that recognises the importance of the human transactions with those settings. These professions include interior and product design, comparative linguistics, and even aspects of criminology and mental health providers.

Like all such implicit and explicit transactions between different domains, a community of interest and support has emerged in which those who cross the boundaries often find they have more in common with other transgressors than with their mother disciplines. This has given rise to common means and forms of communication, with a shared understanding of the issues and approaches that are of value. Although, of course, these are not always understood in the same way by all those involved,

The *Ethnoscapes* series of books provides a forum for these multifarious, cross-disciplinary, determinedly international, studies and practices. Each of the books takes on board one or more of the environmental challenges that that individuals, societies and cultures are facing. Emphasising a social perspective, rather than the dominant 'hard' science viewpoints embedded in physical, geological and climate changes.

It may now be regarded as rather prescient that it was over three decades ago that the need and importance was recognised of bringing together the many strands of environmental social research and practice. But there is no doubt that there were academics and professionals exploring Ethnoscape topics, going back to the 1960s, often in isolation and with little recognition, that are today front-page, and podcast, news. The challenges in the environmental social sciences that Ethnoscapes explores are just as pertinent now as they were when initially identified.

The series, in essence, deals with four challenges the environmental social sciences embrace.

1. Addressing "the awareness of governments and public alike of the problems of environmental degradation and pollution."

This includes the challenge of providing acceptable housing and related environmental conditions that also encompassed the support for environmental and related cultural heritage. It also requires detailed consideration of the assessment and evaluation of designs and design proposals as well as background research on policy related issues.

2. Developing ways of conceptualising human interactions with the physical surroundings.

This may seem somewhat abstract but has practical implications. The dominant view that people are passively controlled by their surroundings supports a paternalistic, management of what it is assumed people need. That ignores the active way in which people make sense of their environment, drawing on cultural and historical influences. This recognises the importance of user participation in decisions about built and natural settings. That, in turn, requires a much richer understanding of how people interact with where they are or want to be.

3. A much wider range of ways of exploring people's transactions with the environment is needed to contribute to policy and practice as well as developing richer insights into human experiences.

The stock in trade of surveys, or the inevitably artificial laboratory-based experiments, whilst of value for some explorations, need to be augmented by methodologies that enrich an understanding of what the experiences are of being in, acting on, and developing places. They need to connect not just with the endeavours of individuals but also with how cultures and societies express these transactions.

4. Finding ways to enable practitioners and researchers to express their own encounters with the contexts they are influencing or studying.

Much of the research that is carried out in what are curiously called 'Ivory Towers', even when it is studying the big wide world, allows the pretence of distancing from the direct experiences of the issues being studied. Yet the challenges of moving across disciplinary boundaries are as much personal challenges of finding new ways of thinking, communicating, and acting, as an academic demand to develop more effective intellectual systems. The Ethnoscapes series recognises the value of exploring these challenges by hosting a variety of formats. Many of these go beyond the staid and limited formulations that academic discourse assumes to be the norms.

The Ethnoscapes series brings together a vibrant mix of cutting-edge explorations, from all over the world, of human transactions with the built and natural environments. This includes, for example, consideration of vernacular architecture that contrasts with the architecture and urbanism of the colonial enterprise, the meaning of home, aesthetics, well-being and health, and consideration of how environmental psychology has become 'green'. All of these topics, and more, provide an exciting basis for dealing with current challenges in the environmental social sciences.

Note

[1] Not to be confused by the term *Ethnoscape* later concocted by Arun Appadurai in 1990, to refer to **human migration**, the flow of people across boundaries. This includes migrants, refugees, exiles, and tourists, among other moving individuals and groups, all of whom appear to affect the politics of (and between) nations to a considerable degree. Ignorant of the lexicographical origins of the term 'scape' he rather confusingly added it to many ideas of flow, such as the flow of technology – technoscapes and the flow of ideas ideoscapes. Appadurai, A. (1990). "Disjuncture and difference in the global cultural economy." *Theory, Culture and Society* 7(2–3): 295–310.

Routledge Library Editions: Ethnoscapes

1. *Environmental Perspectives* David Canter, Martin Krampen & David Stea (Eds) (1988) ISBN 978-1-032-81616-6

2. *Environmental Policy, Assessment, and Communication* David Canter, Martin Krampen & David Stea (Eds) (1988) ISBN 978-1-032-81635-7

3. *New Directions in Environmental Participation* David Canter, Martin Krampen & David Stea (Eds) (1988) ISBN 978-1-032-81646-3

4. *Vernacular Architecture: Paradigms of Environmental Response* Mete Turan (Ed.) (1990) ISBN 978-1-032-82023-1

5. *Forms of Dominance: On the Architecture and Urbanism of the Colonial Enterprise* Nezar AlSayyad (Ed.) (1992) ISBN 978-1-032-84164-9

6. *The Meaning and Use of Housing: International Perspectives, Approaches and Their Applications* Ernesto G. Arias (Ed.) (1993) ISBN 978-1-032-84781-8

7. *Placemaking: Production of Built Environment in Two Cultures* David Stea & Mete Turan (1993) ISBN 978-1-032-86434-1

8. *Environmental Psychology in Europe: From Architectural Psychology to Green Psychology* Enric Pol (1993) ISBN 978-1-032-83324-8

9. *Housing: Design, Research, Education* Marjorie Bulos & Necdet Teymur (Eds) (1993) ISBN 978-1-032-86388-7

10. *Architecture, Ritual Practice and Co-determination in the Swedish Office* Dennis Doxtater (1994) ISBN 978-1-032-81774-3

11. *On the Aesthetics of Architecture: A Psychological Approach to the Structure and the Order of Perceived Architectural Space* Ralf Weber (1995) ISBN 978-1-032-82034-7

12. *The Home: Words, Interpretations, Meanings and Environments* by David N. Benjamin (Ed.) (1995) ISBN 978-1-032-86411-2

13. *Tradition, Location and Community: Place-making and Development* Adenrele Awotona & Necdet Teymur (Eds) (1997) ISBN 978-1-032-84608-8

14. *Aesthetics, Well-being and Health: Essays within Architecture and Environmental Aesthetics* Birgit Cold (Ed.) (2001) ISBN 978-1-032-86577-5

Other Ethnoscapes series titles also available:

Integrating Programming, Evaluation and Participation in Design: A Theory Z Approach Henry Sanoff (1992) HBK 978-1-138-20338-9; EBK 978-1-315-47173-0; PBK 978-1-138-20339-6

Directions in Person-Environment Research and Practice Jack Nasar & Wolfgang F. E. Preiser (Eds) (1999) HBK 978-1-138-68674-8; EBK 978-1-315-54255-3; PBK 978-1-138-68677-9

Psychological Theories for Environmental Issues Mirilia Bonnes, Terence Lee & Marino Bonaiuto (Eds) (2003) HBK 978-0-75461-888-1; EBK 978-1-315-24572-0; PBK 978-1-138-27742-7

Housing Space and Quality of Life David L. Uzzell, Ricardo Garcia Mira, J. Eulogio Real & Joe Romay (Eds) (2005) HBK 978-0-81538-952-1; EBK 978-1-351-15636-3; PBK 978-1-138-35596-5

Doing Things with Things: The Design and Use of Everyday Objects Alan Costall & Ole Dreier (Eds) (2006) HBK 978-0-75464-656-3; EBK 978-1-315-57792-0; PBK 978-1-138-25314-8

Rethinking the Meaning of Place: Conceiving Place in Architecture-Urbanism Lineu Castello (2010) HBK 978-0-75467-814-4; EBK 978-1-315-60616-3; PBK 978-1-138-25745-0

Ethnoscapes: Volume 1

Environmental Perspectives

Edited by

DAVID CANTER

Department of Psychology
University of Surrey

MARTIN KRAMPEN

Department of Aesthetics
Hochschule der Kunst, Berlin

DAVID STEA

School of Architecture
University of Wisconsin

Avebury

Aldershot · Brookfield USA · Hong Kong · Singapore · Sydney

Published by

Avebury

Gower Publishing Company Limited
Gower House
Croft Road
Aldershot
Hants GU11 3HR
England

Gower Publishing Company
Old Post Road
Brookfield
Vermont 05036
USA

ISBN 0 566 05080 3

Printed and bound in Great Britain by
Athanaeum Press Limited, Newcastle upon Tyne

Contents

SECTION TWO
Social Histories of Built Form

SECTION THREE
Aesthetics and Meaning in Architecture

New directions in environmental research

THE ENVIRONMENTAL SOCIAL SCIENCES

The domains of Behavioural and Perceptual Geography,
Environmental Psychology, Urban Sociology, Social
Anthropology, Urban History, Social Ecology, Behavioural
Archeology, Urban Planning, Behavioural Architecture,
Landascapes Architecture and various aspects of design
have all developed marauding sub-groups who move freely
across each others borders, carrying ideas almost like
contraband, without declaring that they have crossed any
disciplinary boundaries. Like all such hidden trade it
has built up a community of interest and support, and as
frequently happens, this has lead to some traders having
more in common with each other than with their
professional compatriots. A common means of communication
has evolved together with an unfolding understanding of
the issues and approaches that are worth examining and
transmitting.

Throughout history, both civil and intellectual, such
informal bands have often coalesced into a coherent force
in their own right, becoming a significant agent for
change in the places of their birth. There are many signs
that this process is well advanced within the academic

and professional domains that speculate on the transactions between people and their physical context. We therefore believe that environmental social scientists now have enough common cause to warrant a series of books that serves the interests of this cross-disciplinary, cross-national community.

By its very nature a community of scholars and professionals that moves readily across disciplinary boundaries is one that sees the value in the challenge of different perspectives. This challenge comes through methods as much as theories and concepts. It is as much a personal challenge to find new ways of thinking, communicating and acting, as an academic demand to develop more effective intellectual systems.

This series will therefore include a variety of volumes in a number of different formats, covering many different aspects of current challenges in the environmental social sciences. Some will be collections of contributions covering theoretical perspectives. Others will focus on methodology. We plan some single authored monographs that look in depth at issues such as social environmental studies in the third world, and others that deal with approaches to design participation with disadvantaged groups.

CURRENT CHALLENGES

The intention is that all the volumes in the series will, with different degrees of emphasis, reflect four related challenges. One is the challenge of responding to emerging environmental problems throughout the world. These are now as varied as providing acceptable housing for those third world countries that have moved beyond the desire to provide only simple shelter, exploring new ways in which environmental heritage can be brought alive and presented more accessably than in traditional museums, or examining the awareness of governments and public alike of the problems of environmental degradation and pollution.

A second challenge is to develop a richer and more effective understanding of the ways in which people and their surroundings interconnect, than has been possible when relying on the perspective of a single discipline. This is, in effect, the challenge of elaborating models of person/environment transactions. Models that move beyond explanations in terms of people responding directly to environmental stimuli or being moulded by environmental pressures.

The range of such explanatory systems is growing rapidly and now includes emphases on the interprative capabilities that people have, consideration of the social and cultural forces that shape the significance of our surroundings and examinations of the historical processes that underlie the changes in our relationships to the world in which we live.

Besides the practical and theoretical challenges the third challenge is methodological. Many of the methods of data collection and analyis that have been used to study people and places have had their origins in one of the parent disciplines and have, typically, been borrowed piecemeal. In particular the procedures used by planners and architects to develop design proposals have been kept quite seperate from the procedures endemic in research. As a consequence most people have had difficulty in moving between the academic and the professional disciplines, although this, of course, has not stopped many trying.

The current methodological challange is therefore to develop ways of collecting information and ways of analysing it that will respond to the cross-disciplinary problems characteristic of the environmental social sciences. Many such attempts are now under way, often first developed with the objective of increasing user participation in the processes of shaping their surroundings.

These new procedures often start life as simple or more direct ways of collecting information about the significance of environment, but researchers then find that new demands are placed on them to draw patterns and generalities out of their data. So new forms of analysis and presentation of results emerge in response. The series will encourage a wider dissemination and use of these and other methodological innovations.

There are also a fourth set of challenges that are essentially personal which are involved in current environmental social sciences. The new theories, methods and realms of application put demands on researchers, authors and practitioners that go beyond the intellectual challenges they face. New cultures, other professional groups, the pressures of responding to existing, immediate problems, all draw upon aspects of ourselves and our ways of dealing with the world that are not often stretched within the confines of many existing academic discussions. In order to understand the contributions that writers are making it is therefore often of value to recognise their own personal voice and to allow them to use forms of expression that may not always be modelled on the neutral, academic stereotype. The series will welcome all effective forms of written communication.

ETHNOSCAPES

The interplay between the processes of action and place is what must be studied if we are to understand, and so shape the role and significance of, physical surroundings in human affairs.

We feel that, this provides a distinct enough enterprise to require a unique, identifying label. Existing terms for our focal concerns, such as "environmental psychology" or "behavioural geography", either emphasise behavioural, psychological perspectives or environmental ones, all of which are not misleading. Labels drawn from more practical considerations, as in "social architecture" or "participatory planning" give emphasis to professional activities that are also inappropriate. Other terms have grown to embrace the flavour of some of what will be covered in future volumes, notably "humanistic geography", and "phenomenological psychology", but on closer examination these terms are both too restrictive in their ideological implications and too ambiguous in their conceptual focii.

We therefore decided to take a terminological step back and look at some of the roots to words current in the literature that had the distinctiveness which we will be encouraging. This led us to realise that the Greek root ethnos, that originally had a strong meaning of race or culture and that is reflected in the term ethnology, has in recent years begun to mean more in terms of the particular attitudes, perceptions and spirit of a people or social sub-group. In this latter meaning it draws from the original meanings of its semantic colleague ethos, so that there is now much overlap in the commitments of "ethnography and of ethogenics" both of which share orientations and methods with many of the current challenges in our arena.

It is also clear that what we will be presenting in future volumes are perspectives on, and visions of, the place related experiences of the people participating in the studies reported. Something like the sub-cultural landscape, or social representation of a setting as experienced, were the notions we felt a title to the new direction would reflect. The suffix "scape" has come to take on just that meaning through important uses such as "Townscape" and "Humanscape". From these considerations "Ethnoscapes" was born. The slight, whimsical hint that it offers of escaping from existing rubrics also attracts us.

Out of consideration for future lexicographers, we provide a formal dictionary definition:

eth.no– <u>combining</u> <u>form</u>. indicating race, people or cultured

–scape <u>suffix</u> <u>forming</u> <u>nouns</u>. indicating a scene or view of something.

eth.no+scapes <u>pl.n</u> scholarly and/or scientific explorations of the relations between people, their activities and the places they create and/or inhabit; historical, psycholgoical or sociological studies of the experience of places, attitudes towards them, or the processes of shaping, managing or designing them.

OBJECTIVES

The series then, has the following objectives:

(1) To bring together work that is international both in terms of the contributors and of the places and populations studied;

(2) To treat cultural, socio-economic, and dynamically evolving aspects of human/environment relations.

(3) To provide a critical, appraisive, and evaluative (rather than assertive) approach to the issues under study.

(4) To integrate theory, research, design/planning practice, and policy.

(5) To represent a broad range of disciplines, and

(6) To outline a framework that is fundamentally dialectical, and explicitly ecological.

"Man" and "environment" are not viewed dualistically as separate entities; neither are urban and rural phenomena, nor the various scales of natural and designed environments.

Our goal, is to point the way, to establish some alternative directions, rather than to define the destination.

THE OPENING TRILOGY

As an opening to the series three related volumes are being published edited by the same three editors. They bring together specially commissioned contributions that cover much of the range of topics that the series as a whole will cover. So although all future volumes in this series will not have the same format, this opening trilogy does give a reasonable overview of what is to come, whilst also providing a broad base for future authors to build upon.

The first of these volumes focuses. essentially, on theory. It brings together papers covering our growing understanding of the ways in which human actions are integrated within our knowledge of the places in which those actions occur. The contributors also explore the social historical antecedents that give meaning to our everyday surroundings, as well as the psychological underpinnings to aesthetic experience.

The second has a more practical orientation. Its contributions deal directly research on those environmental matters on which government agencies and other organisations formulate policies or develop design strategies. This therefore covers the assessment and evaluation of designs and design proposals as well background research to policy issues.

For the third volume in this opening trilogy we have
chosen to deal directly with current developments in
environmental participation. This brings together
contributions that range from studies of hands-on user
participation to explorations on a much broader scale of
the role we all play in shaping our environment. The role
of communication, education and research in the
participation process is motif that is apparent
throughout the contributions.

THREE RELATED CONCERNS

These three volumes range over a very wide domain. But
underlying all the material three related themes can be
identified. These themes also serve to characterise many
studies of Ethnoscapes. Often they have been dealt with
seperately but there is growing recognition that their
links should also be understood.

One is the concern for the protection of the biosphere.
The environmental concern that first captured newspaper
headings through the activities of Friends of the Earth
or Greenpeace, has grown into a political movement,
especially in German where the Green Party has elected
members of parliament. In volume three Galtung
epitomises this movement with his call for an
Environmental International to parallel the work of
Amnesty International.

If a political perspective were identified for the
second thematic concern it would be that mentioned in the
introduction to the first volume in relation to
Kropotkin: anarchism. The once popular mass media image
of the bomb throwing terriorist obscures a more accurate
view of this perspective reflected in the writings of Leo
Tolstoy, Herbert Read, Aldous Huxley, George Orwell and
many others who were pillars of the establishment in
their day as well as more recent figures in our own field
such as Colin Ward. The concern here is for the direct
influence of people over the decisions that are of
immediate relevance to them. In design terms this is
reflected in many aspects of user participation. Whether
it is work in a Botswana village, in Northern India of in
the United States, to take just three examples from these
volumes, the search is for ways in which local
communities themselves can have their actions and
aspirations integrated into decision processes concerning
the man-made environment.

A third perspective is not far removed from the previous two: this is the desire by researchers to respond directly to pressing architectural and planning issues of critical significance to changes in society around the world. In Third World countries these are demands for more and better housing and for responses to other crises brought on by rapid urbanisation and uneven development, itself a product of migration (some would say overdeveloped) countries of the North Atlantic basin, and in Australia and parts of South-East Asia, the analogous problem is the rapid increase in the aging population. In both cases the concern is to understand what housing forms will best answer the needs of new, expanding and special generations of urban dwellers. This requires both an understanding of their way of life and of the processes by which these people can effectively contribute to the shaping of their surroundings.

A CALL FOR CONTRIBUTIONS

The direction and content of the first three volumes has been shaped in response to the material the editors became aware of at various conferences and meetings throughout the world and by the age old acts of personal communication. In that respect it is as much a response to a growing area of action and study as a predetermined framework into which solicited material was slotted. We consider this interactive, organic approach to be absolutely essential to the development of these domains. Like all good traders throughout the ages we see the benefit in considering, without prejudice, any new merchandise that will foster the international, interdisciplinary links that is at the heart of all successful enterprise. As editors we welcome any suggestions or proposals that may further the very broad aims of this series. For us the current and constant challenge is to discover environmental social scientists who are saying intelligent and valueable things to each other and to develop the means by which they can communicate with a wider audience.

David Canter   David Stea

University of Surrey   Santa Fe
Guildford, U.K.   New Mexico, U.S.A

Editors' introduction

A NEW EMPHASIS

One of the central challenges in the environmental social sciences is how to further our understanding of the complex interplay between people and the physical contexts in which they live their lives. It is therefore very appropriate that, as a first volume in a new series, this volume addresses that issue directly from a number of different perspectives. A variety of psychological, social historical and aesthetic perspectives are brought together in their respective sections. Together they illuminate a rich vista of accounts and explanations that assist in our understanding of the significance of our physical surroundings.

Most people would agree that merely understanding person/environment transactions is not enough. The exploration of environmental policy and the associated study of environmental evaluation and assessment is of at least equal importance. Further, the examination of how people may be actively involved in the shaping of their environments is also a worthy part of the overall endeavour. Policy and participation, however, introduce so many of their own challenges, that we have reluctantly assigned each of them their own volume. Policy, assessment and evaluation is dealt with in the second volume of the series. New directions in environmental participation is the third volume.

As editors we were reluctant to have distinct volumes because so many
of the themes, theories and methods run through all three volumes.
There is also much to be learnt from the interplay between the
different types of study. Our desire for didactic clarity, however,
overcame our enjoyment of the richness of intellectual cross-
fertilization, when we realised how luxuriant each seperate volume
would be anyway. Each clearly stands alone as a valuable volume in its
own right.

Despite the separation into three volumes we are confident that the
chapters they include all have in common an emphasis that is different
from that which has been dominant in many earlier studies. Human
action and the places in which it occurs are seen as the focus for the
studies reported rather than "Environment" and "Behaviour". This is
no mere play on words. "Action" draws attention to the fact that
human activities are shaped by intentions, social and cultural
processes, and structured by the meanings that people derive from the
contexts in which those actions occur. Places, an aspect of that
context, are given form and significance by all those who participate
in the experience, management, creation and use of those places.

An Environment and Behaviour perspective focuses, for example, on
the effect of lighting levels on performance or on defining the
parameters of some landscape that will cause it to be rated as
"attractive". Whilst such studies have some value, we believe the
perspectives presented in the following pages broaden considerably the
vision of human interactions with the physical context.

At the outset we must make it clear that our concern is with
understanding what is the nature of the processes that give the
physical context its human implications. The verbs available for
describing the connections between people and their milieu carry with
them epistemological assumptions that we consider counterproductive.
To write of environmental "influences" and "impacts" of environments on
people, to discuss "interactions with" the environment or "transaction
between" people and environments, all have been adopted as the favoured
phrases of one theoretical school or the other. Each group of
researchers, in attempting to clarify the meaning of the terms they
wish to embrace, have inevitably denied that term with different
nuances to others. We wish to avoid this debate by moving to a
position from which such definitions are less relevant. We believe
that this new position provides a view of paths different from those
that have been traversed in the past, even if the vision is rather hazy
at present. At least it revitalizes for our use some of the words in
the English language!

The vision made apparent by the new outlook is a vital, challenging
one that is not well reflected in most existing publications. As a
consequence, a major aspiration of this and subsequent volumes is to
help redefine and reshape that study of human activities and
experiences that deals with the places in which they happen. This
aspiration is not solely academic. We see direct practical gains to
be achieved by re-directing the emphases in the study of person-
environment relationships.

The need for a coherent publication that recnogised the new emphasis was conceived in 1984, with its birth delayed more than two years. That's the gestation period of an elephant. The analogy is perhaps not that far-fetched, if we consider the parable of the blind men and the pachyderm, each feeling only a part of the beast and thus giving different emphases to their interpretation of what it was. The study and practice of human-environment transactions, is not new, but its form is still vague and, as we have indicated, in need of reshaping, of redefinition. Each of the contributors has tried to "feel" that form, to understand it, even to remold it in some way. Each contribution is a partial effort. Only in the totality of the contributions can we begin to grasp the "nature of the beast". The contributors represent a broad range of people with an even broader range of interests, but they are in truth a selected sample: it is "our beast". The credit for the perspectives on its form and function belong to the contributors, but the responsibility for its integration, its only partially revealed topography, rests with us, the editors.

We had the feeling that a new kind of research domain was beginning to take shape, and that if we invited a broad enough range of people to contribute, each of whom in his/her own way was trying to give form to that new domain, we would ourselves learn more fully what was happening. In so doing we believed we would nudge this rather hidden set of concerns into a more public being. We have been impressed by the vitality of what came out of this process and much encouraged by the prospects for the future that it heralds.

A SERIES OF TEXT BOOKS

In creating a format that we think will make this and subsequent volumes useful as texts we have broken a number of molds traditionally used for such enterprises. We do not start with some notion of fundamental, basic aspects of human behaviour to which more complex processes can be reduced. Nor do we embrace a uniquely psychological view of people. Indeed the contrast with what might now be considered "conventional" environmental psychology may help the reader to understand our own perspective.

We ourselves and many colleagues have, in the past, contributed to environmental psychology text books. Such texts, rather unintentionally, sometimes create the impression that the people studied and depicted in such a text were simple minded, isolated robot-like creatures, living in a coercive, essentially threatening environment that they are desperately trying to "personalise" and control. On occasion, there is suggestion that in order to function, these robot creatures seem to respond only to gross aspects of their surroundings such as its "complexity". The text hints that these responses connect internal circuits that are map-like, inevitably distorted representations of their environments. These internal "circuit boards" are then used as a basis for navigation when carrying out daily activities. Any such activities appear to be aimed at maintaining their separateness and privacy from any other robots they may happen to meet. They are also under great pressure to cope with "overload", the threat to their sensitive circuits produced by being crowded with so many other navigating robots.

Admittedly, this science fiction-like parody of environmental psychology is somewhat exaggerated. Few theories or models subscribe to all the aspects we have drawn upon, but many readers will recognise the relationship to much research and theory in that field. In particular, the essentially impoverished vision of humanity will be apparent from our parody. The present volumes provides different visions of people and their physical context.

These alternative visions do, of course, have their origins in many different domains of interest and a variety of disciplines (and, as the reader will perceive, they also benefit from a variety of styles and tones of presentation). Additionally, a number of our contributors have been arguing for alternative perspectives for some time. After all, the study and practice of human-environment interactions can no longer be presented as some new, infant discipline, feeling its way with hesitant steps. The first course on "Behaviour and Environmental Design" was taught at Stanford in 1964. The first "Directory of Design and Behavior" was published in Rhode Island in 1965, containing names of some 70 people then working in, or interested in the area. It is over 15 years since graduate programmes in Environmental Psychology, were established, for example, at City University, New York and at Surrey University, Guildford. We old-timers have grandstudents and great-grandstudents. The U.S. based Environmental Design Research Association (EDRA) has now held close to 20 annual conferences, meaning that some of its younger participants may not even have been born when the first conferences were held. The European-based conferences, held every couple of years now number more than ten. The journal <u>Environment and Behavior</u> is well into its nineteenth volume and the newer <u>Journal of Environmental Psychology</u> is in its seventh.

It should come as no surprise, then, that the themes being exposed here have a long and respectable parentage. One fascinating link to earlier days helps to clarify the special characteristics we see in the material we have brought together. This link takes us, fruitfully, to another time and another place.

KROPOTKIN'S ETHICS - COMMUNITY NOT PRIVACY

In 1918, shortly after the Soviet revolution, in the small, secluded village of Dmitrov, some 60 versts from Moscow, Prince Peter Alekseyevich Kropotkin settled down, after years of wandering and imprisonment, to summarise his thought and ideology. This renowned anarchist and preacher of revolution saw, in the early days of the new Soviet empire that his most important work was to present a full and coherent account of his ethical philosophy (Kropotkin 1968). Given Kropotkin's commitment to action and change it may seem strange that, while many of his compatriots were actively furthering the new age of communism, he determined instead to prepare a major philosophical text. It was the vision inherent in this act that makes his work so relevant to us.

Besides being a major political philosopher Kropotkin was also a significant scientist. For example, in 1873 he published a map and paper in which he proved that the existing maps of Asia entirely misrepresented the physical formation of the country, the main structural lines being in fact from South West to North East, not from North to South or from East to West as had been previously supposed.

As a scientist he recognised the power of fundamental theories in guiding thought and actions. He believed that the Soviet revolution was already, in its early days, foundering because it had not clarified its fundamental ethical position. He also clearly saw that many of the alternatives provided by political systems based on the power of capital were no more, and often less, ethically justifiable.

But, as a scientist, he recognised that polemic and broad assertions provide no lasting basis for any argument. He saw the need to base his conclusions on the study and understanding of the natural world. Inspired by the empiricism of Francis Bacon and the observations and formulations of Charles Darwin he saw in the emerging science of the late 19th century fundamental principles for his ethics and his politics. He highlighted a theme in evolutionary biology that Western capitalism and Marxist materialism alike had ignored, a theme that some socio-biologists are, perhaps belatedly, re-discovering to-day.

The dominant interpretation of Darwinan theory that has influenced so much psychological, social and political science is of a battle for survival, each species defending its territory and fighting against predators and environment to secure its supremacy. Indeed, it was Herbert Spencer, a railway engineer turned philosopher, who actually coined the term "survival of the fittest" in his 1864 book Principles of Biology. It was Spencer who did so much to argue for the social significance of his principle and to see in it a reflection of the importance of the potential conflict between the individual and the society of which that person is a part. The power of the conception of inherent conflict can be seen in explanations of human actions as wide-ranging as super power politics and Oscar Newman's (1972) views of "Defensible Space". Robert Ardrey's (1966) "Territorial Imperative" gave a spurious pseudo-scientific impetus to the popular belief in these notions.

Beyond Ardrey, when some of the more empirically based approaches are considered, the pervasiveness of this view can be discerned in the study of people and their man-made and natural surroundings. For example, the widely quoted work of Altman (1975) focuses on privacy, on the separateness of individuals and how it is maintained. When the term was first introduced to the design literature in the book by Chermayeff and Alexander (1963), "community" was seen as the dominant partner to "privacy". But theoreticians of the social sciences, steeped in the pervasive competitive ideology, soon lost "community". Such other environmental psychology themes as "crowding" and "personal space" also drew on the Spencerian idea that the individual, potentially threatened by physical and social surroundings, must be behaviourally "fit" in order to survive transactions with those surroundings.

Kropotkin (1968) emphasised that for Darwin the _dominant_ process in nature was actually one of _mutual aid_ within a species. He quotes the founder of animal psychology, Lloyd Morgan, as saying "the primeval germ of the social community lay in the prolonged coherence of the group ..." (page 38 footnote 6) reminding us that the first proposition of Darwin's ethics as cited in The Decent of Man is that the foundation of all moral feelings are "in the social instincts which lead the animal to take pleasure in the society of its fellows, to feel a certain amount of sympathy with them and to perform various services for them." (page 33) The seminal work of the ethologist Allee (1938, 1951) reiterated the same theme.

Recent studies in animal behavior provide support further for this perspective. They show that the vision of nature "red in tooth and claw", of a competition between environment and behaviour in which each tries to shape the other, is a misreading of evolutionary theory. The survival of the fittest is a minor, secondary phenomenon that only comes into play when the forces that lead to positive, effective adaptation are not available. Much of our scientific endeavour has mistaken the theme and confused the figure with the background.

Such confusion leads to a differentiation between environment and behaviour, a focus on the individual as a separate organism with minimal group or social commitments. It leads to explanations that emphasise single, linearly-determined causality rather than systems of inter-related influences.

Not surprisingly, many people have been unhappy with the viewpoints, theories and methods of environmental-behaviour study that have emerged from such a limiting and insupportable framework. These attacks have taken the form of diatribes against "positivism" (Relph, 1976), or attempts to develop radically different methodologies (Canter's 1985 "facets", Korosec-Serfaty's 1984 and Seamon's 1982 versions of phenomenology). From these outpourings there is emerging a new loosely-knit community of scholarship and action that, even though diverse and varied and certainly lacking in intense cross-fertilisation and close coherence, nonetheless is recognisably distinct.

In some regards, as already noted, the core that this community shares is identifiably humanistic, especially as the notion of a humanistic science is interpreted by geographers. In a recent far ranging review Chokor (1986) emphasises that humanistic geography represents a movement away from the objective analytical techniques of science and attempts to explore place evocations and descriptions and "to evoke the qualities of locale in the context of human experiences and fulfilments". But whilst most of our contributors would endorse these attempts, they share with Chokor some of the misgivings that he finds in the strong individualistic bias and methodological confusion of much humanistic geography, revealing on occasion, as Chokor puts it "only the trivialities of everyday life".

However, these criticisms of some of the weaknesses in practice of the humanistic approach do not negate the values of its objectives. In particular the emphasis given by humanistic social scientists to the understanding of the context in which people experience their world, and how people interpret that context, is central.

CHARACTERISTICS OF THE "NEW" STUDIES

The present book, then, brings together diverse studies reflecting this newly redirected field of inquiry. Although all the studies in this volume do not have all the characteristics of this new direction each does have a number of them. The characteristics can be summarised as follows:

1. Recognising the collaborative nature of human action, the concerns expressed are firmly based in cultural, social and inter-personal frameworks. The isolated individual acting on a personally defined world is replaced by a person who plays a role in society and whose understandings and aspirations are structured by, and structure, that society and its context.

2. The work reported is overtly cross-disciplinary. Historians draw on social theories, psychologists on philosophy, sociologists on design theory and so on.

3. The ethical dimension of social action leads to the view that all research is, at least implicitly, aimed at bettering the human lot. One consequence is that studies with this perspective are also unashamedly cross-professional. Writers move from design considerations to scientific ones and back again.

4. The recognition of the significance of group processes extends to the view that design is fundamentally a social process, that the furthering of community activity in design is of great significance.

5. It follows from the above that the explanations given of human transactions with their physical surroundings find their roots in cultural and interpersonal processes and that they are also inevitably explanations of systems. Perhaps the most psychologically focused contribution to this volume is the examination of perception by Landwehr [2]. Yet, he still sees the essence of perception as within the environmental and ecological system of which an individual is a part.

The present book, then, contrasts deliberately with other previous and recent texts on environmental psychology, behavioural geography, urban sociology and so on. It does not start with an atomistic recounting of fundamentals out of which more complex systems of explanation can be developed and to which they can be reduced. Further the authors of many of the chapters readily give up their supposed academic neutrality and argue, sometimes fiercely, for their particular perspectives. Beyond knowledge it is necessary to get understanding, but, beyond even this, there is an end towards which understanding is

directed. It is unlikely that all the contributors to this volume
share a common view of that future which they would like to see, but
they do all have such a view. As scientists they study the world as it
is: but as, in many cases, action researchers, they also recognise the
gap between the "real" which they study and the "ideal" that represents
their future vision.

One of the ironies of this volume is that our perspective allows us
to bring together, comfortably, accounts of a number of activities that
are now typically published under separate covers, although they were
combined when human implications of environmental design were first
actively studied. Examination of the first proceedings of the
Environmental Design Research Association, for example Archea and
Eastman (1970), will reveal that design participation exercises rubbed
shoulders with scholarly research; that historical analysis shared
covers with psychological theory; and that all were seen as valuable
contributions. Such miscegenation has been rare since those early days
and we are delighted to have encouraged it once again. This new
"coming together" signifies that there is no longer a supercilious
belief by different "researchers" that they have nothing to learn from
participation and action, or by "practitioners" that theory is
irrelevant. Like Prince Kropotkin, both sides are concerned with
praxis: theory, research and practice mutually assisting each other.

To us as editors this cross-fertilisation caused some problems. A
number of contributions would sit happily in more than one section of
this volume, or even in other volumes in this series. But we felt that
a clear sectional structure was essential in order to help people
identify some of the themes underlying the diversity. The section
headings are therefore deliberately phrased to be didactic and
instructive rather than merely passive descriptions of the papers
contained within those sections. The sections deliberately draw
attention to substantive themes that run through this work. As such,
they facilitate the use of the text as a basis for teaching as well as
an aid for future research.

It might seem unusual to have a volume consisting of a variety of
contributions brought together from many different sources, often
contributions that first saw the light of day in earlier versions as
conference papers, could be presented as a teaching text. But we argue
that a program of teaching should be built around the community of
scholarship which characterises the field being studied. The usual
monolithic view, expressed by one individual, that pretends a neutral
stance on a whole field, has its limits in the explorations of the
implications of our surroundings. No one person can conceptualise and
summarise fully such a natural diversity of perspectives and concerns.
What we have attempted to do is to bring together in an organised form
the mixture of studies, arguments, perspectives, and indeed writing
styles and modes of debate, that characterise dominant aspects of a
realm of discourse and action at a particular point in time. It is
this representation of a community of scholarship that we have sought
to reflect.

Undoubtedly there are omissions. Each of the editors can list his pet vacancy. Undoubtedly there are also distortions produced by the particular sample we have brought together. However, we believe that there is enough coherence, through the major themes.

The first section deals with the ways in which actions and the locations in which they occur are closely intertwined. As we have argued, by putting the emphasis on location and action we are drawing the focus of debate away from an environment caricatured as a set of stimuli, and behaviour as an associated set of responses. Locations have an existence within a spatio-temporal zone and actions an existence defined by the characteristics of individuals and of the social and cultural groups to which they belong. The importance of this principle is illustrated in a very diverse set of examples.

Canter [Chapter 1] opens the first section by showing that actions and places are not two separate entities that influence each other at some single point in time. Instead he argues that they interconnect in such a way that each contains the seeds of change in the other. It is the dialectic of this constant interplay that generates the stable yet evolving experiences of the world.

This process is well illustrated in two subsequent chapters. Landwehr [2] shows how we can understand environmental perceptual processes by relating perception directly to its ecological context and so draw upon the developments in psychological theories of perception. By contrast Chokor [4] illustrates how the form and pattern of Nigerian cities is a product of the interaction between social proceses and physical constraints. Further light is thrown on these processes by Giuliani and her colleagues [3] in their studies of rooms in the middle class suburbs of Rome and Paris. They show what intence and subtle significance can be assigned to domestic layouts from the social processes that they house.

The second section begins by looking at the social and historical processes giving rise to the built forms that characterise the world in which we live. By drawing on perspectives that run across Europe, from Greece by way of Switzerland and Belgium to Great Britain and by including historical studies in Australia, it is possible to see that a number of different scholars have identified critical cultural processes that are reflected in the environments in which we live. The physical surroundings are placed firmly into an historical and a cultural context. We can no longer look at the shape of a building simply as a set of stimuli to which an organism is reacting, we have to consider the way in which socio-cultural processes have given rise to that particular form and the way in which those same processes are active to-day.

Writing of cinema design, for example, Thorne [11] shows how the social processes that structure commercial architecture must be understood if we are to understand the designs so produced. He also makes a very significant point. Such commercial concerns often require a sensitivity to the reactions of building usrs that environmental psychologists have long advocated.

Housing is a central issue in discussions of the social histories of built form. Possibly because it represents and reflects social processes so directly. To take one example of a very particular architectural form, the Bungalow, this bridges the realms of the First and Third Worlds. Starting as a description of a house of the Bengal type, drawing on the Hindi word for such a house bangla, King [5] points out, that the bungalow became a symbol of colonial control and that some of that imagery contributed to that housing form eventually finding its way into English suburbia, where it is now favoured as a retirement retreat.

These interconnections do not happen only at the level of the transmission of cultural symbols. A number of authors point out in this and later volumes that the very fabric of the experienced environment is a product of locally focused, global interconnections. Squatter settlements develop not just because of the attractions in third world cities that Western goods and a Western style of life incites, but as a result of the impoverishment of rural areas, and the needs of the burgeoning areas, and industries there, emerging to supply the developed world. The "reserve army" of the unemployed (and underemployed), that inhabits the favelas of Brazil or the kampong of South East Asia and most of the other squatter settlements of the third world, is a direct result of the first world's desire for cheap, mass produced third world products.

As editors who have been born, and now live, thousands of miles away from each other, and who have developed this book through face-to-face discussions on three continents, we are perhaps more directly aware than many of our colleagues of the unity of the global environment and the commonality of the issues to be faced around the world. Discussions for this book took place between pairs of editors in Caracas, London, Berlin and Yogyakarta. We have had to work on English text written by people whose own native languages include Estonian, Greek, Hebrew, German, Italian, French and Spanish, and who are working in contexts where local languages include Russian, Hindi, Yuroba, and obscure African dialects. This book itself is a product of global interconnectedness.

The third section shows how much further research must go in order to explore aesthetic phenomena fully. Harries et al [12] argue strongly that much of architectural debate is superficial and faddishly facile. Smith [13] takes this argument further by showing the subtleties that he, as a practicing arcitect, must consider.

How much further the debate can proceed is illustrated in two of the probably most difficult and demanding contributions to this volume, those by Walcher [16] and Peled [15]. The authors start from different points to show how all-embracing are human actions on the world and their associated thoughts and feelings. They reveal how much of social and psychological significance is invested in the interplay between actions and places. This means that the exploration and the conceptualisation of this interplay must be as rich as is scientifically possible. The variety of tonal systems, to which reference was made, are not just an enrichment of our ways of looking at action/place relationships, they are a necessity if we are to tackle the complexity of the problems at hand. The really dramatic and uplifting musical harmonies come from many different voices singing together.

It is this diversity that also makes developments in theory both possible and essential so that theories can act as the anvil on which practical solutions are hammered into a useable shape. These theories cohere around two related problem areas: first, the ways in which social rule systems shape our experience of the world and second, the place that aesthetic phenomena, particularly those directly linked to visual perception, play within those experiences. We know from work reviewed in this volume that both social, role related rule systems, and reactions to aesthetics and meanings are context specific. Indeed, as Peled [15] and Groat [14] show in quite different ways that it is the relationship between a building and its context that is central to the reactions people have to it. The implications of materials, or of window shapes, for instance, can only be understood in terms of their socially embedded significance for linking that building to others.

A VARIETY OF VOICES

Within the academic community it is all too easy to take for granted these varieties of contexts and national sources. Because the communications are in English and the dominant style is Trans-Atlantic, Anglo-Saxon we expect all accounts of the work conducted to fall into this mold. Without any doubt we have suffered from this prediliction. Interesting material from researchers in countries not included in this volume was available to us but we had neither the resources nor the temerity to shape it all into a form we believed most of our colleagues could digest.

We were, though, acutely aware of this lack and of the need to give voice to themes and harmonies that are rarely heard because they do not use a tonal system with which we are all familiar. As mentioned before, this does mean that styles of presentation vary and are sometimes rather different from what would be expected in the conventional British or North American Journal. In one sense we welcome these different voices as one would a distinguished visitor who might not command the subtleties of our language but nonetheless has an important message to bring. In another sense we see these less orthodox forms of communication as the inevitable first steps in breaking through an orthodoxy that defends itself with rituals that are not always necessary.

Much of the research done in earlier years, and the books that resulted, reflected the values of Western social science and environmental design quite well. Much of this research accepted with little question the values of middle-class consumer society. We failed, in fact, to question certain implicit biases in our concepts, ideology, and procedures. Users and those who shape the environment - architects - are viewed as individuals. This has been termed the "individualist bias", and characterizes university-level education in social science and design. Similarly, as architects endlessly enter competitions, or compete for business, clients and users "compete" for space - the "competitive bias", expressed in the "territorial imperative" and to a lesser extent in the concepts of "individual distance" and "population pressure". Again in the literature of decades past, the research on the social science - design interface was for universal characteristics of human behaviour (cognition, preference, etc.) those which could be relied upon by architects in all places at all times - the "universalist bias". Finally, there was the hope that psychology, among the social sciences - particularly perception and social psychology - would reveal the human phenomena of most interest to environmental designers in the most scientific way - the "psychological bias". This bias has also contributed to our past tendencies to emphasize behaviour rather than action, space rather than place. The "new view" explicitly recognises that behaviour is but a component of action, that all spatial interactions occur somewhere and that "somewhere" (place) plays a critical role.

There has been a tendency, then, to characterize man-environment relations, or the human-environment dialogue, or the roles of environment-behaviour studies, as universal, individual, psychological, and competitive. We are over-simplifying this view of course. Few, today, would accept it as stated, and even those are losing ground. Increasing attention is now being given to the alternative views we have discussed and that are elaborated in various ways in the present volume.

Nearly everyone remembers the communes of the late 1960´s and early 70´s. Their almost universal failure is attributed to "human nature", but is more probably the result of people with backgrounds in Western industrialized society - the vast majority of the communards - creating artificial communities contradictory to well-ingrained Western values. The communes failed, in other words, because they did not "work". They satisfied their members´ eventual needs, goals, and aspirations less well, within their larger contexts, than prevailing social organisations, and failed to recognise the essential pluralism of their members. In many ways, they were communal without being cooperative, anti-individual but inadequately collective.

The cooperative enterprises represented in many of the chapters of this book - cooperation among users, between users and environmental specialists, and among environmental specialists themselves - "work" because the cooperative mode (whether people cooperate collectively or as individuals) "works" better than its alternative. They "work" because they recognise that there are definable, understandable, essential, and interesting differences among groups of people (cultural groups, socio-economic groups, age cohorts) that transcend merely annoying "individual differences"; and, in recognizing these group differences, they use the information in productive ways. They recognise, too, that places and their component resources possess both uniqueness and commonality, in dialectical relation. Even more, they recognise that the set of dimensions or system of categories underlying the perception of commonality differs from one group of specialists, or of users, to another, in accordance with their world views. "Every man a scientist", said the psychologist George Kelly (1955); whether this ethnoscience harnesses repertory grids, phenomenology, facet theory, historical or literary analysis, or other approaches, it remains the system by which people use and value their environments.

Action and Place, then, are both social phenomena; that, in the final analysis, is the most fundamental message of this book. It is the start of a new direction built upon the closing stages of earlier journeys: an opening epilogue.

Bibliography

Allee, W. C. (1938) <u>The Social Life of Animals</u> New York: W. W. Norton.

Allee, W. C. (1951) <u>Cooperation Among Animals with Human Implications</u> New York: Schuman.

Altman, I. (1975) <u>The Environment and Social Behaviour</u> Monterey: Brooks/Cole.

Archea, J. and Eastman, C. (1970) <u>EDRA TWO</u> Carnegie-Mellon University Office Services Department.

Ardrey, R. (1966) <u>The Territorial Imperative</u> New York: Athenuem.

Canter, D. (1985) <u>Facet Theory: Approaches to Social Research</u> New York: Springer-Verlag.

Canter, D. (1986) "Putting Situations in their Place: foundations for a bridge between social and environment psychology" in Furnham, A. (ed) <u>Social Behaviour in Context</u>, 57, 460-462.

Chermayeff, S. and Alexander, C. (1963) <u>Community and Privacy: Toward a New Architecture of Humanism</u> New York: Doubleday.

Chokor, B. A. (1986) "Research Policy and review 7. Developments in environment-behaviour-design research: a critical assessment in the context of geography and planning with special reference to the third world". <u>Environment and Planning A</u>, 8, 5-26.

Kelly, G. (1955) <u>The Psychology of Personal Constructs</u> New York: Norton.

Korosec-Serfaty, P. (1984) "The Home from Attic to Cellar", <u>Journal of Environmental Psychology</u>, 4, 303-321.

Kropotkin, P. A. (1968) <u>Ethics: Origin and Development</u> New York: Benjamin Bloom.

Newman, D. (1972) <u>Defensible Space: People and Design in the Violent City</u>, London: Architectural Press.

Relph, E. (1976) <u>Place</u> <u>and</u> <u>Placelessness</u> London: Pion.

Seamon, D. (1982) "The Phenomenological Contribution to Environmental Psychology" <u>Journal</u> <u>of</u> <u>Environmental</u> <u>Psychology</u>, 2, 119-140.

1. Action and place: an existential dialectic

DAVID CANTER

PRELUDE

As indicated in the introduction to this volume, a number of authors have recognised the limitations imposed upon the development of a psychobehavioural science that can contribute effectively to environmental policy and design, in the assumed dichtomy between environment and behaviour. In this chapter this argument will be developed to show how we can replace it with a view of the dynamic interplay between action and place. It will be urged that in our design activities and in our research we should be looking for dialectical processes which continuously create changes in the patterns and meaning of actions in relation to places.

Central to these processes are conscious intentions shaped by a person's awareness of self and role in a given context. Intentions and actions are themselves structured by place related rules, negotiated with others, their outcomes reflected in expressed satisfaction with or pleasure in a given place.

Within this framework research cannot stop at asking what people do where, or how satisfied they are with what they have. Design cannot be seen as a neutral shell for containing particular behaviours. Physical forms should actively reflect and express the action/place transactions

---

*The organisation of this paper reflects Bach (circa 1720) in dynamic intentions.

1

of which they are a part. The spatial relationships between places should derive from and contribute to the role/rule networks which give those places their integrated distinctness.

These many themes have their origins in giving human agency pride of place. Engels (Wertsch, 1981) wrote of human labour having the character of "premeditated planned action directed towards definite ends known in advance". The British psychologist William McDougall (1908) made a similar perspective central to his writings. He saw the need to examine the goals that focus motivations if we are fully to understand human activities.

Like many more recent psychologists, McDougall saw consciousness and the human mind as being central to this process of goal orientation. Unfortunately, he saw the essence of this goal orientation in innate needs, yet he did not underestimate the role of mindful processes in human activities. As he put it "the essential nature of mind is to govern present action by anticipation of the future in the light of past experience". This theme was taken up in the fifties by George Kelly (1955) an American psychologist whose ideas have been influential in both British environmental psychology and behavioural geography. Kelly said we should not have to invoke any special notions such as drives, or forces to explain why people do not remain inert. He emphasised the dynamic, active nature of the human experience. Like McDougall he saw the importance of our understanding the sense which people make of their past as well as their anticipation of their own possible futures.

ALLEMANDE

McDougall and Kelly and a number of present-day psychologists throughout Eastern and Western Europe, who we shall be considering later, all reflect an approach to humanity which was first clearly articulated in the far reaching writings of Hegel (Singer, 1983). Hegel saw development and change as central not only to an individual's life-long experiences but to the whole process of human civilization. His ideas have been so profound and influential that major themes in both scientific and political thought can be traced to his argument; I am referring to the ideas of biological evolution and social revolution.

I am not so courageous or foolhardy as to deliver a disquisition on Hegel. So all I will draw from his vast and profound writings is the idea that in order to understand, explore and influence important individual, social and political processes we must harness concepts which are fundamentally dynamic. It is important that we, self-consciously, use a language of human action, in and on the world.

Hegel drew on the philosophical tradition of dialectics, which goes back at least to Socrates. He showed that in order to understand any active, changing processes it is necessary to consider at least two interacting systems. Within Hegel's dialectics these two systems have a natural relationship to each other, such that each is a direct consequence of antagonisms (or as Mao calls them "contradictions" 1967) inherent in the other. It is through the interplay of these symbiotic

2

opponents that change, and in Hegel's (and later Marx's) terms, progress emerges. From this perspective most of the major theories of 20th century psychology, sociology and anthropology have a dialectical quality to them. Just to stay within the realms of psychology, Piaget, Freud and Skinner all see development and human growth as a product of the interactions between two fundamentally distinct and inherently opposing systems. Of course, the great Russian psychologists such as Leont'ev (Wertsch, 1981) have taken an even more overtly dialectical perspective on human action and experience.

We have much to learn from this approach to the problem of studying and shaping human actions in the world. After all, our central concern is precisely with the actions which decision makers perform on behalf of other people. Change and intervention is central to the themes of the present volume

Yet an examination of the Environment Behaviour literature reveals theories and findings that are stubbornly stable. Our scientific metaphors, for example, are taken from the concrete and permanent. Systems of thought which are inherently concerned with variations over time, such as those within music (Karolyi 1981), are hardly ever drawn upon. The traditions of ecological psychology with its behaviour settings and standing patterns of behaviour; the study of mental maps with their static two dimensional qualities; the determination of acceptable levels of performance for lighting or noise; the assignment of meaning to various symbolic forms, all these and the great majority of other studies within our area are conceptualized and presented as phenomena which exist across an indefinite time period. With the notable exception of the writings of Lynch and some of the "chronogeographers", such as Parkes and Thrift (1980) it is rare to find discussions of origin, modification, variations over time, evolution, development and decay.

This omission has two important and related consequences. One consequence is that as researchers we are always chasing changes which others are bringing about. In the U.S. open-plan schools were studied once they were already an established part of architects' vocabulary. In Britain high-rise housing became a research focus when many decision makers had already recognised its failures. Even issues such as meaning and symbolism in built form only became dominant areas for research once the rhetoric of the architectural and planning professions had already accepted them.

The second consequence is that from the practical point of view this limitation on our ways of thinking means that the design and planning professions stumble from one fashion to another. They are not driven by any evolving theory. An almost random series of changes shape our towns and cities. Whether a city centre is destroyed and rebuilt from scratch, or rehabilitated and modified in relation to what already exists, is often an accident of interest charges and political whim.

Yet the opposing forces, the dialectical colleagues, out of which growth and change emerge are everywhere to be seen in the study of person environment relationships. After all, our field is frequently identified by being called the study of environment and behaviour. These two labels have virtually generated their own realms of study, but are seen to interact in some poorly defined way to create the world we experience.

Yet this is precisely where the fundamental difficulty in understanding the dialectical process lies. Hillier (1973) indicated it many years ago, when the pointed to the confusions inherent in the use of the term "environment", but he did not challenge the term "behaviour" as well and he did not emphasise the significance of dynamic person/place transactions. Furthermore, many of even the most avowedly interactionist students of environment and behaviour accept a Cartesian dualism in which there is the world of physical entities an "environment" and there is a world of "behaviour". This is a perspective which is part of the general metaphysical stance that Mao (1967) upbraids as "mechanical materialism" and "vulgar evolutionism". This dichotomy between environment and behaviour in which mental and social processes have no clear presence, or indeed location, is the fundamental confusion which must be clarified before we can produce an active framework of direct relevance to the realities of actions and decision making.

COURANTE

In order to produce a more active, dynamic range of explorations, I take as our starting point the fact that human experience is paramount. It is what each individual knows and does and feels within the world which creates the reality for that individual. But the problem is that such a reality cannot be brought into simple connection with a notional, scientifically measured, "objective" environment. The world as experienced has its own laws of objective existence. Thus, whenever we try to develop causal explanations which show environment and behaviour influencing each other, we find it difficult to proceed very far or very fast and we frequently find very little empirical evidence for the environmental influences for which we search. So many researchers fall back upon "levels of significance" which account for insignificantly small proportions of the measured variation, hiding behind statistical tests for fear or facing the epistemological questions their work raises.

I would suggest that one of the emerging realizations which characterizes the conference in Berlin, and which we must not allow to dissipate, is that instead of dealing with environment and behaviour we must deal with action and place.

Action and place are both products of our experience of our transactions woth the world. The notion of action is distinct from that of behaviour in many ways, but one of the most important is that actions integrate conscious objectives. A person's acts include intentions of what it is wished to achieve with those acts. So, for example it may often be more fruitful to classify actions in terms of their objectives rather than their content. Walking may be an observed behaviour, but going for a walk is a different act from walking to school, because of this purposive nature of human actions an act must always be directed to some entity or process outside of itself. In order to act we must distinguish between ourselves as subjects and the objects of our acts.

4

Action requires a distinction between the entity carrying out the act and the entity on which the action is carried out. In other words, as human beings, in order to be able to act on our surroundings, we need to make a distinction between ourselves and our surroundings. We must also, however, distinguish the active significance of differing surroundings. This is a theme central to Kaplan's (1983) cognitive model of environmental transactions. Unfortunately he does not point out that in order to know what is possible we must experience the consequences of our acts. It is by acting on our surroundings that we make sense of them.

This point is made quite clearly, and directly linked to a dialectical framework, in the study of the Meaning of Things carried out by Csikszentmihalyi and Rochberg-Halton (1981). They specify that in acting on the world a differentiation is being made between the world outside the individual and the world of the individual. This differentiation is the first stage in a process which makes it more possible to integrate the world into further actions. Thus the process of differentiation and integration, which in their ways Piaget and Darwin saw as fundamental to growth and evolution, is also clearly central to the human process of acting on the world.

At an earlier European conference Grauman (1976) took this theme directly. He argued that differentiation and integration are combined in the notion of appropriation, providing a fruitful way of exploring the nature of person/place transactions. He produced a long list of forms of appropriation, showing that actions including everything from "looking" to "emigrating" reveal qualities of environmental appropriation.

One of the major research implications of this is that we need a fuller understanding of the categories and classifications that people use in order to be able to act on the world (Canter, 1986). We need to know what distinctions that make between various building forms: How the personal taxonomies which people utilize for their location decision making are drawn upon to facilitate action, and pleasure in action inaction, in the world. Groat (1982) has carried out some interesting studies along these lines, but a great deal more is possible.

One of the applied consequences is that passive participation in design is of little value. The border between participation and education by doing should be readily crossed. Action itself is a process of distinction and separation. But what we act on is a world which is experienced and understood through that action. Those qualities of it which are perceived as objective and independent of the individual are a product of the subjective, mindful activities of that individual.

As I see it, the value of dealing with human action, instead of behaviour, is that action is driven by an individual; a person. Action is the product of a particular person wishing to achieve certain objectives in a directed and intended way. Action thus encompasses both the concepts of objectives and goals as well as consciousnes and intention. As I have said, this view has remarkably old antecedents. In his outline Psychology published in 1892 James Sully (1892) wrote

the following. "Besides the factor of active consciousness all the
more complex processes of volitions ... [have] other ingredients as
well.   These consist of psychical antecedents, that is, mental
processes proceeding, as well as those accompanying the action. This
antecedent factor may in general be described as a forecasting or
prevision of the action itself and of some at least of its results
under the form of an 'end'".

Self

So, actions contain conscious components which relate to the
anticipated outcomes of those actions. Harre and von Cranach (1982) in
their recent publication have emphasised this point and shown the need
to take these conscious components into account and to collect
information on them in any explanation of human action. At an even
elementary tactical level, then, surveys which ask how much people
like what they have, or bipolar adjectival ratings, lose all contact
with the fundamental questions about what people want to do in given
locations and what cognitions relate to those intentions.

But, as I have already argued, these actions are built upon a
differentiation of the individual self from the world in order to be
able to integrate the world at a more general level. I decide what is
a personal view and what is an audience for that view so that I can
then express the view to the audience. Thus all actions contain some
component of self-clarification or self-definition. By acting on the
world we learn more of the nature of the people we are; our
capabilities, our worth, our potential (Peled, 1976). It is in this
sense that I see actions on the world as fundamentally existential
(Valle and King, 1978).

Proshansky (1983) and his colleagues have written about the role of
place identify for self identity. In their symposium on the Theory of
Place at this Conference Sime and others take this theme further. I
would only, at this stage, like to draw attention to the fact that many
writers (Gergen, 1971) on self concepts have been made clear the
distinction between the self experienced in a subjective form the "I",
and self as an objective, social entity having temporal and spatial
existence that relates directly to other temporal and spatial entities,
the "me". We need to sort out the implications of these different
facets of self for different person/place transactions, because here
lies one clue to the strong emotional qualities places can elicit.

Role

The focus on self also helps to emphasize the critical importance of
the social processes within which an individual acts. From Herbert
Mead (1934) and beyond it has been emphasized that the concept of self
is in part defined by contact with other individuals. George Kelly
echoes this and resonates with some of Hegel's arguments when he points
out that it is the individual's awareness of and interactions with
other selves which helps to clarify and formulate that individual's
self concepts.

6

Kelly sees the self as one of a number of roles of which the individual is aware. What I am arguing here is that the actions which an individual performs are structured by the possibilities made available through the role structure of which that individual is a part. Another way of thinking of this is that, roles enshrine the dominant objectives which an individual feels required to achieve. As a consequence, in understanding people's action on the world we need to understand the role they see themselves playing and their understanding of those roles.

This has direct research consequences. It shows that rather than focusing on individual differences, on personality variations, in order to explain the different patterns of actions and understandings which people perform we should be looking at their role within a given social and organisational context. Indeed in a great deal of research that we have done we have been able to demonstrate quite categorically that role differences are reflected in different patterns of activity and in different conceptualizations of transactions with the surroundings. At the Louvain la Neuve conference I (1979) called this the "second law of environmental interaction". Within this framework, for example, age, sex and membership of various special interest groups are all most fruitfully seen as aspects of role variations which may be important for shaping person/place transactions.

One of the most significant role differentiations is between the individual who has responsibility for changing places (the architect or manager) and the individual who is expected simply to suffer those changes (the user or resident). There is a superordinate relationship in which the designer, planner or architect who has responsibility for place modification is actually attempting to interfere with the existing person/place transactions. If the designer does not know anything about the patterns of action and objective which are characteristic of existing transactions then their design can only be inappropriate. If designers further misunderstand their own role in relation to place modification we have a receipe for confusion and unproductive change.

Rules

What is fascinating is the extent to which design actually does work. The frequency with which people _can_ make use of building forms created by people with little understanding of those who will use them. The key to this consistency is not some notional "flexibility" of buildings or "adaptability" of human beings. It is the coherent and conscious social structuring and inter-personal negotiation which makes place use possible. What is crucial here is that daily use of places reveals that consistent patterns of human actions (Canter, 1984) on the world are an observable product of the processes I have been discussing.

We would expect rules and related role definitions to give rise to an observable set of consistencies. It is the short term stabilities, the plateaux which a process reaches before it changes, which can be observed in standing patterns of behaviour. Thus ecological studies pick up superficial qualities of human actions. We can examine the processes which generate these much more directly by looking at what rules guide human actions and what objectives shape them. In doing this we do find remarkable consistencies across differing cultures (Canter, 1986).

The great interest in studying privacy in the United States can be seen as a function of the power which rules relating to privacy do have in structuring the acceptability of where people can act within that culture. More direct studies of rule formation, development and change, asking what may happen in which place, are already beginning to show us the significance of differing building forms in different social contexts. The layout of a theatre requires an understanding of the roles being performed front-of-house as well as those back stage. Such explorations can also lay the foundations for participation and design guidance.

In other words, it is now possible to turn away from identifying the amount of space needed for a particular class of behaviour, or only to allow participation in planning to focus on what activities will be housed in a given location, and turn towards consideration of the rules that will guide actions in places and to elaborate the pattern of place-role relationships which give places their structure and organisation.

GAVOTTE

The process of differentiation and subsequent integration through acting on the world is also mirrored in the creation by the individual of internal representations of the world as experienced. The famous quotation from Marx serves to illustrate the critical relevance of this point to person/place transactions:

> "what distinguishes the worst architect from the best of bees is this, that the architect raises his structure in his imagination before he erects it in reality."

For designers as well as others the emergent reality leads to a reshaping of the imaginative representation, bringing together an understanding of actions and the locations in which they occur. It is this integrated representation of actions within a physical context which I have called in earlier publications "places" (Canter, 1977).

Places are not only locations. They are categorizations of experience. They are differentiations made by an individual in relation to possible acts to which that person may aspire. By distinguishing between a person's actions and possible places for those actions we are able to create a more effective integration of the two.

Let us consider a real example here to illustrate this central theme. The managers of an organisation come to the conclusion that they should increase their marketing activities. They examine their current place of work and decide that it is inappropriate for these new objectives. They have made a distinction between desired actions and current places, leading to the definition of a new place within which their new objectives can take root.

However, once the new place has been created it will take on a different definition both from the actions which are actually associated with it and from the social processes of place-rule negotiation. This will lead to the emergence of new objectives. These objectives, and their associated actions, will once again be distinguished from their context requiring further modifications to the place as experienced.

To the distant observer, such as an architect being briefed by a client, the above process may look like an organisation discovering it does not have enough space for marketing and commissioning an addition to its building. The architect may then be surprised to discover that the new extension, when built, is immediately assigned to central administration, not marketing at all. The dialectics of action and place, however, indicate that the amount of space involved is only a reflection of certain states of the person/place transactions.

What is true of space in an office is true of other environmental resources, whether it is the Brazilian rain forest or urban open spaces. What we see is only a reflection of the current state of the differentiation and integration of actions and places.

Let me just reiterate the central message I am putting forward here. The research literature of person/place interactions, over the past few years has shown that there are a number of consistencies and stabilities. Standing patterns of behaviour, mental maps, processes of control and space definition have all been identified. Now we must move on to explore the processes of transaction and change which those stabilities we have identified so poorly capture.

It has always been characteristic of our area of activity that our starting point is that we wish to change that which we study. We are not concerned with a solely neutral, objective stance. We are committed to improvement and development, we are committed to modification. But in the past although we have accepted the desire to change what we study we have done little to study what it is that changes. We must work harder at developing models that are inherently unstable. But in order to do that we must go beyond mechanical models of cause and effect. By taking active human agency as our starting point we are logically required to see human actions as central to the change process.

We have already seen that action requires the notion of goal and intent, with their associated exploration of the internal models of the world we inhabit. In other words, by separating off a reality on which action operates, in order to help clarify the self from which the world has been differentiated, we must build up patterns of location for potential actions and their likely consequences. Thus, just as we find consistent role related patterns of behaviour, with their associated rules and development mechanisms, we find consistent conceptualisations of places. These conceptual systems which people employ would, as a consequence, also be expected to have a structure and stability to them and one of which people are aware.

The geographers, such as Relph (1976) and Seamon (1979), who have espoused a phenomonological framework, are some way along the road towards this perspective. The literature on mental mapping indirectly and often in a very confused way, non-the-less demonstrates that if you ask people what happens where they can reflect on their internal representations and generate symbolic configurations which summarise the understandings they have of the world in which they operate. We also know from many studies that physical locations are loaded with emotional connotations. The book shops contain many general accounts of places (Blythe) that have had significance for individuals and from which meanings can be derived. Yet within our literature there is remarkably little overlap between studies of behaviour in various settings and studies of the internal representations on which people can draw for various contexts. Yet at even a banal level, the dialectic proposed here indicates that we could fruitfully explore the relationship between behavioural maps and cognitive maps (Canter, 1977).

The Cartesian distinction between subjective and objective has lead to a confusion about the nature of "place". This has been aggravated in the writings of geographers such as Relph by the use of a romantic elaboration of the notion of place. When I use the term "place" I see it as a technical term to describe a component of experience that has distinct coexisting aspects to it. These aspects are drawn from the fact that by acting on the world the individual makes a distinction between human activities and the world. So a place always contains, in an integrated form, an individuals' preconscious and conscious awareness of both likely actions and their outcomes and the physical form with which those actions may be integrated.

We have thought too much about cognition and looked to closely at perception. Places are aspects of experience. It is important to emphasise that places can be neutral or emotionally charged. They can be experienced as highly relevent to a particular individual such as in the writings of Lym (1980), or they can be the type of "placeless" places which Relph discusses. Part of our task in influencing design is to understand the special qualities which particular places require for particular activities and goals.

In exploring the way in which places are experienced, two important processes which link these experiences to human actions are worth noting. One is the symbolic qualities which places have. The way in which they represent both the individual who uses them and the type of activities which are possible. Architects have always been aware of these qualities of places, frequently expressing this awareness through a discussion of "expressiveness". Indeed, as in many other, probably all, forms of art they have found joy and rapture in the way these expressions are actually generated. There is no opportunity here to discuss the profound and important questions of aesthetic reaction. However, I would suggest that Krampen's (1979) arguments about the meaning which style itself carries, is one step toward understanding the peasures of place.

GIGUE

Beyond the symbolic qualities of places we must consider also consider the way the structure and organisation of places are integrated with role relationships of the people using different places (Canter, 1984).

Architects and planners have always been aware of the importance of understanding the relationships between places, within a building or within parts of a city. But what is clear now is that we are talking about relationships between the different roles which an individual might take on and the different roles which individuals play in relation to each other. By examining the patterns of shared objectives and the areas of conflict we can identify the topological form which is appropriate for any given organization at any given point in time.

By acting on a place we demonstrate our separateness from it and thus increase our opportunity for controlling it. When I rearrange the furniture in a room I reveal that the seminar I wish to hold in that room consists of something more than my own thought processes and involves a set of role relationships which have spatial implications. But in shaping the room I create a reorganisation of my experience of that place which, in its turns requires me to act on it in a particular way. Thus my actions and my conceptualizations are always in dynamic tension. Insofar as I am sane in my experience of the world, and insofar as I share a common set of conceptualizations with others who share places with me, I will be part of a process which has short-term stability. However, this short term stability has in it the seeds of long term evolution, development and change.

Part of the seeds of the change come from the fact that my definition of place use and action will not be identical to everybody elses. Certainly people who have different role relationships to any given place will have a requirement to negotiate the nature of that place and the actions which are permissible within it. The results of that negotiation produce a higher order stability which in its turn leads to a redefinition of the nature of the place. Such a redefinition will have biases to it and be more closely identified with some actions than with others. These biases will lead to further development and change. Further attempts to adjust the place or to redirect actions will eventually ensue.

Where then, does this leave us? A recognition that all is flux has more than methodological implications. It suggests that the results to date that have characterised person/environment transactions are only a reflection of dynamic processes at a particular stage in their evolution. That there are common structures which exist across changing circumstances is to be expected, but certainly all those frameworks and perspectives that assume the possibility of a static set of transactions fall into doubt. This includes, notably, the concept of a brief for a design. The possibility that the form of a place can be specified at a given point in time and then designed must be questioned. Instead the processes and structures of which the building, the neighbourhood or the city are a part must be articulated as a basis for creating a design process. The action research which Bob Sommer advocates in his presentation can, in this light, be seen as far more than an adjunct to the design process, but as an integral part of it.

Also the cry for conservation takes on a new light. Professor Galtung in his presentation quite appropriately points to the need to monitor environmental modifications. But modifications are at the core of person/place transactions. They do have goals/objectives which direct them and will be reflected in the role relationships which manage them. They will accommodate conceptualizations of what is to be achieved at any given point.

I am advocating an integrated set of person/place studies, which assimilate both an ecological framework and a cognitive one, which absorb the emotional components derived from pleasure in places and the possibility of conscious human volition. These studies will recognise that the places people experience have symbolic and representational components which reflect the role relationships that their actions and those places play and the ways in which they play those roles (Canter, 1984). All this will be within a set of activities which take design decision making as an integrated part of normal events. This evolving process will lead to the overlap between design and research becoming greater, as both increasingly are seen as the same process of the interplay of action and place leading to the clarification and growth of role and self definition.

BUILT FORM: SOME CONSEQUENCES* FROM THE EXISTENTIAL DIALECTIC

In general, the approach described here does not lead to a specific identification of a particular physical form being the 'correct', or best, one. Instead it proposes that certain relationships between actions and places are more appropriate than others.

1. Relationships between Places

A strictly functional (effort minimising) pattern of links between locations will be less effective than one which responds to the pattern of user role differentiations.

2. Symbolic Interpenetration

The access from one place to another place should reflect/symbolise the distinctions between the activity objectives that users of those places are likely to have.

3. Structured Flexibility

That component of an action pattern which is quintessential to its existence should be central to a design conception, elements of flexibility should be left to the design of those component places which are less significant.

4. Internal Objectives

Within a place the patterns of activities typical of that place will have a set of related objectives. These objectives will have appropriate meanings associated with them. The form of a place should thus reflect these activities and meanings.

5. Internal/External Relationships

The identification by a person of what relates to them and what not is the starting categorisation. This creates a division of what is inside a given place and what is outside. Thus the ways in which a design handles the relationship between its inside and outside is critical.

----

*In this brief, general paper there is not the space to elaborate all the specific consequences of the proposed approach. However, in the belief that an action theory should have direct implications for human acts I am including some tables which indicate a few of the conclusions to which I see the perspective leading

SOME METHODOLOGICAL IMPLICATIONS

1. Conscious Intentions are preferable to descriptions of behaviour.

2. Role differences are the key aspect of individual variation to be studied.

3. The rules which govern the use of places are critical aspects to examine in most studies.

4. The use of descriptive and case oriented studies are likely to be far more fruitful than experimental research paradigms.

SOME RESEARCH DIRECTIONS

1. The role of place differentiation for those individuals whose sense of self may be less secure than average (e.g. children, the elderly, the handicapped) is worthy of study.

2. The consequences of effective action in specific places for later adjustment in other places requires exploration. (e.g. are place linked actions in therapeutic settings predictive of later health?).

3. All the issues listed in the three other tables are directly amenable to study.

4. Is a pattern language possible? It seems feasible that, at least within a give culture, there are place/action transactions which are so stable that particular physical forms can be suggested as most appropriate for them. Research can identify what these might be expected to be from an examination of individual's taxonomic schemes and then look at the consequences of their presence or absence.

DESIGN PRACTICE

1. Transactions with Clients.

During the process of design all parties are involved in a process of action differentiation and self-definition.

2. Beyond the Static Brief.

The basis for the design of a place is an analysis of the role/acivity patterns which have given rise to the requirement for a place to be built and the inherent transactions out of which changes will emerge.

3. Participation is Education.

Given that people come to understand the relevance of places for their actions by making decisions about those places, the process of participation in design is always one of self-education. Its planning and timing should therefore facilitate and accommodate that educational process.

4. Implicit Design Through Selection.

Many design decisions are made through selection. It may be through the selection of an architect to do the design or selection of a place in which to live. Design practice should therefore enhance the differentiation and integration on which effective selection can be based.

5. Role/Rule Negotiation.

The design process should itself encourage the negotiation of place use, especially between different role groups.

6. Symbol Sharing.

The expressive qualities appropriate to any place need to be explored with interested parties as much as the functional "brief" does.

7. Representations of Action.

In order to act on place proposals the possible actions as well as the potential physical form should be represented. As much effort should go into representing what the experience of a place will be as in representing what it will look like.

Bibliography

Bach, J.S. (circa 1720) Six Suites a Violoncello Solo senza Basso: Number 6 in D major.

Blythe, R. (ed) Places: An anthology of Britain Oxford: Oxford University Press.

Canter, D. (1977) The Psychology of Place New York: St. Martins Press.

Canter, D. (1977) "Children in Hospital: a facet theory approach to person/place synomorphy, Journal of Architectural Research 6 (2).

Canter, D. (1979) "Y a-t-il des Lois d'Interaction Environnementale?" in J-G Simon (ed) Experiences Conflictuelles deL'Espace Louvain-La-Neuve: Universite Catholique, 391-398.

Canter, D. (1986) "Putting Situations in their Place: foundations for a bridge between social and environmental psychology" in A. Furnham (ed) Social Behaviour in Context London: Allyn and Bacon.

Canter, D. (1984) "Intention, Meaning and Structure: Social Action in its Physical Context" in M. Ginsburg et al (eds) Discovery Strategies in the Psychology of Social Action.

Von Cranach, M. and Harte, R. (eds) (1982) The Analysis of Action London: Cambridge University Press.

Csikszentmihalyi, M. and Rochberg-Halton, E. (1981) The Meaning of things London: Cambridge University Press.

Gergen, K.J. (1971) The Concept of Self New York: Holt, Rinehart and Winston.

Grauman, C.F. (1976) "The Concept of Appropriation (Aneignung) and Modes of Appropriation of Space" in P. Korosec-Serfaty (ed) Appropriation of Space published by Universite Louis Pasteur p113-125.

Groat, L. (1982) "Meaning in Post-Modern Architecture" Journal of Environmental Psychology, 2(1), 3-22.

Hillier, W.R.G. and Leaman, A. (1973) "The Man-Environment Paradigm and its Paradoxes" Architectural Design August.

Kaplan, S. and Kaplan, R. (1983) Cognition and Environment New York: Praeger.

Karolyi, O.(1981) Introducing Music Harmondsworth: Penguin.

Kelly, G.A. (1955) The Psychology of Personal Constructs New York: W.W. Norton.

Krampen, M. (1979) Meaning in the Urban Environment London: Pion.

Lym, G.R. (1980) A Psychology of Building Engelwood Cliffs: Prentice Hall.

Lynch, K. (1972) What Time is This Place? Cambridge: MIT Press.

Mao, T-T. (1967) On Contradiction Peking: Foreign Language Press.

McDougall, W. (1908) Introduction to Psychology London: Methuen.

Mead, G.H. (1934) Mind, Self and Society Chicago: University of Chicago.

Parkes, D.N. and Thrift, N.J. (1980) Times, Spaces, and Places New York: Wiley.

Peled, A. (1976) The Place as a Metaphoric Body Haifa: The Technion.

Proshansky, H.M., Abbe, K., Fabian, A.K., and Kaminoff, R. (1983) "Place-Identity: Physical world socialization of the self" Journal of Environmental Psychology 3(1) 57-83.

Relph, E.C. (1976) Place and Placelessness London: Pion.

Seamon, D. (1979 A Geography of the Lifeworld London: Croome Helm.

Singer, P. (1983) Hegel New York: Oxford University Press.

Sully, J. (1892) Outline of Psychology London: Longmans, Gren and Co.

Valle, R.S. and King, M. (eds) (1978) Existential-Phenomenological Alternatives for Psychology New York: Oxford University Press.

Wertsch, J.V. (ed) (1981) The Concept of Activity in Soviet Psychology New York: M.E. Sharpe.

2. Environmental perception: an ecological perspective

KLAUS LANDWEHR

SUMMARY

This paper is intended to provide an ecological perspective for
environmental psychology. Environmental psychology is taken to be
aimed at predicting behaviour by environmental variables. The
ecological approach advocated can be identified with J.J. Gibson's
contributions to the field of perception, where the study of perception
is regarded to be basic to the study of any other psychological issue.
Gibson's approach is introduced by explicating his basic methodological
tenets, his unusual terminology, and his 'theory of space perception'
which redefines that issue in terms of "perceiving the layout of
surfaces". Special attention is drawn to the way Gibson deals with the
ubiquituous fact of "serial vision", i.e. the co-perception of
egolocomotion and spatial layout, and to what it means to perceive
"affordances", i.e. opportunities for action. Finally, the
applicability of Gibson's analysis to environmental perception research
is illustrated by two examples, the first one dealing with how to
analyze any real world scene in order to highlight the main features
which seem relevant to the architect's and to the user's concern, the
other one dealing with the more specific question of how we manage to
perceive the climbability of a staircase. In conclusion it is argued
that the task of environmental psychology no longer ought to be trying
to predict behaviour in arbitrarily chosen physical terms but, rather,
defining the constraints of action with regard to what an environment
affords, the environment and the actor being described at a level
reflecting their mutual compatibility in the first place.

INTRODUCTION

This paper is based upon the thesis that environmental psychology in general and environmental perception research in particular are n o t ecological in perspective according to a definition of "ecological" which I shall try to explain.

I shall not try to prove my thesis by criticizing previous research and theorizing, rather, I shall provide an alternative by giving an outline of, and elaborating upon, the late James J. Gibson's ecological approach to visual perception (and perception and psychology more gene-rally; Gibson 1961, 1966, 1979), leaving it to the reader's discretion to detect the differences between this and traditional approaches.

Taking my thesis for granted, for the moment, one might well ask: how could this happen? Obviously, the present state of affairs is due to environmental psychologists' adoption of non-ecological research para-digms and methods. These were drawn from the kind of psychology that dominated the field when environment-behavior science was first est-ablished as a new sub-discipline.

It is true that social and environmental psychologists have played a central role in trying to have their science convert to new standards (Barker 1965, 1968, Milgram 1970, Secord 1972, Proshansky 1976, Wapner and his associates 1976, and, more recently, Canter 1977, 1984a, b, are among the most influential individuals in this respect). However, as will become clearer in a moment, even their attempts do not suffice to really redirect previously misdirected efforts.

And admittedly, environmental perception researchers have always tried to turn to the more ecologically inclined approaches in perception psychology (cf. Avant & Helson (1973) and Gregory (1974) for an over-view), most notably Gestalt theory (e.g. Arnheim 1954, 1977, Prak 1977) and Transactionalism (Ittelson 1973, 1978). None of these theories, however, provided us with a conception of the perceptual processes which would generally be applicable and acceptable across all phenomena at all scales.

Gestalt theory, or more exactly, Gestalt phenomenology, which is what has been adopted from Gestalt theory proper, limits itself to rather artificial conditions, only paying attention to formal, geometrical relations considered solely with regard to static perception (paradig-matically: a static observer looking at line drawings on a picture plane). This self-imposed limitation of the scope of experimental in-vestigation is partly due to the adherence to a certain theoretical framework. Gestalt theory proper centers around the idea of psycho--physical or, more exactly, psycho-physiological i s o m o r p h i s m , i.e. a correspondence of the "phenomenal percepts" with organizing, thus primary, "field forces" in the brain. The theory can be said to be main-ly constituted and/or summarized, for the German speaking scientific community, where it originated, by the writings of Wertheimer (1912, 1922, 1923), Köhler (1920), and Metzger (1953), for the Anglo-American audience by those of Koffka (1922, 1935) and again Köhler (1929).

Transactionalism, starting from questionable empiricist presupposit-ions, soon shifted its interest to environmental i n t e r p r e t a t i o n without relating its findings back to inter-individually identifiable, non-disputable stimuli. This makes it especially hard to derive implic-ations and guidelines for design from that approach.

Note that Empiricism, although it holds that all our knowledge of the world stems from individual experience, nevertheless supposes this to be based upon preexisting as well as acquired principles of inference and association, thus making perception more the result of "set", assumptions, hypotheses, or personality than a function of stimulation (the classic reference is Helmholtz 1866, cf. Hochberg 1981 for a modern statement and again Hochberg 1962 for a historical treatment of the issue). Paradoxically, nativism, especially in its modern versions of an evolutionary epistemology (e.g. Lorenz 1973), tries to analyze possible pre-experiential constraints on knowledge acquisition empiricly or, for that matter, by means of logical reconstruction believed to mirror actually terminated or ongoing evolutionary development or present stages thereof.

Psychophysics (Fechner 1860, Stevens 1975, also Gibson in his earlier writings 1950a, 1959) can be said to sidestep the problem, favoring a direct approach (naive empiricism, if you want). Gibson in his later writings (from 1966 onward) would score as a nativist, but also favoring direct realism. Classifying theories along the empiricism-nativism dimension is complicated by its cutting across the stance theorists take as regards the materialism-idealism issue (the mind-body dichotomy), where psychophysics, in my view, counts as reductionistic materialism, the ecological perspective is a dialectical approach (cf. the section on Gibson's basic tenets in this paper).

I do not want to suggest that we should quickly do away with the above mentioned theories (Gestalt and Transactionalism). Rather, it can be shown that they incorporate valuable aspects. However, Gibson's work provides us with the promising outlook of being able to incorporate these aspects into a more general and systematic framework, where, among other things, a clear-cut distinction can be drawn between environmental p e r c e p t i o n and other forms of cognitively appraising the environment, e.g. looking at pictures or answering questions about it.

Most environment-behavior scientists do not seem to be interested in the visual, auditory etc. perception of social events but, rather, presumed social effects on perception/cognition. Regarding their field as dealing with historical, socially constituted reality, say, architecture, towns, etc., they tend to care more about defining variables at a sociological scale than they do about the perception process itself. In fact, by using the standard methodology of questionnaires, rating scales etc. they no longer deal with perception but environmental d e - s c r i p t i o n . While this certainly is a valuable contribution in its own right we should also look for how these two activities, environmental perception and description, relate to each other (Landwehr 1985c). For this task, a powerful analysis of perception is needed in the first place, because before inventing or learning a language to talk about something that something has to be perceived.

PRELIMINARY TERMINOLOGICAL CLARIFICATIONS

My definition of psychology was implicitly stated in the introduction. The way I use the terms perception and environment is closely linked to what I want to introduce as an ecological perspective on these topics. The full meaning of "ecological" can only be grasped by becoming familiar with the analyses to be presented. In order to avoid gross misunderstandings, however, some defining remarks may be necessary.

The concept of ecology originates from biology (the science of living, i.e. self-reproducing organisms) where it denotes that sub-discipline which investigates the interaction or interchange between some species or group of species and their respective surroundings. This includes an inventory of biological and environmental constraints on what might be a possible habitat for these species (where habitat is to be read as

"way of life" and/or "place to live in"). To propose an ecolⓞgcial perspective, thus, is to consider behavioural phenomena in the context of
complete or partial ecosystems, species-in-environments.

The co-called Chicago School of Sociology (Park et al. 1925) tried to
apply this idea to social phenomena, say, to sociologically categorized
activities of humans in their specific "self-made" (or self-moulded) environments, especially cities. McKenzie (1925) defines "human ecology"

> "as a study of the spatial and temporal realtions of human beings as
> affected by the selective, distributive, and accomodative forces of
> the environment" (say, of a town; Park et al. 1925, p. 63f.).

And it is in this specialized sense that Barker (see 1965, 1968 for the
most concise statements of his approach) introduced this idea into
psychology. He was interested in what people d o (together) and can do
in a community with all its formal and informal institutions (rules
for interaction), and especially how many people are required to keep
some collective activity going. This is the only environmental dimension
identified by Barker and his associates to be important, simply because
the only environmental variables they consider are behaviours of other
people.

Gibson, on the other hand, being interested in what people p e r -
c e i v e with respect to their material surroundings (of which other
people are also a part), goes back to a geographical, i.e., in the last
resort, a physical and chemical description of the environment (physics
and chemistry at an intermediate scale, i.e. human scale; see next section), leaving social events largely out of focus. I propose to call
Barker's approach s o c i o - e c o l o g i c a l   psychology and Gibson's
b i o - e c o l o g i c a l .

J.J. GIBSON'S ECOLOGICAL APPROACH TO PERCEPTION

Basic tenets

Gibson (1966, ch.1, 1979, ch.1) proposes to describe and analyze the
environment or, "what is there to be perceived" in physical and chemical
terms a t   t h e   s c a l e   o f   millimeters, meters, and perhaps kilo-
meters; this is roughly the human scale or that appropriate to animals
comparable to us. A useful terminology for this has been handed down
over centuries as "common sense physics", comprising the decomposition
of the world into its basic components of earth (land), water, wind
(air), and fire, by the Greeks. A more updated and sophisticated analysis refers to the different aggregate states of matter and distinguishes
media, substances, surfaces which separate the two, and various forms of
energy distribution (Gibson 1979, ch.2).

Note that this is a r e l a t i o n a l   terminology acknowledging the
m u t u a l i t y   of the words animal (or man) and environment. "Whatis
there to be perceived" is so f o r   u s , and different species may see
the world differently (Uexküll 1920, 1963). For example, the air is a
medium to move through for us, the water is the same to the fish, while
for us it is a special (liquid) substance. The very distinction of an-
imal/man and environment is itself an exertion of a p e r c e p t u a l
ability at our disposal, and I shall show later that there is optical-
-visual information not only available but really unavoidable to force
this separation upon us.

Relating specifics of an environment to the perceptual activities of
some animals, therefore, must not be confused with the stimulus-response

21

research paradigm of psychophysics or behaviourism. There, stimuli and responses are defined purely in a formal mathematical manner for abstract organisms, here, environment and perception/behavior is being investigated for concrete species in their biotope or habitat. Thus, we shall not look for general laws of behaviour (functional relations between stimuli and responses), unspecific to place and time, rather, we shall try to define constraints on the modes of perceiving and the routes for acting, here: for humans, in specific situations. These, too, may be lawfully related, but ecological laws will have to be formulated at a more complex, systems-theoretic level (Turvey et al. 1981).

There is another important characteristic of humans and a lot of other animals, too, to be taken into account in this context, namely, their ongoing exploratory activity. Thus, the paradigmatic case for an ecological inquiry into environmental perception is a m o v i n g observer looking around for something in his or her e v e r y d a y surroundings (or, listening to etc.). This led Gibson to abandon the idea of stimulation being imposed onto passive receptors and replace it by his conception of active perceptual systems o b t a i n i n g , picking up a v a i l a b l e information (Gibson 1966, ch.2 and 3).

After all, perception has to fulfill a d a p t i v e functions, so special attention is given to those aspects of an environment which constitute necessary or favorable conditions for the species' survival and welfare. Again, these "a f f o r d a n c e s " , on the one hand can be defined in physical terms, on the other hand they are defined relative to an animal species only. E.g., a certain kind of ground surface, relatively flat, not scattered with rolling stones, etc., is run-over-able for most mammals, but certain kinds of steps can be jumped down by some but not by others, certain kinds of holes are hiding places for rabbits but not for deer etc. It is here that most clearly o n t o g e n e t i c , developmental changes come in: a usual chair, for example, affords sitting for an adult but not necessarily for small children, because of their different bodily constitution; a typewriter affords quick and clearly printed writing, but of course only to the skilled and trained.

Gibson is convinced that we can build up a theory of perception along these lines. We start with an eco-physical description of the terrestrial environment, then, still in physical terms, try to identify in which way the attributes of the environment are specified in the structure and flow of energy distributions ambient to an observer, e. g., in reflected light, air compression, etc., and finally try to find out whether or not an individual observer actually picks up this available information.

It is Gibson's firm belief that generally the ambient energy arrays will be specific to properties of the environment, thus providing "new reasons for (the philosophical doctrine of (direct)) realism" (Gibson 1967). I shall not comment on the lively discussion on this tenet in this paper (see Shaw et al. 1982 for an elaboration), for the present purpose suffice it to say that the realist epistemological bias seems to be sympathetic to the practical concerns of the design professions.

Perceiving the layout of surfaces

Literally the most basic attribute of the terrestrial environment is the g r o u n d which extends about 4.6 km in radius around your place of observation to the h o r i z o n (for average eye height of 1.7 m and an idealized plane surface of a sphere with the approximate diameter of the earth). This surface exhibits some of the most salient features that most other (solid) surfaces on earth do also have: it is

rigid, cannot be penetrated without effort, and cannot be seen through.
Now normally the ground will not be level and even but rather slanted,
"wrinkled", and "cluttered", i.e. broken up into partial surfaces which
either (for the human scale!) are fixed and not removable, so they can
be considered as a bulge in the ground surface, or else they belong to
a detachable object. This makes for one important additional feature of
a layout of surfaces related to the general non-transparency of solids
- the co-called o c c l u d i n g   e d g e : depending on your place of observation you will see some surfaces, but not others, and for your movement along a p a t h   o f   o b s e r v a t i o n   some surfaces will go out
of sight and others will come into sight. Note that in general this procedure is r e v e r s i b l e   and so can be distinguished from going out
and coming into existence which is what sometimes (visually) happens at
the transitions between aggregate states (see the section on events).
The issue of how we are able to (visually) perceive the spatial
arrangement of objects, distances across the ground surface, its inclination, etc. traditionally has been dealt with under the heading of
d e p t h perception. Gibson has proposed for quite a time (see Gibson
1950a where, however, he still considers the theory to be developed as
a complex psychophysics) that a concise account of these problems cannot
be given within the framework of classical physics and geometry, starting with an empty space filled up with abstract objects or mathematical
solids. Instead, he argues, space a n d   object perception should be
analyzed in terms of the perception of s u r f a c e s   (and their edges).
But how do we perceive surfaces in the first place, and how do we distinguish (for static viewing conditions) between, say, the adjoining
of two different surfaces in the same plane and the partial occlusion
of one surface by another? Gibson has bothered himself with questions
like these for decades (see Gibson 1950b, 1979, 1982) and he has come
up with several attempts at exhaustively characterizing surface (for
more detailed references see Landwehr 1985b, 1986).
The most important attribute of "surfaceness" is t e x t u r e , i.e.
structure, differences in different directions, at a micro-level specific to the substances a surface is composed of. Sometimes this micro-
-structuring at the physical-chemical level may be beyond our capacities
of visually scrutinizing it, nonetheless, the resulting patterning
of the surface's colouredness (spectral light reflection) and of the
shadows cast upon it enables us to discriminate one substance from
another by their characteristic surface appearance.
Furthermore, textures tend to be regular, so that repetitions across
the surface's extension can be observed at multiple levels on "breaking
it into elements". Viewed in perspective, then, this results in the
well-known t e x t u r e   g r a d i e n t s , i.e. the stochastic decrease in
texture coarseness at larger distances. This is also to say that the information for increasing distance is exactly the stochastic decrease in
texture coarseness at a defined level of texture elements!
This gives us a first generically ecological principle of how information about the world can become available to us. Different textures reflect light differently and within some limits of thresholds for differentiation all we have to do is pay attention to these differences in
different directions specifying what is there. And the different directions ar n o t   constituted by initially apprehending empty space but
by the observational behavior of the perceiving subject (his/her turning
of the head, locomotion, etc.).
As we have already seen, the differences of the spatial layers of surfaces objectively being arranged one behind the other can be and eventually have to be detected by movement of the observer (or, alternative-

23

Table 1
Varieties of optical stimulus information which specify spatial layout
for static and kinematic viewing conditions

Texture gradients/
Optical flow

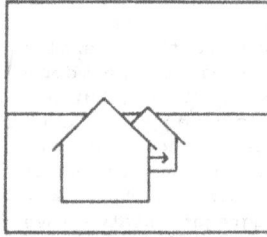

Interposition/
Occlusion

"Aerial perspective",
Cast shadows

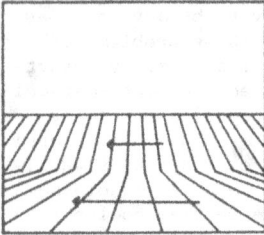

Stretching and com-
pression in texture/
flow gradients

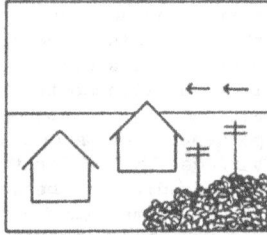

Relative height of
figural lower edge/
"Common fate"

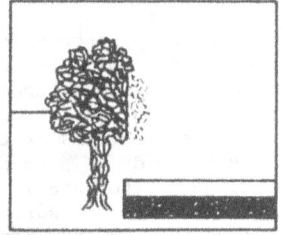

Transparency proper

Discontinuities in
texture/flow gradients

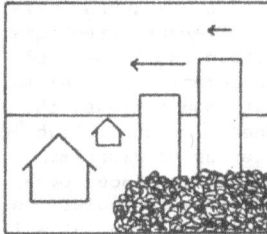

Relative size/order

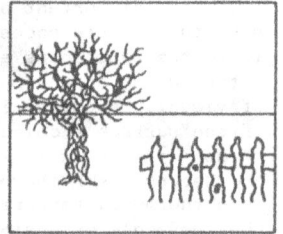

Semi-transparency

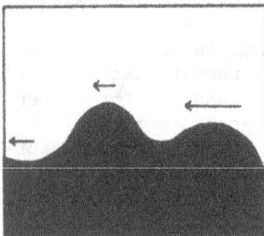

Stretching and com-
pression in contours
of textureless surface

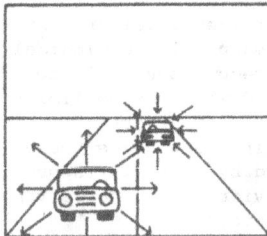

Optical magnification
or minification

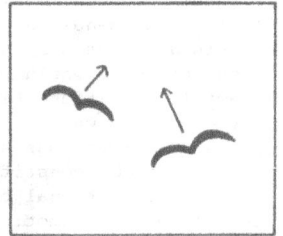

Relative motion

ly, the surfaces), leading to the o p t i c s o f o c c l u s i o n where
it is the continuous accretion and deletion of one texture relative to
another which experimentally has been shown to be sufficient for perceiving an occluding edge (Kaplan 1969, Gibson 1979, p. 76-86 and ch.
11).

In a similar way it is possible to find other principles of ecological
environmental perception, all in terms of modes of surfaceness and modes
of movement only, and to reinterpret and systematize the classical,
hopelessly confused lists of (empirical, monocular) depth cues (see
Table 1).

The perception of egomotion

Dealing with a complex layout of surfaces as we do in architecture,
town planning, etc., and/or given the possibility of breaking texture
into elements at different levels, from microscopic to gross patterns,
an additional description and analysis of the ambient optic array becomes feasible, where edges or contours, more generally, discontinuities
in the overall texturedness, define generalized optical-visual c o n e s
when centrally projected from the surfaces to the (moving) place of observation. Figure 1 (cf. Gibson 1966, Fig.10.6, p.196. and Gibson 1979,
Fig.5.4, p. 72) depicts the essentials of this geometrical analysis
which in fact dates back at least to Euclid (see Burton 1945 in order
to acknowledge Euclid's geometry as a theory of perception!). As you can
see from the drawing, all of the n e s t e d s o l i d a n g l e s , projected for the p a t h of observation, change and are transformed into
new angles of different shape (different outlines of the bases and of
the envelopes of the visual cones), however, leaving certain r e l a t -
i o n s u n c h a n g e d ; this is why Gibson refers to what is really re-
gistered in perception as transformational i n v a r i a n t s .

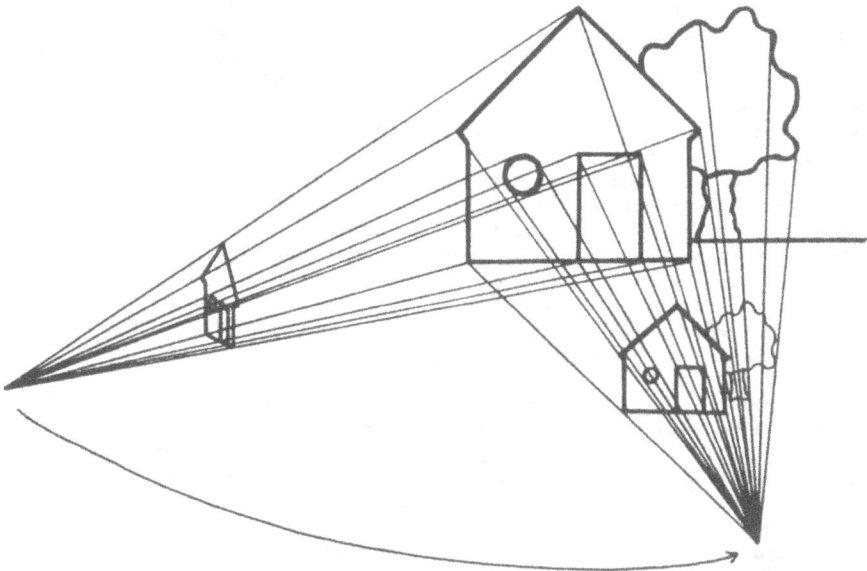

Figure 1: Transforming visual cones (nested solid angles) obtained by
          movement of the observer

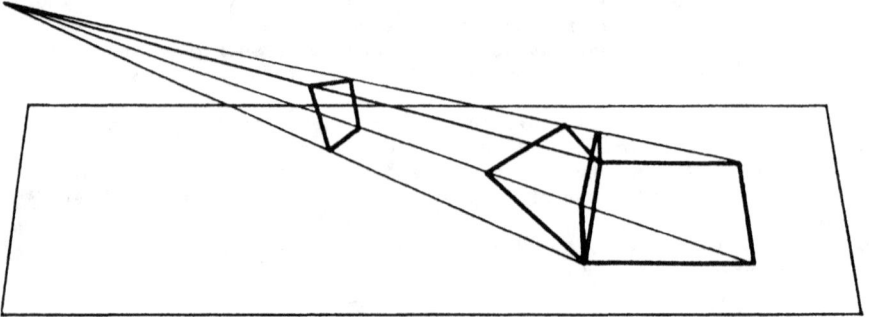

Figure 2: The argument of equivalent configurations

Some time ago Ittelson (1960) put forward the argument of equivalent configurations (see Figure 2) which would render the geometric analysis proposed somewhat dubious, since there would not be an unequivocal specification of surface inclination, form, and distance, if Ittelson was right (cf. Ittelson 1960, Fig.s V-1 and V-2, p.67, and Gibson 1979, Fig. 9.7, p.167). But obviously his argument only holds for either textureless or completely transparent, framed glass surfaces or else for wire figures, and even then only if these are considered in isolation. Under normal circumstances we meet an uninterrupted, closed, continuously connected layout of textured surfaces which is rich enough in information to also specify minor textureless or transparent surfaces scattered over the field of view (like the windows in houses) and of which the transformations in the pattern of visual cones exactly specify b o t h its unique layout a n d the path of observation.

Consequently, for a moving observer there is always coordinated information concurrently available both about the environment and about him- or herself. The same also holds for other kinds of movement of the observer rather than for locomotion only, e.g. sitting down, standing up, leaning forward, and so on. The other types of visually relevant observer activities, turning your head and moving your eyes, are simply specified by a change in what is within your field of view and very little or no relative displacement of the surfaces looked at.

The use of (Euclidian) geometry by Gibson should not be misinterpreted as if he inadvertently turned his theory into a formal, non-ecological approach. As his rejection of the argument of equivalent configurations shows, it is not the "ghostly" layers of mathematical planes defined by intersecting lines or sets of points in the three dimensional coordinate system, on a strictly axiomatic reading of Euclid, which are of interest, but the material surfaces with their edges and visible patches of texture. It is a kind of occlusion geometry which is needed (cf. Lang 1974, opaque geometry).

The reader is adivsed to meet another variant of a geometrical analyses even more cautiously (cf. also Gibson's own warnings in Gibson 1966, p. 198). You can also project surfaces point by point (minimal texture element by minimal texture element) which will give you what is called an optical f l o w f i e l d , i.e. a distribution of trigonometrically calculable vectors - and again it was Gibson who introduced this idea (Gibson et al. 1955). The flow velocities are graded with increasing distance from the observer, as already noted by Helmholtz (1866) in his discussion of motion parallax as a depth cue. Gibson (1950a, E.J. Gibson et al. 1959) more precisely talks about motion perspective as in-

formation about surface layout (cf. Table 1). For a "cluttered" environment, however, again not only are there discontinuities within the flow
pattern (corresponding to some of the edges in the static case, but also
some points, i.e. textures or parts thereof, will no longer project to
the path of observation because of occlusion.

Geometrical analysis, then, for Gibson is a useful method rather than
a meaningful theoretical account and it should not obscure the conceptually different ecological perspective on the problems. For our purposes, however, it has the additional advantage of corresponding to
one of the architect's major tools of specifying his or her design
to the construction workers, thus establishing a common language and
making communication easier.

The perceiving of events

In the two preceding sections it was supposed that the surfaces and
their layout be rigid and persistent. Clearly this is not always the
case. What about elasticity and change? Gibson (1979, ch.6) provides
us with a classification of terrestrial e v e n t s   at three levels:
(1) changes in layout, (2) changes of colour and texture, (3) changes
of surface existence. Events of the first type can be further analyzed
along the dimensions of (1a) translation/rotation, (1b) deformation,
and (1c) disruption. There are some very interesting intermediate cases,
some of which are also contained in Table 1 because they help to specify
spatial relations, most notably (observed) collisions (a special case
of relative motion) and approach/recession of an object, which optically
is defined by texture magnification/minification relative to a backround.
And, of course, the facts of occlusion also have to do with events.

You may want to say that locomotion of the observer should also be regarded as an event because there, too, something changes or something is
going on. It is wise, however, to distinguish two perspectives, your own
on what you do, or your own on what happens around you. The two can be
distinguished on optical grounds. Observer movement (to him/herself) is
characterized by an optical flow field defined over texture patches or
by transformations of nested solid angles defined over surfaces, the
displacements and transformations occuring coordinatively with the observer's locomotion and being distributed across the whole field of view
("everything flows"). Object motion (of which the movement of an observing person when being observed by another person is also an instance)
is characterized by a local disturbance in the optical structure (for
static viewing) or in the optical flow (for the observer also moving at
the same time). Now note that occlusion comes in both cases. When there
is simultaneous movement and motion there are few situations where a
particular occlusion event cannot be clearly attributed to either of the
conditions. Normally, however, the two can be unequivocally separated.

Changes of texture and color are also very important because they
point to changes in the substantial composition of the surfaces involved. It is mainly the greening, flowering, and fading of plants (their
leaves) which impress us in our environment, but we are also concerned
which how fast our cars are prone to get rusty and about dirt and pollution. And there is information in light about most if not all of these
events and their long-lasting effects.

The changes of surface existence are mainly brought about by changes
in the state of matter, e.g. melting solid to liquid and evaporating
liquid to gas, but biological growth/decay and mechanical construction/
destruction also belong to this category. Obviously these are of central
concern to the design professional!

The perception of affordances

So far we have considered surfaces and their layout, ego locomotion, and events, mainly in terms of their simply being there, although at a level of description intended to recognize our being compatible with the world we evolved to live in. More specifically, however, and cutting across the distinctions made we ought to look for the functional significance of the way things are to us, i.e. what kinds of actions they afford, what they enable us to do.

The nomenclature Gibson (1979, ch.3 and 8) proposes to describe the m e a n i n g f u l environment, however, must not be confused with a taxonomy or classification of objects along the categories of the vernacular or any other system in which things would be grouped according to abstract common features (generalized similarity). The terminology Gibson uses although s e l e c t e d from the vernacular is still amenable to more precise analyses in terms of surface layout, optical flow, and transformational invariance, in short, in terms of surface geometry.

The literal primacy of the ground has already been referred to. The environment it constitutes can either be open or else cluttered with obstacles or barriers. In order for a human observer to pass through, the ground has to afford footing and the barriers must be so arranged as to leave open a path. Possible barriers include water margins and brinks (the edges of cliffs). Ascending the steep slope of a hill may call for mountaineering equipment. Modern architecture is responsible for barriers which can be seen through but do not afford going-through, to wit, glass doorways. I illustrated the visual transparency of fences which also prevent coming-in in Table 1. In the natural surroundings only few environments can be found which are concavely wrinkled so as to form an enclosure but humans have built millions of them to afford shelter. It is a non-trivial observation that houses ought to have one or more entrances/exits which can easily be identified and found.

The elementary affordances of water and fire or other forms of energy are obvious. To analyze any object, tools, other animals/people, and displays (i.e. pictures, the TV screen, etc.) in terms of their affordances which can literally be seen at t h e s u r f a c e might seem less convincing. But look at one of Gibson's examples:

"A rigid object with a sharp dihedral angle, an edge, affords cutting and scraping: it is a k n i f e ." (Gibson 1979, p.133)

And note that a dihedral convexity of larger size, e.g. the edge of a wall, affords hiding and peeping, whereas a concave dihedral, depending on its size, angle, and orientation, among other things, affords leaning your back against it while sitting.

Affordances in principle then can be described in eco-physical terms although for some situations the analysis will be fairly complex. Furthermore, the examples given have been oversimplified because the detection of an affordance makes use of the invariance structure of the things or situations seen from different perspectives (places of observation). Thus, the way we are able to take advantage of the available affordances is not so easily spelled out. A planner, e.g., might think that a park he or she designed affords walking through, taking a rest, and many other things, because it is all recorded on a map, perhaps in appropriate terms, but will people be able to see the continuation of the path when entering the place from different directions? Will it be evident where to find the calmest region, and so on?

It is essential in this context to keep in mind that the ecological approach conceptualizes perception to be independent of needs, purposes,

or goals. It is coordinate with action, and intention. For example, to
post a letter will guide your observational behaviour so as to optically magnify a post box in which to drop the letter. Walking past a
post box without having a letter to post does not mean that the possibility of doing so could not be apprehended, indeed, given appropriate
viewing conditions, it almost certainly will be.

Some implications of Gibson's theory

"Perceiving", says Gibson (1979, p.249), "is a (continuous) registering
of certain definite dimensions of invariance in the stimulus flux together with definite parameters of disturbance." It is an activity of
an observer fulfilling adaptive functions rather than being the end
result of imposed stimulation. Invariants and change are thought of as
being directly made use of rather than being meaningless input which
would have to be processed and interpreted. Consequently, a good many
conceptions taken for granted in traditional theories, are questioned.
For example, there may be no such thing as stimulus overload, because
stimuli are no longer conceived of coming in as a sequential input to a
processing system with limited capacity. Gibson concedes that there may
be selective attention (cf. Gibson 1966, ch.13), but the perceptual
systems are thought of as being designed to be capable of tuning themselves to the information available, however complex it may be. And only
exceptionally can there be uncertainty and illusion.
     There is perceptual learning in the sense of being able to further
discriminate minor differences but it is believed not to rely on memory
in the sense of fixed imprintings or semantic categories. "Perceiving
goes on" (Gibson 1979, p.253), as long as information is available,
and the information which i n f a c t is available, can certainly be
said to be i n e x h a u s t i b l e . Finally, the metaphor of extracting invariants can be extended to the variants of "knowledge at second
hand" (cf. Gibson 1966, ch.11, Gibson 1979, p.258-263 and pt.IV), perception aided by instruments, picture perception, and knowing mediated
by descriptions.

THE ECOLOGICAL PERSPECTIVE APPLIED TO ENVIRONMENTAL PERCEPTION RESEACH

How then to we put the ecological approach to work for the tasks of the
designer and the concerns of the environmental psychologist? Since Gibson emphasizes the perception of the objective geographical layout of
material surfaces (replacing the traditional conception of space or
depth perception), questions of o r i e n t a t i o n in an environment,
wayfinding, place differentiation, and recognition, etc., should lend
themselves to an ecological analysis. The second domain is events.
Especially very slow events which go on for quite a time are hard to
perceive. For instance, the changing of the seasons in Northern regions
often goes unnoticed because planners have removed all the flowering and
leaf-changing plants or replaced them by non-changing "greenery". The
ecological perspective reminds us to be aware of possible events in an
environment and care about the conditions of their perceivability. Another example are the changes in daylight illumination which go along
with changes in the distribution of lighted and shaded areas. The perception of flowing traffic, pedestrian movement, etc., may contribute to
our choosing a specific course of action. Finally it is the affordances
of an environment for specific purposes which matter.
     The peculiar thing to note about ecological methodology is that there

are no hypotheses about what people w i l l do but only about what they
c a n do. Thus, the aim of ecological research is n o t to p r e d i c t
behavior but to l i n k p o s s i b l e r o u t e s f o r a c t i o n to
the coordinate constraints of the environment and the species' dispositions. In this sense it is in sharp contradiction to environment-behaviour science in general, and a new research technology is called for.
Within the ecological framework you are more likely to come up with an
inventory of the ways an environment looks from different observation
paths, the ways it offers opportunities for certain activities, the way
it changes and whether this can be seen, than you are with a statistics
about how many people do (did) what in the presence of which stimulus
conditions. Thus, implications for design guidelines and recommenda-
tions, on the one hand, are more direct, on the other, they are more
liberal. You will not be in a position to say, "A majority of people
prefers this.", rather, "Given this, people are free to choose alternatives a to n."

The main advantages of turning to the ecological perspective, in my
view, are, first, that you can specify the relevant environmental attributes very precisely and all within a single generic terminology. This
translates directly into one of the most common languages of the design
professions - geometry. Secondly, there is a non-arbitrary way of delin-
eating higher-order stimulus variables by looking for transformational
invariants across paths of observation (rather than lines of reasoning
or imagination). Thirdly, for any evaluative judgement you are forced to
ask for its perceptual basis (objective affordances instead of subjective valences). Fourthly, in talking about behaviour and action you will
not obscure other determining factors besides stimulus information by
aggregating data statistically. Rather you will try to trace back the
individual biography of occupied places and paths of observation together with the history of events during that time.

I shall demonstrate some of these points by describing two examples
of research carried out explicitly from the ecological point of view.

Decomposition a static view of a real world scene (Landwehr 1985b,c)

As was evident from Table 1 there is both static a n d kinematic information for perceiving the layout of surfaces, and an ecological
approach to environmental perception has to take into account both
types. I devised a method for decomposing a static view of a real world
scene into its most salient features as identified in the ecological
anylsis of the surface layout. Table 2 gives an abbreviated version of
what might be included.

A perfectly static view is equivalent to a photograph or realistic
picture, except for the latter arresting possible events and except for
its once and forever limiting of the field of view. L o o k i n g 'a t a
picture, further delimits the correspondence to really observing a place
because there is information both about what is depicted as well as
about the fact that there is depiction, i.e. that you are looking at a
special kind of surface so prepared as to make available s o m e of the
information available "out there" (Gibson 1979, ch.15). The decomposition method, therefore should n o t be regarded as directly mirroring
or being completely equivalent to (statically) looking at some scenery
while paying selective attention to specific aspects. Rather, it is an
illustration ("pictorization") of a conceptually guided analysis aimed
at guiding your observational behavior along the dimensions differentiated.

The procedure is as follows: a picture of a scene is taken and pro-

30

Table 2
Analyzing optical stimulus information as decomposing a static view
of a real world scene into its most salient aspects and recombining
them in multipel ways

Start

A real world scene

Enduring aspects

Texture

Temporary aspects

Mirror reflection

Edges

Shadow

Figural lower edges

Recombination   End

jected or printed at a convenient size. Then a set of transparencies is overlaid on which (separately) the important aspects, as far as they can be seen in the static view, can be depicted in keeping with the scale and optical perspective of the picture. For the example shown these are texture(s)/gradients, contours/edges, and, as a subset of the latter, the so-called figural lower edges of identifiable, principially removable (detachable) objects, which define the relative height in the field of view of these objects and thus are co-specifying their spatial arrangement. These are the enduring, persisting attributes of the surface layout; shading and mirror reflection are temporary conditions. The latter one is not contained in Table 1 because in general it does not specify much about layout but material qualities and direction and angle of prevalent illumination. These specifications are somewhat intertwinded, however.

The scheme shows how the isolated features can independently be recombined in multiple ways. The recombination of all the aspects differentiated, of course, approximates the original. The purpose of this method is to demonstrate the impact of single qualities on the way the whole appears. In this case, for example the two types of natural texture, grass and leaves, make for a clear specification of the slant of the hill, whereas the artificial gradients at the building's surface (the window frames and the outlines of the facades) give an impression of "far away" to the forest. Imagine the same scene with more structured facades and the woods extending upto the building or the hill scattered with small houses! As regards the figural lower edges they are approximate points, thus specifying relative lack of objects. The main direction in their distribution is horizontal, thus enhancing the specification of the discontinuous steps (streets) along the hill range. Finally the adverse shadow conditions are very impressive (the picture was taken at the end of October).

I believe that analyses like these can help us understand differences in judged "legibility" (cf. Lynch 1960, Kaplan & Kaplan 1982) as well as in judged aesthetic preference (cf. Zube et al. 1975, Kaplan & Kaplan 1982). The method is limited, however, in that it does not take events and movement of the observer into account. And implications for modified design cannot be directly deduced because the method operates at a pictorization level, not the level of identified transformational invariants. Thus, it is only Gibsonian in spirit if used with a sophisticated understanding of the way pictorial forms relate to objecitve layout and its perception.

Perceiving affordances: visual guidance of stair climbing (Warren 1984)

While the foregoing piece of work was intended to tell us something about possible ways of optimizing a whole environment at a larger scale, Warren (1984) more specifically addresses the question of how an ubiquituous piece of design might in fact be optimized so as to meet the purposes it is designed for. He is looking for the optimal layout of a stairway so that it affords climbing with minimal energy expenditure, and finally whether this affordance is perceivable.

Figure 3 gives the ingredients of Warren's biomechanical analysis of the situation (modified after Warren 1984, p.685). As should be evident from even a casual look at the schematic drawing a given riser height will afford easy climbing only if it is appropriately scaled relative to the person variables, most notably the length of the legs. Warren proposes to express this relation in terms of an intrinsic measure, so-called

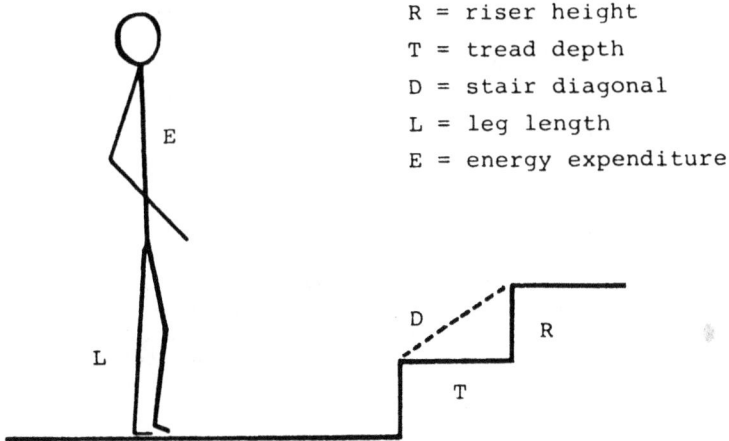

R = riser height
T = tread depth
D = stair diagonal
L = leg length
E = energy expenditure

Figure 3: The climber-stair system and its parameters

dimensionless pi-numbers, arrived at as ratios between any two variables initially measured in the same units. Running two groups of Ss with
different leg lenght, then, first he obtained judgements as to the
climbability of stairs of different riser heights. As might have been
expected, "The results demonstrate that both short and tall observers
judge stairways as unclimbable at a riser height that is a constant
proportion of their leg lengths." (Warren 1984, p.690); π = R/L = .88.
Astonishingly enough the Ss were able to arrive at their judgement on
the basis of looking at photographs (slides) of the respecitve staircases.
    In order to determine the optimal riser height a set of anthropometric
data were collected and Ss run on an adjustable stairmill over a range
of riser heights between 12.7cm to 25.4cm with the stair diagonal being held constant at 34.3cm (cf. Fig. 4). Plotting the data on energy
expenditure relative to the intrinsic measure R/L gives the same minima
for both short and tall Ss. Thus, empirically the optimal riser height
can be determinde to be about one quarter of leg length (π = .26), and
it is found to be considerably higher than those which seem to have become standard among architects designing co-called monument steps with
very low riser height and very deep treads.
    Further another preference jugdement task revealed that Ss are also
able to perceive the optimal stairway by comparing two photographs. As
regards possible implications for improving design you should not be
irritated by Warren's use of statistical methods in order to make his
point, namley to demonstrate the usefulness of intrinsic measurement
and the existence of invariants to specify affordances in the first
place. Once an intrinsic measure is established as a constant ratio of
some variables involved in an animal/man-environment system the consequence is that there cannot be o n e optimal design for all people.
Rather, it is the other way around: every individual, strictly speaking,
needs his or her own staircase! Of course, in the case of constructing
public stairways we can and entually will have to turn to an average
person but we should keep ourselves aware that a body-scaled metric can
satisfy best only for the individual case.

33

THE RECEPTION OF GIBSON IN THE ENVIRONMENT-BEHAVIOUR LITERATUR

There is only scant recognition of Gibson's contribution to an ecologically valid understanding of environmental perception by environmental
psychologists. The "classics" (Proshansky et al. 1970, 1976, Canter
1973, 1974) either do not mention him at all or just classify him as
haveing added a new depth cue or perhaps even solved all the problems of
depth perception and then leave it at that. The same holds for current
textbooks (Ittelson et al. 1974, Bell et al. 1978) and handbook articles
(Hooper 1978). Consequently you will not find papers referenced as
Gibsonian in perspective in reviews (Craik 1973, Stokols 1978, Russell
& Ward 1982) or state-of-the-art book series (Altman & Wohlwill 1976pp).
   Partly this is due to the approach being relatively new and documented only in quite recent publications (mainly the 1966 and the 1979
book of Gibson's plus Mace 1974, 1977, and Michaels & Carello 1981).
Furthermore, some people exclusively associate Gibson's name with the
type of a psychophysical program he in fact advocated in the 50s (Gibson 1950a, 1959) and of which they are critical. They fail to see how
this can be reinterpreted within the ecological framework. Finally,
Gibson is not all to popular among perception peychologists in general,
although he is credited as an outstanding experimenter; but only a (now
rapidly growing) minority follows his theoretical interpretations and
philosophical conclusions. And lastly he never pointed out exactly how
his approach might be applied in any of the domains of inquiry with
which environmental psychology is concerned .
   But obviously he i s dealing exactly with these domains and in some
specialized texts you will find a positive reception of Gibson. For instance, (Lang 1974) devotes most of his paper on the implications of
theories of perception for "formal design" to the ecological approach.
More recently, the Kaplans (Kaplan & Kaplan 1982), albeit critically,
have discussed some possible applications of the concept of affordances
in the context of their preference studies. And finally Jules (1984) has
provided a comparison of the applicability of the ecological and Gestalt
approaches to architecture, more specifically how they relate to the
design guidelines of the Ecole des Beaux Arts and the common convictions
of the Modern Movement.
   Things are completely different if you look into the architectural and
geographical literature. Although there is no (or almost no, depending
on how you classify some authors) mention of Gibson's name or the term
"ecological", examples are abundant where architects, planners, etc.
argue and work along similar lines. This is most obvious, in the writings of Lynch (1960) and Cullen (1961), to go back to the classics, as
it is in the more recent contributions of, Zube and his associates
(1975) and Appleyard & Fishman (1977). The work of Thiel (1961) and that
of Appleyard et al. (1964) also deserves special attention in the context of this paper because they are directly concerned with the "experience" of sequences of stimulation (as is Cullen, too), for example a
walk along a street or a drive down Highway 61. This, then, gives a
promising outlook for the take up of a good deal of previous research
and the reinterpretation of it within the broader ecological framework.
   It is important, however, to be clear about the differences which
still might remain. To the ecological perspective it simply is not e-
nough to take the physical environment seriously, nor does it suffice
to give primary attention to the fact that most of our urban experience
is gained during locomotion. What makes an analysis an ecological one is
to define its terms with reference to a concrete species, to note the
mutuality of action-perception coordination, and the emphasize the func-

34

tional, adaptive significance of perception and behaviour.

CONCLUDING REMARKS

There is one serions shortcoming of the ecological approach which, I
believe, has become obvious in the paper, Gibsonians as yet do not take
social, historical aspects into account. An environment is what it is to
humans as an animal species, not what it might be to them as a cultural
society. This, on my view, does not, however, imply that the approach is
useless as soon as we become concerned with historically moulded environments. After all, a l l environments on earth now are man-made,
but they have not turned into something absolutely new, in the process.
Historical development does not turn off the functioning of the human-
-environment system at its biologically evolved level. Its influence
seems more like s h a d i n g the transactions which take place. History
itself is an ongoing grand event comprising multiple levels of intertwined subevents, and in order to apprehend its influence, its outcome,
and its prospects, we have to attend to available stimulus information
not the least important of which is optical-visual.

REFERENCES

Altman, I., Wohlwill, J.F. (Eds.) Human behavior and environment. Ad-
    vances in theory and research. New York : Plenum 1976 (Vol. 1)
Appleyard, D., Fishman, L. High-rise buildings versus San Francisco:
    Measuring visual and symbolic impacts. in: Conway, D.J. (Ed.)
    Human response to tall buildings. Stroundsburg: Pa.: Dowden, Hutch-
    inson, Ross 1977, 81-100.
Appleyard, D., Lynch, K., Myer, J.R. The view from the road. Cambridge,
    Mass.: MIT Press 1964.
Arnheim, R. Art and visual perception. Berkeley; University of Califor-
    nia Press 1954
Arnheim, R. The dynamics of architectural form. Berkeley: University of
    California Press 1977
Avant, L.L., Helson, H. Theories of perception. in: Wolman, B.B. (Ed.)
    Handbook of general psychology. Englewood Cliffs, N.J.: Prentice-
    -Hall 1973, 419-448
Barker, R.G. Explorations in ecological psychology. American Psycholog-
    ist 1965, 20, 1-14
Barker, R.G. Ecological psychology: concepts and methods for studying
    the environment of human behavior. Stanford, Calif.: Stanford Univ-
    ersity Press 1968
Bell, P.A., Fisher, J.D., Loomis, R.J. Environmental psychology. Phil-
    adelphia, Penn.: Saunders 1978
Burton, H.E. (Ed.) The optics of Euclid. Journal of the Optical Society
    of America 1945, 35, 357-372
Canter, D.V. (Ed.) Architectural psychology. London: RIBA 1970
Canter, D.V. Psychology for architects. New York: Wiley 1974
Canter, D.V. The psychology of place. New York: St. Martins Press 1977
Canter, D.V. Putting situations in their place: foundations for a
    bridge between social an environmental psychology. in: Furnham, A.
    (Ed.) Social behaviour in context. London: Allyn and Bacon 1984a
Canter, D.V. Intention, meaning, and structure: social action in its
    physical context. in: Ginsburg, M. et al. (Ed.) Discovery strateg-
    ies in the psychology of social action. 1984b

Cullen, G. Townscape, New York: van Nostrand 1961

Euclid see Burton

Fechner, G.T. Elemente der Psychophysik. Leipzig: Breitkopf und Härtel 1860 (2 vols.)

Gibson, E.J., Gibson, J.J., Smith, O.W., Flock, H.R. Motion parallax as a determinant of perceived depth. Journal of Experimental Psychology 1959, 58, 40-51

Gibson, J.J. The perception of the visual world. Boston: Houghton-Mifflin 1950a

Gibson, J.J. The perception of visual surfaces. American Journal of Psychology 1950b, 63, 367-384.

Gibson, J.J. Perception as a function of stimulation. in: Koch, S. (Ed.) Psychology: a study of a science. New York: McGraw-Hill 1959 (Vol. 1)

Gibson, J.J. The concept of the stimulus in psychology. American Psychologist 1960, 15, 694-703.

Gibson, J.J. Ecological optics. Vision Research 1961, 1, 253-262

Gibson, J.J. The senses considered as perceptual systems. Boston: Houghton-Mifflin 1966

Gibson, J.J. New reasons for realism. Synthese 1967, 17, 162-172

Gibson, J.J. The ecological approach to visual perception. Boston: Houghton-Mifflin 1979

Gibson, J.J. What is involved in surface perception? in: Beck, J. (Ed.) Organization and representation in perception. Hillsdale, N.J.: Erlbaum 1982, 151-157

Gibson, J.J., Olum, P., Rosenblatt, F. Parallax and perspective during aircraft landings. American Journal of Psychology 1955, 68, 372-385.

Gregory, R.L. Choosing a paradigm for perception. in: Carterette, E.C., Friedman, M.P. (Eds.) Handbook of perception. Vol. 1: Historical and philosophical roots of perception. New York: Academic Press 1974, 255-283

Harré, R., Secord, P.F. The explanation of social behaviour. Oxford: Blackwell 1972

Helmholtz, H.v. Handbuch der physiologischen Optik. Band 3: Die Lehre von den Gesichtswahrnehmungen. Hamburg: Voss 1866 (engl. transl. by Southall, J.P.C. New York: Optical Society of America 1925)

Hochberg, J.E. Nativism and empiricism in perception. in: Postman, L. (Ed.) Psychology in the making. New York: Knopf 1962, 255-330

Hochberg, J.E. Representative sampling and the purposes of perceptual research: pictures of the world, and the world of pictures. in: Hammond, K.R. (Ed.) The psychology of Egon Brunswik. New York: Holt, Rinehart, Winston 1966, 361-381

Hochberg, J.E. On cognition in perception: perceptual coupling and unconscious inference. Cognition 1981, 10, 127-134.

Hooper, K. Perceptual aspects of architecture. in: Carterette, E.C., Friedman, M.P. (Eds.) Handbook of perception. Vol. 10: Perceptual ecology. New York: Academic Press 1978, 155-189

Ittelson, W.H. Visual space perception. New York: Springer 1960

Ittelson, W.H. Environment perception and contemporary perception theory. in: Ittelson, W.H. (Ed.) Environment and cognition. New York: Seminar Press 1973, 1-19

Ittelson, W.H. Environmental perception and urban experience. Environment and behavior 1978. 10, 193-213

Ittelson, W.H., Proshansky, H.M., Rivlin, L.G., Winkel, G.H. An introduciton to environmental psychology. New York: Holt, Rinehart, Winston 1974

Jules, F.A. A comparison of the application to architecture of the ecological and Gestalt approaches to visual perception. Milwaukee,

Wisc.: The School of Architecture and Urban Planing of the University of
    Wisconsin-Milwaukee 1984
Kaplan, G. Kinetic disruption of optical texture: the perception of
    depth at an edge. Perception and Psychophysics 1969, 6, 193-198
Kaplan, S., Kaplan, R. Cognition and environment: functioning in an
    uncertain world. New York: praeger 1982
Koffka, K. Perception: an introduction to the Gestalt-Theorie. Psycho-
    logical Bulletin 1922, 531-585
Koffka, K. Principles of Gestalt Psychology. New York: Harcourt, Brace
    & World 1935
Köhler, W. Die physischen Gestalten in Ruhe und im stationären Zustand.
    Erlangen 1920 (abridged engl. transl. in: Ellis, W. (Ed.) A source
    book of Gestalt psychology. New York: Harcourt, Brace & Co. 1938/
    1955, 17-54)
Köhler, W. Gestalt psychology - an introduction to new concepts in mo-
    dern psychology. New York: Liveright 1929
Landwehr, K. Wahrnehmung und Sprache: evolutionäre Logik und historische
    Grammatik. in: Marek, J.C. et al. (Eds.) Philosophy of psychology.
    Vienna: Hölder-Pichler-Tempsky 1985a, 580-582
Landwehr, K. A comparison of the principles of analysis of optical
    stimulus information in Gestalt theory and in ecological optics.
    in: Sanchez-Sosa, J. (Ed.) Proceedings of the 23rd International
    Congress of Psychology. Amsterdam: North-Holland 1985b
Landwehr, K. A grammar of the optical stimulus information specifying
    "depth" and the ordinal spatial layout of all possible surfaces on
    earth during ambient daylight or artificial illumination and in the
    night. Poster presented during the Third International Conference on
    Event Perception and Action 1985c (copy available from the author)
Landwehr, K. Die ökologische Auffüllung der Welt - Ein Vergleich der
    Prinzipien der Analyse optischer Stimulus-Information in der Gestalt-
    theorie und in der ökologischen Optik. Gestalt Theory 1986 (in press)
Lang, J. Theories of perception and "formal"design. in: Lang, J., Burn-
    ette, C., Moleski, W., Vachon, D. (Eds.) Designing for human behav-
    iour: architecture and behavioural sciences. Stroudsburg, Pa.:
    Dowden, Hutchinson, Ross 1974, 98-110
Lorenz, K. Die Rückseite des Spiegels - Versuch einer Naturgeschichte
    menschlichen Erkennens. München: Piper 1973
Lynch, K. The image of the city. Cambridge, Mass.: MIT Press 1960
Mace, W.M. Ecologically stimulating cognitive psychology: Gibsonian
    perspectives. in: Weimer, W.B., Palermo, D.S. (Eds.) Cognition and
    the symbolic processes I. Hillsdale, N.J.: Erlbaum 1974, 137-164
Mace, W.M. James J. Gibson's strategy for perceiving: ask not what's
    inside your head, but what your head's inside of. in: Shaw, R.,
    Bransford, J. (Eds.) Perceiving, acting, and knowing. Hillsdale,
    N.J.: Erlbaum 1977, 43-65
McKenzie see Park
Metzger, W. Gesetze des Sehens. Frankfurt am Main: Kramer 1953
Metzger, W. Das einäugige Tiefensehen. in: Metzger, W., Erke, H. (Eds.)
    Handbuch der Psychologie. Band 1: Allgemeine Psychologie I. Der Auf-
    bau des Erkennens. 1. Halbband: Wahrnehmung und Bewußtsein. Göttin-
    gen: Hogrefe 1966, 556-589
Michaels, C.F., Carello, C. Direct perception. Englewood Cliffs, N.J.:
    Prentice-Hall 1981
Milgram, S. The experience of living in cities. Science 1970, 167, 1461-
    1468
Park, R.E., Burgess, E.W., McKenzie, R.D. The city. Chicago: University
    of Chicago Press 1925

Park, N. The visual perception of the built environment. Delft: Delft University Press 1977

Proshansky, H.M. Environmental psychology and the real world. American Psychologist 1976, 31, 303-310

Proshansky, H.M., Ittelson, W.H., Rivlin, L.G. (Eds.) Environmental psychology: man and his physical setting. New York: Holt, Rinehart, Winston 1970

Proshansky, H.M., Ittelson, W.H., Rivlin, L.G. (Eds.) Environmental psychology: people and their physical settings. New York: Holt, Rinehard, Winston 1976

Russel, J.A., Ward, L.M. Environmental psychology. Annual Review of Psychology 1982, 33, 651-688

Secord see Harré

Shaw, R., Turvey, M.T., Mace, W.M. Ecological psychology: the consequence of a commitment to realism. in: Weimer, W.B., Palermo, D.S. (Eds.) Cognition and the symbolic processes II. Hillsdale, N.J.: Erlbaum 1982, 159-226 (+227-236)

Stevens, S.S. Psychophysics - introduction to its perceptual, neural, and social prospects. New York: Wiley 1975

Stokols, D. Environmental psychology. Annual Review of Psychology 1978, 29, 253-295

Uexküll, J.v. Theoretische Biologie. Berlin: Springer 1920

Uexküll, V.v. Nie geschaute Welten. Die Umwelten meiner Freunde. Berlin: S. Fischer 1936

Thiel, P. A sequence-experience notation for architectural and urban space. Town Planning Review 1961, 32, 33-52

Turvey, M.T., Shaw, R., Reed, E.S., Mace, W.M. Ecological laws of perceiving and acting: in reply to Fodor and Pylyshyn (1981). Cognition 1981, 9, 237-304

Wapner, S., Cohen, S.B., Kaplan, B. (Eds.) Experiencing the environment. New York: Plenum 1976

Warren, W.H. Perceiving affordances: visual guidance of stair clinbing. Journal of Experimental Psychology: Human Perception and Performance 1984, 10, 683-703

Wertheimer, M. Experimentelle Studien über das Sehen von Bewegung. Zeitschrift für Psychologie 1912, 61, 247-250

Wertheimer, M. Untersuchungen zur Lehre von der Gestalt. I. Prinzipielle Bemerkungen. Psychologische Forschung 1922, 1, 47-58 (abridged engl. transl. in: Ellis, W. (Ed.) A source book of Gestalt psychology. New York: Harcourt, Brace & Co. 1938/1955, 12-16)

Wertheimer, M. Untersuchungen zur Lehre von der Gestalt, I. Psychologische Forschung 1923, 4, 301-350 (abridged engl. transl. in. Ellis, W. (Ed.) A source book of Gestalt psychology. New York: Harcourt, Brace & Co. 1938/1955, 71-88)

Zube, E.H., Brush, R.O., Fabos, J.G. (Eds.) Landscape assessment: values, perceptions, and resources. Stroudsburg, Pa.: Dowden, Hutchinson, Ross 1975

3. Home and the theory of place

VITTORIA GIULIANI, MIRILIA BONNES, FLORA AMONI and
YVONNE BERNARD

This chapter illustrates the results of several studies of the domestic interior in the light of the theoretical perspective offered by the concept of place. It is argued that this theoretical framework can profitably be used to examine, in a molar way, the dwelling unit as a dynamic relationship of physical aspects, activities and evaluations.

The first study presented focuses on the patterns of physical features differentiating space appropriation behaviour through a comparison of living room layouts in Rome and Paris. These patterns are seen to be affected both by the national context and by social variables. Furthermore, the comparison sheds light on notable analogies between the layout behaviours of similar social groups in the two countries.

Starting from the results of this research, subsequent studies examine different aspects of the Italian situation, mainly through an analysis of verbal behaviour of the inhabitants. The manner of naming those rooms which constitute the daytime part of the house is investigated. It is hypothesized that the label used symbolises the adherence to the system of values linked to a certain home arrangement.

The differences of the perception of aesthetic attributes and livability attributes of the home is interpreted as a conflict between two role-related attitudes towards the home.

Finally, the ways of expressing attachment to the home are related back to a dialectic relationship between an 'animistic' and a 'narcissistic' attitude in the process of appropriation of the home.

THE ENVIRONMENTAL UNIT

The considerations which Vygotsky sets as the basis of the study of language and which are based on the assumption that a complex phenomenon such as language must be analyzed in units and not in elements, can, without too much forcing of metaphors, be applied to the study of environment. 'By <u>unit</u> we mean a product of analysis which, unlike elements, retains all the basic properties of the whole and which cannot be further divided without losing them. Not the chemical composition of water, but its molecules and their behavior are the key to the understanding of the properties of water.' (Vygotsky 1962, p.4) The need for what might be termed the 'molar approach' has also received favour in the field of environmental psychology (Craik 1970; Stokols 1978; Ward and Russell 1981). Indeed, the 'absolute integrity of person/physical setting events' is considered by Proshansky (1976) as the most critical of the methodological requirements inherent in the problems to be studied by the environmental psychologist. Just as Vygotsky proposes using the <u>word</u> as the unit in the study of language, so the unit in environmental psychology studies may be taken as the <u>place</u> (Canter 1977; forthcoming).

Insofar as it represents a psychological unit of environment (Russell and Ward 1982), the place is defined on the basis of its relationship with people, both individual and groups, in terms of a) perceived physical attributes (representation of the physical properties); b) activities carried on there and the rules governing the way this is done (representation of the functional and temporal properties); c) evaluations (representation of the affective properties).

Although this subdivision into three constituents is perhaps more the result of attachment to the magic number three than of completeness of analysis it can nevertheless be assumed that one of the ways of making a molar approach to the study of the environment is precisely to consider the environmental unit as a dynamic system composed at least of physical, functional and affective properties, i.e. as a place. As a result 'interventions in any part of the system can reverberate throughout the system' (Altman and Chemers 1980, p.11).

Precisely because of its relational, or 'transactional', nature (Stokols and Shumaker 1981), the place is inseparable from the individual experiencing it. In this sense place identity becomes part of the individual's self identity and therefore reflects 'his or her unique socialization experiences in the physical world as well as those experiences common to all individuals and specific groups of individuals living in particular kinds of physical settings' (Proshansky 1978, p.155). The place is thus culture specific in the sense that different place categories may correspond to different cultural systems, or the same category may have different contents as a function of differences in the cultures, subcultures or roles of the individuals involved.

Although this theoretical framework is widely shared, nonetheless a considerable gap between theory and practice of research is to be noted, and as a result 'the numerous environment-behavior relations (EBR) studies have not been cumulative' (Rapoport 1985, p.253). Stokols and Shumaker identify this gap as 'investigations of the molar environment typically proceed by isolating... specific dimensions of the sociophysical milieu' and 'Rarely are the objective and subjective elements of the environments considered within the same analysis' (1981, pp.444-5).

On the basis of this criticism, in the following, we shall present the results of our studies which, using different lines of research and

methods, are aimed at studying the home interior by means of the
construct of place, that is, at gaining insight into the processes as a
result of which the domestic interior appears as a dynamic unit composed
of physical properties, activities and evaluations. Our study begins
with a comparison of living rooms in Rome and Paris, and subsequently
goes into some particular aspects of the Italian situation.

A CROSS-CULTURAL ANALYSIS OF THE HOME INTERIOR

Whatever the restrictions imposed by the space available, by the
necessity of objects being able to carry out determinate functions, by
the economic resources of the individual and by the offers of the
market, every human being personalises his/her own domestic space, that
is, effects choices that materialise the representation of his/her
system of needs and of the way to satisfy them in relation to this space
(Stokols 1978). Needs and way to satisfy them are structured as a
function of the social identity of the individual (Tajfel 1981), that
is, of the complex of norms and values shared by the social group(s) to
which he/she belongs. The application of these norms and values to the
choices relative to the organisation of domestic interior tends to
produce stable configurations which we can call psycho-physical models.
    The cross-cultural approach appears particularly appropriate to
describe such models. The comparison of the dwelling behaviour of
different cultural groups sheds light not only on the specificities of
attitudes towards the home due to cultural specificities of the groups,
but also on the existence of cross-cultural patterns shared by subgroups
of different cultures (Duncan and Duncan 1976; Moore 1979).
    As argued by Canter and Lee (1974), comparison of the different
cultures can be carried out more easily by means of analysis of non
verbal behaviour, i.e. in our case, through the choices made in the
course of furnishing and decorating the domestic space. The considerable
amount of evidence accumulated in recent years not only points to the
importance of the architectural and furnishing variables in determining
one's perception of the quality of the domestic space (Acking and Kuller
1972; Baird, Cassidy and Kurr 1978; Kaye and Murray 1982), but also to
the different ways in which attitudes, beliefs and sociocultural values
affect the use, structure and decoration of the domestic space (Rapoport
1969, 1982; Laumann and House 1970; Bernard and Jambu 1978; Duncan and
Duncan 1976; Duncan 1981a; Lawrence 1981; Weisner and Weibel 1981).
    These ideas have been developed along two lines (Bernard et al. 1982):
1. On the basis of a set of domestic interiors, each described by a
large number of features, the analysis must identify the structurally
significant properties differentiating the space appropriating
behaviour. These properties are not the same as the features used to
describe the original set but complex functions of this set of features.
The main purpose of the comparison of two countries is not, therefore,
to see how the subjects behave vis-a-vis each variable, but to observe
whether it is the same variables or groups of variables that structure
this differentiation in each country.
2. Having defined the patterns of variables into which the typical
furnishing choices are translated, the second objective is to link those
choices with specific groups of subjects and to see whether the
individuals thus grouped on the basis of their furnishing choices can be
characterized by common sociological variables.
    The city of Rome, for Italy, and Paris, for France, were chosen as two
similar large urban environments, with a comparative sample of

inhabitants matched for age, and educational and professional levels. In each country, a sample of 55 homes was examined: the more 'public' room was chosen, that is, the room used to receive people from outside the family circle. The analytic descriptive system developed to describe the layout of this type of room (Amoni et al., forthcoming) consists of the total number of repertory features (objects present and their characteristics) and relationship features (relations between the objects) likely to differentiate the inhabitants' behaviour in connection with the satisfaction of several fundamental needs, in particular, the need in the home for a suitable setting for privacy regulation and interpersonal relationships (Altman 1975), and the need to receive sufficient perceptive and aesthetic stimulation from the environment (Wohlwill 1976; Mehrabian 1976).

The system used for coding relationship features was divided into three main subsystems: a) a space structuring code, taking into consideration the features that are apparently aimed at modifying the perception of the space ; b) a space functional organisation code, relating the functional arrangement of the furniture in the room to the kind of interpersonal behaviour it favours, namely, the number, location and reciprocal orientation of the sitting places, the zoning pattern as far as the sitting area or the dining area are concerned, and the identification of the focal points (Canter et al. 1974); c) a space decoration code, describing those features that seem more specifically aimed at obtaining an aesthetic fulfilment from the spatial arrangement. Particular attention was paid to those features that are related to the collative variables of complexity and ambiguity (Berlyne 1971; Wohlwill 1976).

Each room is thus described by a set of features denoted as present or absent. The contingency tables are then subjected to a multivariate technique of analysis called correspondence analysis (Benzecri 1980; Fénélon 1981). For the purpose of giving priority to specific patterns found in each country, the two groups are treated separately and the variable patterns emerging from the analysis then compared.

Living room typologies and cross-cultural rules

The first objective of the research (i.e. to identify the properties differentiating space appropriating behaviour) was pursued by comparing the factorial structures obtained for the two different national subject samples (Bonnes et al. 1985). The factorial axes were extracted in order of importance, i.e. as a function of the weight of the variance displayed by the variables determining it. The proximity of the variables could be represented by spatial configurations of points (figures 1 and 2): two points are closer the more often the variables they represent are found in association, i.e. simultaneously present in the same room.

The variable patterns thus identified allows us to define characteristics and internally coherent modalities whereby the arrangement of the living room is organised in each country. Such organisational modalities have been interpreted as rules implicit in the organisation of the domestic space that vary in relation to the national traits of the inhabitants.

The most important rule which emerges in both countries concerns the functional organisation of the layout and defines two modalities characterised respectively by the importance given to elements aimed at favouring social interaction centered around mealtimes (for Italy: figure 1, configuration A; for France: figure 2, configuration C) rather

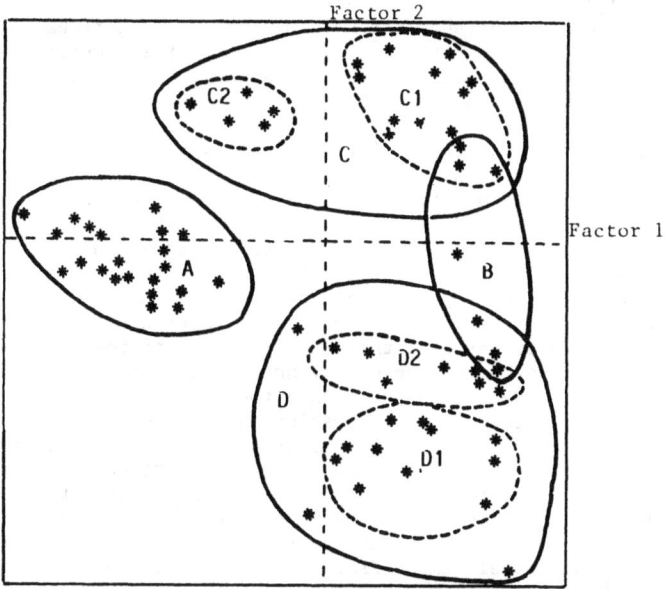

Figure 1 Configurations of variables for Italy (factorial axes 1, 2)

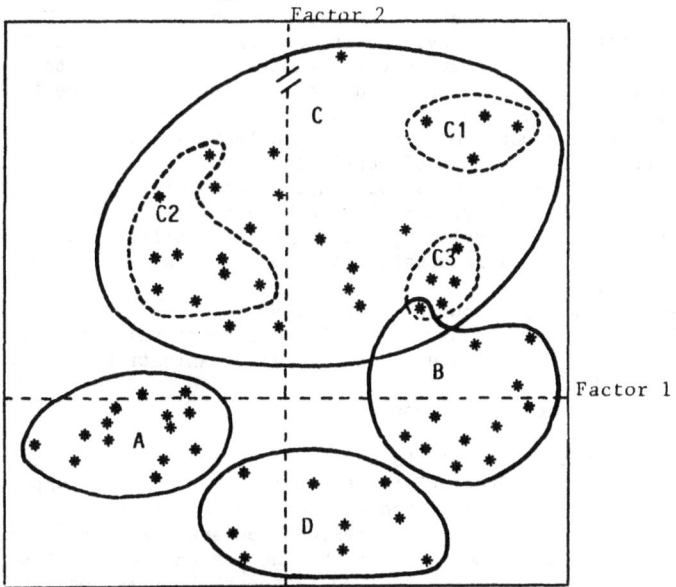

Figure 2 Configurations of variables for France (factorial axes 1, 2)

43

than around conversation (for Italy: figure 1, configuration B; for France: figure 2, configuration D). This type of functional organisation appears as the first discriminating factor in Italy, while in France it is secondary to decoration, which dominates in the first factor.

In addition to this general rule of functional organisation there are several other rules which apply specifically to one country. In Italy, the two different modalities of functional organisation (with the presence or absence of a conversation area) are accompanied by two different modalities of the structuring of the total space: 'opening up' of the walls where the conversation area predominates (figure 1, configuration B) vs marked and differentiated treatment of the various parts of the shell (floor, walls, ceiling) when the dining area predominates (figure 1, configuration A).

In France, the different functional organisation seems to be accompanied by a diversified treatment of the interior as regards decorative aspects: where the dining area predominates (figure 2, configuration C) there is a preference for low level relational ambiguity and complexity (configuration C3) and for rather highly decorative repertory elements (configuration C1). The treatment of interior decoration aspects appears in any case to be the strongest discrimination criterion in France, determining the first factor. This first factor emerges from a definite preference for low relational complexity and ambiguity (symmetry, rigidity) accompanied by the presence of antique elements (figure 2, configuration B), at one end of the axis, and a preference for a high degree of relational ambiguity and complexity (flexibility, heterogeneity) accompanied by the presence of modern elements (figure 2, configuration A) at the other.

The repertory elements seem, in Italy, to carry greater weight in discriminating the choices of the interior layout: in particular, the characterisation of such elements as either 'modern' (figure 1, configuration C) or 'antique' (figure 1, configuration D), enables us to pinpoint the second principal dimension which emerges. In France, this characterisation is less evident and overlaps relational choices regarding both the decoration (with particular reference to the degree of ambiguity of the interior) and the structuring of space (relative to the density of occupation of the walls and surfaces).

Furthermore, in both countries, though less clearly in Italy than in France, repertory elements of particular complexity (richly decorated antique objects) appear as a rule in a context of low level ambiguity and complexity (rigidity, symmetry, centrality); conversely a highly ambiguous and complex relational context (flexibility, asymmetry, disorder, dissonance) is created together with sober repertory elements (modern or plain).

In general, in both countries the rules of structuring of the available space seem to have less discriminatory value than the rules of decoration (for France) and of functional organisation (for Italy).

Living room typologies and social groups

The second aim of the analysis was to see how furnishing patterns linked to factorial axes differentiated the subjects. For this purpose an automatic classification method was applied to the set of subjects, using the same metric as for correspondence analysis. By means of this classification it was possible to examine the entire set of subjects based on their furnishing behaviour patterns. This method begins by isolating the closest point pair(s) (i.e. the subjects with the most similar furnishing behaviour patterns) and then successively adding other points to the original point pair(s) based on their proximity to the original pair(s). The result is summarized in the form of a dendogram. This procedure was applied both separately to the two national sets of subjects and to the French and Italian subjects taken together.

Examining the two dendograms representing the classification of the Italian subjects (figure 3) and French subjects (figure 4), it is possible to make a first significant comparison between the three subgroups (A, B, C) into which each dendogram divides after the first two nodes. The furnishing behaviour patterns characterising each subgroup can be defined in terms of the dimensions that emerge from the interpretation of the first two axes of factorial analysis, i.e. mainly from the type of functional organisation of the room, from the style and decorative treatment of the furnishings. The three Italian and three French subgroups display very similar sociological patterns, and both socio-professional status and educational level are seen to be highly discriminant. However, age seems to be distributed uniformly over the three subgroups.

The Italian subgroup A (figure 1) and the French subgroup A (figure 2) are mainly upper class in composition (executives or professionals). The Italian subgroup C and the French subgroup B are composed of manual and clerical workers. There is some difference between the two countries as far as the distribution of clerical workers is concerned: in Italy they tend to be grouped with the blue collar workers while in France they are spread over a wider range. The Italian subgroup B and the French subgroup C vary more extensively in their socioeconomic composition, although both are characterised by the presence of all (in France) and nearly all (in Italy) the architects and those following artistic professions. These are the subgroups which display less traditional furnishing choices (polyfunctional living room, no predominance of either the dining area or the conversational area, simple objects and relational patterns, flexibility, prevalence of modern style). In both countries, although more markedly in Italy, there is seen to be a close relationship between furnishing patterns and the occupant's social class. Nevertheless, while the more traditional patterns differentiate subgroups of opposite socioeconomic status, the innovative pattern corresponds to a subgroup displaying a greater

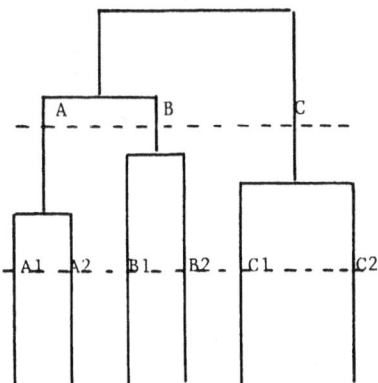

Figure 3 Classification of Italian subjects

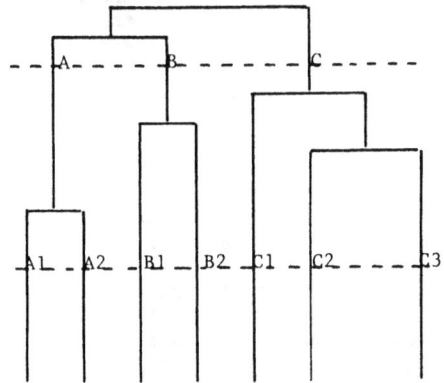

Figure 4 Classification of French subjects

socioeconomic spread and characterised mainly from a cultural point of view.

Further breakdown of the three subgroups reveals more subtle differences in furnishing patterns. However, while there continues to be a relationship between the macrosociological variables in Italy, this is not true in France, where more subtle sociological variables would probably be needed in order to find significant differences between the groups (Duncan 1981a; Amaturo et al. 1985).

If each of the three Italian subgroups is divided into two the discriminant sociological variable is seen to be age. This could be interpreted in the sense that the furnishing models show greater dynamism. The lower age portion of each group displayed a tendency towards polyfunctional arrangement with a less well defined opposition (compared with the corresponding older age group) between the predominance of the dining area (in the lower class) and the predominance of the conversational area (in the upper class). In the upwardly mobile modern working class (Rainwater 1972) the transformation of the room in a polyfunctional direction (based mainly on a dining area and a TV area, with a furnishing and decorative pattern that has no equivalent in France) does not seem to correspond to greater flexibility in the way the internal domestic space is subdivided, but rather to the exhibition of a degree of affluence reached only recently.

CATEGORISATION AND LANGUAGE

As pointed out by Canter and Lee (1974), the fact of taking as central data 'the residue of human action on the environment' leaves open the question of how the environment is actually conceptualised by people. It is from this point of view that we analysed a series of interviews with the inhabitants of the homes that constitute the Italian sample of the studies reported above. An examination of the material reveals that the interviewees choose from a wide variety of terms to name the room(s) constituting the daytime part of their home, although the choice of a particular label does not correspond univocally to the characteristics of the room, either in terms of physical features or behavioural setting (Giuliani 1985; Giuliani and Puglielli 1985).

The hypothesis suggested by the discourse analysis is that the name of the room is assigned on the basis of the hierarchy of rooms in the reference model, rather than on the basis of the current layout and modalities of use. By reference model we mean the sum of the design characteristics and behaviour patterns related to domestic space which is associated with that system of cultural values that are claimed to pertain to the social group to which the individual identifies himself/herself.

It is presumed that this diversity in linguistic behaviour derives from the dynamic relationship between the components of three basic dwelling models, each one attributing a different hierarchy of values to the type of social interaction linked to the categories of rooms designated with the different labels.

The three models can be denoted as 1) middle class traditional; 2) lower class traditional; 3) modern. While the traditional model can be subdivided into two distinct types in reference to the social groups that express it, the dwelling model that we can consider currently the leading one is publicised by the media as a model for a wide range of social strata. Both traditional models are characterised a) by a clearcut separation between a private part of the home, not in view to strangers, and a public part, designed to receive guests; and b) by a marked tendency towards monofunctionality of the rooms, that is, as far as possible, towards assigning one room to one function. However, the models differ in the hierarchy assigned to two different modes of social interaction: eating and conversation. In this way, while the room assigned to receiving guests is the sala da pranzo (dining room) in the lower class model, probably as a result of the persistence of values related to a more collectivistic rural culture (Duncan 1981b), in the bourgeois model priority is given to the salotto (sitting room).

The modern model rejects the traditional distinction between public part and private part of the house on behalf of an increased functionality and more rational use of space and of a greater spontaneity and reduced formality in social relations. The sala da pranzo and the salotto thus tend to be replaced by the soggiorno (living room) where one can have meals and entertain friends, and also watch television, read a book or relax and listen to music, i.e. activities that are not tied to any interaction with outsiders. This implies a change both in the 'temporal qualities' (Werner et al. 1985) of the rooms and in the territoriality patterns (Sebba and Churchman 1983), especially as far as children are concerned. The ritual behaviour in respect to space, expressed as the rigid dependence between events and spaces, gives way to an individualisation of space. Corresponding to a greater request for personal space there is a greater flexibility of use of rooms and a greater uniformity in their temporal qualities.

This model constitutes a stimulus for change, but the real situations may be very distant from it. The individual responses to the trend toward change are mediated by the culture of the social group one belongs to or came from, and can vary from a total assimilation of the model to its rejection, or to a greater or lesser integration with the preceding model (Berry 1980). Many intellectuals are found to deliberately avoid those specific terms for labelling the rooms above mentioned. Instead, they turn to generic terms like 'area', 'zone', 'space', and 'environment' to symbolise in this way the negative value attributed to the adherence, not to any particular home model, but to any preconstituted model at all. The plurality of actual situations is due not only to a greater or lesser acceptance of the new model, but also to the fact that modifications in the layout, in dwelling habits, in the cognitive and affective representations of the areas in the home and in the lexicon that labels them do not proceed necessarily at the same pace. A traditional label may thus be found to correspond to a non traditional layout and/or modality of use and vice versa.

AESTHETIC DIMENSION AND LIVABILITY DIMENSION

The desire to implement in one's own home decorative patterns corresponding to the reference model often leads to situations of conflict. The most frequent type of conflict is that between the desire to have a beautiful home and that to have a comfortable one, where one enjoys living. Analysis of the interviews (Giuliani 1983)points to the existence of a widespread stereotype in which the beautiful home is equated with a set of precious antique objects or, if modern, signed, original, and in any case expensive. Particularly at the lower sociocultural levels they are not denoted as objects having any definite physical characteristics. At best they evoke a vague impression of decorative overabundance, of magnificence, of 'impressiveness'.The presence of these objects implies a formal style of behaviour (Goffman

1959) which is incompatible with the presence of children (they break things, dirty the place, etc.) and which clashes with daily needs and with the equally widespread desire to have a 'warm, cosy and comfortable' home. The majority of interviewees (mainly women) declared that, in furnishing their homes, they had given priority to the criterion of functionality, or to other criteria closely related to practical functions. Only a small number of persons admitted giving priority to an aesthetic criterion or, mainly in the lower class, that they had furnished their house 'according to their own taste' or 'following the latest fashion trend'. The search for 'beauty', although not explicitly rejected, is frequently limited and discounted, and somehow held at a distance. In general, the priority given to an aesthetic criterion is equated to the desire to exhibit one's economic status and is evaluated negatively. Interviewees from the lower class, and to a lesser extent from the upper class, did not always seem to follow this trend, which was more typical of the middle class. Although including many who equate beauty with lack of practicality, lower class people tend to consider convenience more as a necessity than an absolute value: the lack of space and money does not permit much freedom of choice, so one has to make do.

The numerous contradictions in the interviewees' discourses nevertheless led us to think that these differences were due not so much to a different way of resolving the conflict between aesthetic needs and functional needs but rather to the lower class being more willing to admit their desire to 'cut a fine figure', and to appear as 'a person of good taste'. The disavowal of aesthetic intentions on the part of middle class people can be considered as a ploy to ward off negative judgements of their choices, reflecting the bourgeois myth that good taste is innate (Bourdieu 1979).The result that is presumed aesthetically positive is then carried off as something totally unplanned, as an involuntary by-product of preferences motivated by the desire to render one's own home warm, cosy and comfortable.

In order to investigate more fully the difference between a 'beautiful' home and a 'livable' home in a situation where the individual's actual behaviour is not directly involved, a second survey was made with a different sample of subjects (Giuliani and Rullo 1985). The subjects (180 persons equally distributed according to sex and divided into two age groups and three social levels) were shown ten colour photographs of living rooms and were asked to indicate which rooms, if they were sitting on a jury to assess their beauty, they would give first and last prize to, and why (aesthetic condition). They were then asked to indicate in which they would be glad to live personally and why (livability condition). The answers were analyzed both in terms of frequency and crossing with the social variables, and through a correspondence analysis.

The most interesting results in this connection can be summed up as follows: a) the comparison of preference ratings obtained for the different homes shows that the change of condition has a significant effect on the responses; b) half the subjects selected two different homes in the two conditions, this result being unaffected by social variables; c) higher preference ratings for the aesthetic condition than for the livability condition cannot be related back to the presence of antique and precious objects, even though the social prestige effect (Child 1969) is more likely to determine the aesthetic preference than the livability preference; d) aesthetic preference seems to be favoured by a definite homogeneous stylistic connotation of the room (Whitfield and Slatter 1979), whether modern antique, which discourages the

livability preference; e) the subjects use a significantly higher
proportion of affective terms (Russell, Ward and Pratt 1981) to justify
their livability preference than the aesthetic preference; f) the social
variables have a different weight in the two conditions: age and sex
affect the responses related to the livability condition, while
education (especially that of the father) affects the aesthetic
responses.

These results are interpreted in the sense that the two conditions
bring out two different role related identities in the individual
(Proshansky 1978), which are characterszed by a different degree of
interaction with the place (Canter 1983). In making an aesthetic
evaluation of the domestic environment the individual takes a detached
view of it as a passive observer and adopts the criteria learned from
his own cultural world in order to make an aesthetic judgement of any
object at all. When it is a matter of evaluating livability, the
environment is viewed actively, as a result of definite choices, and
what is evaluated is the consistency between these choices and what
he/she would have done or could do to make the environment in question a
satisfactory one in the light of one's own living experience.

This active relationship with the domestic environment is precisely
one of the conditions necessary, in our opinion, for the making of that
particular bond of attachment which turns a house into a home.

THE BASES OF ATTACHMENT TO THE HOME

The study of attachment to the home (Amoni 1986) carried out through an
analysis of its verbal expression has shown that this attachment is
produced not so much as a response to the physical and functional
characteristics of the home but according to the way the individual
appropriates and personalises his dwelling (Korosec-Serfaty 1975; Hansen
and Altman 1976).

During the appropriation process a dialectical interaction is set up
between the occupant and the dwelling with a varying stress being laid
on these two poles according to the way the affective relationship is
structured. When the dwelling is stressed, it is perceived mainly as a
shelter, a primary territory, the centre of the space-time orientation
of the subject (Dovey 1985); when the occupant is stressed, the various
components of its/her identity are alternately exhibited.

We define the first attitude as 'animistic', in view of the primitive
and magical associations with the concept of shelter or lair, and the
second as 'narcissistic', in view of the present models of reference
involved in defining the occupant's self image.

We use the terms 'animistic' (Durkheim 1912) to refer to a series of
attitudes which could be considered as based on the belief that the home
has, if not a soul, at least a 'personality' or some other quality
peculiar to the world of the living. This concept covers a number of
attributes of a maternal type (a kind of sacralisation by contact due to
the fact that the home is a place in which highly emotionally charged
events occur, e.g. weddings, births, and conceptions) as well as certain
explicit statements referring to a personality resistant to
appropriation in the form of a hypothesised product of a previous
history (Barbey 1983). In this type of 'animistic' attitudes, which are
distributed throughout the sample without distinction as to social
status or age, the dwelling appears as the decisive factor in a
relationship in which the individual is subordinate to the extent of
verging on regressive tendencies.

In the case of narcissistic attitudes, on the other hand, the accent is placed more on the subject and on his/her actions directed towards furnishing and decorating the home. The affective relationship grows up around these actions, which are perceived as the expression of personal qualities and are such that the domestic space is fashioned in one's own image. The process of appropriation or personalisation seems to coincide with the manifestation of signs of a positive Self. The subject's identity, which now appears as a social identity, thus takes on a culturally mediated character, in a mainly normative or ideal acceptance of the term, projected onto shared values to which prestige and status are linked. As a result of this cultural connotation the affective investment is qualitatively and quantitatively diversified as a function of the social group to which the individual belongs (Pratt 1981).

The typical features of the two ways of referring to the home can coexist in the same subject as different components of the affective relationship with one's own home. They are summarised in Table 1.

Table 1
Components of attitudes towards the home

ANIMISTIC ATTITUDE	NARCISSISTIC ATTITUDE
pre-eminence of dwelling	pre-eminence of individual
passivity	activity
regressiveness	normativity
self identity	social identity
subjective time	historical time

The expression of feelings of attachment, therefore, indicates the existence, in the occupant/dwelling interaction, of a complex of features characterised by the opposition of the salient features. This opposition is not a contradiction but rather a complementarity; the alternation between animistic and narcissistic attitudes, and between the perception of the dwelling as a 'shelter' or as a 'mirror', seems to be due to the intrinsic dialecticalness of the process whereby a physical space becomes an appropriated space, that is, in a home.

CONCLUSIONS

The proposed aim of using the concept of place as a theoretical framework to reconstruct the integrated and dynamic environmental unity represented by home has only been partially achieved.

In the studies presented here the attention is focussed now on observing the physical aspects of a part of the domestic space, from which the relative patterns of activities and evaluations can be inferred ('A cross-cultural analysis of the home interior'), now on the evaluative aspects ('Categorisation and language') and 'Aesthetic dimension and livability dimension') and now on the symbolic aspects ('The bases of attachment to the home'). The interrelation between these aspects and the agreement between our results and those drawn from the literature on the home confirm the validity of the theoretical choice of the concept of place as a unifying construct. Nevertheless, several relevant aspects have not been covered by our analysis. Two of these deserve special mention.

In the first place, our studies have focussed almost exclusively on the more public part of the house and have neglected the more private areas. The division of the home interior into parts which can be public or private to varying degrees leads to that dialectical dimension of openness/closedness (Altman and Gauvin 1981) which seem to be one of the major levels at which cultural specificity of the home is expressed.

A second topic only touched upon in our study is that of the differences in the conceptualisation of the home which arises and is developed as a function of the role played by the individual inside the home.

We believe that both the above aspects will have to be developed in future research if the meaning of the home in its entirety is to be fully grasped.

REFERENCES

Acking, C.A. and Kuller, R., 'The Perception of an Interior as a Function of its Colour', Ergonomics, vol.15, pp.645-54, 1972.

Altman, I., Environment and Social Behavior: Privacy, Personal Space, Territory and Crowding, Brooks/Cole, Monterey, California 1975.

Altman, I. and Chemers, M., Culture and Environment, Brooks/Cole, Monterey, California 1980.

Altman, I. and Gauvain, M., 'A Cross-Cultural and Dialectic Analysis of Homes, in Liben, L.S., Patterson, A.H. and Newcombe, N. (eds), Spatial Representation and Behavior Across the Life Span, Academic Press, New York 1981.

Amaturo, E., Costagliola, S. and Ragone, G., 'Furnishings and Status Attributes: A Sociological Study of the Living-Room', in Giuliani, M.V. and Bonnes, M. (eds), Psychosocial Approaches to the Home Interiors, Istituto di Psicologia del C.N.R., Roma 1985.

Amoni, F., Le basi dell'attaccamento alla casa, Istituto di Psicologia del CNR, Roma 1986.

Amoni, F., Giuliani, M.V., Bonnes, M. and Bernard, Y., 'Environment domestique et comportement habitatif', Architecture et Comportement, forthcoming.

Baird, J.C., Cassidy, B. and Kurr, J., 'Room Preferences as a Function of Architectural Features and User Activities', Journal of Applied Psychology, vol.63, pp.719-27.

Barbey, G., 'Exploration phénoménologique de la relation individuelle à la chambre', Paper presented at the First Anglo-French Housing Symposium, London, September 1983.

Benzecri, J.P., Analyse des Correspondences, Dunot, Paris 1980.

Berlyne, D.E., Aesthetics and Psychobiology, Appleton Century Crofts, New York 1971.

Bernard, Y., Bonnes, M., Giuliani, M.V. and Amoni, F., 'A Cross-Cultural Approach to the Study of Domestic Space', Istituto di Psicologia del CNR, Rome 1982.

Bernard, Y. and Jambu, M., 'Espace habité et modèles culturels', Ethnologie Française, vol.8, pp.7-20.

Bonnes, M., Giuliani, M.V., Amoni, F. and Bernard, Y., 'Cross-Cultural Rules for the Optimization of the Living-Room', in Giuliani, M.V. and Bonnes, M. (eds), Psychosocial Approaches to the Home Interiors, Istituto di Psicologia del CNR, Roma 1985.

Berry, J.W., 'Social and Cultural Change', in Triandis, H.C. and Brislin R.W. (eds), Handbook of Cross-Cultural Psychology, vol. 5, Allyn and Bacon, London 1980.

Bourdieu, P., La distinction. Critique sociale du jugement, Editions de Minuit, Paris 1979.

Canter, D., The Psychology of Place, Architectural Press, London 1977.

Canter, D., 'The Purposive Evaluation of Places', Environment and Behavior, vol.15, pp.659-98, 1983.

Canter, D., 'Putting Situations in their Place: Foundations for a Bridge between Social and Environmental Psychology', in Furnham, A. (ed), Social Behaviour in Context, Allyn and Bacon, London, forthcoming.

Canter, D., Gilchrist, J., Miller, J. and Roberts, N., 'An Empirical Study of the Focal Point in the Living Room', in Canter, D. and Lee, T. (eds), Psychology and the Built Environment, Architectural Press, London 1974.

Canter, D. and Lee, K.H., 'A Non-Reactive Study of Room Usage in Modern Japanese Apartments', in Canter, D. and Lee, J. (eds), Psychology and the Built Environment, Architectural Press, London 1974.

Child, I.L., 'Aesthetics' in Lindzey, G. and Aronson, E. (eds), Handbook of Social Psychology, vol.3, Addison-Wesley, London 1969.

Craik, K.H., 'Environmental Psychology', in Newcombe, T.M. (ed) New Directions in Psychology, Holt, Rinehart and Wilson, New York 1970.

Dovey, K., 'Home and Homelessness', in Altman, I. and Werner, C.M. (eds), Home Environments, Plenum Press, New York 1985.

Duncan, J.S. and Duncan, N.G., 'Housing as Presentation of Self and the Structure of Social Networks', in Moore, G.T. and Golledge, R.G. (eds), Environmental Knowing, Dowden, Hutchinson and Ross, Stroudsburg, Pa. 1976.

Duncan, J.S. (ed), Housing and Identity, Croom Helm, London 1981a.

Duncan, J.S., 'From Container of Women to Status Symbol: The Impact of Social Structure on the Meaning of the House', in Duncan, J.S. (ed), Housing and Identity, Croom Helm, London 1981b.

Durkheim, E., Les formes élémentaires de la vie religieuse, Alcan, Paris 1912.

Fénélon, J.P., Qu'est-ce que l'Analyse des donnés, Lefonen, Paris 1981.

Giuliani, M.V., 'Reticence and Stereotype in the Expression of Aesthetic Values', Paper presented at the International Conference on Psychology and the Arts, Cardiff, G.B. September 1983.

Giuliani, M.V., 'Naming the Rooms: Implications of a Change in the Home Model', in Giuliani, M.V. and Bonnes, M. (eds), Psychosocial Approaches to the Home Interiors, Istituto di Psicologia del CNR, Roma 1985.

Giuliani, M.V. and Puglielli, A., 'The Lexicon of 'Living Space'', in Hoppenbrouwers, G., Seuren, P. and Weijters, A. (eds), Meaning and the Lexicon, Foris, Dordrecht 1985.

Giuliani, M.V. and Rullo, G., 'The Aesthetic Dimension in the Evaluation of Home Interior Arrangement', Paper presented at the 9th International Colloquium of Empirical Aesthetics, Santa Cruz, Calif. August 1985.

Goffman, E., The Presentation of Self in Everyday Life, Doubleday, Garden City, N.Y. 1959.

Hausen, W.B. and Altman, I., Decorating Personal Place: A Descriptive Analysis', Environment and Behavior, vol.8, pp.491-504, 1976.

Kaye, S.M. and Murray, M.A., 'Evaluations of an Architectural Space as a Function of Variations in Furniture Arrangement, Furniture Density, and Windows', Human Factors, vol.24, pp.609-18, 1982.

Korosec-Serfaty, P., 'Comment définir le concept d'appropriation de l'espace?', Bulletin de la Société Française de Sociologie, vol.2, n.5, pp.24-26, 1975.

Laumann, E.O. and House, J.S., 'Living-Room Style and Social Attributes: The Patterning of Material Artifacts in a Modern Urban Community', in Laumann, E.O., Siegel, P.M. and Hodge, R.W. (eds), The Logic of Social Hierarchies, Markham, Chicago 1970.

Lawrence, R.J., 'The Social Classification of Domestic Space: A Cross-Cultural Case Study', Anthropos, vol.76, pp.649-64.

Mehrabian, A., Public Places and Private Spaces, Basic Books, New York 1976.

Moore, G.T., 'Knowing about Environmental Knowing. The Current State of Theory and Research on Environmental Cognition', Environment and Behavior, vol.11, pp.33-70, 1979.

Pratt, G., 'The House as an Expression of Social Worlds', in Duncan, J.S. (ed), Housing and Identity, Croom Helm, London 1981.

Proshansky, H.M., 'Environmental Psychology and the Real World', American Psychologist, vol.31, pp.303-10, 1976.

Proshansky, H.M., 'The City and Self-Identity', Environment and Behavior, vol.10, pp.147-69, 1978.

Rainwater, L., 'Fear and the House-as-haven in the Lower Class', in Gutman, R. (ed), People and Buildings, Basic Books, New York 1972.

Rapoport, A., House, Form and Culture, Prentice Hall, Englewood Cliff, N.J. 1969.

Rapoport, A., The Meaning of the Built Environment, Sage, Beverly Hills, Calif. 1982.

Rapoport, A., 'Thinking about Home Environments: A Conceptual Framework', in Altman, I., and Werner, C.M. (eds), Home Environments, Plenum Press, New York 1985.

Russell, J.A. and Ward, L.M., 'Environmental Psychology', Annual Review of Psychology, vol.33, pp.651-88, 1982.

Russell, J.A., Ward, L.M. and Pratt, G., 'Affective Quality Attributed to Environments', Environment and Behavior, vol.13, pp.259-88, 1981.

Sebba, R. and Churchman, A., 'Territories and Territoriality in the Home', Environment and Behavior, vol.15, pp.191-210, 1983.

Stokols, D., 'Environmental Psychology', Annual Review of Psychology, vol.29, pp.253-95, 1978.

Stokols, D. and Shumaker, S.A., 'People in Place: A Transactional View of Settings', in Harvey, J.H. (ed), Cognition, Social Behavior, and the Environment, Lawrence Erlbaum, Hillsdale, N.J. 1981.

Tajfel, H., Human Groups and Social Categories, Cambridge University Press, Cambridge 1981.

Vygotsky, L.S., Thought and Language, M.I.T. Press/Wiley, New York 1962.

Ward, L.M. and Russell, J.A., 'The Psychological Representation of Molar Physical Enviromnents', Journal of Experimental Psychology: General, vol.110, pp.121-52, 1981.

Weisner, T.S. and Weibel, J.C., 'Home Environments and Family Lifestyles in California', Environment and Behavior, vol.13, pp.417-60, 1981.

Werner, C.M., Altman, I. and Oxley, D., 'Temporal Aspects of Homes: A Transactional Pespective', in Altman, I., and Werner, C.M. (eds), Home Environments, Plenum Press, New York 1985.

Whitfield, T.W.A. and Slatter, P.E., 'The Effect of Categorization and Prototypicality on Aesthetic Choice in a Furniture Selection Task', British Journal of Psychology, vol.70, pp.65-75, 1979.

Wohlwill, J.F., 'Environmental Aesthetics: The Environment as a Source of Affect', in Altman, I. and Wohlwill, J.F. (eds), Human Behavior and Environment. Advances in Theory and Research, vol.1, Plenum Press, New York 1976.

4. Cultural aspects of place consciousness and environmental identity

BOYOWA A CHOKOR

INTRODUCTION

Humanistic studies of the relationsips between man and environment have been very few in the African context. Despite the varied historical, socio-economic and cultural landscapes of the people, only few studies have evaluated the built form in the context of the social aspirations of people (Chokor, 1986a). Within the architectural and anthropological field, for example, the few studies that have emerged have been primarily concerned with the cultural symbolism of the built environment. Must buildings and landscapes be visualised solely as products or symbols of certain cultures and peoples alone; is the social, cultural symbolization of buildings and landscapes more important than the experiential relationships of the person to the environment? In a sense, studies have failed to evaluate how ordinary people themselves inhabit buildings and places and think about them.

   This paper argues that a fuller understanding of small and large-scale man-created environments in Africa requires knowledge of the sense of orientation and attachments to places and that analysis of such attachments may provide insight into the identity of buildings and landscapes created by different groups. A theoretical exposition of the neglected theme of place attachments and environmental identity is supported with a case study drawn from Ibadan, Nigeria.

THE SELF THROUGH ENVIRONMENTS

The notable concentration of vernacular architecture in developing countries, particularly in remoter rural centres, has stimulated wide ranging interest amongst anthropologists most notably, (Rapport, 1969) in the similarities rather than the interaction between house form and culture. As a consequence of this concern, the built environment is rarely visualized as consisting of centres of meaning with significance for the life of the individual and capable of eliciting various attitudes, feelings and attachments. How various environments produce place-related values in the cycle of life has largely been ommitted from the evaluation of the cultural attributes of landscapes, instead there has been a remarkable concentration of research work on the behavioural, geometric properties and the symbolic logic of built form in relation to the cosmos and biological being (Duly, 1979). Yet the various ways in which social life and the identity of people find expression in the environment should be viewed as equally important in the social understanding of the nature of houses and environments. Often, in the past, the house has been taken as an entity with its own autonomous cultural symbols. It has not been common to construct the built environment as centres of interaction with significance to the life of the person.

In the African environment, the relevance of the few theoretical issues raised above for environmental meaning may be seen in the inter-play between traditional architectural landscapes, modernization and the identity of people. The growth of cities through Western-based forms of modernization represents a significant intrusion into the life of the African and his traditional settings. Increasingly, the original traditional village, ethnic and cultural landscapes have been destroyed and replaced by new forms. People have moved to the cities and have acquired new values and tastes. Such a change has affected the orientation of the African to buildings and places, new sets of relationship between people and milieu are emerging with places, given the variety of contacts and the architectural transformations. The 'ethnoscape' of the African must be informed by the variety of place consciousness and place-related values exhibited by them.

Indeed, the African 'ethonscape' consists of vital nodes such as the house shell, village, hometown or neighbourhood which his cultural, ethnic, social background and other modern demands enable him to create, recreate and within which he experiences multiple identity and sense of belonging. These are existential qualities and relations which affect the interpretation of houses and the meanings of built form to both inhabitants and users. Certainly, how buildings and places serve as anchors and project the identity of people is paramount to the understanding of environmental experience and attitudes in Africa.

The suitability of various settings and housing for different cultural characteristics and groups also demands clarification. On the practical side of policy, the ethnic diversity of African cities and the equally diversified social identities of residents is one reason why conflicting interests must be distilled and articulated to provide more livable environments. For example, the need to redevelop old districts, slum environments and squatter resettlements to meet modern ideals of planning and at the same time maintain the identity of inhabitants is a clear demand which many redevelopment schemes have failed to meet (Marris 1961). Contemporary urban form and design also seem to encourage transient migrant living rather than full

identification with city life, while public housing schemes have failed
in Nigeria partly as a result of insensitivity to the values and
cultural life of people (Chokor, 1986a, p. 17).

Although it has been argued that geographical appraisal of the man-
millieu bond has been lacking in the context of the developing world,
recent developments in sense of place studies particularly in the West
provide some insight into how such a valuable exploration might be
achieved. Geographers have now begun to appreciate that the
environment consists of places at different scale and levels of
experience rather than a static three-dimensional form. Thus, as the
individual self moves in the world and grows up in life, he exhibits
place-related values. A vital task of the geographer is to uncover or
orchestrate those values and intentions as they are revealed with
respect to environments by the individual or group (see Buttimer, 1974;
1976). Existential geographers (see Samuels, 1978, 1979) have argued
that the consideration of place-related values affords the geographer
an approach to understanding how man enters and establishes
relationships between himself and the outside world; how the 'lived-
space' (existential space) of the person becomes significant and
attributed with meaning. As he concludes "human history is geography
of movement, of uprootedness, of collapsing or changing reference
points in the lives of men" (Samuels, 1978, p. 34).

Geographers with a phenomenological background (Ley, 1977) have also
attempted to reveal how man lives and dwells. According to Seamon
(1979, p.79), the body is the foundation of rootedness; through the
recurring cycle of departure and return, body-subject comes to know the
placement of home and its relative location in terms of paths, places,
people and things. With the observed differences between the 'sense of
place' of natives and outsiders (Duncan, 1978) geographers more than
ever are concerned with what makes a locale (at any scale) distinctive,
or the close ties of place to the individual and group sense of
identity (Saarinen et al, 1982, p. 525).

But, perhaps, fuller insight into the nature of place in relation to
existence is beginning to emerge in works undertaken in some related
fields. Environmental psychologists are beginning to embrace with
greater vigour the existential qualities of environments as the
foundation of environmental meaning. Researchers now lay stress on the
existential relations between man and place; purposeful or conscious
intentions create places and affect the relation to environments, all
of which may draw from an awareness of self, relation to others and
society. Such qualities or "dynamic interplay between action and
place" will obviously determine one's satisfaction and pleasure derived
from place (see Canter, 1984, p.1). As Canter further argues action
and place are both products of our experience of our transactions with
the world (Canter, 1984, p. 4).

The resurgence of place studies in the West through attempts to
rationalize the self, the house and the world through the context of
'home' by architectural psychologists and landscape researchers has
provided added spur to the elaboration of the contextual relation
between man and milieux. From the world of confusion and uncertainties
surrounding us the house has been given an existential interpretation
as the centre, the locus, the fixed reference point; 'home' has assumed

56

that centre, "a sure refuge between journeys" and where identity, security and stimulation are most felt (Porteous, 1979, p. 388; Dovey, 1978). Thus, the home has become the extension of the self and self-identity (Hayward, 1978; Appleyard, 1979).

It may be concluded that issues of self, identity and existential interpretation of places provide a key answer for the reexamination of the meanings and values which the built environment communicates to people and thus highlights how the cultural relations of people to the built environment shape the evolution and nature of houses form and neighbourhoods. In the African city context, for example, migrants, ethnic or social groups may develop attachments and affection for places, use space and identify with milieux differently. Territorial behaviour and cognitive, affective relationships to place or symbolic identification with the city, neighbourhood or home are good ways of uncovering meanings and experiences in the built environment (see Chokor 1986a, p. 12). These themes though prevalent in the literature have not been extended further in any meaningful empirical investigation. The Ibadan case study that follows provides a context in which to elaborate the implication of sense of place and home attachments for environmental, housing indentity in Africa.

Methodology

Although recent studies have attempted to explore the subjective experience of people through adoption of phenomenological methods and participants discussion with small groups of people (Seamon, 1979, MacDonald 1981), the need has also arisen to move from the search for an 'absolute pre-suppositionless inquiry" (Entrikin 1976, p. 16) to that which enables the researcher to critically interprete the relation between man and landscapes with humane, people-sensitive concepts and propositions. I have earlier pointed out that most environmental methodological tools developed to date in the West are largely unreceptive to the cultural context of Third World inhabitants and have advocated the use of descriptions founded on the historical, symbolic associations, beliefs, customs and traditions of the people (Chokor, 1986a, p.19).

To study and elucidate the sense of place in Ibadan, Nigeria, I employed a range of investigative methods that related to the cultural life of the people. Ibadan is located in south-western Nigeria in the heartland of Yorubaland. I started off with an investigative questionnaire survey of environmental attitudes and beliefs of 415 residents, exploring the significance of various places to the life of the people; from the house to the neighbourhood and then to the city and in relation to places outside the city. Simple questions were used to explore the various purposeful activities and action undertaken by people within the environment. This level of investigation provided a forum for the researcher to arrive at some generalizations on environmental attitudes, dispositions and beliefs. Surrogate stimuli photographs of locales in the city were also used to "jog" peoples' memories about places and this provided a context for people to relate to building types, their symbols and relevance to social life in the city. At the next stage, I developed an intensive, detailed discussion on the environmental experiences and feelings of people with a select 45 respondents. This level of man-place corroboration was designed to

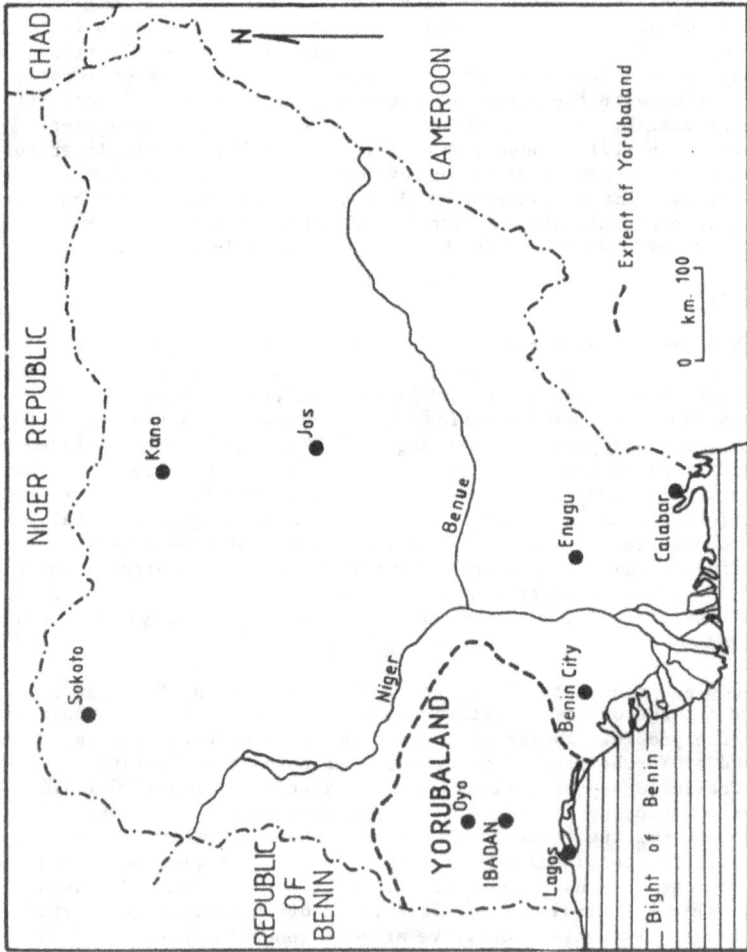

facilitate a more empathetic understanding of environmental situations, in addition to elucidating certain concepts and ideas evident in the structured questionnaire survey. A 'people-place autobiography' was recorded and person-to-person discussion of issues ensued. These discussions tended to convey the time/historical dimension of experience in the trajectories of life.

To elaborate the cultural context of environmental experience, cited earlier on, people with whom discussion and interview were developed, were encouraged to use the languages of social intercourse and cultural expressions of social events, including the employment of proverbs, riddles, poetry, songs, stories and short vivid statements. Such expressions are in tune with the every-day social life which the people live (see Chokor, 1986b). A riddle such as "a pile of shit on a leaf, and cover with leaf", for example, symbolizes humanity between heaven and earth (Beir, 1970). Riddles like other forms of expressions are attempts to qualify and make vivid related environmental attributes and issues as unique but 'intersubjectively' shared experiences in the community.

Finally, to provide some framework for the comparison of reseach results, of the 415 respondents in the survey, 200 were drawn from the indigenous Ibadan Yoruba ethnic group, located in the eastern core section of the city, being permanently resident in Ibadan; one hundred and five predominantly newer residents drawn from the Yoruba ethnic group of migrants resident in the South-Western suburban section of the city and who migrated from within the Yorubaland. The remaining 110 consisted of earlier Yoruba migrants to the city with a high concentration of other Nigerian ethnic groups (Ibos, Urhobos, Edos, Efiks and Nupes) resident in a Northern suburban section of the city and who had migrated from different parts of the country. I had detailed discussion with 15 people each, from the three main groups. Role variations, including age, sex and distance of migration, may affect group sense of place and environmental identity, so also is time, range and depth of experience important, as place itself provides links between the past, the present and the future. Summary characterisations of the three groups is given in Table 1.

The sense of place is primarily a product of a shifting balance between individual's visual, aesthetic evaluation of environments of contact and a more intimate insider's appreciation of them, which is capable of giving rise to affection and attachment to particular localities. The researcher's role in this context is to undertake a critical interpretation of the range of expressions made by people. The meaning of place is the symbolic, connotative college of ideas sifted out of the web of expressions. In this report, the more general identification with buildings, localities and the city are explored

Table 1

Characteristics of the Sampled Groups

TYPE	Suburban Migrants (South-West of the city	Suburban Migrants (North of the city	Core Indigene Group
% with no education	20.00	25.46	51.50
% with primary education	35.24	39.09	28.50
% with secondary education	25.71	28.18	19.50
% with higher education	19.05	7.27	0.50
% self-employed/immobile house-base businesses, artisans and craftsmen	19.05	23.64	34.00
% mobile petty trades, market people/hawkers	22.86	25.45	39.50
% Intermediate clerical, ministerial/teaching staff	16.19	35.45	24.00
% Professional, Managerial higher cadre executives	41.90	15.46	2.50
% Born in Ibadan	8.57	14.55	83.50
% Born outside Ibadan	91.43	85.45	16.50
% Yoruba ethnic group	92.38	58.18	100.00
% non-Yoruba ethnic group	7.62	41.82	-
% 1-5 years of residence in Ibadan	20.95	11.95	-
% 6-10 years of residence in Ibadan	21.90	15.45	-
% 11-15 years of residence in Ibadan	34.29	38.18	-
% 15 + years of residence in Ibadan	22.86	34.55	100.00
BASE (TOTAL) 415 =	105.00	110.00	200.00

A SENSE OF PLACE: CULTURAL VALUES AND ENVIRONMENTAL IDENTITY

A sense of origin of the self, associated with a recognized or known locality permeates the attitudes and environmental consciousness of people in Ibadan. This section explores the consciousness that both immigrants and indigenes have of their places of origin, pointing out the underlying reasons for the environmental attitudes they demonstrated. In addition it describes a series of contextual judgements made about localities in Ibadan, exploring the underlying values behind those judgements.

Attitudes Towards Ibadan and its Localities:

Ibadan is seen by both Yoruba Ibadan indigenes and Yoruba/non-Yoruba migrant groups as a city of many peoples; different communities who have moved and built the city at different stages to fulfill personal, economic and social goals and ambitions. Migrants of all ethnic background are acutely aware of the claims of the Yoruba Ibadan indigenes to be descended from the original inhabitants of Ibadan while indigenes refer to the people who live in suburban locales as 'strangers' from various parts of the country. In general, migrants have very poor images of core localities. The majority have not lived there, do not have daily transactions there and do not wish to live there, describing them as dirty, cluttered with dilapidated old buildings; saying that these ill-maintained and poor indigenous compound housing areas are difficult to live in because they lack amenities and structural beauty. On the other hand, many Yoruba Ibadan indigences see suburban locales, as areas where newcomers to the city have constructed more sophisticated modernized buildings for themselves. They find such buildings attractive and many wish to live there but family and social obligations prevent them from doing so. Indigenes feel that the suburban localities are popular amongst groups only for their physical attractiveness, newness and amenity value. Social or community life is believed to be absent in such areas. Although modernized urban buildings were symbolic of a more regimented and routine way of life, at least life there would be a prosperous one.

Origins of Self, Family and Place Attachments:

The analysis of the survey and discussion results revealed an apparent estrangement of migrants from the city and their pre-occupation with their places of origin. I will explore these issues by examining first, the individual's lives and aspirations. Second, the series of practical steps taken to accomplish goals or symbolize place identity are examined.

An important distinction people drew between places arose from the recognition of two primary environments. The first is more or less a fixed, familiar and known cultural/geographical area which links people with an ancestry, both on arrival and on departure from the world. The second environment comprises a more mundane set of places in which the individual lives, works and moves in response to the prevalent economic and social necessities of life. Since the first has an image of permanency associated with it, it was seen as constituting a key, secured, reference point or centre within existence, full of important cultural meanings or symbols. The second by contrast, were judged to possess transient values or qualities - transit points or stations on the socio-economic paths of life. There was in general no variation on the basis of sex, status, ethnic background and religion to issues of meaning of family houses, home place and personal indentity within the city, representing a latent cultural disposition of people in society in the interpretation of environments.

Though most migrant ethnic groups have been resident in the city for a period of over ten years, an overwhelming majority (97%) claimed they still had a real home outside Ibadan. Within Ibadan over 75% live in rented apartments, the majority built by other rich migrant landlords; others by indigenes and wealthy non-Ibadan residents. For all Yoruba Ibadan indigenes interviewed in the core, Ibadan and nowhere else was emphasized as real home.

One important exception in the migrant group was a 75-year-old Yoruba man who moved into Ibadan at about the age of 12 with his mother. Although he was able to identify the Oyo country in the Yorubaland as the place of his birth and descent, he made infrequent contact with it and subsequently lost communication on the death of relatives. He was, however, quick to stress that he is a non-Ibadan by descent while in fact finding it difficult to come to terms with his inability to identify his people or trace his genealogy.

The definition of ancestral home varied amongst groups but basically a home is a zone with a ring of shared meanings, established precepts, and blood relationships with a recognized ancestral head, and family house or houses. There is oneness of purpose, family tree, family records and continuity. This promotes a sense of belonging and commitment, enabling people to form social relationships and settle disputes more harmoniously. For the migrant non-Ibadan Yoruba people home is the village or town from which they migrated or claimed descent within the Yorubaland. Most non-Yorubas on the other hand, point first to the ethnic areas; states or local areas of origin where they have blood relations before identifying themselves with the villages or towns containing ancestral homes. This point emphasizes the fact that they not only perceive themselves as separate and culturally, linguistically distinct from their host Yorubas but also see themselves as originating from different geographical regions.

Apart from the real cultural and thenic differences between these people, an important point to note is that politics and societal organization equally influences the identity of people. The former political arrangement up to 1966 was founded mainly on ethnic and regional consciousness; the military and post-military civilian regime while not eliminating this consciousness altogether defines people by states of origin and local government areas, so it is quite possible that people, most especially non-Yorubas are also responding to the politics and policies reflected in these arrangements (such politics for example influence the life chances of people in terms of work, ownership of property and claims). For example, the overwhelming majority of migrants (76%) are of the opinion that it is much easier, safer and probably more convenient to acquire land for property development in their various places of origin than in Ibadan (a point which was strongly emphasized by the non-Yoruba migrants). Politics combined with a system of land inheritance or birthright, produce affection or endearment to place; the individual migrant or indigene is not only well-known and accepted in areas of origin but forms part of the history and traditions of a locale.

Attachments Amongst Yoruba Ibadan Indigenes:

Patterns of place attachment and home descriptions made by the core Ibadan Yoruba indigenes bore a marked similarity to those described for the Yoruba and non-Yoruba migrants in the city. Over 80% were born in the town and the majority (89%) have lived continuously in Ibadan. Most (94%) describe identifiable lineage, family compound houses in sections of the city as permanent immovable home grounds which link them with an ancestry. (In fact, 65% live in properties owned jointly by the lineage family and 20% in personal houses). Not only are these cluster of houses or compounds seen as symbols of personal belonging to the town, they also represent continuity with its history and evolution - after all, many maintained, we are located in the central region of the city where the city began and where the original founders are generally acknowledged to have lived. Both a common social and cultural history together with family houses weld people into place; and people and buildings are more united because of the common sense of belonging it creates for groups.

On the one hand, buildings or compounds are infused with a history of personal identity symbolizing the lives, past and future of a geneology; whilst on the other it is the actual level where family groups focus their daily lives and interact to continue this identity. About 50% felt that it would be breaking an important tradition to reject the father's or lineage family compound in favour of rented apartments elsewhere. A typical response was; 'You cannot say that your father's house is bad or derelict and adandon it for other places'. Many equated this with a rejection of one's personal identity, roots and the very symbols that represented it. To be deprived of one's lineage home was read and interpreted by a few as something amounting to 'emasculation' which crippled not only the person's identity but eroded as well his personal history and links with the family past. This environmental attitude and sense of place of the indigenes has had remarkable implications and consequences for the created form in the core of the city (Chokor, 1986c). Having no other place to call home, the compound or agbo-il usually consisting of rectangular houses with adjoining rooms enclosing a courtyard and encased by a wall was popularly adopted to take care of the extended family and the maintenance of a lively network of social ties of the people. The 'conflict' between the cultural values of the Yoruba Ibadan indigenes and the house form is reflected in the core housing landscapes that later emerged.

Older generation indigenes recalled very well how compound family houses met their social/cultural life. This congruence to them is reflected in the complex relationship and harmony between social organisation, people and housing, since to them a compound houses a group of patrillineally related families with a named founding ancestor and a head called Bale who overseas the activities of the compound; the interests of the lineage family and their social life were enhanced and integrated into the built environment. Together with the privacy and social functions afforded by the central courtyard, the meaning of the compound was carried beyond the ordinary physical shell. The past and the contemporary spirit of the people was built into the family compound. The people in a sense found not only that their past and present was represented in the compound but also that the future social/cultural identity of the person is only made certain and coherent by this association.

However, the cultural attachment to the compound and the refusal to move elsewhere has led to subsequent modification and erection of additional rooms, especially within the courtyard (erstwhile use for social exchanges, children's evening play and economic activities). Walls were also demolished in the absense of space for expansion, open spaces were utilized for additional rooms or houses to accomodate anticipated increases in family size. The major effect of both this attitude and initial refusal to accept regulated modern planning in the core was the marked destruction of functional, human, culturally-rooted compound designs and, later, the gradual emergence of a physical oppressive landscape characterized by increasing congestion, dilapidation and general environmental decay, limiting the quality of life of the people (Chokor, 1986c, p. 109). As a consequence, because people are less aware or pay less attention to the tension between their social values and urban form, it would be impossible to redress emerging housing problem in the core of the city without proper attention to these attendant values. The majority of the indigenes I talked to expressed profound attachment to their physical compound and are highly protective of their compound/neighbourhood area, excluding any external/outside urban developers from coming into their housing areas.

Family, common history and cultural socialties and not physical circumstances were the most important reasons for indigene attachment to core compounds and locales. A significant proportion of younger adults were however more radical in their views. The majority felt that it was part of their human existence and identity within the wider world to locate a home in town as Ibadan indigenes but that this did not close the option of moving away when the need arose. However, living in personally built houses as well as family houses creates some form of residential inertia, as the range of dwelling places open to people are restricted to a narrow geographical area, either as a result of economic considerations or family obligations.

It is not that Ibadan indigenes are immutably restricted to one locality, it is rather that it forms part of their cultural identity. Past and future aspirations or realities of life define place to the individual and the meaning of place has value only when both emotional (lineage family life) and cultural components are incorporated, to explain the underlying motives for strength of attachment to place. First, homes or family compounds are important centres of life because extended family relationships form a significant aspect of social interaction within the culture and the physical construction is a symbol of family union to the people. Second, without a uniting central home, social life, cultural life based on lineage family would be meaningless and perhaps impracticable - more discrete, impersonalized and devoid of common bonds, which is the antithesis of extended family life. One traditional chief with 50 years of residential experience in one family compound and locality sums it up:

'these are no attachments, these are places we live as ordinary people as circumstances and opportunities of life offer us; provide a better place for me in the context of my life and family situations - I will make it up'.

Home Identification Among Yoruba and Non-Yoruba Migrants:

The situation of migrants living in the suburbs is rather different in that they originate from localities outside Ibadan. Their responses reflect this origin but do still bear comparison with those indigenes.

A vast majority of all ethnic background (74%) were amazed when asked if the migration to Ibadan may be considered as being permanent with no prospects of moving back. 'No!' many exclaimed. 'Ibadan is not my home. I am going back'. 'Why?' 'Home is the best'. Is there somebody without a home,?' 'do you hate your home?' 'He who goes to the market goes back home'. These simple, symbolic and sentimental responses demonstrate the difficulties migrants experience in stating why they must return home. The analogy of the market and the home place reveals however the strength of personal feelings involved. First, the movement to the city of Ibadan, they claim, was motivated essentially by economic needs. This being so, the stay in the city was synonymous to paying a visit to the market-place in which a return home was expected. Second, about 88% of migrants claim they were living in their respective areas of origin prior to the move to Ibadan and 94% were certain they still had some attachments to these areas (predominantly small towns or country-side villages).

The attachment of migrants to respective home areas and preparedness to go home is clearly symbolized in the house form in which they live within the city. Rather than family compounds as in the core, developers seizing on the 'transient' status of migrants in the city have evolved tenement houses for poorer migrants and self-contained flats for richer groups. These designs have none of the social attributes of compounds. The majority of migrants do not view their houses in the city with any social and symbolic importance, as they hope to build family houses back home when enough money has been accumulated in the city. If anything, urban houses symbolized their temporary sojourn in a 'foreign' land. Thus, they cherish modernity and new designs and find the functional character of modern buildings meaningful and are proud of the amenity value. The tenement housing itself is also highly symbolic of the cosmopolitan life of the city.

Migrants are conscious of the family life they are used to at home which is not represented in the urban housing form. The tenement buildings which are rectangular in shape are normally two or three storeys high, with approximately 15-30 rooms which may accommodate 10-15 migrant families of different ethnic and social background. The co-existence of many different migrant families within the same housing unit, implies that the ties between people and building is weak, and a decreasing role for the extended family as the social basis for neighbourhood interaction. Indeed, in place of the extended family, ethnic neighbours and the hometown groups have become more important settings in which public and private social interaction is developed, providing the basis for a sense of orientation and place consciousness in the urban environment.

The most important factors producing home attachments were family obligations and emotional bonds (90% of those who claim they have attachments). About 74% also attributed it to some sentimentally laden phrase such as "my hometown", "my place of origin", "where I was born", etc; while 50% also mentioned family houses, properties, investments, part-time occupation, personal or family businesses. This, however, seems to suggest the over-riding importance of cultural, social and family bonds over economic opportunities or physical necessities. The majority of migrants in fact stressed the extended family ties which nurtured them, within which they grew up and around which meaningful social, economic, cultural-religious life still revolves. Social events that are far from being replicated in Ibadan. Such attractions and commitments made the apparent quest for home more real.

The link between development of city life and family culture thus affects the place identity of people. Cosmopolitanism creates universalized ideals whilst eroding local culture and customs of the people. Since cosmopolitan and inter-ethnic city life is a much more recent phenomena than traditional bonds of extended family, focused on a locality and place of origin, a high percentage of all migrants (62%) felt that city life forms an extension of the person's relationship to the outside world and cannot replace a sense of belonging elsewhere. About 59% of migrants also tend to marry from home-town or home area which increases family attachment to place.

The great majority of immigrants continue to hope that they might one day return home after their economic activities in the city. The majority view this goal as a realistic one and thus when asked if it was probable that they will carry it out, 90% were sure that they would. It is difficult to determine the amount of sentiment involved in the urge to retreat to homes of origin. Most are actually involved in the social and economic life of the city. There are also significant differences between groups of people. The majority of migrant people with higher education and with professional managerial jobs (86%) show a clearer appreciation of the situation. They claim attachments to areas of origin and indicate willingness to return home but argue that people are in general victims of the systems of ethnic, family, land and economic relationships put upon them by society. People are responding to those pressures which emphasized or fostered ethnic allegiances, family ties and cultural identity.

Educated younger people amongst non-Ibadan Yorubas also tended to adopt a more liberal interpretation of home attachment. Some 33%, of the 74 between the ages of 21-35 interviewed, suggested that home was simply the place where one worked and was happy. Despite these independent sentiments issues of family village commitments still predominate.

Several patterns of behaviour also indicate the migrants' intentions to return home. First, the majority visit these place on a regular basis including those who have spent over 15 years in the city. Secondly, the frequency of visit alongside the purposes reflect a continuing commitment and affection for those places. In general, the Yoruba migrants visited more frequently (about once fortnightly). The non-Yorubas went home more on a seasonal basis – once or twice a year on the average. Generally those who have lived in Ibadan for more than

15 years or less than 5 years visited less frequently. The latter probably need to settle down and be more economically secure before undertaking visits.

However, it is useful to differentiate between routinized visits as outlined above and other less regimented, visits, particularly those undertaken in connection with unforseen events or circumstantial demands. In both cases, most people attributed visits once again to family relationships, e.g., 'my people are still living there', followed by economic ventures, although these reasons often had family related or cultural issues invovled. An important factor necessitating visits arose because people envisaged the home places and family land/houses as capable of fulfilling basic life needs such as feasts, festivals, holidays, rest, spiritual uplift and renewal in addition to serving as intimate centres for caring and sympathetic retirement and burial (accounted for 51% of reason for continuing relationship to home areas).

Perhaps the most clear indication of the migrants' attachment to home areas is provided by the home improvement associations. Analysis shows that 58% of migrants interviewed belonged to village, ethnic or home improved unions, which solicit or subscribe money for the development of ventures in the areas. Most of the associations (64%) have as their primary objective the industrial, commercial and physical development of areas of origin. Further, the associations act as pressure groups to bring in amenities and bolster the locational advantages of the towns and villages for services of government sponsored programmes (44%). Such associations are also interested in promoting communion and good social life among its members (18%). All associations or unions whether those organised by Yorubas or non-Yorubas have commmon aims of taking care of the interests of people in the home areas through group and personal efforts, acting as a kind of forum for fellowship and social interaction amongst members. This in essence preserves and extends the identity of people beyond their locality of origin and makes life in the city more meaningful and purposeful. Migrants of all ages, status, and no matter the length of residents in Ibadan belonged equally to home associations.

The immigrants did not believe that such associations alienated them from the interests of Ibadan City. Rather, they argued that associations formed along similar lines to their own could be a way of resolving the complex management and physical problems of the core indigenous city.

CONCLUSIONS AND IMPLICATIONS

This paper has highlighted the value of a humanistic geographic evaluation of peoples' experiences for the appreciation of the complex bonds between man, housing and places. In the African city, in particular, it has illuminated the socio-cultural influences which affect the sense of place in the modern city. In summary, ethnic groups, depending on their spatial, ancestral origin, share a strong attachment for home whether 'home' in the city, or towns and villages of origin outside the city. All ethnic groups feel that their experiences, environmental identity and relation to district/buildings are affected by a variety of cultural and social backgrounds. Both Ibadan Yoruba indigenes and Yoruba, non-Yoruba migrants identify with specific localities and buildings and percieve home places of origin in particular, as meaningful, supportive, immutable centres of existence from which the biological being emantes, moves and returns after life's gruelling journeys and activities.

There are a variety of implications of these results for the interpretation of buildings, districts, and even far-away places. The home concept is central to the African identity and social survival and consequently affect attitudes to and appreciation of urban form, housing and changes. The attachment of core Ibadan indigenes to their compounds and family houses enables one Yoruba ethnic group to protest landscape destruction or redevelopment. Planners often propose such schemes as a way of alleviating slum conditions, because they are not apt to discern and appreciate the peoples' ability to achieve psychological/emotional orientation in the world through linked association with such places. Thus, while family compound environments in core Ibadan are in need of improvements and inhabitants are conscious of the poor physical quality of the buildings, the significance of such buildings to their family heritage and pride increases the value of the ordinary physical shell and precludes any meaningful demolition, reconstruction or slum renewal works. At another level, the migrant Yoruba and non-Yoruba ethnic groups being far away from home in the city, pay less attention to the social significance of new functional architectural designs and are proud to live in them, but continue to recall their home places with a great affection and hope to return some day.

One major value of this exploration is that studies of the sense of place and orientation of people to man-created milieux will facilitate fuller understanding of the nature of housing designs and the spatial organisation of buildings at the small-scale for different social groups. The analysis of place attachments and the bond of cultural relationship of people to buildings at the community level or city level should be of prime importance to the architectural/environmental psychologists who often are too preoccupied with the overt behaviour of people in design settings. While buildings and neighbourhood area affect behaviour and satisfaction, the behavioural setting has often been over-emphasized. Buildings and landscapes have too often been projected as having certain social and cultural symbols which are peculiar to certain social or cultural groups. The Ibadan study shows, in the African context, that it is the social meanings and cultural significance of built form to the everyday life and identity of people (rather than their cultural signification in building or environments per se) that affect the initial value, attitudes, responses and attachments of residents to constructed form. Thus, while buildings and environments are created or designed with certain cultural, social and functional human needs in mind, such qualities alone are not sufficient to produce attachments and meanings. The social norms, identity and family circumstances of the people must be explored to find out the attributes of places. Anthropological studies of buildings and landscapes must move beyond considerations of built form as symbols of certain cultural groups or cosmic thought, to embrace components, including the symbolic identification with milieu by human groups for a variety of social needs.

At the level of policy, architectural psychologists and urban designers must aim to appreciate the vital linkages between social, ethnic groups, origins or heritage and built form. In order to design and improve environments in the African city, architectural psychologists, planners and designers must incorporate notions of family circumstances, ethnic allegiances, and group identity into the planning and spatial organization of houses, since such factors procure affect, attachments and significance for places.

Overall, this study has a number of implications for the development of environmental theory and education. Environmental theorists must aspire to incorporate notions of place attachments and personal, social identity into conceptualizations of environmental meaning. The built environment has social and physical meanings for people and personal social identity is built into them. Social life is expressed in the ordinary physical setting. Culture values and bonds of affection for place are important factors in deciding how any locale or building should be changed or recreated. Accounting from Yoruba indigenes and migrants to Ibadan provide insight into the influence of culture and social life on environmental images, intentions, actions and identity. In the African context, cultural attachments to a locality and lineage family commitments, constitute vital influences shaping the value and meanings of places and building to the individual, within and outside the city.

Bibliography

Appleyard, D. (1979) "Home" Architectural Association Quarterly, 11, 4-20.

Beir, U. (1970) Yoruba Poetry: An Anthology of Traditional Poems. Cambridge University Press.

Buttimer, A. (1974) Value in Geography. Washington: Association of American Geographers; Resource Paper No. 24.

Canter, D. (1984) Action and Place: The Existential Dialetic; Paper presented to the I.A.P.S. 8, 8th International Conference on "Environment and Human Action", West Berlin, July 25-29, 1984. Chapter,[1] of the present volume.

Chokor, B. A. (1986a) "Developments in environment-behaviour-design research: a critical assessment in the context of geography and planning with special reference to the Third World" Environment and Planning, A, 18, 5-26.

Chokor, B. A. (1986b) "Environment-behaviour-design research techniques: an appraisal and review of the literature with special reference to environmental and planning-related information needs in the Third World" Environment adn Planning, A, 18 (forthcoming).

Chokor, B. A. (1986c) "City Profile: Ibadan" Cities 3, 106-116.

Dovey, K. (1978) "Home: An Ordering principle in space" Landscapes, 22 (2) 27-30.

Duly, C. (1979) The Houses of Mankind: London, Thames and Hudson.

Duncan, J. S. (1978) "The social construction of unreality: An interactionist approach to the tourist's cognition of environment", in Humanistic Geography: Prospects and Problems Eds. D. Ley, M. S. Samuels. Croom Helm: Beckenham, Kent, pp. 269-282.

Entrikin, J. N. (1976) "Comtemporary humanism in geography" Annals of the Association of American Geographers 66, 615-632.

Hayward, D. G. (1978) "Home as an environmental and phychological concept" Landscape 22, 2-9.

Ley, D. (1977) ¨Social geography and the taken-for-granted world¨ Transactions, Institute of British Geographers: New Series 2, 498-512.

MacDonald, R. (1981) ¨A study inside the English working-class home¨ Architecture and Comportment, Architecture and Behaviour 1, 49-65.

Marris, P. (1961) Family and social change in an African City: A Study of Re-housing in Lagos, London: Routledge and Kegan Paul.

Porteous, J. D. (1976) ¨Home: The Territorial Core¨ The Geographical Review 66, 383-390.

Rapoport, A. (1969) House Form and Culture: Englewood Cliffs, N. J., Prentice-Hall.

Saarinan, T. F., Sell, J. L. and Husband, E. (1982) ¨Environmental perception: International efforts¨ Progress in Human Geography 6, 515-546.

Samuels, M. S. (1978) ¨Existentialism and Human geography¨ in Humanistic Geography: Prospects and Problems, Eds. D. Ley and M. S. Samuels, London: Croom Helm. pp. 22-40.

Samuels, M. S. (1979) ¨The Biography of Landscapes: Cause and Culpability¨, in The Interpretation of Ordinary Landscapes, Eds. D. W. Meinig, New York: Oxford University Press. pp. 51-88.

Seamon, D. (1979) A Geography of the Life-world, London: Croom Helm.

5. Cultural production and reproduction

ANTHONY KING

SUMMARY

The paper draws on recent structuralist approaches in urban studies to propose a framework for historical and cross-cultural research on societies, environments and the relationship between them. It directs attention to the need for studying processes of change in societies and environments, of the relationships between them and the conditions of production. Two spheres of research are proposed and related: the political economy of the built environment and also, of social and cultural change. The emergence of a global system of production in the twentieth century requires that urban and building developments in 'first' and 'third world' environment and concerns about 'westernisation', 'modernisation', 'bourgeoisification', 'deindustrialisation', 'counter-urbanisation' be seen in a single perspective.

INTRODUCTION

Over the last two decades, a large body of research has been published concerning the relationship of people to their physical surroundings. Where at one time in the human and social sciences the physical and spatial environment was either ignored or taken for granted or, in architecture and urban planning, design decisions were based on unquestioned assumptions about how environments might be used, today much more is known about these issues. Since the 1960's, many studies have been made of the environment-behaviour relationship, highlighting the way in which, for example, culture, class, gender and other variables affect attitudes towards and preferences for particular environments and hence, the way they are perceived and used.

Yet in this particular research tradition, very little attention seems to have been given to examining three basic assumptions

1) How are these 'physical surroundings' produced in the first place? While questions are asked, for example, about environmental perceptions and the design of environments (whether these are high rise apartment buildings, office interiors or residential suburbs), the actual 'hardware' of the built environment is often taken as given.

2) Likewise, in examining values, attitudes and images in relation to particular environments, the resultant cognitive data (or 'software') is also taken as given, representative of a particular population, in a particular place and at a particular time.

   Yet how, in the long historical term, has this hardware of the built environment and the software of the cognitive culture been produced in any given society? And especially, what function or role does the built environment perform in helping to produce that cognitive culture or alternatively, what role does the culture (a set of values, beliefs, preferences, attitudes or ideology) play in helping to produce, and reproduce both the society and the environment? (King, 1984b).

3) Finally, in examining the relationship of 'people to their physical surrounding's, a third assumption often taken for granted concerns the political economy of the state. In the overwhelming majority of cases in this particular field of research, the investigations are dealing not just with the heavily urbanised environments of industrial society but, with country or culture-specific variations, the environment of industrial capitalism. and whilst there are indeed significant cultural and political variations between different market societies, it is also obvious that there are many similarities which - what we can call 'Western industrial capitalism' - has introduced on a global scale (Smith, ed., 1984; Fielding, 1982; King 1984). Such similarities are not only in the built environments themselves (high rise housing, suburbanisation, inner city decay) and the comparable economic, social, political and technological forces which produce them (uneven development, de-industrialisation, and capital flight or investment) but also in the software of institutions, values, attitudes and practices which have accompanied the historical

73

development of market institutions (as well as responses to them) round the world (Sunkel and Fuensilada, 1979).

In short, we need to know much more about the way in which particular economic and social forces such as, for example, capital accumulation and a concern with property have been reflected in changing cultural values: in increasing concern with privacy, diversions between public and private, community decay and the development of individualism. What, in short, these comments imply is the development of a historical understanding, not only of how environments as well as cultures are produced but also, an understanding which recognises the central role played by political economy in that process.

The three initial issues provide a natural introduction to the second main concern of this paper: the disfunctionality of disciplinary specialisation.

Divide and rule: the effects of the fragmentation of knowledge.

The immense generation of knowledge over the last century, and especially in the last two or three decades, concerning both environments (generally urban) and the relationship of people to them, is clearly a response to the immense growth in urbanisation and economic development, first in Europe and North America, and increasingly in other parts of the globe. Though definitions of 'urban' may vary, we can generally accept that before 1850, no country was predominantly urban. In 1900, only Great Britain had crossed that threshold. By 1920, 14 per cent of the world population was urban; by 1980, 41.5 per cent and by 2000, 51.1 per cent of the world's population are expected to be urban dwellers (Renaud, 1981:13).

Broadly, such knowledge can be divided between those professions and disciplines dealing directly with the construction of that environment - engineers, planners, architects, surveyors, administrators, and the equally many theoretical disciplines, from urban anthropology, economics, geography, psychology, government, sociology, to law, history and others which investigate urban phenomena. In the circumstances, it is perhaps surprising that the gap in conceptual knowledge and understanding between these two broad divisions of professional knowledge (of those largely in practice and others, largely in theory, though the two categories obviously overlap) is not wider than it is; what is more to be deplored is the gap in understanding which has developed in the knowledge, and especially professional education, between the different disciplines in these two broad fields.

For example, attention has recently been drawn to the two ways in which urban and regional development gets analysed. The first 'sees social processes in space as products of, and integral to, broad structural relations and changes such as in class, intraclass and gender relations; the second approach focuses on how people experience, interpret and change what is happening to them. This second approach includes questions of design, architecture and visual interpretation, and the concepts through which people give meanings and reference points to their everyday lives. Yet with few exceptions, these two approaches never encounter one another' (Dickens, 1985: 443).

The first approach may be seen to characterise the now substantial body of work in urban political economy (e.g. Walton, 1979; Smith, 1983; Smith, (ed) 1984; Fainstein et al: 1983; International Journal of Urban Regional Research, 1977 -); the second, the equally substantial body of work produced in man (sic) - environment studies, the conferences of the Environmental Design Research Assoociation (EDRA) or of the International Association of the Study of People and Their Physical Surroundings (IAPS). Yet this is only one kind of division: in much of the work in urban political economy in the last decade, for example, little attention has been paid to the built environment as such, let alone questions of design (King, 1984: 431). In architecture, educators discuss problems of education for 'Third World' students independently of other specialists who study questions of 'development' (Louw, ed. 1983); likewise, in the field of development studies, whilst much attention is given to urbanisation, planning and problems of housing, the relation of these issues to architecture, cultural form and urban design is largely unexplored. The vast literature on 'urbanisation in developing countries' (principally by social scientists) generally excludes (except perhaps in reference to self-help housing) questions related to construction engineering, the pursuit of which is left to engineers (Ive, 1985).

Of course, this may be over-stating the case, for it will be recognised that there are 'inter-disciplinary' conferences and projects; yet such generalisations do prompt questions concerning the powerful social factors which promote the exclusiveness of professional identities, whether as architect, geographer, engineer, sociologist, psychologist etc., the educational curriculae which support these identities, the institutional arrangements (such as separate departments or faculties) which maintain them, and the physical and spatial arrangements (such as buildings and campuses) which ensure that particular people are kept together or apart. Nor is this to forget the plethora of specialised journals, publishers or institutionalised practices whereby career advancement depends on developing specialist knowledge.

The reasons for this fragmentation of knowledge are both deep-seated and complex, raising issues and explanations which go far beyond the scope of this paper: knowledge, like any other commodity, is produced in an ideological context, for different reasons, and paid for (or not paid for, as with the current constraints in educational policies) according to different criteria and priorities.

The consequences of this fragmentation of knowledge are, however, far more simple. The active subject of my sub-title, 'Divide and rule' (i.e. who or what is dividing and ruling) can be left to the reader's imagination, but it will tend to be 'structure' rather than 'agency' (Beauregard, 1984): that is to say, unless human agents - people, communities, representative governments - are able to develop an adequate and comprehensive theoretical grasp over what is happening to environments, as well as those who live in them, by incorporating all forms of knowledge, 'structural forces' - bureaucratic inertia, mindless technology, and in particular, market forces - will certainly gain the upper hand. The fragmentation of knowledge, the result of a relentless and excessive academic division of labour, is a weapon in the armoury of chaos: when no-one understands the overall picture, the chances of changing it become increasingly remote. Without an understanding of the larger economic, social, political and cultural processes which are now, not least with the steady expansion of the capitalist world economy - though there are other factors too - reaching into every corner of the globe, questions concerning local communities and cultures make little sense. Individual cultures and communities can be recognised and provided for only if we have an understanding of the larger processes affecting us all.

Towards a political economy of societies and their built environment.

Such issues suggest an ambitious research agenda. We need, firstly, an adequate understanding (some of which already exists) [1] of the historical development of the built environment, particularly since the emergence of industrial capitalism in the 16th century, an understanding which gives full recognition to what Walton (1984:78) calls 'modes of socioeconomic organisation and political control' and Abu-Lughod (1984:94) 'modes of production'. Like Abu-Lughod, I do not attach any particular ideological significance to this phrase (nor do I wish to get into problems of definition) except to recognise that any system of economic organisation has (or is part of) a division of labour and social structure, with accompanying social relations of production. Such a system of 'socioeconomic organisation and political control' will also be spatially expressed and leads to particular settlement, urban and building forms.

For example, Abu-Lughod (1984), shows how different types and forms of urbanisation in the Arab world are best explained by reference to the particular 'mode of production' characteristic of each: these she describes as 'neo-colonial', 'state socialist', 'charity cases' and 'oil and sand'. In the 'neo-colonial' cases (Tunis, Morocco), political independence has made little difference to colonial urban structures: the promotion of tourism has channeled investment into hotels and resort facilities, labour continues to be exported, economic stagnation in the countryside has encouraged further urbanisation and contrasts in economic status in the cities are reflected in the expanding bidonvilles and public housing projects. In the 'state socialist' countries (Algeria, Iraq), previously imbalanced urban growth has been checked by the promotion of planned secondary cities; national ideologies have promoted a more egalitarian and balanced development which has used local labour to link urbanisation to economic development. Abu-Lughod's 'charity cases' (Israel, Jordan, Egypt) are each subsidised from outside. In Jordan's case, patterns of urbanisation cannot be predicted from the analysis of internal resources whilst in Israel, urbanisation is seen as a tool for military and political purposes rather than as a concomitant fo changes in the mode of production. The 'oil and sand' economies (Saudi Arabia, Kuwait) manifest a variety of urban characteristics (such as the barracks used for housing immigrant labour, carefully segregated from indigenous residential zones) dependent on the role these economies play within the international market economy.

Colonialism likewise, in its various historic and cultural forms, has also a physical and spatial expression: firstly, in the way in which inland market towns, oriented to their surroundings, were undermined by the establishment of colonial port cities, oriented to the metropolis; secondly, in the classic structure of the divided city, segregated according to race, as well as economic, social and spatial provision; thirdly, in the built environments, embodying, in various forms and places, the distinctive institutions of a colonial political economy: the plantation with its 'coolies lines', the military cantonment with its barracks and jail, the 'civil station' with its Club, race course and bungalows of the colonial officials, the 'hill station' with its built forms of recreation and leisure (Abu-Lughod, 1976; King, 1976).

Similarly, familiarity with the particular right or left oriented policies of 'advanced' European or American governments in recent years clearly demonstrates the way in which, within an existing cultural matrix, the interests of capital and labour have affected urban and building development. In Britain, for example, the freer reign accorded to market principles since 1979 by a right wing government has de-fused planning controls, encouraged industrial high-tech development in specific regions, introduced new work practices, privatised previously state-owned housing, transferred responsibility for the dependent elderly from state to private interests, encouraged private (often overseas) capital investment in consumption-oriented activities, amongst other measures. All these policies can be seen in different types and forms of urban and building development: greenfield factories and low-rise industrial estates attract new, owner-occupied suburban housing; decaying inner cities, suffering from the flight of industrial capital, experience further employment decline with the withdrawal of state support for local government; the wooing of foreign investment encourages office building for multi-national headquaters in the City and investment in 'leisure bulding' (theme parks, country clubs and time-share apartments) in the country; privatisation policies result in the sale of public assets; municipal responsibility for housing the elderly is transferred to mushrooming private companies converting mansions for the affluent old; private hospitals attract private investment as public ones suffer economic decline.

At a more general, macro level, state policies favouring greater or lesser public intervention, or growth in heavy industry as opposed to investment in services (banking, insurance, education) also clearly have very different and noticable effects, not only on the built environment but on the ideologies that go with it.

Such an approach, therefore, would trace the changing mode of socio-economic organisation in a given society, and the spatial expression of its division of labour (Massey, 1984) in the production of different urban and building forms, whether these were principally for production (factory towns, foundries, workshops, offices, industrial housing) or for consumption (resort towns, spas, country houses).

It would, in particular, examine the emergence since the nineteenth century of an international division of labour and the development of production on a global scale: a system of production which is equally manifest in built environments round the world. In this context, therefore, can be understood the highly industrialised, urbanised concentrations of Europe and North America, especially those of Britain and the United States, and the more ruralised, cattle, grain or raw material producing areas of Asia, Africa and Latin America with, in the

77

case of the latter, their non-industrial, consumption-oriented towns
(Roberts, 1978; Browning and Roberts, 1980). The development of
Australia's urban, building and dwelling forms is to be seen as part of
the same process of international specialisation (Sandercock, 1975;
King, 1984).

In Britain, the growth of densely-populated, close-built, gardenless
terrace streets of industrial cities (Daunton, 1983; Muthesius, 1983)
providing accommodation for the tea and sugar-consuming factory labour
represents one end of a spatial division of labour at the other end of
which are the plantation economies of East Africa (Brett, 1975), Malaya
or the Caribbean, with their self-built huts accomodating 'native
workers' and the imported, industrially-produced bungalows for the
British planters and supervisors (King, 1984). In a world economy, the
jute mills, shipyards and factories of Dundee (Scotland) are part of
the same process of production, exchange and consumption as the cash-
crop peasant plantations and 'district towns' of Bengal or elsewhere.
The environments where they are situated, not least the 'diffused'
forms of architecture and urban planning (King, 1980, 1984, 1985), are
all part of same process.

Or, to come to the 1980's, we can examine a single system of
production and consumption which incorporates the high-rise,
multistorey aprtments of Hong Kong or Kuala Lumpur, or squatter
settlements in the Phillipines, providing shelter for labour which
produces textiles sold in cut-price hypermarkets on the edge of a
German or British city; the multinational headquarters building in
London, Brussels or New York and the low-cost housing units round the
copper mines of Zambia; or the increase in specialied 'producer
service' employment (in international law, real estate, banking,
insurance) in office blocks of 'world cities' such as Frankfurt, London
or Hong Kong (Friedmann, 1986).

Within this larger economic and social system, characterised by the
transnationalisation of both capital and labour, (Walton and Portes,
1981) there exists a built environment which, on one hand, is
increasingly the same, the result, not just of the 'diffusion' of
architectural forms and styles, but of the spread of institutions - the
office block for commerce, the stock exchange for capital, squatter
settlements or high rise apartments for wage labour (Cohen, 1981) but
also, the spread of ideologies, images and knowledge which these
institutions produce - of planning, design, construction and finance
(Kng, 1984a). The charting of these global processes is now well under
way (Sassen-Koob, 1984; Ross and Trachte, 1983, 1985; Friedmann, 1986).
Yet agaisnt this global background are also national, regional and
local responses, interpretations and resistances to the global whole,
attempts by groups, social movements and minorities (Castells, 1984;
Smith, ed. 1984) to recapture economic, social and cultural identities.

The general point, however, is clear: different forms of socio-
economic organisation and political control, characteristic of phases
of capitalism - or of socialist and other responses to it - have, with
regional and cultural variation, produced forms of settlement and built
environment and the cultural software to go with them.

Towards a political economy of environmental culture. Along with
this understanding of the development of the built environment,

therefore, we also need an understanding of the cultural 'software' which has developed with it: a cultural history of ideas, values, institutions, attitudes which have accompanied environmental change. Such a history must necessarily be wide, broad-based and comparative, taking in not only the history of Europe but, equally the transformation of societies and environments in Africa, Asia, Latin America. It needs to look closely at cultural concepts such as 'privacy', 'communtiy' and 'individualism' in relation to the development of the institution of property, the effects of accumulation on attitudes to community, the development of class and status consciousness in relation to the transformation in settlement patterns and change in the forms of dwellings, and the development of aesthetic consciousness in relation to the commodification of much in daily life. Above all, it requires a massive intellectual effort to examine, within a critical history of ideas, the production of knowledge about environments, the ideologies related to these, of notion of 'taste', 'views', 'environment preferences' and questions of 'design'.

An agenda of such dimensions is, of course, likely to be beyond the capacities on any individual scholar yet studies into parts of the process are clearly possible though they require a far wider historical and geographical framework than has hitherto been the case. Ample research already exists on environmental changes under industrial capitalism in the nineteenth and twentieth centuries to demonstrate the huge value and attitudinal changes which have taken place. Moreover, anyone with a conscious memory extending over the last two decades can (without a detailed knowledge of feudal Europe, or acquaintance with members of societies and cultures at totally different levels of economic development) already observe, between different generations, changed attitudes to the consumption and production of goods, including the use of the environment.

This historical research will be given an extra cutting edge by cross-cultural research, both on built environments, cultural attitudes and institutions, and the relations between them. Such research, however, should focus on questions of **change**: how far is incorporation in the global economy affecting not only environments but also the development of different values?

In proposing these programmes of historical and cross-cultural research (which are complementary and integral, rather than different approaches), emphasis has been placed on questions of political economy: this requires a distinction to be made not simply between crude categories of 'capitalism', 'state socialism' 'Welfare capitalism' or the like, but between a range of variation in economic and social organisation. By examining particular societies over a given historical period and the way in which their environments have been transformed through different and contrasting 'modes of production' (for example, China, Cuba, USSR, Tanzania, Mozambique) an opportunity should be presented of isolating political economy variables, possibly shared by all, from social and cultural variables, specific to each.

Finally, we need to distinguish more carefully than hitherto when conceptual categories such as 'first', 'second' or 'third world' are functional or disfunctional. Effectively, there has only been one world, characterised by an economic system which, especially from the sixteenth century, has transformed Europe, North and South America, Asia and Africa. In the late twentieth century, the transformation of environments is being effected, with degrees of variation, by a simple process - the culture of increased consumption. The recognition of global system of production would enable more precise meanings to be put on a variety of terms: 'Westernisation', 'modernisation', 'Europeanisation', 'bourgeoisification', all of which are part of the same process, as also are 'third world' 'squatter settlements' and 'low-cost' or 'self-built housing' or, in so-called 'advanced industrial economies, processes of 'de-industrialisation' and counter-urbanisation' (Payne, 1977; Ward, ed. 1982; Bluestone and Harrison, 1982; Helding, 1982).

In this context, social science concepts need to be subjected to a rigourous, critical analysis, not only in 'developed' but in 'developing' societies, in free market as well as socialist economies, in present as well as in historical terms. Cognitive processes are obviously learnt, supported and sustained by the environments and cultures, class structures and political economies which produce them. A simple, useful example can be quoted.

The separate or 'detatched', single storey dwelling, located in suburb or country which in Britain and elsewhere is known as a 'bungalow' is a historical artefact, an archetypical product of colonialism and free market processes which, in given cultural contexts, has principally been inserted into the built environments of late capitalism in the twentieth century. During the course of the eighteenth and nineteenth centuries, it developed in India (from the indigenous **bangla**, or Bengali peasant hut) to become the typical, space-consuming dwelling form of the British in India, a product of a colonial mode of production (Alavi, 1980) and a symbol of political control.

Its introduction into Britain as a second, 'country home' for the expanding urban bourgeoisie, was not simply a case of 'cultural diffusion'. In the particular circumstances in which it occurred, temporally, between 1890 and 1914, at the 'height of Empire' and spatially, in a newly-discovered 'country-side' (sic), economically depressed by increasing competition from colonial grain, the bungalow is a unique and tangible cultural by-product of the emergence of an international division of labour. Its subsequent cultural history was as contributor to and product of three social and urban processes which have come to characterise the consumption-oriented market economy of the twentieth century: suburbanisation, 'second homes' and, in the growing trend towards separate dwellings for the wealthy retired, household fission and the fragmentation of kin. All three are social processes which have physical expression: in political economy terms they all mean the same thing - capital accumulation and increasing consumption (King, 1984a, 1984b).

Hence, when in the 1980's cohorts of the elderly are asked to express their housing preferences as a guide to provision by state or private sector developers, or sample populations are surveyed by public and private organisations regarding their preferred housing choice, large proportions of the population express preferences for a bungalow (NHBC, 1984). In short, societies and political economies produce environments; environments then help to socialise people into accepting them; finally, the environments help to produce the culture and ideology which is mutually supportive. Gershuny (1978:6) refers to these processes as 'inertial mechanisms which tend to limit the malleability of the future'. It is in a broad, historical and cross-cultural framework such as this that culture-specific studies of 'individualism' and its relation to community values (Bellah et al.; 1985) might be re-examined.

CONCLUSION

In the notes above, I have suggested a broad, and perhaps schematic range of issues for investigation. Such an investigation or analysis implies an understanding of people's reactions to environments - and the consequent responses to them - which is not conceived within narrowly defined boundaries of either time or space. Developments in global communications in the last decades have given far larger dimensions to the social, geographical and temporal space in which decisions are made and aspirations expressed: it is, for example, no longer a matter of surprise that disadvantaged inner city blacks living on London housing estates identify with the oppressed majority in South African townships; nor that they perceive similar solutions to their problems to be appropriate.

Likewise, relations between people and their physical surroundings cannot be seen 'as of the instant', bounded by a simple time-scale encompassing yesterday, today and tomorrow. They must be seen as belonging to a long historical past, part of a dynamic of historical change which is concerned not simply with solving 'today's problems' (whether of housing, designing 'responsive environments' or employment) in 'today's terms'; they must be geared to a vision of the future which takes in not just local and national, but also global needs and perspectives. And they imply an historical understanding of how people's relationship to the city has also changed (as charted, for example, in recent oral history studies. Oral History, 1985).

Some insight into what is happening to economies and cities in 'industrial' free market economies is already available (Friedmann, 1986; Ross and Trachte, 1983, 1985) Sassen-Koob, 1984; Smith, ed. 1984; Soja et al. 1983; ESRC, 1985; Pahl, 1984 etc). The solutions to the problem of cities, of environments, and of people's relationship to them, are not simply academic and professional but demand a political will (Gilbert, 1984). They demand solutions which are not only short term and local, but long term and international. In the late twentieth century, communities and cultures can coexist only as a part of an international whole.

NOTES

[1] One approach is represented by the Bartlett International Summer School on The Production of the Built Environment, 1979 - to date.

BIBLIOGRAPHY

Alavi, H., (1980) 'India. Transition from feudalism to colonial capitalism', Journal of Contemporary Asia, 10, pp. 359-99.

Abu-Lughod, J., (1984) 'Culture, "modes of production" and the changing nature of cities in the Arab world', in Agnew, J., Mercer, J. and Sopher, D. eds,. The City in Cultural Context Allen and Unwin, London. 94-119.

Bartlett International Summer School (BISS), (1979) The production of the Built Environment. Bartlett School of Architecture and Planning, University College, London WC1. Annual Proceedings.

Beauregard, R. A. (1984) 'Structure, agency and urban redevelopment' in Smith, M. P. ed. Cities in Transformation. Sage, London. 51-74.

Bellah, R. N., Madsen, R., Sullivan, W. M., Swidler, A., and Tipton, S. M. Habit of the Heart: Individualism and Commitment in American Life University of California.

Bluestone, B and Harrison, B (1982) The Deindustrialisation of America. Oxford, New York.

Brett, E. A. (1973) Colonialism and Underdevelopment in East Africa. Heinemann, London.

Browning, H. and Roberts, B. (1980) 'Urbanisation, sectoral transformation and the utilisation of labour in Latin America', Comparative Urban Research, 8. 86-104.

Castells, M. (1984) 'Space and society: managing the new historical relationships', in Smith, M.P. ed. op. cit. 235-60.

Cohen, R. B. (1981) 'The new international division of labour, multinational corporations and urban hierarchy', in Dear, M and Scott, A. J. eds. Urbanisation and Urban Planning in Capitalist Society. Methuen, Andover, Hants. 1981. 287-315.

Daunton, M. (1983) House and Home in the Victorian City. Arnold, London.

Dickens, P. (1985) 'Review of King, A.D. "The Bungalow. The Production of a Global Culture" (1984) in International Journal of Urban and Regional Research, 9, 3, 443.

Hausner, V. and Robson, B. (1985) Changing Cities. Economic and Social Research Council, London.

Fainstein, S. S., Fainstein, N., Hill, R. C., Judd, D. R. and Smith, M.
P., (1983) Restructing the City: The Political Economy of Urban
Redevelopment. Longman, New York.

Fielding, A. (1982) 'Counterurbanisation in Western Europe'. Progress
in Planning. 17, 1-52.

Friedmann, J. (1986) 'The world city hypothesis', Development and
Change (in press).

Gershuny, J. (1978) After Industrial Society? The Emergent Self-Service
Economy Macmillan, London.

Gilbert, A. (1984) An Unequal World. Links between Rich and Poor
Nations. Macmillan, London.

International Journal of Urban and Regional Research (1977) Arnold,
London.

Ive, G. (1985) 'Towards a history of the production of the built
environment in West Africa' Bartlett International Summer School.
1985. Proceedings of the BISS, Bartlett School of Architecture and
Planning, University College, London (in press).

King, A. D. (1976) Colonial Urban Development. Culture. Social Power
and Environment. Routledge and Kegan Paul, London.

King, A. D. (1980) 'Exporting planning: the colonial and neo-colonial
experience' in Cherry, G. ed. Shaping an Urban World. Mansell,
London. 203-26.

King, A. D. (1984a) The Bungalow. The Production of a Global Culture.
Routledge and Kegan Paul, London.

King, A. D. (1984b) 'The social production of building form: theory and
research', Environment and Planning D: Society and Space 2. 429-46.

King, A. D. (1985) 'Colonial cities: global pivots of change' in Ross,
R. and Telkamp, G. eds. Colonial Cities. Nijhoff, Dordrecht and
Lancaster. 7-32.

Louw, H. J. ed. (1983) Architectural Education in Europe and the Third
World. Parallels and Contrasts. European Association for
Architectural Education. School of Architecture, University of
Newcastle upon Tyne.

Massey, D. (1984) Spatial Divisions of Labour. Macmillan, London.

Muthesius, S. (1983) The English Terrace House. Yale University Press
Newhaven, Conn.

NHBC (1984) 'Housing for sale to the elderly'. National House Building
Council Second Report. Prepared for the Housing Research Foundation.
NHBC. 58 Portland Place, London W1.

Oral History (1985) 'Urban Space and Order', Oral History 5, October

Pahl, R. E. (1984) *Divisions of Labour*. Blackwells, Oxford.

Payne, G. (1977) *Urban Housing in the Third World*. Leanord Hill, London.

Renaud, B. (1981) *National Urbanisation Policy in Developing Countries*. Oxford University Press, Oxford.

Roberts, B. (1978) *Cities of Peasants*. Arnold, London.

Ross, R. and Trachte, K. (1983) 'Global cities and global classes: the peripheralisation of labour in New York city', *Review*, 6, 3. 293-431.

Ross, R. and Trachte, K. (1985) *International Journal of Urban and Regional Research* 9.

Sandercock, L. (1975) *Cities for Sale*. Melbourne University Press, Melbourne.

Sassen-Koob, S. (1984) 'The new labour demand in global cities' in Smith, M. P. ed 1984 op.cit. 139-72.

Smith, M. P. 'Structuralist urban theory: a symposium', *Comparative Urban Research*. 9, 5-70.

Smith, M. P. ed. *Cities in Transformation*. Sage, London.

Smith, R. (1974) 'Multi-dwelling building in Scotland, 1750-1970's in Sutcliffe, A. ed. *Multi-Storey Living. The British Working Class Experience*. Croom Helm, London. 207-43.

Soja, E., Morales, R. and Wolff, G. (1983) 'Urban restructuring: an analysis of social and spatial change in Los Angeles', *Economic Geography* 59, 2. 195-230.

Sunkel, O. and Fuenzilada, J. (1979) 'Transnationalism and its national consequences', in Villamil, J. ed. *Transnational Capitalism and National Development. New Perspectives on Development*. Harvester Press, Susses. 1979. 67-93.

Walton, J. (1979) 'Urban political economy: a new paradigm', *Comparative Urban Research*. 7. 5-17.

Walton, J. (1984) 'Culture and economy in the shaping of urban life' in Agnew, Mercer and Sopher, eds. 1984. op.cit. 76-93

Walton, J. and Portes, A. (1981) *Labour. Class and the International System*. Academic Press, London.

6. Urban social history

GILLES BARBEY

ABSTRACT

Urban social history is not defined as a single chapter of history but
is closely related to meanings and values of urban life. This short
essay attempts to demonstrate the wide scope of the field by presenting
parallel cultural perspectives with a special emphasis on French
literature, as France is traditionally renowned for studies in urban
sociology. Following this approach, urban social history is not only
concerned with general studies of historical contexts. It also
involves the individual histories of city dwellers. This research
orientation considers change in concepts and attitudes as a consequence
of town planning and technical progress. Urban order is therefore
pictured as an eminently cultural and social process.

Urban social history deals primarily with the relationship between the city and its population. It is concerned with housing facilities, which affect the existence of the city, but is also concerned with a range of other subject matters, whose intricate articulations can better be defined by the inclusion of a large variety of themes rather than by their exclusion. However towards a better comprehension of such a vast complexity of factors, it would appear advisable to structure them in several general thematic categories which will permit an easier examination of the existing bulk of literature. We would therefore tend to approach urban social history by referring first to the general evolution of urban culture and society. Then it seems appropriate to explore the structure of the urban space as a result of social order. Finally, the meanings and individual experiences of urban life should also be studied.

History can be considered as a combination of objective facts and subjective reactions, incorporating both a macro-perspective and the micro-histories of the inhabitants. The exploration of urban social history follows both an external and internal course. Urban phenomenology is evidently part of the same quest for information.

EVOLUTION OF URBAN CULTURE AND SOCIETY

It is not intended to undertake a thorough investigation of urban history since its first origins, but to analyze what is the specific and recent evolution of the modern city. A series of historical essays about the city envisaged as a totality was published before and just after World War II. Mumford (1938) appears as one of the most influential authors of this period. He was concerned with the linkage of the city's history to the lifestyles of the inhabitants. For example he describes the factors that influenced the daily life in the medieval or baroque city and refers "to the first spread of privacy within the aristocratic home at the end of the 16th century. The change in the constitution of the household manifests itself by a gradual divorce of the home, henceforth a place, for eating, for entertaining, and in a secondary way for rearing children, from the workplace." Mumford successively depicts the urban confusion during the Ancien-Regime and the birth of the industrial town, with the corresponding tensions and oppositions between the social classes. Following the evolving family and society, changes occur in the physical shape of buildings and urban quarters.

Mumford further studies the modern city and suggests that "instead of trusting to the mere massing of population to produce the necessary social concentration and social drama, one must seek these results through deliberate community planning and closer regional linkages." The modern planning of cities should be able to eliminate urban pathology by providing better living conditions and a stronger sense of identity.

Following his own analysis of the historical city, Gutkind (1962) refers to the same considerations as Mumford's. He advocates the natural and organic growth of the city, which can be compared to a human body with its constituent parts growing to their full size. Such an anthropomorphic perspective of the urban scene influenced several generations of pre-war and post-war town planners in their attempt to apply organic concepts in order to achieve decentralized urban planning.

Based on the examples of Ebenezer Howard, Patrick Geddes and Tony Garnier, Giedion (1941) also considers town-planning as a human problem. A new conception of the space-time relationship has recently emerged. Giedion suggests that "the ground plan of the house has been made flexible and informal: the layout of the modern town tends in the same direction." Another famous and earlier historian previously used the same metaphor of the house applied to the city: it was Sitte (1889) who wrote that "the forum represents for the city what the atrium is to the family house." Both authors are using familiar images to suggest more emphasis on the relationship between man and the city. Mumford, Gutkind and Giedion among other historians are concerned with the linkage of urban social history to the practice of town-planning. They claim that the historical analysis of cities may be instrumental in shaping new planning concepts.

Moving away from the belief that the city is like an organic totality, a new generation of urban historians provided a less operational but more specific outlook on the urban scene. Guerrand (1967) discussed the origins of social housing in France. He describes the philosophy of the first entrepreneurs of social housing and the distance between the idealist conception of the phalansterian house based on Fourier's ideas and the actual buildings conceived by the Social Catholic movement in housing. In the first case the community is supposed to build a new social order, whereas in the second case, families are separated as much as possible, in order to secure social peace. Guerrand demonstrates the utmost influence of the sanitary enquiries and reports, such as those of Villerme (1840). The first urge is to cure the overpopulated city and establish healthier life conditions in the houses of the poor. Most of Guerrand's considerations deal with the dwelling units of the lower labour classes and the rise of philanthropic measures to improve their housing conditions.

A similar perspective of social urban history can be found in the work of other French historians sharing the view of Foucault (1961), who approached the history of the institution through the study of illness, madness or captivity. In this perspective, urban pathology is seen as a basic characteristic of the city at the beginning of the industrial era. Hygiene and medical care are considered fundamental in the management of urban space. Such institutions as the hospital or the asylum can help public authorities control the social confusion and establish order. In parallel, the housing of the masses is gradually reshaped. The private space of the dwelling unit is clearly separated from the public realm of the street. Houses are numbered individually so that they can be taxed and controlled more efficiently. A new order is applied to the city. A central police corps replaces the former system of allocating one citizen per house to secure order and peace. The 19th century appears as a slow and continuous move away from the confusion and insecurity of earlier times. The influence of morbidity on the city is known through detailed accounts such as the cholera epidemic of 1832 in Paris described by Leca (1982).

Housing policies during the first half of the 19th century are analysed in detail. They are based on a rigid discrimination and separation
between families and between sexes within the family. A new conception
of dwelling space restricted to the four walls of the apartment allows
an easier control of the inhabitants and an increased degree of privacy
for the families. This was witnessed by Aillaume et al. (1977).

A predominant concern for the fate of the labour classes during the
19th century is also shared by authors studying the history of social
housing in Great Britain. Burnett (1978) describes the new tasks around
1850, which consist in settling the multitude of labourers in houses
built privately, either philanthropically or speculatively. Dwelling
types are examined and living conditions extrapolated from floor plans.
Similarly Gauldie (1974) describes the sudden affluence of rural populations in the already overcrowded slums of the industrial cities.

Since the early 1980's an increasing interest in industrial archeology and architecture has produced a vast quantity of studies on Victorian
housing in almost any major city of the UK. The favoured approach is
usually a confrontation of housing policies and housing types, with a
discussion of such examples as the 'bye-law' or the 'back-to-back'.
Daunton (1983) notices that "the change in the physical structure of the
city relates closely to the changes in the nature of the family. The
emergence of the private, encapsulated dwelling was a physical demonstration of the social value attached to the conjugal family and domestic
life." The principal difficulty encountered was to translate social
aspirations into effective political action. Englander (1983) explores
the landlord-tenant relations within the framework of the class struggle
amongst property owners and non-propertied classes of the Victorian era.

The recent proliferation of literature on working-class housing is
not restricted to France and England. Its scope is not only concerned
with economics and policies, but also with social and behavioral
issues. The themes of urban disorder, overpopulation and crowding in
the preindustrial society are becoming familiar. The existing
literature provides interesting opportunities for cross-cultural
observations and studies. The tragic housing and dwelling conditions
of the labour classes are certainly an endless and stimulating field of
research for historians, as they reveal the social mechanisms and
reactions in their full crudity.

A less familiar field of research concerns the living conditions of the
more affluent classes of society. For obvious reasons of discretion and
secrecy the ruling classes do not favour the detailed inspection and
description of their life-styles. Perhaps the most generous source of
information in this domain is available in the novels of contemporary
writers such as Balzac, Dickens or Proust, who portray the everyday life
of the bourgeoisie with great care. A few recent public exhibitions
related to   everyday urban life helped document the domestic culture
of the higher classes and the evolution of the 'beaux-quartiers'.

We also find some indications of the role of the elite in the foundation of the new settlements and urban quarters. Cannadine (1979) demonstrated the role played by the English aristocracy in the middle of the
last century when it was influential in promoting new seaside resorts

such as Brighton, Eastbourne or Scarborough. The construction of the
railway network and the establishment of fashionable resorts were often
combined. The social values and symbols of status are evident from the
architecture and decoration of buildings. The foundation and extension
of thermal spas in France were the theme of various exhibitions in France. For example the 'winter city' at Arcachon near Bordeaux is an interesting example of planning and architecture serving a resort devoted to
leisure and medical care of tuberculosis. Arcachon was promoted by Emile
Péreire who owned the local railroad in 1860. Another exhibition (1985)
retraced the history of the main French thermal spas and displayed an
impressive collection of buildings. The social aspects of affluent life
are powerful in shaping the framework and landscape of such favourite
and exclusive places of relaxation as Vichy, Vittel or Aix-les-Bains.
The artificial milieu of the thermal spa is an ideal setting for the
study of the relationship between human behaviour and the physical environment.

Another important chapter of urban social history deals with the problems of sanitation, domestic hygiene and comfort. The German philosopher
Elias (1939-76) studied the evolution of human behaviour as a consequence
of the process of civilisation and demonstrated its impact on urban
social life. Gleichmann (1976) analysed the gradual improvement of sanitation in cities and revealed the influence of sewage on domestic health.
Guerrand (1985) published a history of the water-closet. The relationship between moral education and hygiene was further explored in its
historical context at the end of the 19th century in Switzerland by
Heller (1979). The originality of the trend of research mentioned above
was its involvement with detailed and sometimes trivial analyses of the
everyday life of the urban population. The accelerated transformation
of domestic behaviour as a result of mechanization and technology, was
also thoroughly investigated earlier by Giedion (1948).

Further questions of urban social history relate to the issues of
parenthood and relations between generations. For example, the changing
behaviour of children in the city is discussed by Aries (1960-73) who
retraced the corresponding attitudes and roles of parents and children
over time. Parr (1967) examined the experiences, or rather the lack of
them, available to modern children in large cities and concluded that
increased urban mobility has reduced substantially their environmental
perception. The tradition of heritage within families is also described
by Gotman (1984) as having specific implications for real estate and
therefore on the urban structure as well.

The transformation of external spaces reflects in turn the history of
outdoor everyday life and the various forms of appropriation of public
zones. For example the planning of a public park in Paris is seen by
Conan (1984) as informative of the relationship between nature and the
city. The use of open spaces and parks is depicted by Ballion (1975) as
a cultural process which can reveal strong cultural differences.

As far as the evolution of the city as a whole is concerned, the
recent tendency of urban social history was to stay away from global
speculation and favour a more detailed analysis of the components or
mechanisms of the city. History was instrumental in shaping research

concepts in urban sociology and geography. Most of the social and historical studies on urban culture are consistent and even convergent in describing the gradual move away from the confusion and morbidity in cities in the middle of the 19th century and the progressive emergence of a new social order which will reach a high degree of anonymity in the second half of the 20th century. It is now important to examine the influence of changing social relations on the morphology of the city.

THE STRUCTURE OF URBAN SPACE

Information regarding the structure of urban space can be borrowed from at least two sources: the history of architecture and the history of planning. Over recent years, research appears to have become more specialised and separated in relation to these two poles. However such complementary historical perspectives should remain closely interconnected, as they appear for example in the work of many Italian historians.

Aymonino (1975) studied the history of the main capital cities in Europe, such as Berlin and London, Paris and Vienna, in order to define the economic and sociological characteristics of the capital city. He contrasts the general tendencies with the specific differences between cities, while discussing the existence of a common model for the major capitals. Aymonino proceeds with the examination of the urban fabric in its successive transformations, which are particularly noticeable in the case of Paris under the leadership of Baron Haussmann. He depicts the emergence of an urban morphology which is translated into architectural terms in the form of building typologies. These tend to cluster around certain predetermined models. This approach favours the acknowledgement of such political and economic forces as the quest for power and profit in urban development.

Benevolo (1978) examined the relationship between architecture and the city by undertaking a survey of international examples of town development, including such utopian illustrations as the achievements of Owen, Fourier and Cabet. Borrowing from the early French and British examples, Benevolo described the nature of the social conflicts which originated in the 18th century. They resulted in the industrial revolution, which in turn helped to shape the industrial towns of the 19th century. Benevolo relates closely social history to the history of urban form, using the pertinent examples of garden cities or further models of urban development, which were basic in influencing the building types. In a similar way but even more specific, Cervellati (1977-81) analysed the social and political processes which influenced the structure of the historical center of Bologna. The same book justifies the selected type of urban renewal in Bologna during the second half of the 20th century, which consists in the conservation and restoration of existing buildings rather than their replacement. The case of Bologna can be looked at as having an exemplary value. It can even be understood as a direct consequence of the analyses of Gans (1962) and Coing (1966), who proved that urban renewal can be disruptive to human relations and values when it proceeds to clear up slums and replace them with new settlements, regardless of the existing characteristics and life-styles of the community.

90

In a somewhat convergent perspective, Bertrand (1980) demonstrates the evolution and internal distribution of housing types in Paris. A new rationality appears in the urban fabric during the middle of the 19th century. This is, for example, evident in the new grid of Paris restructured under Haussmann. It is then obvious that the shape of the houses is no longer influenced entirely by the perimeter and form of the lot, as was the case during the Ancien Régime. Instead, the internal distribution of spaces within the building is beginning to determine its morphology, as evidenced by Castex (1977). This process is not only the result of a change of the physical aspect of the city but also a reflection of different social relations, notably in real estate policies based on the quest for a maximum profit.

In a different perspective, the work of Ledrut (1973) emphasizes the socio-cultural dimension of urban space by showing the city as the result of a network of social relations. This conception of urban history resulting from the social production of space is more closely related to the discrepancies between diverse urban policies than to the recognition of regular patterns. Yet most historical studies are rather concerned with the reapparence of regularities (Lepetit, 1981).

A new orientation in research perspectives since the 1970's has resulted in various important essays on the history of planning. Sutcliffe (1981) undertakes a well documented historical and cross-cultural comparison of the town planning practices in different countries of Europe and the United States. He analyses the theoretical sources which influenced town development in various countries, contrasting, for example, the philosophy of town extension in Germany with the spirit of garden cities in Britain. In a parallel way, King (1976) describes the power of British colonialism in India, defining the morphology of urban settlements or compounds and the widespread circulation of the Anglo-Indian bungalow. Housing forms are closely related to the requirements of a domestic culture, which originated from   military occupation and control. Similar views drawn from a wider context are expressed in a still more general scope by the same author (1982).

Daunton (1983) recognized the importance of the influence of housing in urban history. He suggested that "much of the work of housing reform may be interpreted as an attempt to change social behaviour via physical change." It is evident that "social historians have dealt with economics, politics and society while improving design, whereas architects and architectural historians have overlooked everything except the design of buildings " (Lawrence, 1985). Swenarton (1981) maintains that "both approaches imply that design and society are not involved in a single process but are separate and distinct."

In methodological contrast to the behaviour-oriented studies of urban history the contributions of quantitative historical research are worth mentioning here. The university of Caen in France published a collection of surveys based on urban housing during the Ancien Régime in the French towns of Cambrai and Rouen (Bardet et al., 1971). From documents such as building accounts or tenants' leases it was possible to understand how a majority of houses were actually built, inhabited and maintained, resulting in an entirely pragmatic and well grounded view of the building practices and dwelling conditions before the industrial revolution. This perspective is therefore of great value to urban social history as it describes the housing conditions of the broad mass of people.

Such a brief survey of the sources concerned with the structure of urban space cannot capture the diversity of research perspectives. However, the detailed analysis of planning strategies and measures on one hand, and the study of urban housing and dwelling conditions on the other, are helpful in outlining the issues common to different cities. A comparison is consequently possible.

It is sometimes difficult to identify a delineation between the respective contributions of urban history and urban analysis, especially in such delicate matters as population growth (Seidel, 1984). It should be pointed out that many case studies hardly relate to one another. Therefore a real shortage of consistent and longitudinal studies appears. The following publication is an exception to this observation.

In a brilliant survey of the traditional 'Miethaus' (tenement) in Berlin, from its origins around 1740 to the present time, Geist and Kürvers (1984) retraced the progressive urbanization of the outskirts of Berlin as a direct consequence of the industrial revolution. The study describes the birth of the proletarian 'Miethaus' in the military barrack (caserne), whose building type is gradually adapted to civilian families. The longitudinal study of Meyer's Hof's housing development provides a vivid description of the urban context in the end of the 19th century, as well as the erection of the quarter and its continuous use over a period of almost a century. Such detailed and richly illustrated research is extremely rare, as it involves considerable methodological and practical difficulties. However it is useful in order to testify to the actual history of existing buildings.

From the last mentioned publication, it becomes evident that urban social history cannot limit itself to the study of building policies, but should also take into consideration the changing use and values of the environment. One could therefore conclude that urban social history is not only political and economic in scope, but also social and behavioural. The next section attempts to analyse different perspectives concerned with the experience of urban life.

THE EXPERIENCE AND MEANING OF URBAN LIFE

Urban identity seems to be a multi-faceted concept which deserves to be approached from different perspectives. In 1969, Buttimer redefined the notion of 'social space' with reference to the work of Chombart de Lauwe, Sorre and Durkheim. For Chombart de Lauwe (1960), urban social space connotes a hierarchy of spaces, in which population groups live, move and interact. Based on her empirical study, Buttimer (1972) concludes that "the success of a residential development is contingent on the existential meaning it acquires for its residents." From a somewhat different perspective, Jacobs (1962) investigated the urban scene and studied the use and meaning of city neighbourhoods, whose constituent parts are valued for their capacity for social integration. For example, "it is a matter of what kinds of tangible enterprises sidewalks have, and therefore of how people use the sidewalks in practical, everyday life."

In her field study of Stortorget in Malmö, in Sweden, Korosec-Serfaty (1982) evaluated the new layout of the central square and the 'spatial resources' offered to the population. The variety of activities performed seemed to indicate that the square does not only serve as a recreational space but also allowed the reappropriation of a collective past, rooted in history. This consideration suggests implicitly that the redesign of the square ought to become meaningful to a majority of people. Using the example of an Italian city quarter, Noschis (1984) discussed the concept of affective meaning of the environment for its inhabitants. The urban quarter is identified as a physical milieu and also as a highly symbolized social space.

The concept of place is investigated in a more phenomenological perspective by Seamon (1981), who identified the life-world of the urban population. He suggests the concept of 'place-ballet' which is defined as "a set of integrated behaviours which sustain a particular task or aim", as evident from a market scene for example. Related phenomenological perspective of urban identity are expressed by Mugerauer (1984), and Graumann and Schneider (1984). The convergence of history and the social sciences helps us to understand the complex concept of urban identity. For methodological reasons, i.e. the lack of sources, it is particularly difficult to achieve a true historical observation of a sample of a population over a long period of time. This very goal is pursued by Beerli (1983) in a longitudinal study of a central section of Geneva, Switzerland, between the 13th and 20th centuries. The author attempts to explain how the morphology of the urban environment was gradually shaped and modified. He makes use of various iconographic and literary sources to trace back the daily life of the population at different periods of time. At an even narrower scale, two houses are described in detail and their changing population examined from the point of view of the family structure and the professional activities performed at home. This combined method of exterior and interior observation provides a similar description to the Geist and Kürvers analysis of the Berlin tenement. Detailed records of house occupation can be obtained from Niethammer's survey of working-class housing in Imperial Germany (1977). The authors describe the effects of overcrowded rooms and the constant insecurity due to the necessity of moving into still cheaper premises. A detailed account of the living conditions by the inhabitants themselves is difficult to find, perhaps because the daily life of the working-class was not considered a particularly interesting subject. In a more contemporary urban context, Clerc (1967) analyses the attitudes of large housing developments in France and reveals the conditions experienced in such communities. The actual framework of housing and the corresponding social structures are seen to have critical implications for the behaviour of the inhabitants. Liveability appears to be strongly influenced by the physical setting. Therefore, it is important to understand the complex influence of the urban environment on human behaviour. This problem area must now be further examined with references to the life-styles of the population.

Boudon (1969) compares the present condition with the original appearance of the housing colony of Pessac near Bordeaux built in 1925 by Le Corbusier. The owners modified their houses so radically that they changed the initial appearance totally. The conflicts between the modern image designed by the architect and the ultimate appearance of the buildings after their total transformation by the inhabitants reveal the inadequacy of architectural concepts in terms of culture. They also indicate what symbols and forms are mostly valued by the local population at Pessac.

Another approach to life-styles related to the spatial context of buildings, focusses on the determinants of environmental quality, which serve as guidelines for design. Rapoport (1977) suggests that "there is more constancy at smaller than at larger scales." Hence more can be learned by analyzing small-scale units historically and cross-culturally.

Medam (1977), who is to a lesser extent concerned with the design perspective, explored the changes occurring in the life of families. He noticed that the home has lost part of its earlier signification, not only as a consequence of the change in the internal relations in the household, but also because factors such as the media have helped modify the meaning of the dwelling by offering constant pictures of the outside world in the newspapers or on the TV screen. The home is therefore experienced in a different manner and its protective value is no longer comparable to what it was before. A relatively more complex way of life results in different expectations about home.

On the whole, detailed historical analyses of the evolving life-styles since the industrial revolution are lacking. Based on an investigation of the city as a product of capitalism, Murard and Zylberman (1976) undertook a thorough sociological survey of the resulting human relations. They discuss the emergence of intimacy as a regulating process intervening between human beings to secure social peace and discipline. Their exploration of intimacy and privacy reveals a new orientation in housing policies where space is manipulated intentionally as means of social control. It is obvious that the public-private relationship has resulted in a vast amount of literature that cannot be summarized here.

Another orientation of urban social history worth mentioning can be found in publications which follow a more philosophical or poetic approach to describe the nature of urban life. Williams (1975) considers dialectically the opposition of the country and the city in order to extract the intimate and respective character of both. He uses literary quotations to connote the changing nature of the urban scene in contrast to the rural landscape. Gracq (1985) portrays the French city of Nantes by comparing the physical shape at the present time with his childhood memories of it, in order to achieve a suggestive description of the urban metamorphosis. His survey includes the identification of various familiar places that are felt to be most representative of the city. Similarly, Stokes (1980) makes use of childhood memories to describe subjectively the atmosphere and experience of certain parts of London. His 'inside-out' perspective of Hyde Park favours sensitive impressions which are meaningful to the reader.

The phenomenological analysis of the city by Sansot (1973) presents not only the urban places and institutions, but also the way they are used and the less evident meanings they convey. The text is conceived to suggest sensitive images and feelings that everyone associates with his own experience of the city. This perspective tends to reveal the hidden face of things and results in a subjective vision shared in common by a majority. Such texts are a useful complement to the literature on urban social history.

CONCLUSION

It is obvious that a sample of about seventy bibliographical references cannot provide a comprehensive definition of an epistemological field as vast as urban social history. Such an attempt to synthesize a scientific domain remains questionable from the point of view of its objectivity, since it depends on the expertise or erudition of the surveyor. If he is restricted to one culture and can only reach publications in the same language, chances are that his perspective will remain narrow.

In spite of the difficulty of achieving a well documented account of such a wide field of study, it appears firstly that the scope of urban social history is dependant on the cultural and professional orientation of the observer, and does not correspond to any fixed definition. Secondly, this field of research is further structured according to its goals. If the demand is for example predominantly design-oriented, then the historical context taken in consideration is likely to be reduced to the contemporary period of time. But if the demand is related to an object on a long term basis, then the historical perspective will be extended further back into the past. Thirdly it seems that only few studies cover a systematic field of knowledge. It is then up to the researcher himself to provide the necessary linkages between individual theories, in order to bridge the gaps. Fourthly, although a true cross-cultural perspective is difficult to adopt, it is advisable to balance contributions from one culture with others drawn from different cultural contexts, in order to establish a level of complementarity. Fifthly, in spite of the congenital multidisciplinary nature of urban social history, it is important to remain aware of the dominant orientation selected, be it history, geography or anthropology. Sixthly, urban social history is bound to be primarily concerned with the issues of everyday life such as housing and dwelling. It seems that this survey has revealed most of these orientations.

Bibliography

Aillaume, J.M. et al., Politiques de l'habitat (1800-1850), CORDA, Paris 1977, p. 280.

Ariès, Ph., L'enfant et la vie familiale sous l'Ancien Régime, Seuil, Paris 1973.

Aymonino, C. et al., La città capitali del 19. secolo. Parigi e Vienna, Officina Edizioni, Roma 1975.

Ballion, R., La fréquentation des espaces verts parisiens, unpublished paper, Laboratoire d'économétrie de l'Ecole polytechnique, Paris 1975.

Bardet, J.P. et al., Le bâtiment, enquête d'histoire économique, 14e - 19e siècles, Mouton, Paris 1971.

Barret-Kriegel, B. et al., La politique de l'espace parisien à la fin de l'Ancien Régime, CORDA, Paris 1975.

Beerli, C.A., Rues Basses et Molard. Genève du 13e au 20e siècle, Georg, Genève 1983.

Benevolo, L., Histoire de l'architecture moderne. 1. La Révolution industrielle, Dunod, Paris 1978.

Bertrand, M.J., Architecture de l'habitat urbain, Dunod, Paris 1980.

Boudon, F., Tissu urbain et architecture : l'analyse parcellaire comme base de l'histoire architecturale, Paris 1980.

Boudon, P., Pessac de Le Corbusier, Dunod, Paris 1969.

Burnett, J., A Social History of Housing (1815-1970), David & Charles, London and Vancouver 1978.

Buttimer, A., 'Social Space in Interdisciplinary Perspective', The Geographical Review, Vol. 59, No. 3, 1969.

Buttimer, A., 'Social Space and the Planning of Residential Areas', Environment and Behavior, Vol. 4, No. 3, Sept. 1972, pp. 279-318.

Cannadine, D., 'L'aristocratie et les villes dans l'Angleterre du 19e siècle : les villes balnéaires', URBI 1, Sept. 1979.

Castex, J. et al., Formes urbaines : de l'îlot à la barre, Dunod, Paris 1977, p. 39.

Cervellati, P.L. et al., La nouvelle culture urbaine. Bologne face à son patrimoine, Seuil, Paris (1977) 1981.

Chombart de Lauwe, P.H., 'L'évolution des besoins et la conception dynamique de la famille', Revue française de sociologie, Vol. 1, 1960, pp. 403-425.

Clerc, P., Grands ensembles, banlieues nouvelles. Enquête démographique et psychosociologique, P.U.F., Paris 1967.

Coing, H., Rénovation urbaine et changement social : l'îlot no 4 (Paris 13e), Editions Ouvrières, Paris 1966.

Conan, M., 'Images of Nature in the City: Psycho-sociological analysis in Regard of the Creation of a Public Park in La Villette', in Proceedings of The 8th International Conference on Environment and Human Action, Berlin 1984.

Daunton, M., House and Home in the Victorian City: Working-Class Housing 1850-1914, Edward Arnold, London 1983, p. 37.

Daunton, M., Public Place and Private Space: The Victorian City and the Working-Class Housing, London 1983.

Elias, N., La civilisation des moeurs, Calmann-Lévy, Paris (1939) 1973.

Englander, D. Landlord and Tenant in Urban Britain, 1838-1918, Clarendon Press, Oxford 1983.

Foucault, M., Histoire de la folie, Union Générale d'Editions, Paris 1961.

Gans, H., The Urban Villagers: Group and Class in the Life of Italian-Americans, Free Press Macmillan, New York 1962.

Gauldie, E., Cruel Habitations. A History of Working-Class Housing, 1850-1918, George Allen and Unwin Ltd., London 1974.

Geist, J.F. and Kürvers, K., Das Berliner Miethaus, Vol. 1 (1740-1862), München 1980; Vol. 2 (1862-1945), Prestel, München 1984.

Giedion, S., Mechanization Takes Command, Oxford 1948.

Giedion, S., Space, Time and Architecture, Harvard University Press, Cambridge (1941) 1967, p. 810.

Gleichmann, P., 'Wandel der Wohnverhältnisse', Zeitschrift für Soziologie, No. 5, 1976, pp. 319-329.

Gotman, A., 'Logement, parenté, héritage', in Proceedings of The 8th International Conference on Environment and Human Action, Berlin 1984.

Gracq, J., La forme d'une ville, José Corti, Paris 1985.

Graumann, C.F. and Schneider, G., 'Urban Identity and Identification', in Proceedings of The 8th International Conference on Environment and Human Action , Berlin 1984.

Guerrand, R.H., Les origines du logement social en France, Les Editions Ouvrières, Paris 1967.

Guerrand, R.H., Les lieux. Histoire des commodités, La Découverte, Paris 1985.

Gutkind, E.A., The Twilight of Cities, Macmillan, New York 1962, p. 172.

Heller, G., Propre en ordre. Habitation et vie domestique, 1850-1930 : l'exemple vaudois, Editions d'En-Bas, Lausanne 1979.

Jacobs, J., The Death and Life of Great American Cities, Jonathan Cape, London 1962.

King, A., Colonial Urban Development, Routledge and Kegan Paul, London 1976.

King, A., 'The Social Production of Building Form: Theory and Research', in Environment and Planning: Society and Space, Vol. 2, 1982, pp. 429-446.

Korosec-Serfaty, P., 'Functions and Daily Uses of Stortorget, Malmö', in ARIS, Nova Series, No. 1, Hässleholm 1982.

Lawrence, R., 'Urban History, Housing and Politics in Britain: A Review Essay in Survey 5', Society and Place, Nr. 4, 1985.

Leca, A.P., Et le choléra s'abattit sur Paris, 1832, Albin Michel, Paris 1982.

Ledrut, R., Les images de la ville, Paris 1973.

Lepetit, B., 'Histoire urbaine et espace', L'Espace géographique, No. 9, 1981, p. 45.

Medam, A., 'Loger en famille', in De la construction de l'espace à l'espace de la création, Cahiers de psychologie de l'art et de la culture, No. 22, Paris 1977, pp. 61-75.

Morgan, W., *An Introduction to the Social History of Housing in Victorian Preston*, Preston 1984.

Mugerauer, R., 'Openings in the City, Openings for the City', in *Proceedings of The 8th International Conference on Environment and Human Action*, Berlin 1984.

Mumford, L., *The Culture of Cities*, Harcourt, Brace and World, New York 1938, p. 114.

Murard, L. and Zylberman, P., 'Le petit travailleur infatigable ou le prolétaire régénéré; villes-usines, habitat et intimités au 19e siècle', in *Recherches*, Fontenay, Nov. 1976.

Niethammer, L. and Bruggemeier, F., 'Urbanisation et expérience ouvrière de l'habitat dans l'Allemagne impériale' in L'haleine des faubourgs, *Recherches*, No. 29, Fontenay 1977, pp. 103-154.

Noschis, K., *La signification affective du quartier*, Librairie des Méridiens, Paris 1984.

Parr, A.E., 'The Child in the City: Urbanity and the Urban Scene', *Landscape*, Vol. 16, No. 3, 1967, pp. 3-5.

Rapoport, A., *Human Aspects of Urban Form*, Pergamon, Oxford, New York 1977.

Sansot, P., *Poétique de la ville*, Klincksieck, Paris 1973.

Seamon, D., 'Body-Subject, Time-Space Routines and Place-Ballets', in Douglas D.C. Pocok (eds), *Humanistic Geography and Literature*, London 1981.

Seidel, A., 'Myths in Local Government Toward Urban Growth and the Physical Environment', in *Proceedings of The 8th International Conference on Environment and Human Action*, Berlin 1984.

Sitte, C., *L'art de bâtir les villes* (French translation from 'Der Städtebau nach seinen künstlerischen Grundsätzen', Wien 1889), Paris 1980, pp. 8-9.

Stokes, A., 'Excursions intérieures', *URBI* 4, Paris 1980, pp. xvi-xxix.

Sutcliffe, A., *Towards the Planned City. Germany, Britain, The US and France. 1780-1914*, Basil Blackwell, Oxford 1981.

Swenarton, M., *Home Fit for Heroes: The Politics of Architecture and Early State Housing in Britain*, Heinemann, London 1981, p. 3.

Villermé, L.R., *Tableau de l'état physique et moral des ouvriers employés dans les manufactures de coton, de laine et de soie*, Paris 1840.

Williams, R., *The Country and the City*, Oxford University Press, New York 1975.

7. Socio-cultural aspects of built form

RENA PAPAGEORGIOU-SEFERTZI and ARISTIE
PAPADOPOLOU

SYNOPSIS

A part of this article will be seen as critical in nature, so it must
be stressed at the outset that the intention is to be constructive.
Aspects which regard architectural form as an "expression" or as an
"instrument" will be rejected because they fail to explain it in the
former case, and promote a very partial, therefore unreal, view in the
latter.

A hypothesis which regards architectural form as a "product" of a
certain labour will be developed. In particular it is hypothesised
that: 1) architectural forms are developed though a process of
production i.e. practices of production and consumption of
architectural forms. 2) The process of production of architectural
form is distinguished from the process of production of plastic form.
Architectural discourse is a means of producing this distinction. 3)
The process of production of plastic form can be studied autonomously,
apart from the practice which produces the materiality of the plastic
object.

Taking into account that: 1) The process of production of plastic
forms cannot be uniform for all social groups, since our societies are
hierarchical and internally differentiated, the type of conflicts which
arise during the production of urban plasticity should be investigated.
2) Urban plasticity is not accidental but subjected to certain
statutory rules and control. Thus conflicts arise because of the
different use made by the inhabitants of the statutory planning
regulations. Some dominate while others are dominated. 3) The problem
with which the architect is confronted is: to find a solution which can

overcome the conflict. In other words, with the architectural form he must "create" a fictitious conciliation of the contradictions.

This analysis leads to a triple determination of the architectural form: 1) plastic 2) statutory and 3) fictitious. As a consequence, architecture achieves only a fictitious conciliation of the conflicts produced by social contradictions during the production of urban plasticity, which is in contradiction to the struggle which characterises social reality. It is this struggle which gives the measure, or the limitations of the function of an architectural form as a model.

THE HYPOTHESIS

If we attempt an outline of the positions taken by theoreticians of architecture we may say that some comment generally on the facts of architectural history, while others define the architectural artiface as the object of their study.

In the latter case two approaches can be distinguished: a) the descriptive: i.e. those who describe the object without explaining it, thus producing its duplicate, and b) the explanatory approach: that is, those who attempt to explain the architectural artifact.

In both cases we can agree with D Porphyrio's (1981) critique that:

"Architecture as "object" allows one to assign to the building a unity defined by the boundaries of its physical existence, always assuming that the unity of the building is an instantaneous given, an immediate and homogeneous coherency. Conversely, this notion of architecture as "object" founded on the assumption of a pre-given coherency ... allows architectural history to set as its task the ressurrection of such coherency. Thus, architectural history always neglects the contradictions present in the building and always silences its antinomies ..." (p. 98)

When theoreticians of architecture try to explain the architectural artifact, the following distinctions appear: 1) The position of the theoreticians who assume that the architectural artifacts comprise a unity which can be studied autonomously, that is independently of any other phenomena. In this case architectural artifacts may be regarded in a "spiritualistic" perspective; i.e. as phenomena whose essence surpasses history, thus their appearance remains mysterious. On the other hand architectural artifacts may be viewed in a "positivist" perspective, according to which they are regarded as objective data and knowledge of them depends on the refinement of a sum of technics and methods of analysis and classification. 2) The position of those theoreticians who study their object by attributing it to "another reality, e.g. artistic, technical achievements of the epoque, financial conditions etc. This "other reality" becomes responsible for the form of the architectural artifact.

To some extent this latter approach seems more correct and more compatible to the manner in which we are posing the problem, since our objective is to correlate architectural form to other social practices.

Yet we shall have to distance ourselves from it as will become
apparent.

From a historical point of view it can be argued that it was Hegel
who lifted art and (architectural) from the metaphysical realm within
which it had been debated for centuries, and situated it within
culture. He spoke of art as "proceeding from the absolute idea" and
assigned as its end "the sensuous representation of the absolute
itself". The term "Idea" was used to convey not simply some abstract
Platonic image that lodges itself in the mind as a constitutive a
priori, but on the contrary, to mark a mode and an awareness of
concrete reality. (D Porphyrios 1981).

However, perceiving art as a manifestation of transcendent values
credits the artist with the ability to look at the Idea itself and to
reveal it to others. "Aesthetic transcendetalism", as Gombrich (1981)
calls this process, also presupposes the idea of "historical
colectivism", i.e. the role assigned to the collective, to the nation
or to civilisation which is characterised by its peculiar and
distinctive spirit, its "Zeitgeist", whose overwhelming power holds
everyone in its spell.

Thus the idea of the "transcendency" of art becomes "transparency" in
a secularised form, as the work of art is still seen as the
"expression" of the spirit of the age, which, as it were, remains
visible across its surface. As Gombrich (1981) maintains:

> "The rod "expression", with its elusive ambiguity, facilitates this
> transition, enabling the historian to disclose the philosophy of an
> age, or its economic conditions, behind the work of art. What is
> common to both methods is naturally the connection with
> collectivism, for the way leads from the individual work of art via
> the style, which should now be interpreted as a symptom, a
> manifestation of class, race, culture or the age. (p. 7)

Historical determinism has a powerful role in this approach. To
quote Gombrich (1981) again:

> "One cannot condemn that which is unavoidable ... The history of
> art has been presented along the lines of teleogy of development,
> first in antiquity, then int he Renaissance and also by
> Winckermann, and what at the time was seen as decline can
> admittedly also be interpreted in the relativist sense as yet
> another process of adaptation". (p. 8)

However, the question is: Adaptation to what? Does every collective,
every social group, make identical demands on architects and their
standards? The idealistic philosophy has its answer, since it regards
the "artists" as "world historical individuals" who are managers of the
spirit of the epoque and are thus aware of the necessary next step to
be taken by their world, which step they take through their "creation".
It is obvious that it is not granted to ordinary mortals to recognise
and understand this anticipation of the future in the present. This
means that every criticism of contemporary events is theoretically
impossible since it involves the danger of the future proving it
blasphemy. As Gombrich (1981) very rightfully points out: "All that

remains for the critic in the end is to try and see which way the wind blows".

It is obvious that such criticism can be characterised as "metaphysical opportunism" or "pseudoscientific knowledge". We would like to add to this that the same applies for the artist.

With these analytical categories architectural history has attempted to study its materials. We can thus agree with D Porphyrios (1981) in that:

"The task of such a history of architecture is to perpetuate the ideological foundations of a "humanist" anthropology of creation, which in its turns, helps re-produce the dominant ideology of our conjuction architecture as an 'object' for consumption". (p. 99)

Thus we can say that although Hegel saved art and architecture from metaphysics, he introduced another type of metaphysics, that of creation. He bequeathed his successors with this aspect, the "relation of expression" between the artist and the Idea.

It is exactly this relation which we suspect and oppose, because no scientific knowledge can be based on it. We propose instead the conception of the historical relation between the result and its conditions of existence as a "relation of production".

Once we grasp the relationship of architecture and society not as one of result/cause, effect/origins, form/content, representation/Idea etc, as all idealist theories do, but as one of the production then we have freed ourselves from all the categories of the Hegelian model and the humanist approaches. Accordingly art and architecture is not a man's creation but a product, and the producer/s is/are not a subject centred in his creation but an element in a situation or a system.

Since theory and criticism should not limit itself to immatating reality by representing it in a comment, nor should it limit itself merely to the analysis and classification of its objects, neglecting their production, but on the other hand neither should it attribute its object to "another reality" whose relations to the object remain external. We shall try to answer the question of the relationship between architectural form and social practices with the following hypothesis:

1) The form of the architectural artifact is the result of a practice which is the object of a theoretical approach; i.e. the study of architectural phenomena. By architectural phenomena we mean architectural practices whose result is the architectural form. The basic elements of architectural practice are: the object (architectural form), the subject (architect), the means of production used, and the architect's perspective.

2) There is an intrinsic relationship between architectural practice and other social practices, not of cause and effect but of interaction and interdependence.

We believe that the above hypothesis permits us to avoid both contemporary theories, which regard the architectural artifact as the "expression" of a social formation, and those theories which regard it as an "unpredisposed instrument" which simply serves a certain social formation.

ARCHITECTURAL FORMS AND SOCIAL PRACTICES

If we consider the course of architecture during a given period, especially a recent one, we can see that it consists of a succession of steps, each posing diverse problems. These steps may be great or small, significant or insignificant, obvious or obscure. Yet, the plethora of projects proposed in response to each step, illustrates the route architecture takes and suggests that despite the variety and abundance of architectural solutions something remains constant throughout. That is the critical role of the architect. This role gives him the right and the obligation to master a disequlibrium, or in other words, to take a risk.

If "taking a risk" seems to constitute the existing condition of architecture, then where does this risk come from? Apparently, it is due to the conflicts which develop during the production of urban plasticity. How do these conflicts arise? Apparently, they are due to the contradictory attitudes and postures of the social groups and social categories which are involved in that social practice known as "to inhabit".

If we consider the condition of architecture in this light, then instead of accepting or rejecting the architecture of "functional zones" we should examine it as the compromise devised in response to conflicts of that period. Similarly, rather than applaud or ignore the problem posed by contemporary architects of the "non-architecturality of the periphery", it would be better to examine it as a compromise proposed to face the contradiction between the mass production of the built environment on the one hand and the individual's appropriation of it on the other.

Up to this point we have presented the process of producing architectural form as ex machina. We will now attempt to describe the elements of this machine and its function.

According to our hypothesis, previously presented, architectural forms are said to be submitted to a process of production of architectural phenomena - that is to the practices of production and consumption of architectural form. In the absence of a developed iconology of architecture the concept of form remains ambiguous. Here, when using the word "form", we mean everything that makes the plasticity of an object apparent. We should note that the process of production of architectural form is well distinguished from the productin of plastic forms. By "plastic forms" we mean any kind of physical form which is produced during man's everyday experience in his environment. Every "plastic object" has a form which changes as the object changes. If architecture is to be distinguished from all other practices which produce "plastic form", we must examine the distinct relationships it establishes and the processes which produce this distinction.

Here is what P Macherey (1978) says abou the difference between literature and language:

"The difference between two autonomous realities already constitutes a kind of relationship. All the more so because real differences are dialectical rather than static; They are a continuously sustained, elaborated and recapitulated process, they display a very precise mode of relationship, non-empirical, but none the less real, because they are the product of a certain labour." (p. 53)

We must look for the source of this difference in the separation of intellectual and manual work; what distinguishes architectural practice from other practices that produce plastic forms is the conception/composition of the form of the object on the design board through a transposition in place and time. In this way we can see how architecture organises its knowledge and exerts its power. It can be admitted that architecture is divided into three interdependent subsystems: architectural discourse, architectural form, and architectural artifact. We are now interested only in the processes of production of the architectural form, therefore no particular stress will be placed on the question of architectural knowledge. It is not our intentin to do for architecture what M Foucault (1969) has suggested for painting: "...to prove that, at least in one dimension, it is a discursive practice which takes shape in techniques and effects". (p. 253)

We are looking for the effects of architectural practice in another dimension: In the production of plasticity. What animates the process of production of plastic forms? It has been noted that the process is supported by aspirations, postures and attitudes that arise from the relation of man to his environment. Since man is in the habit of giving a form to plastic objects, we can study this practice autonomously from the practices that produce the materiality of the "plastic object". There is an analogy between the functioning of production of plastic forms and what M Foucault (1969) believes about the utterance:

"The utterance is always given by means of a material substance, even if it is concealed and even if, once revealed, it is condemned to disappear. The utterance is not only in need of this materiality; but it is a necessary dimension of it. In a sense, materiality constitutes the utterance. A phrase composed of the same words, having the same sense, maintaining its syntactic and semantic identity does not constitute the same utterance when spoken in conversation or produced in print". (p. 131)

It is clear then that with rgards to the plastic object we can distinguish three processes whose interdependence must be explained:

- The process of production of architectural forms;
- The process of production of plastic forms;
- The process of production of the materiality of the plastic object.

To pose our question again: How are conflicts produced in the course of the production of urban plasticity? The production of urban plasticity is not accidental but is controlled, selected, organised and redistributed by specific institutional procedures whose constitution and function must be studied for each given social formation. By these procedures we mean the "permission to build". In most cases such permission is not granted if a building does not conform to prescribed regulations. Only beyond these regulations can we find the so-called "liberty of expression". Examples of such "liberty" are the interior decoration of a house and the facade of shops, though they, in turn, must comply to a different systems of codes and values.

We can say that the regulations governing "construction permits" express the control of the production of urban plasticity to ensure its conformation to the intended project. It seems that the authorities propose a "grid" through which urban life is subjected to the vision inherent in this "grid".

The inhabitants face this project which promises to guaranty harmony within the urban space. We can agree with M de Certeau (1980) in that:

"the geometric space of the urbanists and architects resembles the "sens propre" put forth by grammarians and linguists to maintain a standard and normative level to which they can refer all deviations. In reality, this "sens propre" (without any figurative sense) lies unnoticed in the every day usage of a speaker or a pedestrian".

It is clear that in our class societies the conflicts of production of urban plasticity result from the different uses that inhabitants make of the regulations and initial projects. Through those there are some who dominate the man-environment relationship, while others are dominated by it.

Conflicts are not due to the different modes of appropriating space of distinct social groups, but rather to another limitation: The all-encompassing model of life-style proposed by authority is in contradiction to the attitudes, values aspirations habits, and in the last analysis practices of those who are not ready to adopt it.

Thus the architect faces a problem: To overcome, or even better, to avoid the conflict. Here lies the specific role of architecture, to undertake the fictitious conciliation of contradictory positions; that is, to undertake their presentation as if they were not antagonistic so that their cooperation can be achieved in the architectural realm.

Thus it can be appreciated that architecture is submitted to a triple determination: That of the state, of plasticity, and of fiction.

If therefore we wish to study a certain style, a movement or a certain architectural artifact, we must take into account the conflict during its production, the conditions of the conflict's emergence and the function of the permission-granting apparatous during the period. We should also find the forms of conciliation which architecture creates and invests in such statements as: "...recognising the composite character of the edifice as a unifying entity." (Bauhaus), "ornament is a crime." (A Loos)," today's architects lost in the utopian necessity to find new techniques, have abandoned their obligation: to be experts in compromise." (Venturi), "the presence of the past" (1st Biennale of Venice), or "the art of completing cities". (Grunbach).

Thus the architecture of "functional zones" is only the fictitious conciliation of conflicts caused by the contradiction between "luxurious housing" - privilege of a minority and the need for "housing for all", demand of a majority. In contrast to contemporary academic architectural practise, zoning architecture proposed "residence for all". Thus some avant-garde architects oriented themselves to the search for an "ideal type" of inhabitant who could be generalised. They recognised this "type" in the life-style of a wage earner: "living", "working", "moving", "relaxing". The proposed housing suited a conception of society as a sum of "ideal types" who establish predetermined relations with their environment.

It must be noted that the conceptions of the urbanists of CIAM, (otherwise known as the architecture of functional zones), are characterised by the logic of composing initial plans which would serve as the basis for every plastic practice. This opened a specific period in the exercise of authority control over urban space: the "Modern" period. New roles were distributed to the architects and the urbanists and new forms were given to their differentiation.

The Marseille building complex (1947-1952) conceived by Le Corbusier, besides the conflict between the dominant and the dominated, had also to face the fonlict between the plasticity of the past and the new it introduced. Le Corbusier had to find the "hors-lieu" that could serve as a support: Nature. It was in relation to nature that he conceived his work and not in relation to the reality of the city of Marseille. In deciding to break away from the city, he undertook a series of inversions in the interior of the complex, making it into an "upside-down" world:

> "...the columns taper downwards instead of up, the landscape and garden are on the roof instead of the ground, the streets are in the air and internal instead of being external and on the ground, and the shopping centre is on the seventh floor instead of being connected with the commercial life of Marseille." (p. 16)

These are the inversions which Jencks considers as "natural", or better, as "positive creations", for "the closest modern equivalent to the "Greek Temple", where "family life, the domestic, every day life of the home is elevated to the level of a public monument." (p. 15)

Today, still facing conflicts, and still responding with fiction, architects continue to look for the "hors-lieu". We could say that this is a phenomenon common to periods of transition. Charles Moore's perspective is the opposite to that of his predecesors. He introduces the "hors-lieu" in place. Italy, home of an immigrant minority in New Orleans, appears in the form of a marble model which indicates the Piazza d' Italia. Jencks (1980) comments:

"As Italy rises towards the Northern Alps, so do the five orders of
Italian columns, and they culminate in a new Sixth Order which
enframes the future restaurant. Neon necklaces around the neck of
these columns further indicate that this is the 20th century, and
the fact that commercial "bad taste" is a very big part of it". (p.
20)

The island of Sicily is at the centre of a target and serves as the
tribune during celebrations and festivals. This is the conciliation of
the minority and the majority. Italy can only be introduced into New
Orleans as a distorted memory; it can only be accepted as a work of
art, a town monument.

Conciliation between the Italian ethnic factions: The presence of the
north as well as the south; an exchange of values; a creative
coexistance. As Jencks (1980) remarks:

"...For the Sicilians there are references to archetypal piazzas
and fountains; for the Modernist there is an acknowledgement of
skyscapers and the use of current technologies (the neon and the
concrete); for the lover of pure architectural form there are
cutaway imposts finished in speckled marble and a most sensuous use
of polished stainless steel. The overall impression finally is a
sensuous and rhetorical one, every bit as mixed and rich as the
Trevi fountain, another example of architecture, sculpture, writing
fountain, landscape and urban form". (p. 20)

It should be noted that architectural form - when thus established -
functions in a complex manner through the architectural discourse.
Thus the architectural form is not only produced in a determined
process, but enters also a process, of reproduction of other phenomena.
It is not the result only of material causes but has effects on
individuals who are socialy defined. It imposes certain modes of
appropriation of the architectural artifacts over social classes and
social categories; dominant and dominated.

In other words, the architectural phenomenon is not simply situated
in a domain of "aesthetics" or "asthetic judgement" (i.e. aesthetic and
architectural ideas), but gives rise to certain behaviours and certain
ways of consumption and cultural practices.

We thus arrive at the possibility of describing the process of
reproduction in which an architectural form enters. The "raw material"
of the architectural form is the contradictory attitudes in the
practice of "inhabiting" the city. The "effect" of the architectural
form, which has become established as a model, is to invoke similar
forms which are subjected to rules of the models, thus realising the
dominant aspects.

We can say then, that the architectural artifact is an executor of
the reproduction of power relations. It permits a certain kind of
appropriation or a certain way of expression by people who become its
"liberal" agents. The architectural artifact is not imposed
mechanically neither does it dictate its repetition. On the contrary,
it is given for interpretation, for variation according to individual
discretion, and for personal appropriation. As far as the form of the

107

architectural artifact is concerned that is always a matter of
dominance, subjection of individuals to dominant behaviours. It
functions unequally over individuals and most importantly it is
consumed differently by various social groups. "Subjection" should be
conceived mainly in relation to dominated categories and not the
dominant. While architecture appears to be offered to everyone,
practically "subjection" to it means for the members of the elite of
the dominant groups, the acquisition of the ability, or skills to
express themselves through the forms, while for the dominated social
categories "subjection" means domination and elimination through an
architecture which they cannot appropriate because they lack the
cultural means to appropriate it.

This discussion allows us to see the relationship between
architecture and social practice not as a relation of expression, but
as one of interdependence. It should be added that the relationship is
not instrumental. To the extent that architectural forms are a
fictitious conciliation they are found in contradication to the
struggle which threatens every reality.

If this explanation of the production of architectural form allows us
to arrive at which constitutes the conditions of its existence, it also
offers us the means of thinking of the temporary, if not ephemeral,
nature of the architectural artifact.

If the proposals of the charter of Athens are fictitious
conciliations, the resolutin of the contradictions which produced them
being beyond the scope of architecture, is it possible to imagine that
they would not be surpassed?

As we have tried to show, the projects of contemporary architecture
arise from the need to master the conflict between, on the one hand
Modern Movement and authority - which implies the imposition of
homogenous behaviour on urban residents - and on the other, the
persistance of social groups in differentiating themselves. Can we,
then, consider such projects definitive simply because they are
contemporary?

Bibliography

Balibar, E., Macherey, P. (1974) Presentation in Les francais fictifs. Le rapport des styles itteraires au francais national, Collection Analyses, Paris, Hachette.

Certeau, M. (1980) L'invention du quotidien" (1. Arts de Faire), Collection 1/18, Paris.

Foucault, M. (1969) L'archeologie du savoir, Gallimard, Paris.

Gombrich, E. (1981) "Hegel and Art History" in Architectural Design, (On the Methodology of Architectural History), No. 51, 6 July 1981, pp 3-9.

Jencks, C. (1973) Modern Movements in Architecture, Penguin Books

Jencks, C. (1980) "Piassa d'Italia" in Architectural Design (Post-Modern Classicism, 5/6 pp 20.

Macherey, P. A Theory of Literary Production, Routledge and Kegan Paul, London (1978) 1980.

Porphyrios, D. (1981) "Notes on a Method" in Architectural Design, (On the Methodology of Architectural History), No. 51, 6 July 1981, pp 96-104.

8. Building a house or a social universe?

CATHERINE MOUGENOT

Through a systematic inquiry into Belgian State housing policy this
paper focuses on the latent functions of a policy which shapes the
material environment of social life. On reviewing the various existing
theories on housing policy, we cannot find a satisfactory explanation
for the fundamental fact that most families are in favour of this
policy and its implicit urban and architectural forms.

   This paper argues that housing has progressively become adopted as a
means for social expression. Through the home, the individual shows his
social position : this implies that he supports a common social universe
while displaying his own socio-economic status. Considering that the
social representation function is an essential ingredient of housing
policy, we come to see that the representations of social life and
social groups conveyed by housing policy are all the more influential
when materialized in this everyday environment through which the
individual is socially identified.

There are two reasons why Belgium is a particularly interesting case for the analysis of housing policies : firstly, it has a high proportion of one-family houses and home-owners, and secondly there is an impressive amount of state intervention with respect to housing, where most aid is granted to families wishing to purchase or build their homes. All this has led the Belgians to say of themselves that they have 'a brick in their guts' ('une brique dans le ventre'), implying a sort of natural propensity or a national trait of character.

However, nothing is more socially and institutionally constructed than the 'natural' tendency of Belgians to want to build, and all the more so to want to own their own home, preferably a one-family house. We may therefore ask where this 'need' comes from. How did these ideals for housing and habitat which today may be considered to be dominant come to be ? And to what specific material forms do these lead ?

The aim of this text is to answer these questions with a view to contributing to current theoretical analyses of state housing policies with respect to the specific Belgian context.

To inquire into the context in which these housing requirements developed is to deliberately take a sociological and historical viewpoint in as much as neither today's institutions nor today's behaviour can be separated nor separable from the way in which they originated. In other words, we are only interested in this institutional history in so far as it has present-day consequences which, although perhaps more implicit, are probably all the more effective.

To ask this same question also means that we are interested in the latent functions of housing policy other than those officially admitted. To take our reasoning this step further, we must propose the hypothesis that the real functions of government housing policy are not only to produce measures of support or to build but also to create a demand for housing of a certain type which corresponds to certain spatial and architectural patterns. Therefore, the effect of government policy is not only on the supply but also on the demand, i.e. the amount families invest in and what they expect of their houses. If we admit this hypothesis, we must examine all the functions of state housing policy and in particular the way in which the latter defines a need (a home to live in) while providing material means of satisfying it.

THE MATERIAL CHARACTERISTICS OF BELGIAN HOUSING POLICY

It is difficult to talk about the latent functions of state policy without first taking points of reference in order to measure their impact.

The situation in Belgium is characterized both by the amplitude of the measures taken in favour of housing and their diversity. Indeed, one should keep in mind the fact that housing policy if far from limited to the actual building of houses. On the contrary, it can take on very effective forms of action without necessarily being as visible as for instance a state-owned compagny building a housing estate.

We can get a good idea of the specific nature of this aid by looking at a few main aspects.

Table 1.

LEGAL REPORT ON HOUSING AND THE FORM IT
TAKES IN THE EEC COUNTRIES IN 1981

	Number of houses lived in by their owners	Number of one-family houses
Germany	40.5	47.8
France	50.7	54.2
Italy	59.0	- (c)
Netherlands	41.8	64.2
Belgium	67.7 (a)	79.4 (a)
Luxemburg	59.2	63.2
United Kingdom	55.9	79.0 (b)
Eire	74.7	- (c)
Denmark	54.9	57.8

Source : EUROSTAT - Luxemburg

(a) Population and Housing Census
    on 1 March 1981 - INL.
(b) Office of Population, Censuses and Survey,
    Social Survey Division, General Household
    Survey, 1981.
(c) Data missing.

Table 2.

TYPES OF HOUSING AID IN BELGIUM AND NUMBER
OF TRANSACTIONS OVER THE PAST TWENTY-FIVE YEARS

Number of homes built between 1968 and the
1981 survey in Belgium : 1,090,447

Built by the SNL	:	190,185
Built by the SNT	:	35,895
Building grants	:	373,486
CGER loans	:	243,959
SNT loans	:	24,305
Loans from the Ligue des Familles Fund	:	44,727
Purchase grants	:	88,024
Restoration grants (since 1967)	:	27,104
Tax relief	:	data non published
Relief on sollicitors"fees	:	data non published

Source : INL - Building and Housing Statistics.

Quantity

Because of the fact that different types of grants are available and
that therefore some buildings may at different times have been the
object of various different types of aids, and that some buildings are,
for one reason or another, eventually demolished, it is virtually impossible to get a precise estimate of state housing aid in Belgium.
Nevertheless, we may certainly say that the amount is impressive : of
the 3 million homes which at present make up the Belgian real estate
pool, one in three, at some time or other, received aid from the State.

'Grants for bricks'

The grants are essentially aimed at improving the quantity and quality
of housing. In other words, apart from a very small rent support grant
(less than 1 per cent of total housing aid expenditure), the grants are
definitely not intended to cut the expenses of the inhabitant with some
system of financial support (as is the case in the Netherlands, for
example).

Aid for property

Among all the measures taken by the State, only one is clearly aimed at
increasing the amount of housing available for rent : the setting up of
the 'Société Nationale du Logement' (national housing company) just
after the First World War. This initially large investment now comes
to no more than 10 per cent of all housing aid. Furthermore, it should
be mentioned that some of the houses belonging to the SNL are later sold.
All other measures either are aimed at encouraging ownership, or favour
ownership as a necessary condition for access to grants. On top of
support for building, rebuilding and for renovation, we should mention
actual grants for property itself which consist of a system of tax
relief for the purchase of property. The nature of this type of aid

means that its extent is secret : it is not to be found in published financial statistics nor is it accounted for in the data on social housing in Table 2.

Support for the one-family house

Traditionnally, the Belgian people has always preferred to spread out at ground-level rather than vertically. However this is not consistent with the small size of the country or its high population density. Nor is this clear preference for one's own house - terraced or preferably detached when financially possible - the result of a 'natural tendency'. The model of the one-family house has always been strongly preferred by Belgian housing policy, even though as early as 1920 the law admitted that housing for people of 'moderate' income may be collective.

Visible and invisible aid, from a material point of view

Among the measures mentioned, some are clearly physically visible, others not. In Belgium there are three types of inhabitant : those who take on all the expenses themselves : building, purchase or rent, those who take on the expenses individually but with State help ranging from tax relief to loans from social funds - these first two are materially or visually indistinguishable -, and those who live in, rent or buy housing built at State initiative. The latter type of housing is easily distinguishable through its position, density, volume and architectural style. In most cases it is even possible to recognize at a glance which national building society built it (the SNL or the SNT) - (See Table 3). Therefore, up to a certain point one can distinguish a spatial hierarchy with clear-cut steps but also a tendency towards continuity, which can be the basis of a complete system of social identification and exclusion.

Supporting networks

These different forms of financial support come together with a set of specific elements which contribute to the make-up of supporting networks. For example, the intention to forbid public houses and the likes in State-owned housing estates led for a long time to the forbidding of shops in general in these neighbourhoods. The social surroundings were also conditioned by making gardens or small livestock (SNT) obligatory, and by setting up a system of networks which led to the formation of local groups by organizing festivities or collective action such as cooperatives.

The whereabouts of these housing areas, although related to financial constraints, are not unrelated to the leading social world view : State housing estates were built preferably in semi-rural areas, far from city centres and above all far from the symbolic image of the city as linked to the representation of working class power.

Briefly, and especially in relation to the building of State owned housing estates, our intention here is to draw attention to a network of material elements which not only make up Belgian housing policy, but also form the basis for a social world view.

ECONOMIC INTERPRETATION

In the analysis of housing policy, there is a strong school of thought
which interprets government intervention as a function of its economic
role : housing is conditioned by the leading types of production, by
the economic factors concerned (financial and industrial investment,
the building sector ...), and by the economic cycle. Housing may be
encouraged as a consumer product during years of economic growth, as a
means of controlling or of helping certain sectors of the economy, or in
times of economic slump, it may be used directly in the fight against
unemployment. From this economic activity of building and the profits
it may return, one can deduce the factors involved and the form of the
product built.

The analysis of the economic function of housing is specific to the
theoretical starting point : either liberal or Marxist. The former
favors housing in so far as it has an impact on salaries via rent and
examines the fluctuating dynamics of the building sector. The latter
position considers housing as a form of reproduction of labour and as
the scene of interactions between different forms of capital (industrial, financial ...). In one way or another, both perspectives cast
the actors in response to whom the public actor – the state –
intervenes. (1)

With respect to the initial hypothesis, however, there are two limitations to this strictly economic interpretation : the first is that
this approach is not entirely self-sufficient and sooner or later has to
make use of other concepts which often remain vague; take, for example,
the concept of housing conditions : from the Marxist viewpoint, these
must provide the reproduction of labour and depend on 'social needs'
which are both the objective and subjective needs of an objective necessity. (2) These considerations are rather imprecise with respect to our
aim which is to discover what leads to demand and how it is related to
specific material forms. In the same way, economic analysis cannot help
including vague ideological and political effects. In this respect, how
should one interpret the initiatives of a left-wing local government ?
(3) And in a strictly economic interpretation, how should one consider
the role of the state ? Indeed, the state has a twin role : to encourage the growth of capital and to maintain the social order which perpe-
tuates its existence, or in other words, to conserve its legitimacy

through political and ideological means. But according to N. Harloe, these two roles are often incompatible. (4)

The second limitation to this interpretation is that although the general idea that this casting of economic actors always puts the beneficiaries in a marginal role, or worse, even excludes others from the system is certainly true - and has not housing policy always defined itself as building for OTHERS ? - this requires further definition. We should ask, for example, on what conditions have actual or potential inhabitants been able to claim access to aid - and what sort of aid ? The whole question of socially constructed needs must therefore be examined in detail.

HOUSING POLICY : A FORM OF MORALIZATION

In order to evaluate housing demand and the way in which it is conditioned by state policy, we need to look for perspectives which take into account the position of the inhabitants. One particular theory has repetedly been suggested on this basis. It proposes that housing policy is not only intended to achieve its obvious material aim but also to instill 'morals' into the working classes. M. Foucault's theories (5) pointed out the institutions with which society arms itself in order to punish and cure social ills (prison, school, psychiatric hospital). The idea that housing can lead to moral and social peace for working class families was stressed. This is a recurrent theme used to explain the history of housing in Belgium and in all of Western Europe in general. (6) The various material characteristics of housing built either by industry or by the state are intended to bring moral wellbeing to society as a whole and to the lower classes in particular. Thus, for instance, the location of housing (mainly on the outskirts) was intended to allow a sort of return to the earth, giving the working man a healthy passtime and keeping him away from drink and bad company (cf. the negative image of working class power in cities). He might also save money by growing vegetables and keeping small livestock.

And here we find a reason for the 'natural' need for a small family house in the country. This house was to be, like the cane that straightens the plant, the foundation of social life leading the family into a particular way of life by shaping private space and its whereabouts.

On top of these factors is the pressure to attain ownership. As we stressed earlier, this has always been the foundation of Belgian housing policy - unvarying, even though the measures taken and the way they are justified have changed. Up until the 1960's the position was that ownership was a form of social and moral salvation and of deproletarization - 'in order that the worker become conservative, he should be given something to conserve : property is the basis of democracy'. Property was also considered to be a means of ordering the lower classes classes's way of life via the time and money spent on the process of saving and being in debt : 'I don't own my house, my house owns me'.

To see housing policy as a form of systematic moralization requires further definitions and qualification. For instance one might ask how the ruling classes managed to impose this social world view so well and so completely on the lower classes who had shown resistence in other

Table   4.

A FEW POINTS OF REFERENCE CONCERNING BELGIAN HOUSING POLICY

1889 Promulgation of the law on workers' housing. It allows tax relief for workers who own their own homes, creates patronage committees and fixes the role of the CGER (Caisse Générale d'Epargne et de Retraite - general savings and pension fund). These types of intervention are still essential at present.

The first intervention was intended to reply to violent demonstrations by workers (bloody riots in 1886) by displacing the field of proposed solutions towards slightly improving the living conditions of the working classes, for whom the problem was above all political (the fight for universal suffrage).

In everyone's opinion (including the Government's) this law clearly favours the privileged among workers. It only deals with the purchase of property and is far from solving the problems of the poorest.

1920 Creation of the Société Nationale du Logement : SNL (national housing society) (the then SNHBM) whose aim is to approve local building and housing societies. The latter will mainly let housing. Previous housing benefits are maintained and all the legislation is extended to people of 'modest income' rather than simply to workers by profession.

Here was a response to the socialists' and the radical liberals' demands for rented housing. Form models for the construction of this new type of housing spread rapidly and were commonly applied. As a whole these were built on the 'garden-city' model, whereas flats were rare and were only built more extensively following World War II, and then only in big cities.

Furthermore, previous aid was continued (cf. 1889), thus contributing toward further discreet but non the less efficient access to ownership not only for workers but for any person of modest background.

1922 Institution of a system of permanent grants for building or buying a house. The latter grant only applies if the house to be bought is State-owned. Indeed, the SNL soon realized that it could cut down its costs and increase its financial resources by selling some of the houses initially intended to be let.

The building grants, while of course favouring ownership, were only available for one-family houses, and also implied a form model (initially, aid was only granted for houses at least 10 metres apart).

1929 The 'Ligue des Familles nombreuses' (the league of large families), an associative pluralistic movement for the advancement and defense of families, organizes its own housing fund. It starts up through donations, l tteries, etc. In 1969, the State was to officially recognize the housing fund of the Ligue des Familles nombreuses by granting it annual subsidies. The fund is mainly to lend money for purchasing or building houses.

1935 Foundation of the Société Nationale de la Petite Propriété Terrienne (national society of small and land property - now the SNT), intended to take up the activities of the SNL in rural areas. The SNT is to build houses exclusively for sale and to give out loans for building, purchase and restoration.

The SNT houses were also built on a precise form model : detached or at least semi-detached houses spread out in a green area (see Table 3).

1948 In the context of the post-war reconstruction, the system of grants for building is reinforced (the 'Taye law'). From 1967, grants also became available for building flats.

From here (1948) onwards, the involvement of an architect and of town planning became obligatory. Aid was only to be granted after having checked building plans and layout.

1967 A more complex and remodelled system is brought in with the aim of increasing sanitation, improving, and more recently insulating houses.

With rare exceptions, this type of aid was only to be granted to home-owners. Observation has shown that, in practice, houses are usually embellished rather than improved in depth.

areas. In particular, there is a danger in systematically equating a concrete material form to a moralization project proper. Another point is that the ideological discourse on the moralization of the lower classes, with its dogmas and the idea of the social world it defends, should not hide what actually was accomplished : networks which managed to convince better than words of the advantages and the need for a house and a garden.

On the whole, this discourse fades out at the end of the 1950's : the end of a fashion in the way of saying things, but also a proof that there were other forms of action and of promotion which didn't necessarily need saying in order to be effective and to continue producing results.

The SNL houses

THE MATERIALIZATION OF A COMMON SOCIAL UNIVERSE

Another way in which we can understand the impact of the spread of these housing models is by suggesting that housing policy is also a policy for managing the ideas and representations of social groups. In other words, we wish to demonstrate that by changing the material way of life of families, we also change their conception of themselves and of society as a whole.

The first effect of housing policy was to impose upon the whole of society the idea that the home is an essential part of life and thus that to procure a home - and a comfortable one - is an important task into which it is worth investing time, money and effort. The first law on housing for workers in 1889 (see Table 4) was an attempt at solving a political problem and social tensions through measures affecting living conditions. However it was far from clear to the family - particularly to the lower class family - either that housing or better still the house was something that should be claimed, or even simply that it could be thought of as a space from which one might show oneself symbolically : - materially in the local environment, the neighbourhood, but also in a more general way in the global social environment.

117

Especially since the dissociation of work and accommodation, professions are no longer the only criteria for differenciation : housing is becoming a specific criterion for social evaluation. A set of facts and of measures taken with concrete results in space allow us to see how housing policy has instituted housing space as a criterion for social identification and belonging, or again as a social status-symbol by which people measure their position in the social structure.

Furthermore, it is very interesting to note that it was precisely at the beginning of an overall trend towards dissociating housing from the place of work that the idea of a housing policy was introduced, clearly at the initiative of the ruling class.

The common representation is based on the house as an evaluation criterion but also as a mode of social expression available to all. And is not housing policy there to prove it with its system of aid and compensation, by giving more and more people the possibility of taking part in this world of representation.

Thus all the systematic work of nearly the last hundred years may be interpreted as a way of proposing or enforcing a way of life and of expression in society through housing in arbitrary but legitimized forms of habitat : forms which have become evident, naturalized, and which are a part of similarly natural needs. And here we must stress the obviousness of both the choice of housing policy and of popular practise : this is unquestionably the one-family house whose arbitrary attraction is strengthened by aid for building and home-ownership. Here, for everyone (each social group), is the chance and the place in which to invest one's sense of good behaviour : habitat is both a place for concrete behaviour and a basis for mental representation, and all the more so as the one-family house is a form of expression which is lasting while private and personal. The collective sharing involved in this form of expression comes all the more naturally as it is percieved in a more individual way.

SOCIAL DESIGNATION

First of all we must recognize the essential importance to the analysis of the definition of the beneficiaries of aid. Indeed, this definition changes constantly, but neither changes in living conditions nor fluc-tuations in the amount of housing available can be held responsible. Instead, the constant defining and redefining of social classes, of their characteristics and of the relationships between them comes into play. Thus the definitions and oppositions to be found during debates and in documents dealing with housing policy may be held to be decisive. But are there real objective differences between a little manual worker and a little employee ? Between a small landowner and a big one ? Between a worker and a person of modest income ? Are these differences sufficient to warrant discrimination in state aid ? Does not wanting to answer these questions finally mean asking another one : why and how does a society, at a particular point in a historical and social context, stake its all on instituting these definitions and distinctions, and on giving them concrete contents - precise representations - in particular by means of housing policy ?

118

In order to analyse the evolution of the way beneficiaries of housing
aid were defined, we need to compare what is socially at stake in a
society whose morphology has become more and more complex during the
20th century, and what the social implications of this increasing complexity and its representation are. One of the latent mechanism of
housing policy is social recognition of various middle-class fractions,
and especially social recognition of the integration of the upper
fraction of the working class into the definition of 'middle class'.
Thus, for example, the family morals proposed explicitly even by
living in a one-family house were more than simply the practice of the
Christian doctrine to which most of the actors of this housing policy
adhered. It was also a way of giving social existence to the group
which could best identify with it by its way of life : the middle class.

In this respect, a decisive change came about in 1920 when the definition of the beneficiaries of aid was widened to encompass all people
of 'modest income' rather than strictly 'workers'. This opening
towards the middle classes (liberal and self-employed petite
bourgeoisie), especially through the recognition of their way of life
and their housing, is an essential point because this group was about
to fundamentally change its social morphology : after the apogee of
economic liberation, a new group was due to prevail in number : that of
the employees with low and medium salaries. The advantages granted to
the former were soon to become the foundation for the social definition
of the latter - ever increasing in number.

The incorporation of the upper fraction of the working classes into
the middle classes was also at stake in recognizing and defining the
latter. Housing policy made a constant effort to this effect, and this
was clear in 1889 : the law was solely intended to favour home-ownership
among the privileged of the working class. The apparent change of aim
in 1920, when aid became available for renting while earlier aids were
maintained, only increased the apparent distinction between workers :
although the material burden of the poorer among them was lightened by
making housing available for rent, they were nevertheless socially
pointed out by their living in state-owned housing estates.

This reasoning should not, even if it is tempting, take on a machia-
vellian interpretation, nor even be thought to be intentional. We
might also suggest that the more social logics are unconscious and
unintentional, the more effective they are. In fact, the question here
is not which effects were expected by the actors of housing policy and
which were 'side effects'. Our perspective is to propose a social
logic following this policy, and in particular to find out which effects
are still active in today's way of life and in our manner of self-
representation in society.

THE INTERPLAY OF DIFFERENCES

It is apparently contradictory but socially logical that this universe
of representation based on habitat should itself be the basis for a
system of social differenciation which makes this mode of common identity possible and plausible. For this common universe to take over and
integrate a large part of the population, it must allow material differences and allow them to appear as such. Here again, housing policy

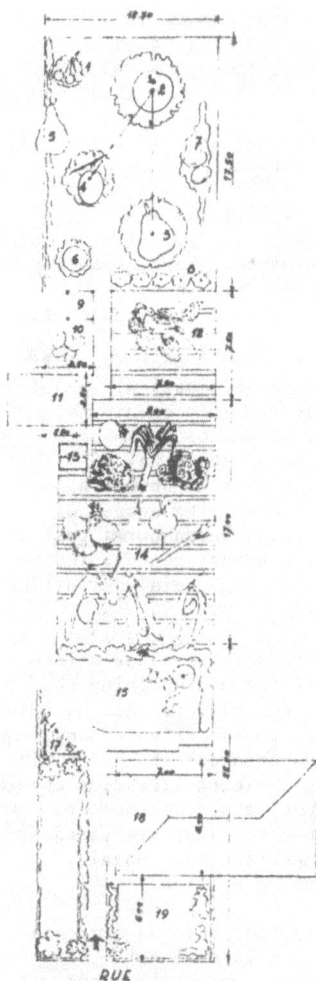

THE SNT HOUSES

'How to lay out a plot of 8 ares in the province of Hainaut in order to produce the vegetables, fruit, flowers, eggs and part of the meat needed for the household', from
the periodical 'Propriété Terrienne' - November 1956.

The first area of the plot groups the house, the flower patches, the lawn (19, 15)
and a bower (17). This space is intended for leisure, rest and for children to play in.
The second area is separated from the latter by a row of high flowers (16) and groups
the vegetable patch (13, 14) together with the henhouse, the rabbit hutches (10,11)
and a compost heap (9). Finally the orchard (1-7) is separated from the rest of the
garden by a hedge of currant bushes (8). The house (18) and the garden sheds (11)
are semi-detached.

The information provided shows how to divide up the plot of land and gives an estimate
of how much one might expect to produce from such a layout.

clearly plays a role by compensating material inequalities while
showing them up : integration within differenciation.

But let us first mention the material form most frequently found in
Belgium : the detached house. This form was inspired from the large
residences of the rich and cultivated. It is typical of Belgium that
even wealthy families always spread out sidewards rather than upwards.
This form model adopted by the rich, enforced by the prescriptions of
state policy, could not have suited diffusion and reappropriation
processes better. It should be noted that the rural nature of this
model was not only able to integrate people who had recently moved to
town but also families still living in semi-rural or even rural areas,
in particular through a very efficient policy of public transport
season tickets for workers.

We must also stress here the diversity of the measures taken
concerning housing, with sharp visual differences but with constant
trends. We can distinguish houses built to be rented : they are all
built on a similar scheme and spaced very closely. Houses to be sold
are also very standard but with much wider spacing (the houses are in
one's or two's). Lastly, there are houses built by individuals from
the smallest to the largest, with or without state aid. Here is a
material typology made up of continuity and discontinuity while
allowing a wide variety of details of shape.

Everyone is offered a housing program which may enable him to identify
with a social level equal or superior to others (to have a house like
so and so's) but most of all, which will enable him to distinguish
himself from what he does not - or no longer wants to be. This is the
essential function of a system which, although made up of continuity,
values difference. The string of measures taken in aid of housing may
be seen as a series of absorptions of different groups into a common
universe while allowing genuine material and social differenciation.
The town planner Van Swaelnen showed intuition about this when he
declared on the subject of temporary housing to be built after World
War I : 'This type of housing is not an isolated problem, but it is a
part of a global concept : from barracks to collapsible huts, from
these to small workers' houses, and from small workers' houses to
workers' cottages, the transition is very natural and happens step
by step ...'. (7)

To favour varied types of access to housing for socially close
groups is to favour social continuity rather than division, and is to
do concrete work towards avoiding a break-up of society and avoiding
strongly or too strongly pronounced oppositions. All of Christian
ideology is to be found here : to harmonize, to render continuous,
while cristallizing the concrete modes of behaviour of the social
groups whose social existence one wishes to ensure. To favour a moral
and individual existence centred on the family not only conforms to
Catholic doctrine, it also and above all ensures social recognition for
the groups who can or wish to conform to this model.

The evolution of material forms, far from having taken place for its
own sake, should also be seen in this light. The 'working man's house'
was more than just the forerunner of the detached house so commonly
desired today; was it not also one of the concrete, material forms of
expression of a redefined society?

It is apparent to us that to control the mechanisms by which we identify in practice with a group or a way of life and our perception of the latter is a means of exercising power, and that in this respect, housing is at the crux of understanding a society.

CONCLUSION

We can neither give a final conclusion here, nor even suggest that the list of possible interpretations of Belgian housing policy is complete. Our intention is simply to ponder over the effects of an impressive policy which has always worked very clearly in the same direction although through a variety of concrete expressions.

Our hypothesis suggests that if the system is so efficient, it is because it fulfils (among other things) a social representation function. The house has become a virtually obligatory - and at least a naturalized form of expression through which we show our position in the social universe. This implies just as much our adhesion to a common order as the expression of differences. The house has turned out to be a form of social definition as well as a way of adhering to this universe.

We may therefore suggest analysing each of the material forms of housing not by mechanically comparing these forms with the social position of the inhabitants (even though interesting statistical links may be observed), but by trying to see how everyone places his sense of moral and above all social honour in them. One might also, in this respect, try to see to what extent other state-owned or partially state-owned places are not only places of practical use but above all the basis for representation and identification with a social world view.

NOTES

(1) Bassand, N., Chevalier, G., Zimmermann, Politique et logement, Collection Villes, Régions et Sociétés, Presses polytechniques romandes, Lausanne, 1984.
(2) Cornuel, D., 'Sur l'intervention de l'état dans le financement du logement', International Journal of Urban and Regional Research - Book reviews, vol.1, no.3, pp.542-555, Edward Arnold, London, 1977.
(3) Idem (2).
(4) Harloe, N., 'Le logement et l'état : récents développements au Royaume-Uni', Revue internationale des sciences sociales, vol.XXX (1978), no.3, pp.626-640.
(5) Foucault, M., Surveiller et punir, Editions Gallimard, Paris, 1975.
(6) Cf. among others a particularly typical analysis of this tendency : Muraro, L., et Zyberman, B., Le petit travailleur infatigable - villes, usines, habitat et intimité au XIXème siècle, Recherches, Paris, 1976.
(7) Cf. Gobyn, R., 'La crise du logement et le problème du logement provisoire en Belgique après la première guerre mondiale', Resurgam - La construction en Belgique, Crédit Communal, 1985.

9. Urban open space

PERLA KOROSEC-SERFATY

INTRODUCTION

During the last decade we have been able to observe a renewed interest
in urban public spaces in general, and most particularly in streets
and squares, both among town dwellers, theoreticians and practitioners
of urbanism and architecture (Anderson, 1978; Appleyard, 1975, 1981;
Jacobs, 1961; Rudofsky, 1969; Whyte, 1980). The term "renewed" is
particularly adequate here as what we see is a reaction to the
conception of urbanism which quite simply ignores squares and describes
the traditional urban streets only as being the central point of an
unbearable disorder (Le Corbusier, 1946; 1957).

To give back life to cities made arid by modern urbanism, three types
of attitudes emerge. Firstly, one which is often put into practice for
instance in French new towns (Chatin, 1975) and which does not
question the theoretical foundations of functionalist urbanism, but
which seeks "an improvement by creating as dense an urban centre as
possible within the new towns (...) An accumulation of retail trade and
collective facilities are arranged around squares. But while squares
are rediscovering their traditional vocation as places for meeting and
meandering, they are nonetheless just one accessory among others"
(Favardin, 1982, p.76).

The second attitude is more critical of functionalist urbanism and
finds its expression in the desire to integrate recent squares into
the history of a given town (Krier, 1980).

Finally, the third attitude occurs in an already existing urban web,
often quite ancient, and involves a programme for the protection of
urban buildings and sites, based on values which were defined from the

XIXth century onwards by the Historical Monuments Service which, for example, was founded in France in 1830.

Restoration and protection concepts have, from the beginning, been a point for controversy (Parent, 1981) because very different answers can be given to the questions they raise at different levels. What makes a "historical landmark"? What building deserves to be restored and protected ? What kind of restoration is the most "authentic" one? Or the most "aesthetic" one? Some architects or art historians favour a strict fidelity to original designs regardless of the modern context of the building or place. Others plead in favour of an interpretation of the architectural, aesthetic or social history of the building, and for the choice of the time when the building was the most "beautiful" or "successful" etc... and technical issues make all answers the more complex.

Questions concerning the social stakes of restoration and protection are added to-day to this still on-going controversy. What is the social cost of protection measures for urban sites ? Who profits from them, and who suffers? What are its consequences for the modes of place appropriation? These are the questions which we would like to discuss in this chapter on the occasion of the study of the practices of three French public squares and a Swedish town square which have recently undergone measures for protection and which have also been reconverted into pedestrian areas.

To do this, we will take as a basis several empirical studies on squares undertaken by the author and the Psychology of Space Study Group in the course of the past twelve years (Decker, 1976; Korosec-Serfaty & Kaufmann, 1974; Korosec-Serfaty et al. 1976; Korosec-Serfaty, 1981; 1982; Korosec-Serfaty & Schall, 1983; Lévy, 1976; Tramoni, 1976). Our aim is neither to describe each of these empirical studies, nor to enter into a detailed account of their results. While each of them was designed to help us attain an understanding of the complexity of each case, we now wish to distance ourselves from the details of the studies, thus allowing us to articulate some of the thoughts they brought to our mind.

We thus offer a reflective piece on the cultural, social and psychological meaning of the preservation of urban places based on our interest for urban open spaces. This is why our intention is not only to compare the usage of these squares as they could be observed immediately before their transformation into pedestrian areas, and their present usage, but also to adopt a wider scope. Indeed, we would first of all like to make an historical detour for each of these squares and to bring out the continuities and discontinuities between the traditional practice of these squares and their current usage.

Secondly, we will discuss from a general point of view the themes of thought which stem from the protection of urban monuments and sites, so as to situate better the squares which form the object of our study into a given doctrine of protection. As a conclusion, we will propose an analysis of the impact of the protection of these sites on their usage and representation.

SQUARES IN STRASBOURG AND STORTORGET IN MALMO

PLACE DE LA CATHEDRALE

The Place de la Cathédrale (Cathedral Square) is the oldest square in town, just as the Cathedral is the oldest monument. Built on the site of a Roman sanctuary, it was destroyed and rebuilt several times. The present Cathedral corresponds to the reconstruction which was decided upon after a fire in 1176. Its building was continued until the XVIth century, the result being a gigantic and complex monument, which constitutes the main dimension of the spatial and architectural identity of the square, and is the symbol of the town (Photo 1). The half-timbered houses which are traditional in this eastern part of France called Alsace, date from the XVth, XVIth and XVIIth centuries and constitute the other fundamental dimension of this identity. They carry the date of construction or transformation and each one is designated by a precise name to this day. The facades are sculptured and carry the owner's initials, thus conveying the social identity of the dwellers. These houses were built and inhabited by traders and artisans. They are alongside XVIIIth century freestone houses with tall and narrow facades, leaving no room for modern buildings.

The Place de la Cathédrale is a "natural" square, stemming from the necessities of various aspects of Medieval every-day life. Up to the XVIIIth century, it was essentially a popular square where markets of all types were held, surrounded by shops and saddlers and second-hand clothes dealers. The Cathedral was a highly active place, where artisans and day labourers were engaged, lawyers gave consultations and the town's authorities gave their audiences. Leaning against the monument itself, there were stalls sheltering all sorts of artisans. Acrobats climbed up its towers and entertained the crowds with their performances. It was in front of the portal that the town's civic authorities were sworn in each year. In the XVIIIth century, the square begins to be transformed: bourgeois houses and shops disappear to make way for a large Jesuit college and an episcopal palace, which was to become for a time during the Revolution the municipality's head quarters. Thus the Place du Château (Château Square) was created and this closed the access to the river Ill (Figure 1). It was also during the revolutionary period that the representatives of the people gave the Cathedral the successive names of the Temple of Reason, the Temple of the Supreme Being, etc... by staging a number of celebrations. It was once again at stake during the wars in which France and Germany were opposed in 1870 and in 1914. In June 1940, Hitler with his suite of Nazi dignitaries took possession of it. In November 1944 the Division under Leclerc, who was at the head of the army which liberated Strasbourg from Nazi occupation, hoisted the French flag on its spire. Since then, we have been able to observe other symbolic gestures such as a red flag, then a black one, floating above the Cathedral during the months of student unrest in 1968, but these gestures were quickly dispatched through the intervention of the local authorities.

PHOTOGRAPH 1 The cathedral constitutes the main architectural landmark of Strasbourg

FIGURE 1

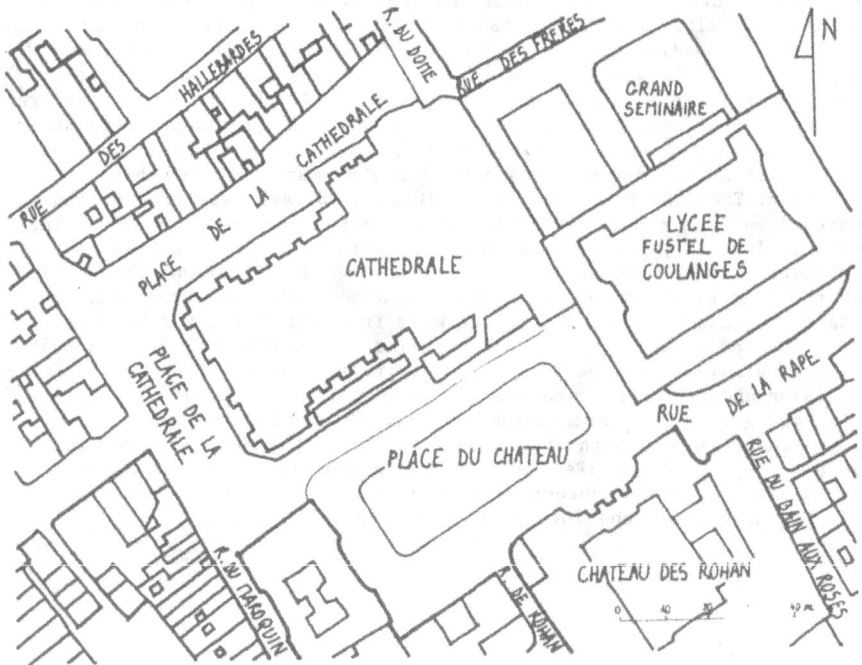

The Place de la Cathédrale is a pedestrian square to-day, integrated into a network of streets and squares (Figure 2) which are also pedestrian and cater to tourists, being lined with shops dealing in luxury items. However, its situation (Figure 1) is such that a large number of trades and services are accessible to the dwellers at a short distance. At the present time it is surrounded by twenty-two trades, of which only one (a chemist's) can be considered as being necessary to fulfill every day needs. All the others are connected with luxury (antique shops, restaurants, etc ...), with pleasure (souvenir shops, cafes), with the presence of the Cathedral (bookshop specializing in Christian literature) and with the preservation and commercial exploitation of regional traditions (a book-shop specializing in Alsatic studies, i.e. in studies concerned with the history, culture and traditions of Alsace, and another shop concerned with the culinary specilities and wines of the region) (Decker, 1976). The Place du Château which, in fact, completes the Place de la Cathédrale, is the home of a museum to which are added the various museums of the former episcopal palace called the Château des Rohan. Only one public service is present in the square: the post office.

The Cathedral is still a place of worship. And yet it is incessantly in the process of restoration, and all the city dwellers are familiar with the slow transference of the scaffolding along its facades throughout the years (Korosec-Serfaty and Schall, 1983). A few times in the year, prestigious concerts are held there. It is also haunted by a large number of tourists nearly the whole year round. As it dominates the town, the Cathedral can be seen from afar and the various developments in the town are supposed to ensure that this will always be the case. A few lines are enough to draw and represent it, and therefore to represent Strasbourg on official paper as well as for the packaging of food-stuffs, emblems and so forth ... (Figure 3).

The square as a whole constitutes the major centre of attraction for tourists in the town (Korosec-Serfaty and Schall, 1983). Decker's systematic study (1976) shows that its dwellers are very much attached to it, and are very proud of living "in the shadow of the Cathedral". They insist on the feeling of pleasure they get from looking at it through their windows. These dwellers belong to the middle-class, some belong to the upper middle-class but most of them are families of modest means living in run-down flats. On the whole, it is a very stable population, and its composition has hardly changed following its conversion into a pedestrian space. This can be explained by several reasons. On the one hand, some buildings whose facades are carefully restored shelter trades which attract a large number of tourists : pastry or souvenir shops, restaurants, etc... (Photo 2). On the other hand, a few buildings, while carefully preserved on the exterior, are relatively little modernized in the interior. Lastly, the rest of the buildings round the square have not been refurbished at all for decades (Photo 3). For the Place de la Cathédrale is still one of those historical urban neighbourhoods characterized by an aging population, due to an easy access to trades and services and to the existence of a large number of decaying dwellings. However, the rapid renovation of the other historical quarters of the town allows us to predict that its gentrification will not be delayed for too long.

FIGURE 3

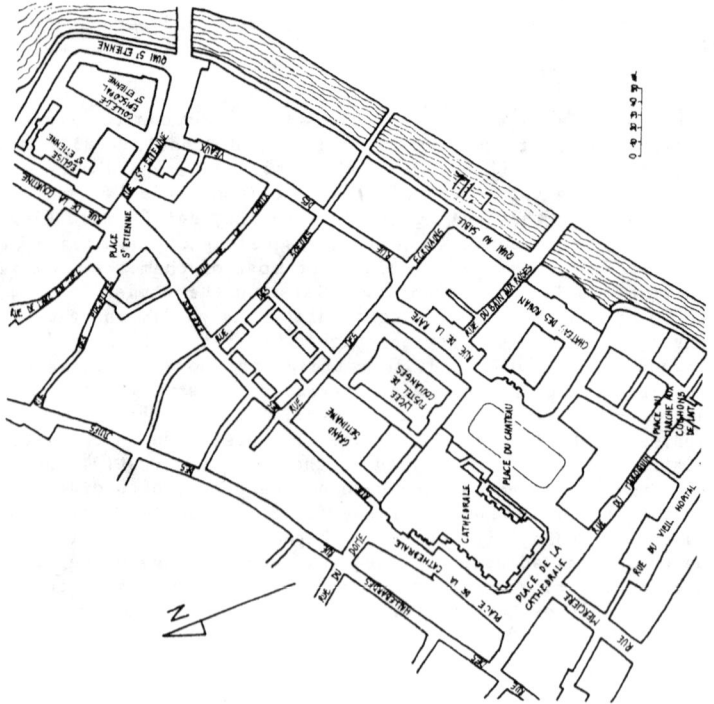

FIGURE 2

PHOTOGRAPH 2 Decaying building,
Place de la Cathedrale

FIGURE 4

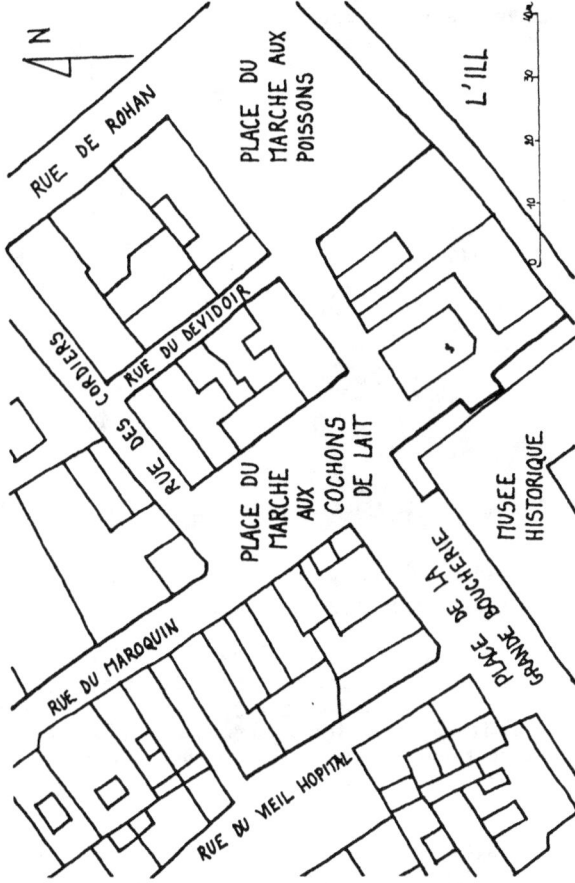

129

PHOTOGRAPH 3 Houses from the XVth, XVIth and XVIIth centuries, Place du Marche aux Couchons de Lait

PLACE DU MARCHE AUX COCHONS DE LAIT

The Place du Marché aux Cochons de lait (Suckling-pig Market Square) can also be regarded as a "natural" square, stemming from the economic necessities of the Middle Ages. Located on the banks of the Ill (Figure 4) it has been for a long time a place for storing wood used for construction, covered with warehouses, but it was also an artisans and commercial square where traders in wine, oil and cooked meats could be found.

It is considered to be one of the town's most beautiful sites by both tourists and Strasbourg dwellers, for its dimensions which make it an intimate space (Lévy, 1976) and for its surrounding houses with their sides covered by sculptured wood from the XVth, XVIth and XVIIth centuries (Photo 4). It has been pedestrian since 1973. In the years leading to the decision to forbid cars access, it was a highly congested square, very busy and, in as much as it is situated a few steps from the Place de la Cathédrale, was much visited by tourists. A co-existence of commercial activities linked with everyday life could be observed (grocer's, electrical goods shop, etc...) as could those linked with leisure, luxury items and tourism. Today, all commercial activity linked with fulfilling every-day needs has been replaced by traders in luxury items and restaurants which endeavour to preserve, or recreate, a traditional atmosphere.

When Lévy (1976) studied the square usage and representations, the dwellers of the square were still the ones who lived there before its transformation into a pedestrian area. They were mostly elderly people of modest means. Some years later another study, conducted by Delor (1982) on the relationships between streets' and squares' names and the dwellers' social identity showed that the new dwellers were much younger and better off. They said they chose to move into the small and recently renovated appartments because the name of the place, its scale, the traditional architecture, its location near the historic center of the town merged to remind them of life in a small village.

PLACE ST-ETIENNE

Equally close to the Place de la Cathedrale, the Place St-Etienne (St. Steven's Square) is in fact one of its means of access, as is the case with Place du Marchèaux Cochons de Lait. It's history is intimately bound with that of St-Etienne's Church which is, according to the legend, the town's oldest religious monument, founded in the VIIIth century (Seyboth, 1971). It has a troubled history, since it became a Protestant temple at the time of the Reform, became a church again aft erwards, then a synagogue, "national property" during the Revolution, etc... Since the XIXth century, the church, integrated with a highschool, has been Catholic.

These religious references constitute one of the identity dimensions of the square, which not only carries the name of a saint, but whose church, according to local tradition, was founded by the brother of Sainte Odile, who has given her name to a regional pilgrimage. All the neighbouring streets carry names which bring religious institutions to mind : rue des Freres (Friars Street), rue des Soeurs (Nuns Street), rue de la Croix (Cross Street) etc... (Figure 5). One of the buildin gs, notable for its size, character and history is the present Residence for Catholic Students, and was inhabited by families of noble birth from the time of its construction in the XVIth century, before becoming the seat of the Nobility Directoire for Basse-Alsace for almost a century. The square, as is the case with its neighbouring streets, has always been inhabited by religious personages and nobles, but also by artists, painters and engravers, who generally belonged to the aristocracy of artisans and were themselves renowned in their time.

Today, the Place St-Etienne is not reserved for pedestrians only. Seen as a "village square" by its dwellers, who idealise it and are very attracted to it (Tramoni, 1976) it is surrounded by XVIth and XVIIth century half-timbered houses and also by elegant-looking stone houses which make it one of the most picturesque squares in the town (Photo 4). It is congested by traffic and is a densely populated square. Up to a decade ago, it was surrounded by a number of artisans shops and small traders (bakers, grocers, a cobbler and a smith) as well as by the upper class artisan (a book-binder and a confectioner) who frequently inhabited the square.

This diversity is today challenged by the proliferation of restaurants and clothes shops and the arrival of a younger and socio-economically more homogenous population, belonging to the upper middle-classes. Numerous students and school children regularly use the square and create a certain animation as well as appropriation conflicts which are renewed daily (Tramoni, 1976).

131

FIGURE 5

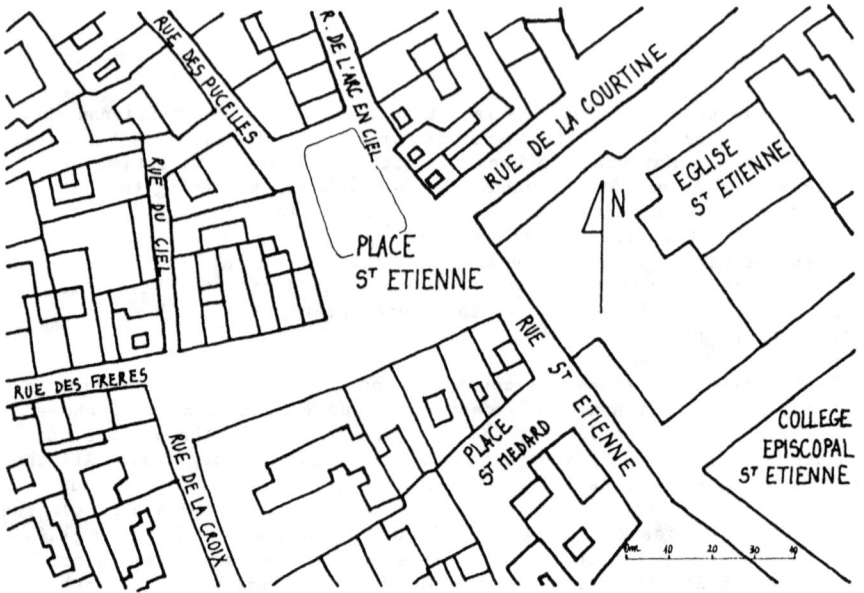

PHOTOGRAPH 4
Place St Etienne is surrounded by various examples of
Vernacular architecture as well as by examples of elite
architecture (`architecture savante`)

FIGURE 6

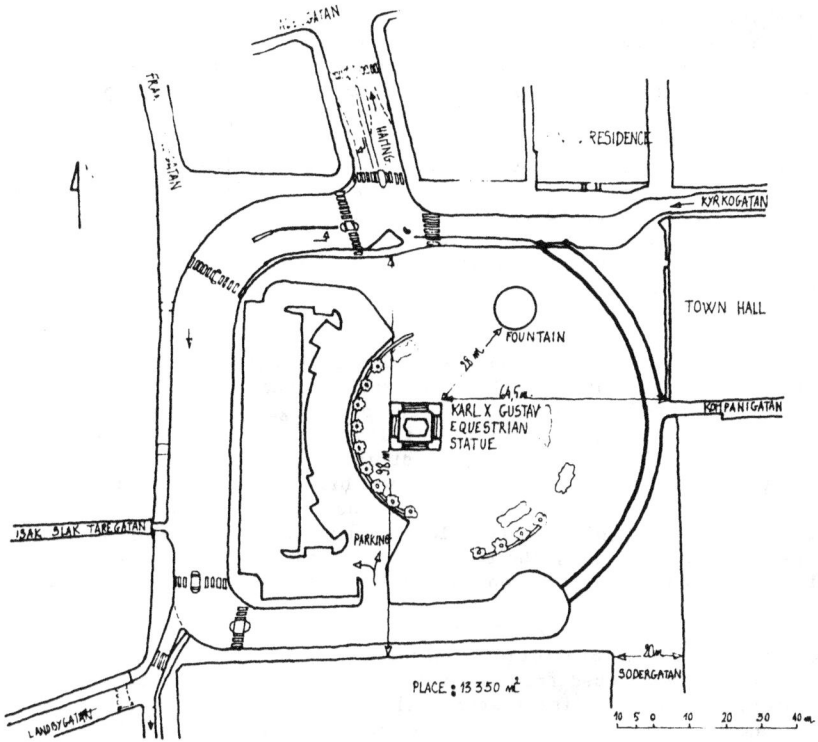

Map labels: FRANGGATAN, HAMNGATAN, RESIDENCE, KYRKOGATAN, TOWN HALL, KOPPANIGATAN, FOUNTAIN, KARL X GUSTAV EQUESTRIAN STATUE, 64.5 m, 25 m, 98 m, PARKING, ISAK SLAK TARGGATAN, 20 m, SODERGATAN, LANDSBYGATAN, PLACE : 13 350 m², 10 5 0 10 20 30 40 m

PHOTOGRAPH 5 Stortget from south-west angle

STORTORGET IN MALMO

The history of the city of Malmo dates back to the XIIIth century. Stortorget (Main Square) was created in 1534 in accordance with a deliberate wish to reinforce its commercial importance. We are therefore dealing with a square which stems from a voluntary policy of space-planning, which is medieval in its conception of a mul tifunctional central square, located away from large traffic flows. However, it is also representative of the spirit of the Renaissance in that it had to constitute an architectural whole. Its location near the town's harbour, whose commercial exchanges focussed on its one true rival, Copenhagen, was decided upon according to an intention to create a new dynamism in the trading routes. From the moment of its creation, it was a square for cottage industry and for both great and small trade.

The affirmation of the square's social and functional identity was rapidly translated into architectural terms since the mayor who inspired the dynamism essential to the projet gained an authorization from the king to demolish certain buildings, which occupied the square's future territory. He also contributed to the financing of the future Town Hall from his own pocket, and his own house, built in 1525, is only separated from the Town Hall by the breadth of the square itself. The building of beautiful-looking houses was encouraged by a system of tax exemption, the existence of a party wall between buildings and an imposition on the building material used and on the layout of the facades.

From the beginning Stortorget was conceived as a square whose monumentality developed from the relationship between its considerable dimensions (Figure 6), its status within the town, its location, the nature and architectural styles of the surrounding buildings (Mogensen in Korosec-Serfaty, 1982) and the ornamentation efforts which were concentrated upon it. The square underwent regular face-lifts and in the XVIIIth century many of the surrounding private houses were grand enough to be called "palaces" by contemporary observers. It acquired the architectural identity which we know today with its often massive and highly decorated houses and the mounted statue of King Charles X Gustav at the turn of the century (Astrand in Korosec-Serfaty, 1982). The statue was installed at the initiative of the town's notable persons, traders and local nobility. A fountain was also installed in 1964. It is the final piece of the principle elements of the square's ornamentation, whereas the decision taken in 1978 to make it into a pedestrian area gives it its current general appearance (Photo 5).

The square is surrounded by buildings whose symbolic value is undeniable, including the Swedish king's residence when he sojourns in the town, the house of the major who was in charge of its creation, and the Town Hall. This latter held for a long time, according to demand, popular entertainments, commercial transactions, meetings of the local authorities and a tavern. Opposite, benches and a pillory were installed for carrying out public punishments. Lastly, the square was a place for elections, demonstrations of power put on by the authorities or for the people in revolt (Henje-Sjoholm in Korosec-Serfaty, 1982).

Today, only seven private persons own buildings in the square, out of a total of twenty-one buildings. At the turn of the century, thirteen of these had been built and were owned by private persons. Five banks were among the list of builders, whereas today we can count seven bank-owned buildings. One insurance company was listed among the builders, whereas four of them are now owners. In the same way, there are now three offficial buildings, whereas there were only two originally. Out of thirty-eight activities represented on the ground floors of the buildings, ten are activities which ar directly associated with luxury: Oriental carpet shops, etc...

YESTERDAY AND TODAY: A COMPARISON OF SQUARE USAGE

MULTIFUNCTIONALITY AND ENCOUNTER

The squares which form our sample have a long history. In two cases this history would seem to be dominated by the monumentality of a building (Place de la Cathèdrale) or the architectural whole which constitutes the square (Stortorget). However, an examination of their traditional practices shows that this monumentality has in no way prevented a considerable social effervescence, for example the gathering of crowds for the acting out of civil and everyday activities and entertainment. In both cases, religious, civil and military powers as well as the representatives of economic powers remain unisolated spatially. On the perimeter of Place St-Etienne the alternation of artisan and commercial houses, of a mansion and a private school, reveals the same state of mind, which not only accepts the encountering of social groups, but also turns its multifunctionality into a quality necessary to collective territory.

Finally, even in the case of the Place du Marchè aux Cochons de Lait, which seems in no way an emblematic space, we find this spatial proximity between the people or institutions who hold a part of the political, religious or economic power and the most down-trodden groups of city dwellers. In the case of the Place de la Cathèdrale, which has ever been a space where the symbols of different powers have been united and where the different forms of popular and elite cultures coexist, this proximity is simply more striking. But the Place du Marchè aux Cochons de Lait is nevertheless outstanding for these two characteristics, since it holds several corporations' headquarters, acts as a refuge for the homeless, etc...

These squares all illustrate the necessity for the poorest poeple, who were the most numerous until quite recently, to work outdoors and this imposed, up to a certain degree, a diverse usage of exterior spaces and led to similar animation in towns situated in very different climates, as is the case here (Korosec-Serfaty, 1986 a). They are all squares for gatherings, contrary to the royal squares of the XVIIIth century, for example, which are both meant to be emblematic and governed by spatial segregation intentions leading in this way to ceremonial and leisure activities (Lavedan, 1960; Leroy-Ladurie and Quilliet, 1981).

In Strasbourg, as in Malmo, our sample squares were to remain active for a long period, in spite of the gradual disappearance of the small

street trades (Massin, 1978) and the progressive restriction of public
sociability and play activities into interior or specialized spaces
which affects the XIXth century. Opera Houses, cafés, parks are designed to offer well defined entertainments, and to ensure a new kind of
public life (Korosec-Serfaty, 1986 b). The XXth century, with motorists and their usage of squares was literally to asphixiate them.
Decker's study (1976) undertaken before Place de la Cathedrale was
transformed into a pedestrian area, underlines the extent of the
conflicts between pedestrians and motorists. However, it should be
emphasized that this state of affairs guaranteed the installation of
various trades and the cohabitation of dwellers belonging to different
socio-economic groups.

From a historical point of view therefore, we see a slow "emptying"
process in these squares, analogous to the one observed in streets
(Korosec-Serfaty, 1985), but it is their transformation into
pedestrian areas which initiates the radical change of the
inhabitants' usage and representations of them. Indeed, for the first
time, their role is not linked with the needs of everyday life, nor to
the expresssion of personal power nor even directly to leisure
activities. Their role now is essentially to materialize the idea of
common patrimony and to reify the values connected to this through
architectural objects or settings. For the very idea of patrimony
implies the recognition of the objects as being precious and therefore
as being worthy of appropriation. The new symbolic value of these
places was translated into a financial value, creating a new housing
market, accessible to another socio-economic group, and which obeyed
only the rules of property speculation. Indeed, these speculations have
always existed. The new factor is that today they are hindered by
local regulations only, issued by a single authority, while for a long
time the power of town administration was held by a number of groups,
whose interests were often contradictory. The conflicts between
groups holding small pieces of power have for centuries upheld areas
of liberty for the town dwellers against all the odds (Barel, 1975;
Leguay, 1984). This liberty has been widely taken advantage of, in
particular when collective appropriation of urban open spaces was
concerned, in order to satisfy the needs of day-to-day living and to
establish the identity of city communities.

PLACE SPECIALIZATION AND DOMINANT PRACTICES

THE RHYTHM OF USAGES

With the exception of Place St-Etienne, all these squares now have a
Winter aspect which contrasts sharply with their Summer aspect, taking
into account the important role played by tourism. In the same way,
the daily rhythm of its usages is closely related to the working hours
of the cafés, restaurants and luxury goods shops. As always, and for
the same reason, the animation is located outside during the day and
inside at night, though to a lesser extent. Only the usage rhythm of
Place St-Etienne is based principally on school hours and the student
calendar during the day, and on the restaurant goers and dwellers at
night.

THE PRACTICES

The dominant practices in the squares are essentially crossing it,
lingering in it (sitting on a bench, or outside a café, etc...),
consumer activities (buying an object, a post-card, etc...), aesthetic
consumption (looking at facades, taking photographs) and play
activities (watching a fire-eater, playing guitar, etc...). These are
marked to a greater or lesser extent according to the square. Play
activities are rare everywhere except in Place de la Cathédrale, where
jugglers and acrobats can be seen throughout the Summer season.
Crossing is the dominant function of Stortorget, which is also during
the short summer season a lingering space. Consumer activities are
especially intense in Place de la Cathédrale and Place du Marché aux
Cochons de Lait, which are similarly the squares which evoke the
highest rate of aesthetic consumption.

PHOTOGRAPH 6 Aesthetic and goods consumption, Place de la
Cathedrale

In all of these places, work is exclusively represented by commercial activities, based on one means of exchange, which allows complete anonymity, detachment and the "objectivity" of the transaction (Simmel, 1971). On the other hand, the play activities are reduced to watching others (passers by or peddlers) while keeping one's distance. They are based on everyone's personal consent to participate in or to withdraw from activities which are mainly aimed at providing some kind of entertainment, some kind of pleasure. This strongly contrasts with the shared games and play which, in the past, were imposed by either the religious calendar, the political power, the civil one or simply by bad weather conditions which made people stop all work (Verdon, 1980). Such games and play implied an active participation of all group members, and an obligation to take part in them. The leisurely participation we observe now is centered on the individual, and comes from him or her, precisely because leisure time itself is considered to be not only a right (Dumazedier, 1962) but some kind of private property.

In other words, although they imply several modalities of space appropriation, the dominant practices are more passive than active. We shall see that this fact has a direct influence on the image the dwellers have of "their" square (Decker, 1976; Delor, 1982; Lèvy, 1976; Tramoni, 1976).

CATEGORIES OF USERS

The users of all the squares belong to every age category. However, it is predominantly old people who linger in Stortorget. They come to sit in the sun for a time, while small children and adolescents are largely absent. Place de la Cathèdrale and Place du Marché aux Cochons de Lait are visited by people of all ages, with young children being very rare. Considered from this angle, Place St-Etienne is the only square which has a balanced representation of the different age categories. Today, there is no notable frequency in the squares of users belonging to the most underprivileged socio-economic categories, altho ugh a few scarce vagrants can be seen from time to time in all of them. Again, this contrasts with what the history of streets and squares tells us about public life. Children of all ages used to be outdoors, as well as women and men, at all hours of the day (Aris, 1979; Farge, 1979; 1986) while we observe today a clear association between indoor places, children and women.

THE INTERACTIONS BETWEEN THE DWELLERS OF THE SQUARES

The dwellers of Place de la Cathèdrale and Place du Marché aux Cochons de Lait say quite simply that "everyone keeps to him or herself". However, in two cases (Stortorget and Place St-Etienne) one neighbourhood association exists and shows an obvious desire to appropriate the squares. They expect the municipality to take their ideas and existence into account. However, even in the case of Place St-Etienne, we witness a contradictory discourse: the majority of the dwellers touch on the "village" quality of the square, and say that "everyone knows each other". But once under analysis, this expression brings us to "nodding" and "knowing by sight" relationships only.

138

However, this contradiction between the discourse and the reality is, on the psychological level, only apparent. For what is witnessed in all cases is the same idealization of the "village life", seen as implying close relationships between the dwellers and the existence of a network of mutual help and care, that can be observed in numerous studies on the social life of urban neighbourhoods (Rosenberg, 1980).

ROLE AND DIMENSIONS OF THE IMAGE OF THE SQUARES

BEAUTIFUL "OLD" SQUARES

With the exception of Stortorget which is considered to be both immense and deserted, the other squares are thought to be beautiful because of their small dimensions, which give the impression of being intimate, and yet, at the same time, open. Their beauty (and in the case of Stortorget their grandeur) is associated with the traditional styles of the surrounding buildings, which are said to incite contemplation. We have stressed that this aesthetic pleasure takes on a particular form in the case of the Cathedral, with dwellers living in the belief that to see it from their windows constitutes a unique privilege. All the dwellers see the care for the facades as a positive action which elevates their own dignity as town and square dwellers.

The squares are also thought to be beautiful on account of their being "historic". The dwellers lend a wide, even vague meaning to this term, by which they mean "old". They do not refer to notable events or great facts which they know have taken place in these squares, but to the fact that they have witnessed a collective past.

This past does not correspond to History as defined by historians, but to a positive image of good old times whose main characteristic is that it constitutes a common heritage from which everyone can draw in his own way, i.e. a patrimony. As such, it allows reference to origins (Jackson, 1980). Because it is a simplified representation it reinforces a collective identity, in this case a regional identity which is not fed with major historical and verifiable events, but with general images of earlier ways of life, or, to use Jackson's terms, of a "vernacular past" (p. 94).

EMBLEMATIC SQUARES

For this reason, we can say it is not this or that old house, or even for instance the Cathedral which is itself a monument in the eyes of the dwellers and visitors, but the squares themselves as places rather than as architectural settings. Indeed, it is what remains of the meaning of the past which gives special and similar character to the way people look at very different objects, like the houses of ordinary men of the "olden days" and "monuments" in the accepted meaning of this term. Therefore, today, the role of these squares is essentially emblematic, for they represent a given vision of a collective identity. Historically, they were appropriated through daily uses, revolts and celebrations, while today they are appropriated through the collective internalization of their meaning as monuments.

All monuments are, by definition we could say, a reminder of something important to a group of men: faith, the adulation of a leader, a victorious war, etc... In this way, they are both linked to an expres- sion of what is sacred, and are also objects which are related to memory, even if the forms of this relationship differ during the course of history and according to culture. The monument is didactic in the case of Medieval and Renaissance churches. It incites respect or loyalty which was the King's due in the Classical period, and is a means of showing the advent of a new era during the revolutionary periods. It may be an object devoid of exceptionally aesthetic qualities, or perhaps we should say that with each monument, its beauty represents an additional consideration, even if, in this as in all other cases, beauty adds another dimension and gives an individual meaning to the object. Thus, the "Little Mermaid" of Copenhagen is a mo nument in that it is the symbol of the town, and most certainly forms part of its identity. Moreover, this example shows that the size of a monument does not necessarily have to be exceptional, even if, once more, large dimensions can directly influence one's experience. Because of its position at the crossroads of the memory, the symbolic and the sacred, a monument implies an ability to appropriate its message, or its meaning. The history of places of collective vocation such as palaces, churches, cathedrals, town halls etc... shows that this ability was shared up to a moment which is generally situated as being towards the second half of the XIXth century (Goetz, 1985; Souchal, 1985). This was the period of great transformations, marked by the acceleration of urbanization and industrialization, when architecture was integrated with functionalist needs, even if it seems extraordinary to our eyes to consider the stations, post offices and Town Halls of this period as being functional (Jackson, 1980).

The loss of this common understanding of the meaning of monuments leave a space for interpretation open to individuals or sub-groups. This leads to controversy and conflicts to which notable persons and economic, religious or political leaders are no longer the only ones to take part. The man in the street also plays his part, through, for example, the Press etc... The formulation of contradictory inter- pretations on the political meaning of a single aesthetic option, as was for instance the case for the monument erected to the memory of soldiers lost in Vietnam (Howett, 1985) shows that agreement is reached only on the notion that a monument is always full of meaning and that it is inside the space left for interpretation that confrontation occurs.

At the same time as the codes for reading monuments become weaker, the traditional functions of monuments are no longer necessarily fulfilled. Sites such as a battle field or statues erected in the name of a category of citizens, as with the Unknown Soldier, are designated as such. We propose the notion of the museumization of public squares, or better still, of urban public places as part of the same phenomenon, and of their emblematic role as a powerful means to internalize an image of a community's past ways of life, whatever the flaws of this image: oversimplification of community bonds, vagueness, romanticism, etc...

We would like to illustrate now some possible configurations of the

dimensions of squares as muzeumized places and thus be led to offer a
better understanding of this concept.

MUSEUMIZATION AND DISENFRANCHISEMENT

PLACE ST-ETIENNE

The dwellers of Place St-Etienne have chosen to live in this square,
sometimes after a few years of waiting, in order to live in an old
neighbourhood. By "neighbourhood" they mean an urban territory with a
strong social and architectural identity, to which the inhabitants are
attached, and where it is possible to form interpersonal links. The
meaning they give to this word covers parts of its definition by
sociologists who see in the neighbourhood a geographical and emotional
reality (Bell and Boat, 1957; Keller, 1968; Metton, 1980). They
predominantly belong to the professions, are architects, students,
teachers, etc... and as such contribute to the evolution of values
connected with urban ways of life.

They regret the departure of the dwellers they have replaced and the
vanishing of small shops that could be visited daily. This is why they
idealize the cake-shop, the only shop on the square they can use
daily, as being in a way the only "natural" support of the
neighbourhood life, which they say is all they could wish for. For
this same reason, they say they tolerate "their" tramps better than
the ones who frequent other squares.

Although pedestrianization would be a relief because of the endemic
illegal parking and the traffic congestion in the square, they are
afraid of it. A pedestrian area attracts tourists who would recaste
their dwellers as theatrical extras against the scenery of an
operetta. Their fear is to see the square rooted in an image, which
would in no way be contradicted by the way in which it would be used
by both the dwellers and passers-by. They refuse the idea that the
value of this square as a fixed point for a collective identity should
be pushed to its limit, in other words, they refuse its complete
museumization and their disenfranchisement. It is because of this fear
that they organize various gatherings of the dwellers. They thus try
to resist the risk they perceive, to act on the vision they have of the
square as a possible convivial place to live in, and to change its
present social reality.

In this case, we observe on the part of the dwellers an understanding
of the environmental messages imparted by preservation in general, and
by preservation associated with pedestrianization in particular. The
risks are those of all official recognitions, in this case it is the
overemphasis of this legitimation of the "nobility" of the place.
Preservation and the ensuing gentrification are major factors in the
museumization process, which nevertheless remains incomplete as long
as the dwellers actively appropriate the place. Through such an
appropriation the dwellers at once act on their own image of the place
to make it real, prevent the possible transformation of a protected
place into a sacred area, and, through the control they gain of the
place they protect their own privileges.

PLACE DU MARCHE AUX COCHONS DE LAIT

It is a completely different case for the inhabitants of Place du
Marché aux Cochons de Lait, who tell us on the contrary that the
presence of tourists should enforce the eviction of the vagabonds and
youths who linger in the square as they alter its "good image". In
other words, they have internalized the sacred dimension which all
museumization implies, and they would like the facade to be devoid of
any flaws. This type of attitude confirms the expropriation of the
inhabitants in favour of the tourists. It is a consented disenfranchisement by a population of more modest means and who didn't chose to
live there following its transformation into a pedestrian area, but
who have been there for a long time. They have made facadism their
own, as is conveyed by protection measures.

This is particularly noticeable on an aesthetic level : the
municipality had a fake well looking like a typical Alsace traditional
well, installed at the centre of the square (Photo 7). Thus, the
elements of the image of an "old traditional and picturesque Alsace
square" are there : the halftimbered houses, the recently laid out
paving stones, the well. The "old" inhabitants think this last object
fits in the square, because it really tells one where one is. On the
other hand, they say the "modern" concrete tubs of flowers should be
removed, for these ornamental elements don't strictly belong to the
"traditional" catalogue, which is precisely the catalogue of popular
post-cards. However, the "new" inhabitants, like the dwellers of Place
St-Etienne who also made comments on this well, say it is "non authentic" since the square never had a well throughout its history. They
insist that preservation should "respect the true spirit of the past".
We thus witness two kinds of social use of the past (Dubost, 1982) and
two conceptions of the material means which should be used to convey
the complex interdependance between sense of place, community identity
and the sense of a shared history.

STORTORGET

This main square is also, up to a point, an important feature of the
good image of Malmo (Korosec-Serfaty, 1982). It features a very ordinary kiosk (Photo 8) where drinks and sandwiches are sold. During the
interviews, the inhabitants of Malmo made negative aesthetic and social
value judgments about it. They also say that the square should be more
lively and that the interactions between users should be much more
frequent. From the phothographic survey it transpired that the kiosk
was one of the most active zones in the square and, from observation of
users' routes and of social interactions, one of the most structuring
areas as well. What is rejected therefore, on the level of
representations, is the contrast between the now revered historical
character of this symbol-square and the banality of the kiosk where
people buy a type of food perceived as popular. We are thus confronted
by what people say and what we observe : if the kiosk represen ts, on
the aesthetic level, "an error of taste", yet, it creates precisely
the kind of liveliness the users say should take place in the square.
This rejection of any "wrong note" is due to the fact that all
museumization puts the museumized object at a distance from its
potential user and creates in the latter an essentially contemplative

142

behaviour, which quite naturally evolves towards a demand for a logical attitude : the contemplated object (to which one no longer relates through the gestures of daily life and necessities) must be perfect, or integrated in a flawless whole, i.e. perfect because it is untouchable and untouched.

PHOTOGRAPH 7 Fake well, Place du Marche aux Couchons de Lait

PHOTOGRAPH 8 Food kiosk on a grand scale

CONCLUSION

In the case of Strasbourg as well as in Malmo, we have a fair amount of
evidence on the role played by local authorities and notables in the
final decision to protect the squares. However, a policy, be it of
historic preservation, is not a phenomenon which appears ex-nihilo. It
is integrated in the dynamics of values, ideas and attitudes specific
to a given culture and time. In the 50's and 60's, the Strasbourg
political leaders belonged to the same political trend which is in
administration today. As a matter of fact, the town has had the same
Mayor for the last quarter of the century. Fifteen or ten years ago,
his administration agreed to have high rise buildings built and old
quarters and structures torn down, while such decisions would be taken
with more hesitancy today. The political world generally assimilates
with some delay ideas which are articulated and spread by other people
than political leaders. Therefore we should rather reflect on the
cultural context which gave birth to the values connected with historic preservation. We suggest an interpretation in terms of power
diffusion of class-related values.

Historically, the idea of preservation was spread by Art historians.
This fact has two implications. One is that preservation of architectural objects or urban sites does not include the people who use
them. Therefore it contains always the temptation and risk to opt for
facadism, turning buildings and settings into sentimental objects
rather than into places for human action and for the dynamism of
social life. The other risk is to make the material environment seem
sacred and this means, one could say by nature, that the various modes
of space appropriation are drastically curtailed. The official
recognition of the value of given places should not mean that they
become fetishes, i.e. that the object is more valued that the actions
and human relationships of which it is only one aspect, at best a
support (Boesh, 1980) and a provisional materialization in a complex
and continuous dynamism (Marx, 1934). The historical landmarks must
be protected against passing times, fashions and individual whims. But
in order not to become the symbol of the "burden of the past" (Ford,
1984), their protection should benefit from a more comprehensive
approach to the various issues raised: profits and inconveniences,
control of real estate speculation, the understanding of conflicting
interests and of the sociological spectrum of the dwellers and users
of the areas are all to be preserved, as well as the possible social
consequences of a flexible application of a historic preservation
policy.

Who might benefit from the preservation of an urban neighbourhood?
Who might be disenfranchised as a result of such an endeavor ? Such
questions should be clearly addressed, since all social groups do not
share the same values. Specialists of popular culture often stress
that the origins of many of its aspects are to be found in elite
culture (Julliard, 1985). The existence of a popular set of values
that evolves in close relation to the diffusion of elite ones implies
that different representations and uses of space exist. Appleyard
(1973) and Goodchild (1974) have found, for example, that working-class
urban residents have function-oriented images of places, while middle-
class residents pay more attention to aesthetic and historical factors.
Such factors contribute to the formation of a sentiment and symbolism

which play a major role in middle-class' housing choices, and thus can be considered as ecological variables (Firey, 1979).

Therefore, the second implication is that the awareness of the aesthetic or historic value of objects and sites, as well as of art objects, paintings and sculpture, etc... is not equally spread among all members of a given society. It is typically class-associated (Sandstrom, 1977; Bourdieu, 1979). In this case, it is a haute bourgeoisie view of the world (Aris, 1979). When, in the XIXth century, historic preservation is formally organized, it was connected to issues like national or regional identities, national pride, as much as to certain ideas about Art, Beauty, and a vision of urban civilization.

Ideas about the preservation of monuments or historic landmarks are first printed in scholarly journals read by small circles of archaeologists and architects before being spread in the society at large. Nature conservation was typically an elite initiative and action (Zube, 1975; 1982). Elite theories on the ideal social use of urban open spaces oriented the design of XIXth and XXth centuries parks (Baillon, 1975; Cranz, 1982) in spite of evidence that these theories do not necessarily coincide with popular environmental attitudes and use (Foresta, 1980).

All the squares under consideration here have been protected according to an elite conception of historic urban centers. They are also used according to middle-class conceptions of public sociability. We have stressed earlier that the bulk of activities which can be observed is oriented towards leisure and consumption, which are the two major dimensions of a middle-class image of public life in urban open spaces, and in squares in particular (Korosec-Serfaty, 1985 a; 1985 b) as they allow the users to live the illusion of peaceful coexistence between all social groups. Museumized places are, par excellence, the setting s for such seemingly non conflicting coexistence of people. To conclude, we suggest that the members of the same social class first spread the modern conceptions of architecture and urban planning, then experience disenchantment born from these ideas and their popular rejection, and finally gave a new and stronger impulse to the spreading of historic preservation ideas.

The local political leaders, who often belong to the same social class, only then integrate them to their action. Thus we observe the following general proces:

1. diffusion of values;

2. actualization of values through actual historic preservation decisions;

3. emergence of new environmental "status" and "messages" of protected places, i.e. implications for use, assertion of new aesthetic codes and translation of the "value" of the place to financial standards;

4. internalization by the dwellers of an idealized image of the past;

5. rejection of elements (be they architectural, ornamental objects or behaviours) incongruent with those images.

Finally, a closer analysis has shown that the social class which articulate and spreads the preservation ideas is the one which has the ability to resist their implications, while it is an aged and modest population who not only must leave the place for newcomers but also internalizes without criticism the values conveyed by the museumization. Therefore, they are the only deprived group of dwellers, and their only compensation is in the fact that they participate to the glorification of their vernacular past, their collective past as ordinary people and not the past represented by heroes.

Bibliography

Aris, P., (1979), "L'enfant et la rue : de la ville l'anti-ville", Urbi, II.

Anderson, S., (1978), On streets, M.I.T. Press.

Appleyard, D., (1973), "Notes on Urban Perception and Knowledge", in Downs, R. M., and Stea, D., (eds.), Image and Environment: Cognitive Mapping and Spatial Behavior, Aldine, Chicago.

Appleyard, D., (1975), "Streets : Dead or Alive ?", New Society, July 3.

Appleyard, D., (1981), Livable Streets, University of California Press, Berkeley.

Baillon, R., (1975), "La frequentation des forēts", Revue forestire francaise, Vol. 2. March - April.

Barel, Y., (1975), La ville médiévale, Presses Universitaires de Grenoble, Grenoble.

Bell, W., and Boat, M. T., (1957) "Urban Neighborhoods and Informal Social Relations", American Journal of Sociology, 62, 4.

Boesh, E. E., (1980), "Action et objet. Deux sources de l'identité du moi" inTap, P, (ed.), Identité individuelle et personnalisation, Privat, Toulouse.

Bourdieu, P., (1979), La distinction. Critique sociale du jugement, Editions de Minuit, Paris.

Chatin, C., (1975), Neuf villes nouvelles. Une expérience francaise d'Urbanisme, Dunod, Paris.

Cranz, G., (1982), The Politics of Park Design, M.I.T. Press, Cambridge, Mass.

Decker, S., (1976), Etude psychosociologique d'une place publique: La Place de la Cathédrale a Strasbourg, Unpublished M.A. Thesis, Strasbourg.

Delor, P., (1982), Les noms de rues, Unpublished M.A. Thesis, Strasbourg.

Dubost, F., (1982), "L'usage social du passé. Les maisons anciennes dans un village beaujolais", Ethnologie Francaise, XII, I.

Dumazedier, J., (1962), Vers une civilisation du loisir?, Seuil, Paris.

Favardin, P., (1982), "La relecture de la place des années 1920-1950", Monuments Historiques, March-April, 120.

Firey, W., (1979), "Sentiment and Symbolism as Ecological Variables", American Sociological Review.

Ford, L. R., (1984), "The Burden of the Past. Rethinking Historic Preservation", Landscape, Vol. 28, 1.

Foresta, R. A., (1980), "Comment: Elite Values, Popular Values and Open Space Policy", American Planning Association Journal, October.

Goetz, G., (1985), "Architecture, urbanisme et sculpture monumentale", Monuments Historiques, April-May, 138.

Goodchild, B., (1974), "Class differences in Environmental Perception", Urban Studies, 11.

Howett, C. M., (1985), "The Vietnam Veterans Memorial. Public Art and Politics", Landscape, Vol. 28, 2.

Jackson, J. B., (1980), The Necessity for Ruins, and Other Topics, University of Massachussets Press, Amherst.

Jacobs, J., (1961), The Death and Life of Great American Cities, Random House, New York.

Keller, S., (1968), The Urban Neighborhood: A Sociological Perspective, Random House, New York.

Korosec-Serfaty, P., (1981), Images de Places, Vol. 1: Etude des representations des formes, fonctions, pratiques et modes de la sociabilité des places publiques. Ministry of Environment, Paris.

Korosec-Serfaty, P., (1982), The Main Square. Functions and Daily Uses of Stortorget, Malmo, Aris Nova Series 1, University of Lund Press, Lund.

Korosec-Serfaty, P., and Schall, D., (1983), Images de Places, Vol. 2: Contribution de la presse regionale à la formation des représentations des places publiques. Le cas strasbourgeois. Maison des Sciences de l'Homme, Strasbourg.

Korosec-Serfaty, P., (1985), Du dehors vers le dedans. Une approche dialectique de l'experience et des pratiques des espaces publics urbains et de la maison. Unpublished Doctorate dissertation. University René Descartes-Sorbonne, Paris.

Korosec-Serfaty, P., (1986 a), "Uses and Representations of Urban Open Spaces. A Cross-cultural Approach" in Goodey, Brian and Del Rio, Vincente ,Designing Cities : International Case Studies of Urban Design Practice, Pergamon Press, Oxford, forthcoming.

Korosec-Serfaty, P., (1986 b), "Offentliche Platze", in Graumann, C., Kruse, L, and Lanterman, E., Okopsychologie: Ein Handbuch in Schlusselbegriffen U, Urban and Schwarzenberg, Munich.

Krier, R., (1980), L'espace de la ville. Theorie et pratique, Archives d'Architecture Moderne, Bruxelles.

Lavedan, P., (1960), Les villes franaises, Metiers Graphiques, Paris.

Le Corbusier (1946), Manire de penser l'urbanisme, Deno 1/Gonthier, Paris.

Le Corbusier (1957), La Charte d'Athnes, Editions de Minuit, Paris.

Leguay, J. P. (1984) La rue au Moyen Age, Ouest-France Universit Rennes.

Leroy-Ladurie, E., and Quilliet, B., (1981), "Baroque et Lumires" in Georges Duby (ed.), Histoire de la France Urbaine, Vol. 3, Seuil, Paris.

Lévy, M., (1976), Places publiques et appropriation par le regard, Unpublished M.A. Thesis, Strasbourg.

Marx, C., (1934), Morceaux choisis, Gallimard, Paris.

Massin, (1978), Les cris de la ville, Gallimard, Paris.

Metton, A., (1980), Le commerce et la ville en banlieue parisienne. Published by the author: 7, Residence Marceau Normandie, 92400 Courbevoie, France.

Parent, M., (1981), "Invention, theorie et equivoque de la restauration", Monuments Historiques, 112

Rosenberg, S., (1980) "Vivre dans son quartier ... quand même", Les Annales de la Recherche Urbaine, 9.

Rudofsky, B., (1969), Streets for People, Doubleday, Garden City, New York.

Sandstrom, S., (1977), A Common Taste in Art. An experimental Attempt. Aris, University of Lund Press, Lund.

Seyboth, A., (1971), Strasbourg historique et pittoresque, Editions des Dernires Nouvelles d'Alsace, Strasbourg.

Simmel, G., (1971), On Individuality and Social Forms, Levine D.N. ed. The University of Chicago Press, Chicago.

Souchal, F., (1985), "La sculpture monumentale", Monuments Historiques, April-May, 138.

Tramoni, M. L., (1976), L'appropriation d'un espace public: La place St-Etienne a Strasbourg, Unpublished M.A. Thesis, Strasbourg.

Verdon, J., (1980) Les loisirs au Moyen-Age, Tallandier, Paris.

Whyte, H. W., (1980), The Social Life of Small Urban Spaces, The Conservation Foundation, Washington, D.C.

Zube, E., Brush, R. O., Fabos, J. G., (eds.), (1975), Values, perceptions and resources, Dowden, Hutchinson and Ross, Stroudsburg, Penn.

Zube, E., (1982), "Changing Views of the Landscape: Policy and Research". Paper presented at the Fith Annual Symposium on Aplied Behavioral Science, Virginia Polytechnic Institute and Sate University.

10. Social architecture — William Morris our contemporary

ALAN LIPMAN and HOWARD HARRIS

The idea of innocence faces two ways. By refusing to enter a
conspiracy, one remains innocent of that conspiracy. But to
remain innocent may also be to remain ignorant. The issue is
not between innocence and knowledge (or between the natural
and the cultural) but between a total approach to art which
attempts to relate it to every aspect of experience and the
esoteric approach of a few specialised experts who are the
clerks of the nostalgia of a ruling class in decline ...
The real question is: to whom does the meaning of the art
of the past properly belong? To those who can apply it to
their own lives, or to a cultural hierarchy of relic
specialists?   (Berger, 1972, p.32)

I have spoken of the popular arts, but they might all be
summed up in that one word Architecture; they are all parts
of that great whole ... mutually helpful and harmoniously
subordinated one to another ... [Architecture is] above all
an art of association ... the true democratic art, the child
of the man-inhabited earth, the expression of the life of
man thereon ... that which springs direct from popular
impulse, from the partnership of all men ... of each one of
us, who must keep watch and ward over the fairness of the
earth ... Unless you are resolved to have good and rational
architecture, it is, once again, useless your thinking about
art at all.   (Morris in Meier, 1978, pp.399-401)

Why William Morris? Why him in the 1980's - in the tide, in the flood
of Post-Modern consumerism; in the decade of space shuttles, of

microchips, of Hi-Tech buildings? Morris the Romantic Poet, the Pre-Raphaelite brother; the champion of Icelandic Sagas, of handicraft, of Gothic Architecture. Morris who denounced Classicism, the Renaissance, the Enlightenment, St Paul's Cathedral. An eccentric, a strange cove who kept distinctly odd company - Eleanor Marx, Peter Kropotkin, Frederick Engels and that outrageous Bernard Shaw.

In the 1950s and '60s Morris was quite a good fellow: all those handsome fabrics, that splendid wallpaper, that fine furniture, and, above all, that remarkably prescient Red House. A socially concerned sort of chap whose name, in the days when we'd never had it so good, could be invoked by architects holding to a social conscience. Later, as we were being steeled in the white heat of technology, he was shelved; an anachronism who would divert us with his dreams of medieval village life.

Why William Morris? Because, tragically, his struggles remain all too apposite. Today, as in his lifetime, architecture - the true democratic art - eludes us. Now as then we are weighed down by useless toil. Now as then we are diminished by acquisitive individualism. Now as then we choke on the shoddy, the makeshift. Now as then we are in the thrall of our machines, our miracles of ingenuity. Now as then we need to educate our desires:

> Again, though many of us love architecture dearly, and believe
> that it helps the healthiness of both body and soul to live
> among beautiful things, we ... are mostly compelled to live in
> houses which have become a by-word of contempt for their ugliness
> and inconvenience. The stream of civilisation is against us ...
> (Morris in Cole, 1944, p.526)

JOY IN LABOUR

For Morris, architecture is the quintessential art, an expression of pleasure in work, an art 'made by the people for the people as a joy for the maker and user'. (Morris in Cole, 1944, p.545) This he asserted in the teeth of all he saw about him; in opposition, that is, to soulless work, to the degrading experience of alienated labour:

> ... the greatest of all evils, the heaviest of all slaveries;
> that evil of the greater part of the population being engaged
> for by far the most part of their lives in work, which at the
> best cannot interest them, or develop their best faculties,
> and at the worst (and that is the commonest, too) is mere
> unmitigated slavish toil, only to be wrung out of them by the
> sternest compulsion, a toil which they shirk all they can -
> small blame to them. And this toil degrades them into less
> than men: and they will some day come to know it, and cry
> out to be made men again, and art only can do it, and redeem
> them from this slavery; and I say once more that this is her
> highest and most glorious end and aim ... (Morris in Cole,
> 1944, p.552)

Morris didn't much care for Victorian notions of work. He rejected **especially** the prevailing reality of his - and our - times, the separation of labour from pleasure, of work from art. Beauty for him arises from, stems from joy in labour:

152

Yet I repeat that the chief source of art is man's pleasure in
his daily necessary work, which expresses itself and is
embodied in that work itself; nothing else can make the common
surroundings of life beautiful, and whenever they are beautiful
it is a sign that men's work has pleasure in it ... it is the
lack of this pleasure in daily work which has made our towns
and habitations sordid and hideous, insults to the beauty of
the earth which they disfigure ...   (Morris in Briggs, 1962,
pp.140-1)

The passé sentiment, the innocence of an antique socialist? Hardly.
Now as then architecture as a joy for maker and user remains beyond
reach, remains a repressed hope - for building workers on the lump, for
factory 'hands' on the line, for typists in the pool ..... for architects at the drawing board, 'pandering to degrading follies for the
sake of profit, wasting their intelligence and energy in contriving
snares for cash in the shape of trumpery which they themselves heartily
despise'.   (Morris in Cole, 1944, p.649)   Few find creative pleasure
in their work or in its use. Architecture continues to rest on
alienated work, 'those externals of a true palace of industry can only
be realised naturally and without affectation by the work which is to
be done in them being in all ways reasonable and fit for human
beings'. (Morris in Cole, 1944, p.649)   Hardly an apt description of
our local car assembly plants - those that remain. Here, as elsewhere,
workers refuse the products of their own labour and counsel others to
do likewise. Continually Ford workers tell us 'never buy a Ford ...
we know what goes wrong with them because we know we don't care how we
do the jobs ... it's a funny feeling riding along in something you
really hated when it was a shell on the line'.   (Beynon, 1973,
pp.109-12)

Motorcars or buildings, it's all the same - it's the look that
counts. The burnished, thrusting bodies of cars, the beguiling looks
masking the pain and loss of production, the joyless labour of the
assembly line; the neat facades of corporate architecture, its entic-
ing look concealing the alienated social relationships of daily life,
'the crispness of the external face is everything it is cracked up to
be, but the view of this skin from the inside is somewhat ordinary -
and perhaps even a little crude ... [This] disjoint between the
interior and the exterior [reflects] ... the management's opinion that
those looking out have less sensitive eyes than those looking in'.
(Campbell and Kay, 1978, p.401)   This, certainly, was not Morris'
vision:

... our factory which is externally beautiful, will not be
inside like a clean jail or workhouse; the architecture will
come inside in the form of such ornament as may be suitable
to the special circumstances. Nor can I see why the highest
and most intellectual art, pictures, sculpture, and the like
should not adorn a true palace of industry. People living a
manly and reasonable life would have no difficulty in
refraining from over-doing both these and other adornments
...   (Morris in Cole, 1944, p.654)

Morris was affronted by much of the 'civilisation' about him; not least by the division, the rupture of art from work, of artist from worker, of designer from builder. He believed that we all have it in us to be creative. Creativity, he held, is not the preserve of artists alone, 'that talk of inspiration is sheer nonsense, I may tell you that flat ... there is no such thing, it is a mere matter of craftsmanship'. (Morris in Meier, 1978, p.398) For him, craftsman-ship entails fellowship; expressly the collaborative making of Gothic architecture:

> In the times when art was abundant and healthy, all men were more or less artists; that is to say, the instinct for beauty which is inborn in every complete man had such force that the whole body of craftsmen habitually and without conscious effort made beautiful things, and the audience for ... art was nothing short of the whole people. (Morris in Morton, 1973, pp.61-2)

> ... from the first, the tendency was towards ... freedom of hand and mind subordinated to the co-operative harmony which made the freedom possible. This is the spirit of Gothic Architecture. (Morris in Cole, 1944, p.484)

Little of this spirit remained in Morris' world. Craftsmanship, the bedrock of creative work in fellowship, was being undermined, subver-ted - was splitting. The majority, their craft skills denied them, were now operatives employed at 'useless toil,' at 'the making of wares which are necessary to them and their brethren because they are an inferior class ... coarse food that does not nourish ... rotten raiment which does not shelter ... wretched houses ... miserable makeshifts ...' A minority, denied socially useful labour, were engaged in 'the puffery of wares,' employed in 'making all those articles of folly and luxury, the demand for which is the outcome of the existence of the rich non-producing classes' - an effete art for a ruling class in decline. (Morris in Morton, 1973, pp.91-2 - emphasis in original) Craftsmanship, the fusion of beauty and use, was being destroyed: the majority were being deskilled, a minority had become trapped in folly and luxury - a denial of social need.

Wretched houses, the puffery of wares, by-words of ugliness and inconvenience - familiar affronts of our times. We live now, all too evidently, with the drab uniformity of much council housing; with the soulless, sleek office blocks of our city centres; with the shoddy nastiness of most factories. We live with homelessness, overcrowding and with unemployment among construction workers; we live with dilapidated, run-down local amenities and with the strained opulence of newly-developed commercial centres; we live with condemned houses, boarded-up homes - reminders of expedient, get-it-up-quick housing quotas. Our lives are weighed down, daily, by denial of social need; creativity has been yet further suppressed, deskilling has intensified:

CHRISSIE: It's a tile, Snowy. Lots of tiles, Brown ones.

SNOWY: Yeah, I know, I know, nothin' special. Just beauti-fully made and precision laid a hundred years ago - and still

like new ... We're all capable of work like that, Craftsmanship
doesn't die out in people, Chrissie. We can all do good jobs,
but we're not allowed to ... There's times when I'm not taken
on because I'm too good. And because I'm good, and I do the job
proper, I refuse to skimp on the stuff and I'm slower than the
bosses want me to be. And then I'm not a profit margin anymore,
I'm a liability ... Sometimes I'm so proud of what I've done, I
put me name on the bottom righthand corner of the wall ...
'Snowy Malone, 1982'. (Bleasdale, 1983, pp.36-7)

The medieval craftsman was free on his work, therefore he made
it as amusing to himself as he could; and it was his pleasure
and not his pain that made all things beautiful ... and
lavished treasures of human hope and thought on everything that
man made, from a cathedral to a porridge-pot. Come, let us put
it in the way least respectful to the medieval craftsman, most
polite to the modern 'hand'; the poor devil of the fourteenth
century, his work was of so little value that he was allowed to
waste it by the hour in pleasing himself - and others; but our
highly-strung mechanic, his minutes are too rich with the
burden of perpetual profit for him to be allowed to waste one
of them on art; the present system will not allow him - cannot
allow him - to produce works of art. (Morris in Cole, 1944,
p.596)

ART AND COMMON LIFE

Culture and society, art and everyday life: Morris refused these distinctions and the banal division between works of art and mere artefacts which they support. He refused to accept as desirable, or
necessary, a world in which culture is privilege, art is luxury; in
which the makeshift is commonplace:

To the Socialist a house, a knife, a cup, steam engine, or what
not, anything, I repeat, that is made by man and has form, must
either be a work of art or destructive to art. The Commercialist, on the other hand, divides 'manufactured articles' into
those which are prepensely works of art, and are offered to
sale in the market as such, and those which have no pretence
and could have no pretence to artistic qualities.

I must ask you to extend the word art beyond those matters
which are consciously works of art, to take in not only painting
and sculpture, and architecture, but the shapes and colours of
all household goods, nay, even the arrangement of the fields
for tillage and pasture, the management of towns and of our
highways of all kinds; in a word, to extend it to the aspect of
all the externals of our life.

... people talk about, and advertise, art pottery, art furniture, art fire-grates, and the like, giving us clearly to
understand by such words, that it is unusual for pottery,
furniture and fire-grates to have anything to do with art,
that there is ... a divorce between art and common life ...
those things that are without art are so aggressively; they
wound it by their existence. (Morris in Meier, 1978, pp.395-6)

The wounds remain. Indeed, commercialism has matured, swollen into the luxury and into the obsolescence of consumerism - producing goods intended either to fall out of fashion or to fall apart.

In architecture, 'the true democratic art,' celebrations of luxury as a way of life are rewarded, displays of fashionable consumption are prized. Accordingly, in yet another of the Royal Institute of British Architects' select exhibitions - British Architecture 1982 - two submissions, Salute Birdcage and Newfield (a modern manor house), were commended. The former - quite literally a 10ft high birdcage - 'is made in stainless steel mesh and faced with mouldings, balustrades, columns, pinnacles and pediments in limewood. The Corinthian capitals and cherubs are in polished brass ... This is not a model of a building, it is a piece of classical architecture with obvious associations ...'. (Figure 1) Newfield (Fig.2), in contrast, is inhabited by people; it is 'a true country house' complete with 'giant Ionic order on pedestals ... Portland stone and stucco ... central doors with a segmental pediment ... carved consoles.' This is 'in fact quite a small house.' (Architectural Design, 1982, pp.200-1) In fact this architect's practice seems to have run to modest commissions - a Baroque birdcage here, a Georgian manor-house there, even a Palladian summer house for the Minister, for the garden of Michael Heseltine's country seat. Architecture, art is being consumed by wealth, is being reduced to luxury.

All this is somewhat distant from common life, from the contrived obsolescence that pervades our daily lives:

LINDA: Well, the fan belt broke, so it was a dollar eighty.

WILLY: But it's brand new.

LINDA: Well, the man said that's the way it is. Till they work themselves in, y'know.

WILLY: I hope we didn't get stuck on that machine.

LINDA: They got the biggest ads of any of them!

WILLY: I know, it's a fine machine .....

LINDA: Can you do anything about the shower? It drips.

WILLY: All of a sudden everything falls to pieces! Goddam plumbing, oughta be sued, those people. I hardly finished putting it in and the thing ..... Once in my life I would like to own something outright before it's broken! I'm always in a race with the junkyard! I just finished paying for the car and it's on its last legs. The refrigerator consumes belts like a goddam maniac. They time those things. They time them so when you finally paid for them, they're used up. (Miller, 1949, pp.35,36,66 and 73)

This for the most of us is lived experience; this is the reality of separating art from common life:

The first point, therefore, in the Socialist ideal of art is that it should be common to the whole people; and this can only be the case if it comes to be recognised that art should be an integral part of all manufactured wares that have definite form

Figure 1

Figure 2

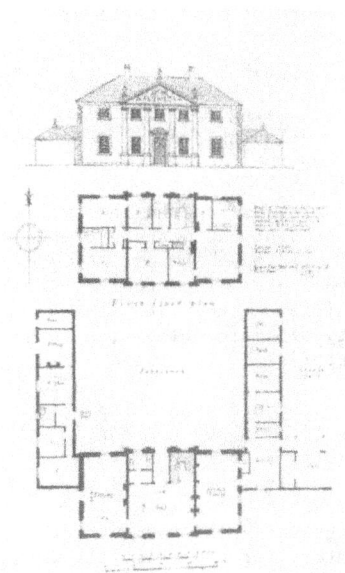

and are intended for endurance.   (Morris in Meier, 1978, p.396)

MACHINES, MIRACLES OF INGENUITY

> I believe machines can do everything - except make works of
> art.   (Morris in Meier, 1978, p.334)

Morris was ambivalent about mechanised industrial production. He wel-
comed the labour-saving potential of machinery; he recognised its
capacity for relieving people from necessarily unpleasant work, of
liberating them for joyful labour, for art. What he saw about him,
however, was machinery in the hands of 'the Commercialist;' he saw
machinery being used for 'profit grinding,' for reducing craftsmen to
'hands':

> Our epoch has invented machines which would have appeared wild
> dreams to the men of past ages, and of those machines we have as
> yet made no use. They are called 'labour-saving' machines - a
> commonly used phrase which implies what we expect of them; but we
> do not get what we expect. What they really do is to reduce the
> skilled labourer to the ranks of the unskilled, to increase the
> number of the 'reserve army of labour' ..... In a true society
> these miracles of ingenuity would be for the first time used for
> minimising the amount of time spent in unattractive labour,
> which by their means might be so reduced as to be but a very
> light burden on each individual ...   (Morris in Morton, 1973,
> p.105-6 - emphasis in original)

> I have spoken of machinery being used freely for releasing people
> from the more mechanical and repulsive part of necessary labour;
> and I know that to some cultivated people, people of the artistic
> turn of mind, machinery is particularly distasteful, and they
> will be apt to say you will never get your surroundings pleasant
> so long as you are surrounded by machinery. I don't quite admit
> that; it is the token of the terrible crime we have fallen into
> of using our control of the powers of Nature for the purpose of
> enslaving people, we care less meantime of how much happiness
> we rob their lives of.   (Morris in Briggs, 1962, p.177)

Morris was spared the full effects of all this on architecture. In
particular, he was spared the widespread abuse of machine production
in building - the extensive use of standardised, mass-produced
components. The architecture associated with this is only too
familiar: the relentlessly repetitive facades, the unrelieved uniformity of office blocks, of schools, of hospitals, of town halls, of
factories ..... These buildings are indifferent to us. We in turn,
are in danger of becoming indifferent to them, of turning our backs on
architecture 'the child of the man-inhabited earth, the expression of
the life of man thereon.' Like towns and cities throughout Britain,
Cardiff - from where we write - is rich with examples. Here, in the
administrative capital of Wales, is the recently assembled addition to
the Welsh Office.   (Fig.3) Here, within sight of its feudal
neighbour - the Norman Keep, Cardiff Castle - is a new, a twentieth-
century fortress complete with 'moat', with guarded entrance, with
armour-plated slit windows. Here, behind a cold facade, administrators
are admitted - via carpeted, wood-panelled offices - to their inner
courtyard complete with coffee shop and hanging gardens. And not two

Figure 3

Figure 4

Figure 6

Figure 5

miles away is Wales' Teaching Hospital (Fig.4), is Wales' Gas Board
(Fig.5), is the head office, the seat, of our local financial baron
(Fig.6) .....

The other side of this stardardised aesthetic is an architecture
fixated by technological innovation, an architecture that is determinedly 'modern'. This is the imagery of 'Hi-Tech' - offering the
finely-tooled, machine-finished looks of, for example, the Inmos
Microelectronics Factory, Newport. (Fig.7) Here a fully rigged aircraft carrier, firmly moored in a Gwent field, celebrates a machine
aesthetic on the flight deck while accommodating personnel below, 'the
building ... a kit of rapidly erectable parts with maximum off-site
prefabrication ... should act as both a high performance, precision,
production machine and as a friendly and stimulating environment for
employees.' And those who prefer the excitements of space travel will
envy the citizens of Louisville, Kentucky. (Fig.8) Here, in Star
Trek style, a 'light, silvery, glowing, rounded' space ship will land
on 'planet earth' at the corner of downtown Fifth and Main Streets,
where it will accomplish such homely missions as 'responding to the
river ..... communicating visually and socially with the community,'
and providing 'spaces for people to identify with'. (Architectural
Design, 1982, pp.136-43 and 83-6)

EDUCATION OF DESIRE

> The untouched surface of ancient architecture bears witness to
> the development of man's ideas, to the continuity of history,
> and, so doing, affords never-ceasing instruction, nay education,
> to the passing generations, not only telling us what were the
> aspirations of men passed away, but also what we may hope for
> in the time to come. (Morris in Meier, 1978, p.407)

> ... it was possible then to have social, organic, hopeful
> progressive art; whereas now such poor scraps of it as are
> left are the result of individual and wasteful struggle, are
> retrospective and pessimistic ..... there is no hope save in
> Revolution. The old art is no longer fertile, no longer
> yields us anything save elegantly poetical regrets; being
> barren, it has but to die ... (Morris in Cole, 1944, pp.596
> and 598)

> ... the leisure which Socialism above all things aims at obtain-
> ing for the worker is also the very thing that breeds desire -
> desire for beauty, for knowledge, for more abundant life ...
> that leisure and desire are sure to produce art, and without
> them nothing but sham art, void of life or reason for existence,
> can be produced: therefore not only the worker, but the world
> in general, will have no share in art till our present
> commercial society gives place to real society - to Socialism.
> (Morris in Briggs, 1962, p.143)

Architecture or revolution? There is a tension in Morris the
designer, the socialist. How to live, where to focus energies - in
artistic struggle or in political action? How best to cultivate
desire, to nourish hope - in art or in education for revolution?
Morris resisted the choice; he worked continuously to make his life,

Figure 7

Figure 8

161

and our lives, whole. He stood against the imposed separation of artistic from political life, of pleasure from labour, of art from common life. He refused the distinction between architecture and emancipation, between 'the true democratic art' and 'real society - Socialism':

> Surely any one who professes to think that the question of art and cultivation must go before that of the knife and fork (and there are some who do propose that) does not understand what art means, or how that its roots must have a soil of a thriving and unanxious life. Yet it must be remembered that civilisation has reduced the workman to such a skinny and pitiful existence, that he scarcely knows how to frame a desire for any life much better than that he now endures perforce. It is the province of art to set the true ideal of a full and reasonable life before him, a life to which the perception and creation of beauty, the enjoyment of real pleasure that is, shall be felt to be as necessary to man as his daily bread, and that no man, and no set of men, can be deprived of this except by mere opposition, which should be resisted to the utmost. (Morris in Morton, 1973, pp.245-6)

Salute Birdcage, the Welsh Office, the Inmos Factory, 'British Architecture 1982, 1983, 1984 ...' - it need not be like this. Art need not be consumed by wealth, reduced to luxury. Architecture can be used to educate desire. This, in the initial phase of modern architecture, is what many socially committed designers sought to do; before, that is, they and their works were incorporated into capitalist consumerism. It is this that the Tecton group - an architects' cooperative - attempted to realise in their innovatory Health Centre (1938-9) for the Labour controlled borough of Finsbury; a building that, in its use as well as in its form, anticipates community participation in health care - an accessible, open service in a welcoming, congenial building. (Fig. 9)   For the Tecton cooperative the building had to be as much a community resource as were the services made available in it. And Walter Gropius and his collaborator Maxwell Fry treated their Impington Village College (1936) in a similar manner, as an educational resource for adults as well as for school children. (Fig.10)   Here too the form and social use of the building anticipate education as a collective, a communal endeavour.

And others, whose buildings did not feature in 'British Architecture 1982', have tried to push design practice yet further. These are the 'community architects' who, in crisis-struck areas of cities such as Glasgow, Newcastle, Manchester, Liverpool and London, are struggling to forge new ways of working; to forge collaborative relationships between designers, building users and construction workers. These are the handful of practitioners who are attempting to enlist active participation in design decisions which are customarily confined to architects.

> Neither in News from Nowhere nor in such lectures as 'A Factory as it might be' or 'The Society of the Future' is Morris offering precise 'solutions'. Nor does it even matter (as a first criterion) whether the reader approves of his approximations. Assent may be better than dissent, but more important than either is the challenge to the imagination to become immersed in the same open exploration. And in such an adventure two things happen: our habitual values (the 'commonsense' of

Figure 9

Figure 10

bourgeois society) are thrown into disarray. And we enter into Utopia's proper and new-found space: the education of desire. This is not the same as 'a moral education' towards a given end: it is, rather, to open a way to aspiration, to 'teach desire to desire, to desire better, to desire more, and above all to desire in a different way'. (Thompson, 1977, pp.790 - emphasis in original)

I have a sort of faith ... we shall have leisure to think about our work, that faithful daily companion, which no man any longer will venture to call the Curse of labour: for surely then we shall be happy in it, each in his place, no man grudging at another; no one bidden to be any man's servant, every one scorning to be any man's master: men will then assuredly be happy in their work, and that happiness will assuredly bring forth decorative, noble, popular art. That art will make our streets as beautiful as the woods, as elevating as the mountainsides: it will be a pleasure and a rest, and not a weight upon the spirits to come from the open country into a town; every man's house will be fair and decent, soothing to his mind and helpful to his work ... . (Morris in Morton, 1973, p.55 - emphases in original)

BIBLIOGRAPHY

Architectural Design, (1982), British Architecture 1982, Academy Editions, London.
Berger, J., (1972), Ways of Seeing, BBC and Penguin, London.
Beynon, H., (1973), Working For Ford, Penguin, Hardmondsworth, Middlesex.
Bleasdale, A., (1983), Boys From the Blackstuff: Five Plays for Television, Granada, London.
Briggs, A., (1962), William Morris: Selected Writings and Designs, Penguin, Harmondsworth, Middlesex.
Campbell, B. and Kay, T., (1978), 'Industrial Democracy and the Architect: the Herman Miller Factory at Bath', Architects' Journal, vol.167, no.9, pp.397-407.
Cole, G.D.H. (ed.), (1944), William Morris, Nonesuch, London.
Meier, P., (1978), William Morris: the Marxist Dreamer, Harvester, Hassocks, Sussex.
Miller, A., (1949), Death of a Salesman: Certain Private Conversations in Two Acts and a Requiem, Viking, New York.
Morton, A.L. (ed.), (1973), Political Writings of William Morris, Lawrence and Wishart, London.
Thompson, E.P., (1977), William Morris: Romantic to Revolutionary, Merlin, London.

11. The environmental psychology of theatres and movie palaces

ROSS THORNE

Architecture which is 'popular' has been largely missing from our environment for the last fifty years. The USSR attempted to impose an architecture which would be appreciated by the masses through its espousal of an architecture of 'social realism'. Of their own volition the architects of movie-palaces of USA in the 1920s were also attempting to provide an architecture or places, the meaning of which would be communicated to and appreciated by the masses. They were conscious of the effects of colour and decoration on people's moods and feelings, perhaps being more aware of 'environmental psychology' than are many of their modern-day colleagues who now exist in a world more populated with social scientists who can assist them to understand what these effects really may be. The evidence available shows firstly, that there exist popular misconceptions as to who experienced the 'de-luxe' highly decorated movie theatres of the 1920s – and secondly, that architects of those theatres in USA, conscientiously attempted to produce environments which would provide the patrons with feelings of well-being.

It will be shown in this study of principally historic documentation, that these architects, their intentions and their buildings have implications for what Architecture and its meaning is, or should be, in a democratic society.

INTRODUCTION

Architects and architectural historians have theorised for many years
about the visual qualities of buildings, suggesting ways of designing
to produce 'good' building appearance or satisfactory 'architectural
composition' (e.g. Robertson 1924). The Modern Movement justified much
of its theory, with the claim that the building forms proposed would be
socially beneficial. This claim was commonly not based on any appeal to
hard evidence about the social consequences of particular building
forms.

When the potential value of input from the social sciences began to
be recognised (as far back as 1962 in Australia (RAIA, 1962)) some
architects became interested in relating theories of perception to
architectural design (e.g. Thorne, 1974 a/b; Prak, 1977). However this
practice has not been widely adopted and Lang (1983) currently finds it
necessary to exhort teachers of basic design to use, in their courses,
appropriate research within the area of perception.

In an effort to confront architects with the idea that they are
producing buildings unsuitable for their users or the general
community, social scientists and others have investigated the
differences in the way architects and non-architects respond to
building design. (See, for examples, **Proceedings of International
Architectural Psychology Conference,** Simon (1979)). Certainly many
architects have now come to the view that the Modern Movement did not
afford solutions to all the problems of 'good' design but, in diverting
their attention to more recent theories (of Post-Modern style) they may
have drifted even further from community acceptance of their work
(Groat, 1982).

The current architectural mode is rich in 'symbolic' use of past
architectural forms and details, the symbolic content of which is
frequently described in thick and obscure language (e.g. Agrest and
Gandelsonas, 1979). Neither the visual forms nor the verbal
interpretations appear to have the meaning for the general public that
is seen in them by the architects, or by certain historians (e.g.
Norberg Schultz, 1980). As Rapoport (1982) has observed, resort to
semiotics to describe the symbolism of buildings has produced more
obscurity than clarity of meaning.

For at least fifty years, architecture has adopted a visual and
verbal language which, although it has a certain internal coherence,
has failed to communicate its supposed 'meanings' to the general public
and has, indeed, aroused dislike. It is instructive to compare two
attempts made, against a socialist background on the one hand, and a
capitalist one on the other, to produce buildings that would be
'understood' by the general public, in the sense of having clear and
widely shared connotations. Kopp (1970), in documenting the
development of the architecture of 'socialist realism' in Soviet Russia
notes that the classical style had been a luxury of the privileged
classes, while modern architecture (whose superiority he assumes) had
been discredited.

But the moderns also had against them the forces of custom and
tradition...; they had against them the fact that they were ahead

of the masses.... And they had left behind not only the masses but
also the conventionally trained professionals, the building
workers... and timid administrators. (p.225)

The vacuum left by the banning of modern architecture was taken up by
"strange Greek, Roman, Florentine, or pseudo-Russian edifices,
supposedly the fruits of applying to architecture the method of
socialist realism" (p.219). Kopp comments that this was not "realist"
architecture but rather a mask of decoration expressing the opposite of
reality.

With somewhat different theoretical overtones this is exactly what
took place in USA from about 1913 to 1932 in the design of the picture-
palace type of theatre. Although it could be argued that their
assumptions were basically similar, the major architects for these
buildings did not defend them in ideological terms. They argued their
case on 'psychological' grounds and evaluated their success through
patronage (or buttocks on seats).

With the hindsight of nearly sixty years it may seem that the great
theatre/cinema architects were naive in trying to use contemporary
psychological theories to provide suitable environments for the showing
of moving pictures. Nevertheless, whatever the poverty of the popular
theories they appealed to, their enterprise clearly 'worked' in every
way. It produced impressive 'places' of great appeal to the users, who
were numerous. As we shall see, they were to facilitate an escape from
reality not only for the lower classes but also for middle and upper
classes in proportionally greater numbers.

Indeed these buildings are excellent examples of a good product of
the design process, according to the criteria set down by Canter (1977)
who states that "we need to identify the initial objectives or goals
for the creation of the place" in question (p.164). In the present
case we can do this from the the writings of the theatre architects
published in the motion picture exhibitors' journals and elsewhere.
Canter then explains that

These objectives will themselves be a conceptual system, no matter
how loosely formulated, of what place the design is to house. The
design team's task is to convert this conceptual system into a
product. In order to do this they will themselves have to
forumulate a conceptualisation of the place to be produced. By
working with this conceptualisation, they give rise to a setting in
which the various users interact. These users, in their turn, will
form conceptions of what the place consists" (Canter, 1977, p.164).

Unlike many of the architects of the later modern and post-modern
movements these theatre architects of USA (and their followers in other
countries) had a conceptualisation, in particular of the interior
environment, which, it seems, was clearly communicated to the users.
That is, the conceptions formed by the users' interaction with the
setting were similar to those of the architects. By contrast, it is
clear that the conceptions of many of those who use or view some
current Modernist and Post-Modernist architectural products are greatly
at variance with the conceptions of their designers (e.g. Groat, 1982;
Purcell, 1984a; 1984b; 1984c).

To dismiss the products of these theatre architects as being pastiches of 'Architecture' or being the non-architecture of commercialisation is an irrelevance. Such dismissal does not confront the interaction issue continuing between society and the building. First, what constitutes Architecture often changes as the age of buildings increases and their uniqueness or social significance is more fully appreciated. This is currently happening in USA with the granting to move-palaces of national monument status (e.g. The Fox Theatre, Atlanta and Ohio Theatre, Columbus).

Second, in considering the interaction of society and building there are the more important aspects of consumer participation and communication. In the design of these theatres consumer participation was involved, albeit indirectly, in two ways: 1) the architects deliberately set out to eliminate the physical separation of social classes, which was a feature of traditional theatres; and (2) indirect participation took place through the market place.

Although the latter form of participation may be anathema to some, it does exert an influence in many Western countries, perhaps especially in the area of housing. In Austalia, for example, the most fundamental way in which people 'participate' in the planning and production of the physical suburban environment is simply through the purchase of detached houses in numbers far in excess of other types of (frequently less expensive) dwellings which are available. (The detached house is desired by 90 per cent and obtained by over 70 per cent of the adult population in Australia (Thorne et al, 1980).

That is, in a relatively free market situation and through the purchase of one type of dwelling rather than another type, a person is participating in the production or design of a physical environment which will contain specific visual attributes. Prototype dwellings are inspected and ordered by prospective home-owners. By demand 'popular' designs and styles continue to be replicated; the unpopular suffer their demise through lack of demand. In much of the same way a demand for palatial movie-theatres was experienced from 1913 when (according to Hall (1961)) the first purpose-built luxury cinema was constructed. Good attendances were seen as a demonstration of demand which was met by the construction of larger and more highly decorated versions of the same up until the Great Depression of the early thirties.

The movie-palace theatre-architects and their exhibitor-clients wished to communicate a number of qualities, in their designs. They wanted the customers from all classes to feel important; they sought to provide all the visual design elements usually available only to the rich, and to afford a total environment consistent with the make-believe, artificiality, or escapist content of the films of the time. Accordingly, discussion of these movie theatres, of the architects conceptualisations (or intentions), and of the buildings' success with the users is dependent upon knowing who the users were and what the film producer/exhibitor companies' conceptual systems, or design expectations were. Also, it is necessary to provide a brief description of the nature of the theatre design that existed before the popularisation of theatre by the silent movies, and the contribution made to it by these architects.

Evidence as to the 'environmental psychology' applied in U.S. movie-theatre design of the 1920s has been derived from reviewing all statements by architects and designers in the major U.S. motion picture exhibitors' journals for the decade, and extracting those which had 'psychological' implications. The words of the architects and designers are quoted at length as data, in order to provide a sense of the involvement they had in this aspect of designing suitable environments for a particular human experience.

THE SOCIOLOGY OF THE CINEMA

Popular writing on the escapist "dreamworld" of the cinema, where underprivileged people with supposedly dreary, unfulfilled lives could while away a few hours in a mock-palatial atmosphere, secretly living out some emotion portrayed on the screen, is colourful. However it may not represent the true story of the cinema. According to Handel (1950) no systematic studies of theatre/cinema audiences were made until around World War II, although Jowett (1976) has found a few earlier studies which attempt, more than anything else, to assess a suspected deleterious influence of movies on children and adolescents. For more comprehensive evidence on the sociology of popular drama, of which cinema was in the 1920s, 30s and 40s, we have to look at the more recent research undertaken on its successor, television (e.g. Goodlad, 1971).

Therefore, with so little contemporary evidence available it could be argued that the popular theory was probably highly influenced by the claims of the film-company advertising copy-writers and the language of the exhibitors' journals, particularly those published in U.S.A. through the 1920s. The purple prose of the exhibitors' copywriters extended, as too did the florid theatre designs, to Australia and other Antipodean outposts such as New Zealand and South Africa. The Regent Theatre, Sydney, Australia, was "erected to the enhancement of the motion picture and allied arts" in 1928. The souvenir programme of the official opening (9th March 1928) provided (in part) the following dedication:

> Today at wish we conjure up glories that are gone; they live again in tense reality upon our screens. There too, we leave a record of ourselves - the mighty and the meek, our prayers and strange despairs. The dreams we have may crystallise and stay for ever.

A few months later at the opening of the more robustly florid State Theatre, Sydney, the hue of the prose became suitably more intense:

> To that priceless, peerless, and enduring spirit of High Romance that uncalled leaps to flame in the hearts of all; that divine spark that perpetually gilds this drab world anew with the glowing fairy web of adventure, courage, endeavour, and fancy free; that primal urge of imagination that shone in the flashing eyes of Jeanne d'Arc....

To this and more the State Theatre was dedicated. If there was a "divine spark" that gilded the drab world anew it was echoed in the descriptive sub-titles given to some of the most palatial movie theatres. It was as if the exhibitors and their architects were aiming for a heavenly solution in opulance. The Rialto, New York, was advertised as "The Temple of the Motion Picture" while its larger more costly successor, The Roxy, New York, was "The Cathedral of the Motion Picture". Not to be outdone in attempting to transcend such ethereal heights some movie palaces in USA were simply called Paradise Theatre (e.g. in Chicago; opened 1928, demolished 1956).

This popular 'sociology' of movies and the environments in which they were exhibited may have been reinforced by the appearance in 1961 of the first major book to provide "the story of the golden age of the movie palace". In this book Hall (1961) provides an enthusiastic account, frequently quoting the extravagant prose of the exhibitors' journals, and contributing his own of a highly descriptive nature. He uses an unattributed quotation, "An Acre of Seats in a Garden of Dreams" as the title for his chapter on the architects and their most outrageous designs. Not only, it seems, did these theatres enhance the dreams of the audience but for Hall (1961) were the outcome of dreams of the architects:

> The United States in the Twenties was dotted with a thousand Xanadus. Decreed by some local (or chain-owning) Kubla Khan, these pleasure domes gave expression to the most secret and polychrome dreams of a whole group of architects who might otherwise have gone through life doomed to turning out churches, hotels, banks and high schools. The architecture of the movie palace was a triumph of suppressed desire and its practitioners range in style from the purely classic to a wildly abandoned eclectic that could only have come from men who, like the Khan himself, 'on honeydew had fed, and drunk the milk of Paradise'. (p.93)

If the architecture of the movie palace was a triumph of suppressed desire those examples exhibiting a wildly abandoned eclectic could only be described as orgasms which, for their enormity, might make blanche the U.S. Legion of Decency – an organisation which, at the time of the construction of such theatres, was exploring every means of establishing control or censorship over the subject matter of motion pictures (Jowett, 1976). Without wishing to deviate into Freudian-style sexual allusions it may seem noteworthy that the USA, for a country of considerable puritanism (when compared, say, to some Scandinavian countries) has produced visual designs of a number of objects from cars through movie palaces to theme parks of unique, unrestrained vulgarity.

Books on the architecture of the golden age of movie theatres published more recently than Hall (1961) say little more than repeat the claims by exhibitors and their architects. Although Atwell's (1980) fine history of British movie theatres is sub-titled, "A History of British Cinemas and their Audiences", there is little about the audiences. Resort is again made to architectural writings which largely summed up the intentions of the original architects.

Atwell cites Sexton's and Betts' writing of 1927 in **American Theatres Today** "The masses, revelling in luxury and costly beauty, went to be thrilled by the gorgeousness of their surroundings which they could not afford in their home life". Returning to the original writing it is

found that these architectural authors continue to make further
important claims on the social role of the theatre-building in the
sentences which follow the above quotation:

> And they are disappointed if they do not find the thrill they have
> come for. Their favorite (sic) 'movie house' is the one which
> gives them the biggest thrill. The management must necessarily
> take this fact into consideration for the biggest part of their
> audience must come from the masses. (Sexton and Betts, 1927, pp.15-
> 16)

Such references to "the masses" may be misleading, allowing assumptions
to be made about the lower or working (mass?) classes being the major
beneficiaries of such escapist environments. As will be shown in the
next sub-section such assumptions are erroneous. However, the notion
that people have favourite movie houses which give them a thrill to be
within is important for it implies that some movie theatres become
places of considerable significance and meaning for many people within
a community.

Goodlad (1971) notes four good effects of popular, escapist, mass
media drama which seem to function positively with reference to social
structure. A highly visually stimulating environment, as were provided
by the major movie theatres, created settings likely to enhance three
of those effects: relaxation; stimulating imagination, particularly of
children; and providing vicarious interaction - particularly for people
in social isolation.

Of course there are people, more vociferous than numerous, who decry
escapist fare as having a "narcotizing dysfunction" (Goodlad, 1971,
p.86). A number of these people were extremely vocal during the 1920s
when the art of the silent motion picture was being refined and the
lavish movie houses built. They were attracted to the simplicity of
the stimulus-response theory which had been a bulwark of embryonic
psychology; but, as Jowett (1976) points out, it was in the 1920s that
social science measurement techniques became more sophisticated thereby
encouraging improved studies of the impact of movies on the community.

Objective as these studies might have been they were not necessarily
accepted by those who believed the content of movies should have been
controlled. "Those who studied the influences of motion pictures
almost always found themselves embroiled in heated arguments between
reformers and the industry. Both sides at times even resorted to
employing their own 'scientists' to produce competing studies or to
refute previously published evidence" (Jowett, 1976, p.213). Although
the evaluation of the moral influence of movies may have differed
greatly, Jowett (1976) notes that these studies seldom varied widely on
their statistical findings for attendance.

THE MOVIE-THEATRE USERS

In 1908 **The Moving Picture World** 2:2, January 11, noted that two
million Americans, one third of whom were children, attended movie
houses each day. It also claimed that audiences included few women
under 30 but many who were middle-aged or elderly. It is not known how

such claims were researched but one of the first few analyses of market
research figures (being of those from 1940 to 1946) show that movie-
going in USA was fairly evenly distributed amongst males and females
and over the range of income groups, with the high-income group
attending more frequently than low-income, while members of the middle-
income group attended most frequently. People with higher education
would attend slightly more often than those with low education (Handel
1950/1976).

Studies made prior to the market research of the 1940s were rather
patchy and were mostly made in an attempt to prove that movies had some
kind of influence on children and adolescents. In 1919 the Reverend
John Phelan made a study of movie-going in Toledo, USA, a city of
260,000 people, estimating daily, weekly and yearly attendance of
45,000, 316,000, and 16,380,000 respectively, noting a high proportion
of those attending were children (Jowett, 1976). In 1929 Mrs. Alice
Miller Mitchell administered a questionnaire to over 10,000 Chicago
children to discover that the average attendance was between once and
twice a week with 90.6 per cent of the sample attending regularly
(Jowett, 1976).

A study of one city prior to the advent of systematic market research
in the movie film industry was undertaken in Newburyport,
Massachusetts, by sociologists Lloyd Warner and Paul Lunt in 1935
(Jowett, 1976). It supported the findings of the later study cited by
Handel (1950/1976) that attendance was fairly equally distributed
amongst males and females, but the earlier study showed a slight
majority of females in the upper-upper class and the majority of males
in the lower-lower class attending. Compared to the respective
percentage which any class group occupied in the then total population
of the city, the breakdown of attendance showed the lowest attendance
was for the lower-lower class and highest attendance for the lower-
upper class group. The latter was followed in rank order by the upper-
upper, lower-middle and upper-lower class groups. However the lowest
class attended more frequently. The great bulk of the audience in
numbers (over 80%) ranged across the upper-middle, lower-middle and
upper-lower class groups (Jowett, 1976).

Confirmation of this tendency for the middle class to attend movies
rather than the lowest class has been demonstrated to some extent by
Gomery (1982) who has used the methods of urban geographers. He has
noted, apart from the large downtown movie palaces, that some of the
largest and most elaborate theatres in New York and Chicago were built
in what were middle class areas in the 1920s, but have since declined
to be termed lowest class. Gomery feels that it has been this decline
of areas which has provided a false indication, obtained in recent
years, that the lavish movie palaces were to encourage the 'escape' of
the lowest class.

Govermy's hypothesis that the most palatial theatres were not
constructed in lowest class areas was able to be tested for the city of
Sydney, Australia. In 1933, the earliest year that the Australian
Census provides data on both income and occupation and therefore an
indication of class, the city possessed a population of 1,235,267 in 50
local government areas. The earliest directory of suburban theatres
and their capacities shows a total of 156 (**Film Weekly Directory,**

1937). Photographs and other historical documentation provide evidence
of the type and richness of decoration for these buildings (Thorne,
1976; 1981; Thorne, Cork and Tod, 1983; Sharp, 1982; 1983).
Classifying the local government areas (LGAs) by income and the
theatres in those LGAs by decoration and seating capacity, shows that
neither highly decorated movie theatres nor a high ratio of theatre
seats per population existed in the suburban LGAs in which residents in
employment had the lowest income. The most highly decorated suburban
movie theatres existed in 8 LGAs ranging from number 5 to 35 in rank
order of LGA by income.

Therefore, as much as can be assessed from the meagre audience
research carried out from 1929 through to the market research of the
1940s, and to the evidence of the correlation of movie theatres
according to the richness of decoration by the class of population (in
the area and at the time they were constructed), it appears that those
in the community most enjoying the escapist qualities of both the
movies and the places in which they were shown, were predominantly
people from lower-upper through middle to upper-lower classes.

THEATRE BUILDINGS EXPRESSING SOCIAL CLASS

The earliest 'environmental psychology' study into theatre design was
carried out in 1902 as an unstructured observational survey of theatre
patrons as they left a performance. From standing at the exits and
listening to the patrons' comments about the theatres' designs the
architects, George and C.W. Rapp (1923), concluded that there should be
a major change in the design of theatres.

It must be remembered that nineteenth century theatre reflected the
new class consciousness of society (Barker, 1971). Rivalling the
Theatres Royal, Covent Garden and Drury Lane, London, in capacity, and
stage facilities, the Theatre Royal, Melbourne, advertised, in 1855,
the attraction of "separate and spacious entrances... provided to the
gallery, the pit, the pit-stalls, the slips, the upper boxes and to the
dress circle" (The (Melbourne) Age, July 16, 1855). Thus there were
six sections of the auditorium for six classes of people who were
prevented from intermixing between entrance and their seating section.
The wide range of seat prices at the time were not so much related to
the ability to gain a good view of the stage but to the purchase of
space and comfort enforcing the separation of the classes in seating,
at the same time (Thorne, 1971).

Visits to old theatres today, and an inspection of old illustrations
of theatre interiors, show a great difference in the environmental
quality intended for the different classes, as evidenced from the
sequence of interior spaces from the respective points of entry to the
seats allocated for them in the auditorium. The stairs and corridors to
the cheapest seats are dingy and devoid of decoration and floor
covering (see illustrations of two entries to Theatre Royal, Sydney);
the seats are unmarked benches with little leg room. In the 19th
century the only 'service' provided to the patrons in the cheapest
seats was more a service to the manager or lessee - 'packers' employed
to ensure that everyone was cramped up as tightly as possible occupying
between 2 to 2 1/2 sq. feet per person or one quarter of a sq. metre

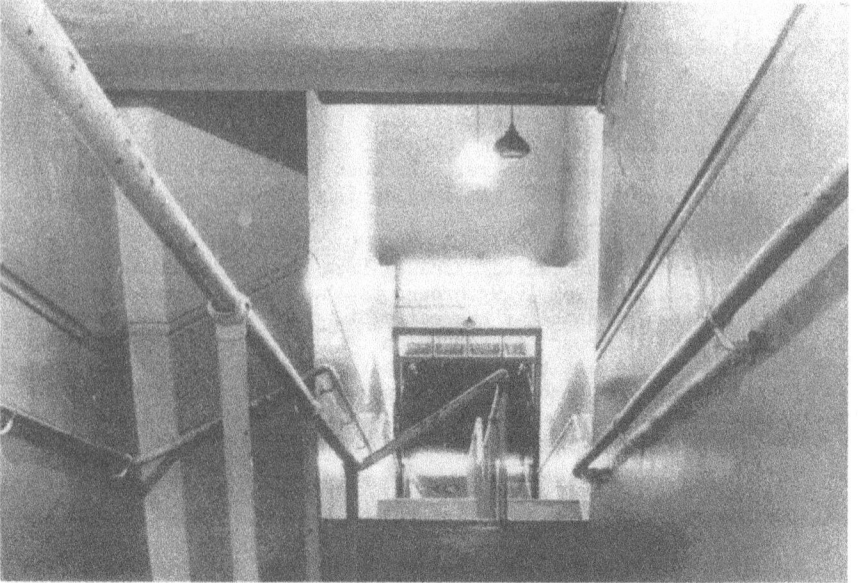

Separate entry from street to seat for balcony patrons; Theatre Royal, Sydney, 1876, redesigned 1921, demolished 1971.

Entry from street for dress circle and stalls patrons; Theatre Royal, Sydney. Prior to 1921 the low priced back stalls seats had a separate entry from a side street.

(Thorne, 1971; 1979, citing Royal Commission of N.S.W., 1887).

Class consciousness in America may not have been as great, or at least as ostentatiously apparent as in Britain or Australia. Some contemporary newspaper descriptions of theatres neglect to describe the quality of the entrances to the galleries yet detail those to the stalls (or parterre/parquet) and boxes (e.g. for Manhattan Opera House, **New York Tribune** November 13, 1892). However, in a description of the American Theatre, New York, it is evident that entrances to different parts of the theatre are quite separate (Birkmire, 1901). Although these two theatres and those mentioned above for Melbourne and Sydney were major city theatres, accommodation invariably was available for the low-income classes, but not in luxurious surroundings. (In the low-income suburbs of London the poor also had their own one class "penny-gaff" playhouses (Wilson, 1954; Sheridan, 1981).)

George L. and C.W. Rapp were to initiate the complete break-down of class distinction in theatre design. The reason for their 'unobtrusive observation' study of 1902 was that they were asked to design a theatre to seat 2,000 in such a manner that each would feel content in his seat". "Night after night the architects and (the client) theatre manager stood in playhouses then famous, watching the expressions and listening to comment as the crowds of theatregoers passed in and out" (Rapp, 1923). The conclusion of their study was that theatre patrons wanted a "clear direct view of the stage" which required the "elimination of all pillars and columns" supporting the various levels in the auditorium.

After over 80 years have elapsed this seems an obvious conclusion but, at the time, theatres such as Wade's Opera House, San Francisco, the theatre known as the Second Boston Museum (Young, 1973) and The Princess's, Melbourne, (Thorne, 1971) all had eight columns from the stalls floor supporting the front edges of the three tiers above thus causing interruption of view to those patrons in the back stalls, dress and family circles.

After their 1902 experience the Rapp brothers continued to monitor theatres and cinemas, obtaining mainly anecdotal but useful evidence. In 1923, when commenting about the design of large movie theatres, George Rapp noted that the

> purchaser of the cheapest ticket (for the gallery) dislikes the feeling that he is isolated from the rest of the auditorium. And so there has been introduced broad and gradually ascending staircases leading up from lofty and impressive lobbies making the way to the upper levels of the auditorium attractive and inviting. (Rapp, 1923)

Elsewhere George Rapp added:

> Here is a shrine to democracy where there are no priviliged patrons. The wealthy rub elbows with the poor ... and are better for this contact. Do not wonder, then, at the touches of Italian Renaissance .... These are not impractical attempts at showing off .... It is richness unabashed, but richness with a reason.

(Morrison, 1974, cited by Herzog, 1980)

Thus the egalitarian theatre design came into existence. However, this design form did not only express a social change: both the architects **and** the exhibitors were wishing to enhance the psychological state of well-being - that sense of occasion when one attends a theatre.

Hall (1961) notes that one major exhibitor, S.L. Rothafel, initiated accessories to the functions of simply attending (for the patron) and showing a then silent film (for the exhibitor). The new design form allowed all classes to inexpensively experience the heel-clicking, saluting, uniformed surrogate servants and footmen who were employed to assist in door opening, direction finding, and ushering (Hall, 1961). All public spaces, including vestibules to lavatories, were to have the same care attended upon them for decoration and furnishing (see, for example, State Theatre, Sydney, in Thorne, (1981)). Members of all classes took the same route through a lofty grand lobby usually to some grander nodal space like a rotunda in which there would be a featured grand staircase. For a few minutes all patrons could be kings and queens in pseudo opera houses or royal palace halls. For example, those who walked through the Grand Lobby of the Tivoli Theatre, Chicago (built 1921), traversed a simulated Chapel of the Palace of Versailles (Weaver, 1921).

Finally, upon entering the auditorium the greatest impact was upon the patrons with the cheapest tickets, being those in the gallery. The space would almost explode upon them - a vast area surrounded by huge curtained imitation windows and coffered ceilings, from which hung some of the world's largest crystal chandeliers. Or, it might be a walled Roman or Venetian garden under a sky across which scudding clouds peppered the azure blue.

These movie palace theatre environments were hardly more than gigantic stage sets in which the members of the audience were the real performers or participants acting out an occasion of watching moving shadows. The architects, no less than the audience and the exhibitors, were most serious about their participation. They strove to produce environments which would communicate to the patron the feelings of well-being and importance (Herzog, 1980).

THE FUNCTION OF THE MOVIE PALACE THEATRE

Most of the theatres for which the architects claimed they used psychological concepts or attributes in their design were movie palaces, the function of which was considerably more than showing silent, black and white movies. Indeed, the movie palace function was quite complex, far more so than a present-day cinema.

Today the exhibitors sell movies, sophisticated with wide-screen, colour and stereophonic sound, but the head of the Loew's/MGM conglomerate, Marcus Loew, is attributed as saying: "We sell tickets to theaters, not movies". (Herzog, 1980, citing Freeman, 1977) And the theatres provided an environment **of** entertainment rather than an environment **for** entertainment.

Palatial grand staircase for balcony patrons at the Fox (movie)
Theatre, Washington, D.C.

Grand marble staricase for balcony patrons at the State Theatre,
Sydney. The stair is situated in a high domed-ceiling rotunda.

For their time silent films were the supreme technological advance in
visually simulating events, just as radio in the 1930s to 1950s aurally
simulated events. Neither can be judged by the yardstick of the
present-day technology of sound film or video. In fact, viewing a
restored silent movie printed from an original undamaged negative,
projected at the correct speed (and not at the faster sound speed to
which we are accustomed) can be an enlightening experience. The
nuances of movement and subtle acting, the visual composition of each
scene, the use of intercutting shots and montage in editing had all
become extremely refined by the mid-1920s. (See, for example, early
films by De Mille (Card, 1971) and those of Lubitsch (Horak, 1975), von
Stroheim and Eisenstein (Manvel, 1972).)

Consistent with movie palaces emulating the style of highly decorated
European opera houses and late 19th century vaudeville theatres, the
motion picture itself was generally called a "photoplay" and presented
on stage as for a theatrical performance. (Herzog, 1980) However, the
showing of a movie was only a part of the function of these theatres.

> Of course the picture is important, and we could not do without it;
> but what we have tried to do is to build around it an atmospheric
> program that is colorful, entertaining and interesting. This type
> of program, with its ballets, musical presentations, stage settings
> and lighting effects, calculated to form a series of pictures
> sometimes contrasting and sometimes gracefully merging into one
> another, was originated by ourselves. (Rothafel, 1925, pp.362-363)

Theatre programmes show that the "atmospheric program" of organ, and
orchestral performances, soloists, revue, intermixed with newsreel and
travelogue films, considerably exceeded the length of the feature film,
and it was the architecture - the sequence of spaces leading to the
auditorial climax - which set the mood of anticipation for this complex
programme. (Hall, 1961; Herzog, 1980) It is summed up by that
entrepreneural originator of the lavish movie presentation, 'Roxy'
Rothafel, when he said that "Theater entertainment... takes place not
only on the stage, but at the box office, in the lobby, the foyer, the
rest rooms, and the auditorium itself". (Herzog, 1980, citing
Rothafel, 1932)

THE ENVIRONMENTAL "PSYCHOLOGY" CLAIMED FOR BY THEATRE ARCHITECTS

Theatre architects of the 1920s had none of the present pretensions of
modernism. They claimed nothing as pure (and so often falsely carried
out) as 'form follows function'. Writing of the theatre architects of
the 1920s Ahlschlager (1927) stated that they attempted to achieve an
"ensemble" effect of colour, decoration, lighting and furnishings.
Their success was judged largely by attendance figures at the movie
theatres. The architects of the more successful theatres were
commissioned to design dozens, even hundreds more. Ann Dorin (1927),
in charge of decoration for one large chain of movie theatres, claimed
that colour was so important that the "wrong" colour in a theatre whose
location catered for a particular class of people could deter them from
attending. She described an example where the audience attendance
increased after changing the colours of the interior of one theatre
(using an unchanged policy of movie exhibition as the control

178

variable). Dorin went so far as to devise a set of guidelines for the use of colour in theatre buildings:

> The warm, or irritating colors – red, orange, yellow – proved the most successful in cases where the community drawn upon was made up mainly of the more primitive classes, while the cool or restful colors, such as blue, green, violet, made the greatest appeal in the more refined neighborhoods. However, there are other considerations. The size of the house, for one thing, the climate, for another, and there is always, of course, the design of the theatre itself to be consulted.... Red of course, is the most generally liked color, though psychologists appear to have established the fact that most women like red, while the male preference is for blue. (Dorin, 1927, no pagination)

Before psychologists take exception to these seemingly confusing claims which have no supporting evidence, they are to be reminded that the aim of the subject matter of this section is to recount the intention and claims of the architects and designers, and **their** belief that they were designing to satisfy psychological needs of the people who attended movie theatres.

The architect–cum–art director for Publix Theatres, Frank Cambria (1927), asked whether "a theatre should be dressed up as a home or should a theatre be a theatre, in its design and decoration as well as the presentations offered there for the entertainment of the public?" (p.2185). In the interview with Cambria the editor noted:

> The fact that the success of artistic decoration in the theatre is measured by its ability to stimulate a pleasurable emotion upon the majority of the people explains the prevalence of the colorful treatments used in the de luxe picture houses....
>
> Designing treatments that will appeal to the mass of the picture goers presents primarily a problem in crowd psychology. (p.2185)

Cambria himself claimed that

> The first impression the theatre should create is one of brightness, gaiety. People coming to a theatre are seeking amusement and they are in the frame of mind to be pleased by effects that make an immediate impression of attractiveness. Objects which quickly engage the attention are therefore needed in the decorative scheme – spaciousness, elegance and the vivid coloring of a fairytale are the elements of the ensemble. (p.2187)

Ahlschlager (1927), in elaborating upon the concept of ensemble design claimed that:

> There must be nothing disturbing in the entire ensemble, and above all in the auditorium itself, the stage must hold the undivided attention of the audience. The architectural and decorative scheme must be such as to draw the audience to the stage and the stage to the audience, thereby giving the production a chance to meet the audience more easily across the line of footlights. The audience must form a veritable part of the stage and as the stage has its

The auditorium environment for balcony patrons at a 'deluxe' picture palace. State Theatre, Sydney; opened 1929.

Picture palace auditorium design used all decorative means available to focus attention on the stage and provide a feeling of expectation. State Theatre, Sydney.

lighting effects so must the audience, yet these effects must not
detract from the stage. (no pagination)

Paul J. Henon, president of the Hoffman-Henon Company, an architectural
firm which had designed 100 theatres by 1928, was concerned with
integrating "beauty, utility, safety and economy of operation in the
theatre plant"

> Beauty, for example, means beauty not in the classic sense. It is
> here used not in the abstract - but specifically to mean that which
> shall be held beautiful by the **particular type of people upon whom**
> the **particular theatre will be dependent for its patronage ....**

> Everything about the theatre must be beautiful and restful and tend
> to put the playgoer in a frame of mind in which relaxation plays a
> large part. If the theatre-goer is to be shocked at the outset, by
> some outre or grotesque ornamentation he will never be in the
> **proper frame of mind** to enjoy what is to be presented to him in the
> way of entertainment. He will not have a good time and while he
> may never trace the cause, he does know the effect and
> **unconsciously will develop an aversion** to that particular
> playhouse. (Henon, 1928, no pagination) Emphasis by this author.

Thomas Lamb who, with John Eberson, was one of the two best known and
successful theatre architects in U.S.A. thought the decorative scheme
of a theatre was the most essential part of building after the
architectural background. He thought that it should be defined "as it
is being used in modern times":

> This being a psychological age, it can probably best be defined in
> psychological terms....

> To make our audience receptive and interested, we must cut them off
> from the rest of the city life and take them into a rich and self-
> contained auditorium, where their minds are freed from their usual
> occupations and freed from their customary thoughts. In order to
> do this, it is necessary to present to their eyes a general scheme
> quite different from their daily environment, quite different in
> color scheme, and a great deal more elaborate.... The theatre is
> the palace of the average man. As long as he is there, it is his,
> and it helps him to lift himself out of his daily drudgery. (Lamb,
> 1928, no pagination)

Although he hardly defines his ideas in psychological terms as he says
he will, it does seem evident that the design of movie theatres may
have been an exercise in architectural determinism which actually was
successful. Yet this was in the 1920s, decades before the phrase was
coined by critics of the architects of the Modern Movement.

Another theatre architect, S. Charles Lee, was also concerned about
the psychological impact of design: "What we must remember is that
every American citizen considers himself a king in his own little
empire. This is the beginning of the psychological analysis of a
theatre building" (Lee, 1929, p.31). Again, however, the "psychology"
is hypothetical or expressed as a type of elemental theorizing which
was not systematically tested.

It was assumed by these architects that their theories were substantiated by the popularity of the theatre through attendance by audience. The client exhibitors also believed this, and employed them to design more and more "de luxe" movie theatres. Lee (1929) was very concerned about the careful expenditure of money, reconciling the need to put the maximum possible number of seats on the site, and provide the impression of luxury and spaciousness to the public spaces. He felt that lobby and foyer space was an "important sacrifice of precious seating room.... When the minimum space to be allotted to this purpose is determined upon, then the architect must use his greatest skill to make this space seem larger...." (p.31). He also reinforced the claim by the Rapp brothers insofar that the balcony patrons should be perhaps more consciously considered than others because they must mount stairs to their seats. He spoke of stairs which enticed people up - in his words "**pull up** instead of **discouraging down**" (Lee, 1929, p.31).

The architect who was most innovative in providing a kind of escapist stage-set environment for the auditorium was John Eberson. For the interiors of what were described as "atmospheric" theatres he denied, in visual terms, the fact that the auditorium was an enclosed space with walls and roof. He tells of how he was struck by the idea expressed in one of the editorials of **Motion Picture News**. It claimed that it is the

> climax of showmanship to be able to make your audience feel at home, to make them feel that they have a most important role to play in the entertainment which they are attending, and that it is most necessary to create a warm and friendly atmosphere in the theatre. (Eberson, 1927, no pagination)

As a result of reading this he turned his efforts towards the "development of a different conception of atmosphere carried out in architectural treatment". The concept was to provide a plain curved ceiling which was to be a simulated sky, together with complex, false surrounding garden walls and building facades, containing grilled openings, niches, pergolas, statuary, artificial creepers, shrubs, and stuffed birds.

Eberson claimed that the "quickly-won popularity" of this style could be "attributed to the fact that these auditoriums are successfully different and are merely dignified imitations of nature glorifying classic architecture". He also claimed that "in an out-of-door atmosphere, in addition to the 'warm' and 'friendly' foreign picturesqueness, the spectator enjoys the natural beauty of skies and flowers he has been brought up to love". (Eberson, 1927, no pagination) He wrote of his diligence in recreating the complex colouring of the Mediterranean built environment using hundreds of shades of pastel colours, but his belief in the "peculiar blue" sky colour selected, and its attributes, could be termed 'psychological', even if it could not be supported with empirical evidence:

> It releases the nerve tension of the audience; refreshes the eye; makes one feel that one can breathe, and it has one hundred and one beneficial effects on the mind and nerves...

Blue is always described as the color of Hope. This is not a
fanciful and trivial sentiment, but a fact which can be
scientifically proved, but it must be a certain defined and
distinct blue on a certain defined and distinct textured surface.
(Eberson, 1927, no pagination)

Although the concept of scientific proof in 1927 may seem
embarrassingly unsophisticated today, the aim of providing pleasure to
the senses or emotions through the colour, texture and form of the
environment was inherent in Eberson's claims, as it was in all those
from the successful theatre architects quoted. They showed themselves
to be articulate, being able to describe their aims in clear,
understandable, if at time colourful language, and produced buildings
which seem to have been understood by, or to have had meaning for the
people who used them. Unlike the architecture of recent years with its
own language of abstract intellectualism to describe its symbolism
and meaning (Rapoport, 1982), the theatre architects of the 1920s never
received the criticism that the general public did not understand or
like their buildings. The criticisms levelled at them were rather that
the buildings were vulgar pastiches of past styles which, for
conservatives, were not archeologically 'correct' in detail (e.g.
Franzheim, 1925), and, for moderns, lacked an abstract purity (e.g.
Schlanger, 1931).

In USA in recent years the general public has gathered around to save
its loved movie palaces which have created so much meaning in so few
historic years. Communities in cities such as De Kalb, Oakland,
Memphis, Aurora, Montgomery, Joliet, Atlanta, Dallas, etc. have
obtained historic classification for them and raised funds to restore
and re-use them as live performance centres (Gruenke, 1983). Such
enthusiasm and hard work is epitomised in the documentation of the
purchase and restoration of the Ohio Theatre, Columbus (Bishop et al,
1978).

CONCLUSION

In discussing an historic example of environmental psychology resort
must be made to evidence which does not conform to the empirical
requirements of today. In the example of the movie theatres of the
1920s in the USA, the words of the architects have been quoted almost
to excess in order to convey their intentions and ideas about designing
for 'psychological' reasons - to create environments which would
provide feelings of emotional well-being. Their success was measured
by buttocks on seats by the exhibitors; and the same architects were
employed to design tens, even hundreds of examples of their concepts,
until the market became saturated at about the time of the Great
Depression. In retrospect, however vulgar their buildings may seem,
however naive or amateur their psychological efforts, it is clear that
these architects and their astute, showmen clients considered the
users, who both attended in great numbers and did not represent any one
class of people. The architects also possessed a sensitivity to the
nature of an environment, and proceeded to communicate to the patron a
strong sense of place. Almost concurrent with the rise of 'social
realism' in USSR these theatre architects of U.S.A. were attempting to
achieve the same objectives as the government decreed style - to design

buildings which would be understood by and communicate meaning for the vast majority of the population. The difference lies in the fact that in U.S.A. these objectives were successfully achieved in the most commercial manner possible.

Picture palace decoration drew on, and mixed all styles of architecture. An entry lobby using predominantly English Gothic elements and Florentine Renaissance style doors. State Theatre, Sydney.

Bibliography

AGREST and GANDELSONAS, 'On Practice (1979)' International
  Architect No.1, Vol.1, Issue 1, 1979.
AHLSCHLAGER, W.W., 'The Roxy, Demonstrating a noteworthy Principle of
  theatre design', Motion Picture News, December, 1927.
ATWELL, D., Cathedrals of the Movies: A History of British Cinemas and
  their Audiences, The Architectural Press, London 1980.
BARKER, C., 'A Theatre for the People', Nineteenth Century British
  Theatre, Richards, K. and Thomson, P. (eds), Methuen, London 1971,
  pp.3-24.
BIRKMIRE, W.H., The Planning and Construction of American Theatres,
  Wiley, New York 1901.
BISHOP, M., COE, F., DAVID, C., ELLIES, C., KIGHT, B., MARSICO,
  J., SALVATO, G. and WOODS, A. (eds), The Ohio Theatre: 1928-1978,
  Columbus Assoc. for the Performing Arts, Columbus, Ohio 1978.
CAMBRIA, F., '...discusses Theatre Design and Decoration in an
  interview by Thomas C. Kennedy', Motion Picture News, June 3, 1927,
  pp.2185-2189.
CANTER, D., The Psychology of Place, Architectural Press, London 1977.
CARD, J., 'The Silent Films of Cecil B. DeMille', in Dentelbaum, M.
  (ed), The "Image" on the Art and Evolution of the Film Dover, New
  York 1979, pp.118-120.
DORIN, A., 'Showmanship and Interior Decoration', Motion Picture News,
  May 1927, n.p.n.
EBERSON, J., 'New Theatres for Old: Originator of the Atmospheric
  Style Discusses the Formula in which Art and Showmanship Meet',
  Motion Picture News, December 29, 1927, n.p.n.
FRANZHEIM, K., 'Present Tendencies in the Design of Theater Facades',
  Architectural Forum, June, 1925, pp.365-368.
FREEMAN, R.E., 'American Movie Theaters, 1894-1977: The Practical Side
  of Fantasy', unpublished paper, 1977, p.8.
GOMERY, D., 'Movie Audiences, Urban Geography, and the History of the
  American Film', The Velvet Light Trap No.19, 1982.
GOODLAD, J.S.R., A Sociology of Popular Drama, Heinemann, London 1971.
GROAT, L., 'Meaning of Post-Modern Architecture: An Examination
  Using the Multiple Sorting Task', J. of Environmental Psychology 2:1,
  March, 1982, 3-22.
GRUENKE JR., B.E., 'The Decorators View', Marquee, J. of the
  Theatre Historical Society: Theater Preservation Issue, Vol.15, No.4,
  1983.
HALL, B.M., The Best Remaining Seats: the story of the golden age
  of the movie palace, Bramhall House, New York 1961.

HANDEL, L.A., Hollywood looks at its audience: A report of film audience research, University of Illinois, Urbana, Ill. 1950; reprinted by Arno Press, 1976.

HENON, P.J., 'The Architect's Service to the Industry: an Interview with', Motion Picture News, December 29, 1928, n.p.n.

HERZOG, C.K., The Motion Picture Theater and Film Exhibition, 1896–1932, Ph.D. Thesis, Northwestern University, 1980; Xerography facsimile copy, University Microfilms, Ann Arbor 1982.

HORAK, J-C., 'The Pre-Hollywood Lubitsch', in Dentelbaum, M. (ed), The "Image" on the Art and Evolution of the Film edited Dover, New York 1979, pp.107–117.

JOWETT, G., Film: The Democratic Art, Little, Brown, Boston 1976.

KOPP, A., Town and Revolution: Soviet Architecture and City Planning 1917–1935, Thames and Hudson, London 1970.

LAMB, T., An Interview with, 'Good Old Days to these Better New Days', Motion Picture News, June 30, 1928, n.p.n.

LANG, J., 'Perception Theory, Formal Aesthetics and the Basic Design Course', EDRA 1983, Proceedings of the Fourteenth International Conference of the Environmental Design Research Association, Amadeo, d., Griffin, J.B. and Potter, J.J. (eds), EDRA Inc., Washington 1983.

LEE, S.C., 'Stretching the Building Fund and the Plot Area', Motion Picture News, December 28, 1929, p.31.

MANVELL, R., The International Encyclopedia of Film, Michael Joseph, London 1972.

MORRISON, C., 'From Nickelodeon to Picture Palace and Back', Design Quarterly, 93 (1974), pp.6–17.

M.P.N., 'Conservative Design Has Lasting Appeal', Motion Picture News, June 22, 1929, pp.43–52.

NORBERG-SHULTZ, C., Meaning in Western Architecture, Rizzoli, New York 1980.

R.A.I.A., Buildings are for People Annual Conference of the Royal Australian Institute of Architects, 1962.

PRAK, N.L., The Visual Perception of the Built Environment, University of Delft, Deft 1977.

PURCELL, A.T., (a) 'The organisation of the experience of the built environment', Environment and Planning B: Planning and Design Volume II, 1984, pp.173–192.

PURCELL, A.T., (b) 'Multivariate models and the attributes of the experience of the built environment', Environment and Planning B: Planning and Design Volume II, 1984, pp.193–212.

PURCELL, A.T., (c) 'Esthetics, measurement and control', Ekistics 307, July/ August 1984, pp.379–387.

RAPOPORT, A., Meaning of the Built Environment: A Non-Verbal Communication Approach, Sage, Beverley Hills 1982.

RAPP, G. and C.W., in Exhibitors Herald Vol.16, May 26, 1923, Better Theatres Section, p.xi.

ROBERTSON, H., Principles of Architectural Composition, Architectural Press, London 1924.

ROTHAFEL, S.L., 'What the Public Wants in the Picture Theater', The Architectural Forum, XLII, 6, June 1925, pp.361–364.

ROTHAFEL, S.L., 'The Architect and the Box Office', The Architectural Forum, LVII, September 1932, p.194.

Royal Commission of New South Wales, 'Construction of Theatres, Public Halls and other places of Public Amusement and concourse', Votes and Proceedings of the Legislative Assembly 1887.

SCHLANGER, B., 'Motion Picture Theatres of Tomorrow', Motion Picture Herald, Better Theatres Section, February 14, 1931, pp.12, 13, 56.

SEXTON, R.W. and BETTS, B.F., American Theatres of Today, Architectural Book Publishing Co., New York 1927.

SHARP, B., A Pictorial History of Sydney's Suburban Cinemas, Barry Sharp, Strawberry Hills, Sydney 1982.

SHARP, B., A Pictorial History of Cinemas in New South Wales, Barry Sharp, Strawberry Hills, Sydney 1983.

SHERIDAN, P., Penny Theatres of Victorian London, Dennis Dobson, London 1981.

SIMON, J.G., Editor Conflicting Experiences of Space: Proceedings of the 4th International Architectural Psychology Conference, Catholic University of Louvain, Louvain-la-Neuve 1979.

THORNE, R., Theatre Buildings in Australia to 1905: from the time of the First Settlement to arrival of cinema, Architectural Research, University of Sydney, Sydney 1971.

THORNE, R., (a) 'Perception and the Architect', A Short Course in Architectural Psychology, Architectural Psychology Research Unit, University of Sydney, Sydney 1974, pp.27-44.

THORNE, R., (b) 'The Perception of the Architects' Space' A Short Course in Architectural Psychology, Architectural Psychology Research Unit, University of Sydney, Sydney 1974, pp.45-78.

THORNE, R., Picture Palace Architecture of Australia, Sun/Academy, South Melbourne, Vic. 1976.

THORNE, R., 'Theatre Buildings as One Indicator of the Social History of Australia', Architecture Australia, September 1979.

THORNE, R., Cinemas of Australia via U.S.A., Department of Architecture, University of Sydney, Sydney 1981.

THORNE, R., CORK, K. and TOD, L., Theatres/Cinemas in New South Wales, unpublished report, Heritage Council of N.S.W., Sydney 1983.

THORNE, R., DIESNER, M., MUNRO-CLARK, M. and HALL, R., Consumer Survey of Housing Demand-Sydney: 18-39 Year Age Group, I.B. Fell Research Centre, University of Sydney, Sydney 1980.

WEAVER, W.R., 'A Visit to the Tivoli' (Chicago), Exhibitors' Herald, Vol.12, April 2, 1921, pp.86-91.

WILSON, A.E., East-End Entertainment, Arthur Barker, London 1954.

YOUNG, W.C., Documents of American Theater History, Vol.1: Famous American Playhouses, 1716-1899 American Library Association, Chicago 1973.

12. Meaning in architecture: Post-Modernism, hustling and the big sell

PAUL HARRIES, ALAN LIPMAN and STEPHEN PURDEN

INTRODUCTORY COMMENT - ON PRODUCING AESTHETIC MEANING

Buildings are meaningful for people: they are endowed with meaning, they carry meaning and, according to some, meanings inhere in buildings. Meaning, then, is a central preoccupation in architectural theory and criticism. For our part, we are uneasy about the ways in which this key concept has been handled recently, particularly by a number of 'Post-Modern' theorists and critics.

Our unease with much of Post-Modern theory centres on the restricted vision of its advocates, on the narrow scope of their social reference. We are especially concerned about their view of people, their audiences, as mere consumers of meaning. In contrast, many founders of the 'Modern' movement in architecture - with whose work Post-Modernists are expressly at odds - manifested a wider vision. For them, architecture was an instrument - indeed, the instrument - for bringing about, for engineering radical social change: a changing architecture for a changing society. They sought to knit architecture to their anticipated social order. They sought a future in which meanings would no longer be treated as marketable objects, as commodities for consumption.

Since the late 1960s, Post-Modernist critics and theorists have advanced prescriptive concepts of meaning. They have marketed a number of ideas and practices. They have attempted to persuade their publics - principally designers - about the relevance to architectural design of matters such as: complexity and contradiction (Robert Venturi, 1977), object fixation and space fixation (Colin Rowe and Fred Koetter, 1978), familiar and unfamiliar (Charles Moore and

188

Gerald Allen, 1976), dual coding (Charles Jencks, 1977), icons and
vessels (Robert Stern, 1981), and semiotic theory (Geoffrey Broadbent,
1977). In our view, these and similar notions cluster around a core
assumption in Post-Modernist thought, that meanings inhere in
buildings. Accordingly, such meanings are treated as commodities; as,
that is, objects to be made available, to be catalogued for designers
to select, to apply, to manipulate.

We contest this view - that meanings inhere in buildings. We
contend that people (including architectural theorists, critics and
practitioners) actively endow their physical environments (including
buildings) with meaning. Thus we question current orthodoxy in
architectural theory. We question the covert - often overt - treatment
of people as passive objects and of physical, spatial settings as
active subjects. We contest the view that people are mere receptors of
aesthetic meaning, that buildings actively generate meanings - that
'objects confer importance to location, and location confers
importance on objects'. (Moore and Allen, 1976, p.51) On the
contrary, for us meanings are constructed socially, they are produced
in specific cultural and historical contexts. Rather than being
innate to objects, meanings are assigned to them. Rather than
containing inherent meanings, buildings carry, they embody meaning.

POST-MODERNISM - THE MARKETING OF MEANING

In focusing on Post-Modern architectural theory we shall examine how a
number of its exponents deal with the concept of meaning. First, we
will discuss how - in their pre-eminently formal emphasis - they treat
of aesthetic issues as surface matters, as superficial phenomena.
They view meaning as residing predominantly in the appearances, the
facades of buildings. Second, we shall consider how this aesthetic of
surface, of shell - this 'facadism' - enables post-modernist critics
to assume the role of aesthetic arbiter. They appropriate aesthetic
meanings, they seize on the decorative aspects of artefacts and, by
abstracting them from the social relations of their use, translate them
into 'the aesthetic'. So, for example, the neon signs and advertising
hoardings of the Las Vegas Strip are treated as if they are
independent of the commercial, the buyer-seller relationships that
give rise to them:

> Las Vegas is analysed here only as a phenomenon of architec-
> tural communication. Just as an analysis of the structure
> of a Gothic cathedral need not include a debate on the
> morality of medieval religion, so Las Vegas's values are not
> questioned here. (Venturi et.al., 1979, p.3)

That is to say, theorists such as Robert Venturi and his co-authors
survey the surface appearances of phenomena in order to select images
which, purportedly, represent the phenomena.

In concluding this discussion of contemporary, Post-Modern architectural theory we will argue that, having objectified and appropriated
acts of aesthetic endowment, Post-Modernist critics market their
interpretations - they offer themselves as entrepreneurs of meaning.

In our experience Post-Modernist discourse consists primarily of
comment on the appearance of buildings. Contributors to the debate

indulge overwhelmingly in what, in another context, the architectural historian Peter Collins referred to as 'pictorial criticism, that is to say appraisals concerned with the appearance of buildings ..... judging buildings largely according to their "appeal to the eye"'.   (1971, p.263)   Consider, by way of illustration, Robert Venturi's Complexity and Contradiction in Architecture, acknowledged as a singular contribution to architectural thought.   (Vincent Scully, 1977, p.12; Robert Maxwell, 1978, p.22; Annette LeCuyer, 1981, p.2)

Complexity and Contradiction is a theoretical treatise, one that is predominantly visual in focus and in subject matter. The book is, in Maxwell's words, 'for the most part a survey of the architectural effects [aesthetic meanings?] which Venturi himself has most enjoyed, taken from a variety of examples both ancient and modern'.   (Maxwell, 1978, p.23)   Venturi scans various geographic locations, a range of historical periods and numerous cultural contexts in order to identify recurring visual effects; effects which he treats as aesthetic constants. Reference to such constants, such quasi-universals, enables him to formulate specific design precepts - tenets for conveying aesthetic meanings. Buildings designed according to these canons stand, Venturi claims, in opposition to 'orthodox Modern architecture'. So - under the rubric 'Complexity and Contradiction vs. Simplification or Picturesqueness' - he argues for a distorted, ambiguous, conventional, accommodating, redundant architecture of 'messy vitality' to replace a straightforward, articulated, designed, excluding, simple architecture of 'obvious unity': compromise, he contends, replaces clean, hybrid replaces pure, less is a bore replaces less is more ..... richness of meaning replaces clarity of meaning.   (Venturi, 1977, p.23)

For Venturi, an architecture of messy vitality conforms with, acknowledges such design tenets as 'both-and' (pp.23-32), 'double function' (pp.34-40), 'superadjacency' (pp.56-68) and 'inflection' (pp.88-105). He uses these and similar notions to account for the constituents of complexity and the elements of contradiction that he assigns to the buildings illustrated and discussed in his text. Thus the maxim 'both-and' refers, we are told, principally to 'the relation of the part to the whole', it 'emphasises double meanings'. Here Venturi contrasts the 'either-or' exclusivity that is characteristic, he claims, of orthodox modern architecture with the 'both-and' inclusivity of his 'valid', abstruse architecture. Modernism, he argues, is clear and directly explicit: 'a sun screen is probably nothing else; a support is seldom an enclosure; a wall is not violated by window penetrations but is totally interupted by glass ...'. He, in contrast, advocates paradox and ambiguity; an 'hierarchy, which yields several levels of meanings among elements with varying values ... simultaneous perception of a multiplicity of levels involves struggles and hesitations for the observer [the spectator], and makes his perception more vivid'.   (pp.23 & 25)

Venturi derives his maxim of 'both-and' from the recurring visual effects, the aesthetic constants which he ascribes to a range of buildings. Thus he cites Hawksmoor's Christ Church at Spitalfields as evidence of the 'both-and' phenomenon because the tower is both wall and tower: at street level it terminates a vista while, above, its spire dominates the skyline. And in the case of the Bruges Cloth Hall, whereas the scale of the building at street level 'relates to the

immediate square' the 'disproportionate' scale of its tower 'relates to
the whole town'. A similar argument is advanced for the Philadelphia
Savings Fund Society Building where, Venturi observes, 'the big sign
sits on top ... and yet it is invisible from below'. (pp.30 & 32)
Evidence of a like order is assembled from such disparate geographic,
historical and cultural sources as Le Corbusier in Ahmedabad and at
Poissy; Lutyens and Vanbrugh in Oxfordshire; Michelangelo, Bernini and
Borromini in Rome; Hawksmoor, Wren and Soane in London; Neumann in
Banz, Vittone in Turin, Fischer von Erlach in Vienna, Furness in
Philadelphia ..... and the Hagia Sophia in Istanbul. (pp.23-33)

In Collage City Colin Rowe and Fred Koetter treat of urban layout in
a not dissimilar manner. (Rowe and Koetter, 1978) They too derive
precepts for designers by surveying the recurring visual effects which
they attribute to a range of urban settings, 'fragments'. They too are
at odds with the Modern Movement: settings designed according to the
tenets they advocate stand in opposition to ideas of 'total planning',
'total design'. Thus, in their chapter 'Crisis of the Object:
Predicament of Texture', they invoke the notions of 'object fixation'
and 'space fixation' to contrast Le Corbusier's plan for Saint-Die
(1945) with the plan of medieval and Renaissance Parma. Whereas the
former 'illustrates, as clearly as possible, the dilemma of the free
standing building, the space occupier attempting to act as space
definer ... a kind of unfulfilling schizophrenia ...', the latter
exemplifies 'the apparent virtues of the traditional city: the solid
and continuous matrix or texture giving energy to its reciprocal
condition; the specific space; the ensuing square and street acting as
some kind of public relief valve and providing some condition of
legible structure; and ... the very great versatility of the supporting
texture or ground'. (pp.60-63) Like Venturi, Rowe and Koetter do
not reject modernism in toto. Rather than opting for the 'either-or',
on the one hand, of object fixation or, on the other, of space
fixation, for them '... the situation to be hoped for should be recognised as one in which both buildings and spaces exist in an equality of
sustained debate'. (emphasis in original - pp.151-181)

Having called on other, similar notions - such as 'figure-ground',
'solid-void', 'bricolage', 'collision city' - the arguments in Collage
City culminate in a 'list of stimulants, a-temporal and necessarily
transcultural ... possible objets trouvés in the urbanistic collage';
items such as Stabilzers, Potentially Interminable Set Pieces,
Ambiguous and Composite Buildings, and Nostalgia-producing Instruments.
(pp.151-181) These too are assembled from diverse geographic
locations, historical periods and cultural contexts. Thus we are
informed that nostalgia 'may be "scientific" and of the future,
"romantic" and of the past or ..... simply elegant vernacular or "Pop"'
and is to be induced by reference to images drawn from The Strip at Las
Vegas, offshore oil rigs, the pyramid of Caius Centius in Rome, Galena
in Illinois, Cape Canaveral, Vignola's garden temple at Bomarzo and the
walled fortifications at Montlouis and at Briancon.

In Dimensions, a further contribution to the Post-Modernist argument,
Charles Moore and Gerald Allen (1976) convey a similar preoccupation
with facadism, with the aesthetic of surface. Their book, they write:

    ... is a series of architectural walking tours. The buildings
    described are from widely different times and places, and they

are in the low and middle styles, as well as the high one.
They are linked ... by a small set of general concepts we
think are useful in looking not only at them, but at any
buildings. (p.vii)

The authors of Dimensions - like Venturi and like Rowe and Koetter -
treat of buildings primarily from the standpoint of observers,
stressing their 'appeal to the eye'. They also survey examples drawn
from disparate sources (from, for instance, Hadrian's Villa to Main
Street in Disneyland) to illustrate recurring visual effects,
aesthetic constants. Not least among such quasi-universals - for
example 'place', 'inclusive and exclusive' - is their notion of
'familiar and unfamiliar':

> ... it seems to us useful to regard design as the choreography
> of the familiar and the unfamiliar - the chance to massage our
> sensibilities with shapes that are likely to be familiar to us
> (whatever their specific connotation to our individual lives)
> and shapes or relationships full of surprise, which call us
> to attention and response, readying us for choice.   (p.15)

Designers, apparently, are active - they choreograph, they direct:
their audiences respond, they consume. The former produce familiar and
unfamiliar meanings ('in the low and middle styles, as well as the high
one') to induce appropriate reactions in the latter (low, middle and
high!). Having had their sensibilities suitably massaged by the
arrangement of shapes, people are, apparently, called to attention,
they are readied for choice. For Moore and Allen, Disneyland, 'the
most important single piece of construction in the West in the past
several decades', epitomizes the range of such choice. Here a 'whole
public world' is on offer (for those able to pay); a public realm
which allows people to be both spectators and 'participants', to
respond to opportunities for 'big and little drama, hierarchies of
importance and excitement ..... at the speed of rocketing bobsleds
..... or of horse-drawn streetcars'. But, we are reminded,
Disneyland 'does not offer the full range of public experience':

> The political experience, for instance, is not manifested
> there. Yet there is a variety of forms and activities
> great enough to ensure an excellent chance that the
> individual visitor will find something to identify with.
> (pp.116-119)

Disneyland is for Moore and Allen what Las Vegas is for Venturi et
al - a Post-Modernist exemplar of public place; a place primarily for
purchase and entertainment, a market-place of meaning. Customarily in
such places, freedom of choice is limited to selection from commodities
made available to people; it precludes 'the political experience' -
their active control of what might be relevant to them. For us,
however:

> Freedom is not merely the chance to do as one pleases;
> neither is it merely the opportunity to choose between set
> alternatives. Freedom is, first of all, the chance to
> formulate the available choices, to argue over them - and
> then, the opportunity to choose. (C. Wright Mills, 1978,
> p.193)

Charles Jencks (1977), historian and theorist of post-modern

architecture, has made the current ethos of marketing explicit; indeed,
for him, it constitutes the 'theoretical base of Post-Modernism'.
Jencks embraces the notion of aesthetic meaning as marketable commodity, he repeatedly depicts architects as producers of meanings ('high'
and 'low') for consumption by others:

> A Post-modern building is ... one which speaks on at least
> two levels at once: to other architects and a concerned
> minority who care about specifically architectural meanings,
> and to the public at large ... who care about other issues
> concerned with comfort ... and a way of life .....
> architects can read the implicit metaphors and subtle
> meanings ... whereas the public can respond to the explicit
> metaphors and messages.

In illustrating this 'definition of Post-Modern building', this
'visual formula', he invites us to consider a pediment of the Temple of
Artemis, Corcyra (6th century BC). Here, we are told, is a 'billboard'
containing a mixture of meanings, 'popular' and 'elite'. Popular
'audiences' are presented with the 'dramatic' story of Medusa, complete
with snakes and rampant lion-panthers, rendered in strong colour.
Elite audiences - concerned minorities - are addressed on a different
'level': they read 'human proportions, visual refinements and a pure
architecture of syntactic elements'.   (p.6)

Not surprisingly, then, our reading of Post-Modernist theory and
criticism is that its proponents evince a patronising, a condescending
view of 'the public at large'. They consider themselves arbiters of
meaning. They posit that people's aesthetic views, the aesthetic
meanings with which people endow buildings, are mere induced responses.
Architects, they contend, build meaning; people are regarded as consumers of meaning who passively receive messages. In contrast,
theorists and critics produce meaning, select appropriate messages;
they identify recurring visual effects from which they derive design
prescriptions for architects to assemble and manipulate aesthetic
meanings. They furnish designers with packages, catalogues of meaning
- with inventories such as Robert Stern's (1977) 'paradigms and principles' and Venturi et.al.'s (1979) 'types of change' (pp.34 & 35),
their 'ingredients of architectural monumentality' (p.47), their
categories for assessing whether or not 'boring architecture is
interesting' (p.72).

Uncertainty about the demand for and distribution of popular meanings
may, we are informed, be resolved by consulting 'social research'.
Thus Jencks (1977, pp.129-130) urges architects to call on opinion
pollsters (market researchers such as Conrad Jameson) in order 'fully'
to understand 'the values of the local ... the semiotic group', 'the
language of the tribe'. On the other hand, Geoffrey Broadbent (who
interprets social research for architects) refers designers to the
apparently more precise potential of environmental psychology.
(Broadbent, 1977)   He evokes a variety of research procedures -
including semantic differential, repertory grid and semiotic analyses -
to identify the meanings that buildings 'carry'. As a case-in-point,
he cites a study of, among other buildings, the Parthenon in which
participants were required to appraise, on seven-point scales, whether
this historical monument is 'hot' or 'cold', 'fast' or 'slow', 'strong',
or 'weak', 'good, clean, valuable' or 'bad, dirty, worthless'. Of
course, 'these scales can only be applied metaphorically'; but this,

Broadbent claims, is their 'strength' - 'they help us get past the opinions we <u>thought</u> we had' (emphasis in original).

For Broadbent the prospects are promising - Post-Modernism is on the brink of meeting the demand for aesthetic meaning so long frustrated by the Modern Movement:

> Theoretical studies of meaning in architecture and deliberate attempts to again build architecture with meaning are coming together in the work of architects such as the Venturis ..... Robert Stern and Charles Moore.

We view these preoccupations in design theory and criticism as facets of contemporary consumerism. They are the specifically architectural forms of what Raymond Williams (1981, p.362) has termed the 'dominant cultural styles appropriate to consumer capitalism'. We regard the advocates of post-modernism as purveyors of packaged meaning, as vendors of stylisms. They are part of and contribute to a dominant orientation in consumer society; an orientation directed overwhelmingly toward marketing commodities for mass consumption:

> The term Post-Modernism is ideological and its coinage as a slogan by Jencks and others surely has the aim of reducing culture to consumerism ..... Post-Modernism as a polemic, consciously or unconsciously intends the destruction of the resistance of architecture and its reduction to the status of one more consumer good.   (Kenneth Frampton, 1980a)

THE MODERN MOVEMENT - UTOPIAS INCORPORATED

Post-Modernism is, we contend, a celebration of consumerism. The founders of the Modern Movement - the objects of much Post-Modernist denunciation - viewed architectural meaning rather differently. They treated of aesthetic meanings as harbingers, as visions of a new society; as expressions of their utopias.

The ideas and practices central to the Modern Movement were rooted in the social context of the two decades following World War I, a period marked by expectation of social change; indeed, in certain Central and Eastern European instances, by the actual emergence of new social orders. Members of the architectural vanguard - for example, Eric Mendelsohn and Walter Gropius (with his colleagues at the Bauhaus) - interpreted this context in a similarly anticipatory way:

> From 1914 on, the new architecture, expressing the new and necessary facts on which our future will have to be built ... has embraced its duty with rightful determination to reshape our earth in accordance with the social needs of today ... this, in fact, is what the world expects from the architect: to form the signs, the symbols of a new age.   (Mendelsohn, 1944, p.31)

> Together let us conceive and create the new building of the future, which will embrace architecture <u>and</u> sculpture <u>and</u> painting in one unity and which will rise one day toward heaven from the hands of a million workers like the crystal symbol of a new faith.   (emphases in original - Bayer et.al., 1959, p.16)

And others among Mendelsohn's and Gropius' contemporaries expressed their commitment to societal change in, on occasion, similarly gauche rhetoric:

> Our modern system of production is imposed labor, a senseless
> pursuit, and, in its social aspects, without plan; its motive
> is to squeeze out profits to the limit ... the chase after
> money and power influences the form of life ..... the penning
> up of city people in treeless barracks, in an extreme contrac-
> tion of living space ... city life has brought with it
> herding into barren buildings without adequate open space, an
> emotional choking of the inhabitants ..... Not the product,
> but man, is the end in view ... Not the occupation, not the
> goods to be manufactured, ought to be put in the foreground,
> but rather recognition of man's organic function ..... We
> then lay down the basis for an organic system of production
> whose focal point is man, not profit.   (Maholy-Nagy, 1947,
> pp.15&17)

In short, influential Modernists sought a new architecture for a new society; for, that is, their socialist utopias – a commitment which has been documented by such varied commentators as Nikolaus Pevsner (1960, pp.19-39), Kenneth Frampton (1980b, pp.130-141), Anthony Jackson (1970, pp.36-43) and David Watkin (1977, pp.37-61). The pioneers of modernism viewed architecture as a means of social libera- tion. The aesthetic meanings which they assigned to 'modern architecture' were socially emancipatory – 'a vital architectural spirit, rooted in the entire life of a people, represents the inter- relation of all phases of creative effort, all arts, all techniques'. (Bayer et.al.,1959, p.20)   Accordingly, unlike Post-Modern theorists, early advocates of the Modern Movement sought to look beyond the appearances, the surfaces of objects. They viewed aesthetic meanings as being rooted in social life:

> The road that runs into the ... [Van Nelle tobacco factory,
> Rotterdam, 1927-29] is smooth, flat, bordered with brown
> tiled sidewalks; it is as clean and bright as a dance floor.
> The sheer facades of the building, bright glass and grey
> metal, rise up ... against the sky ....   The serenity of
> the place is total. Everything is open to the outside.
> And this is of enormous significance to all those who are
> working, on the eight floors inside .... The ... [factory],
> a creation of the modern age, has removed all the former
> connotations of despair from that word 'proletarian'. And
> this deflection of the egoistic property instinct towards a
> feeling for collective action leads to a most happy result:
> the phenomenon of personal participation in every stage of
> the human enterprise. (emphases in original – Le Corbusier
> in Frampton, 1980b, p.134)

Whereas Post-Modern theorists focus, primarily, on the appearance of buildings in order to prescribe assemblages of visual effect; theorists of the Modern Movement focussed on social needs in order to formulate design principles. For instance, confronted with the issue of high density housing for 'urban industrial populations' – 'the penning up of city people in treeless barracks' – Gropius analysed relationships between the spacing and the heights of apartment buildings and, on this basis, advanced design guidance intended to

ensure improved 'conditions as to air, sun, view and distance'.
(Gropius, 1962, p.99)   And in stating their formally explicit principles of design (in, for example, Les 5 points d'une architecture
novelle) Le Corbusier and Jeanneret (1943, p.128) evidenced a similar
response. They argued for:

1. pilotis to elevate the mass of a building off the ground
2. a 'free' plan realised by separating load-bearing
columns from sub-dividing, internal, walls
3. a 'free facade', the counterpart in the vertical plane
of the free plan
4. horizontal strip windows and
5. a flat roof, preferably landscaped, to replace the
ground covered by the building.

That is to say, they attempted to integrate technological innovation,
radical architectural form and changing patterns of space use. They
sought, via principled design, to liberate stylistic form and anticipate changing social need. This contrasts markedly with Post-
Modernists' preference for the free-market; for, that is, their
capricious, their wayward selection from whatever has been made
available:

The main justification for honky-tonk elements in architectural order is their very existence. They are what we have.
(Venturi, 1977, p.42)

Any middle-class urbanite in any large city from Teheran to
Tokyo is bound to have a well-stocked, indeed over-stocked,
'image-bank' that is continually restuffed by travel and
magazines ... it seems ... desirable that architects learn
to use this inevitable heterogeneity of languages. Besides,
it is quite enjoyable. Why, if one can afford to live in
different ages and cultures, restrict oneself to the
present, the locale? Eclecticism is the natural evolution
of a culture with choice.   (Jencks, 1977, p.127)

In seeking a unity of aesthetic and social goals, theorists of the
Modern Movement (like their radical predecessors, such as William
Morris and others of the Arts and Crafts movement - Cole, 1944)
attacked established cultural symbols, they challenged the dominant
cultural ideas of their time. In opposing the 'outmoded' design
conventions of academist architecture, they attempted 'rationally' to
harness architectural design to contemporary industrial production.
For the founders of the Modern Movement, then, aesthetic meanings
arose from and were integral to their critical appraisals of and
interventions in their social milieux. They regarded aesthetic change
as part of social change - a unity of form and content. Accordingly,
the meanings with which they endowed their buildings were utopian in
character, and they anticipated that others - their publics - would
interpret these buildings similarly. Their aesthetic, their utopian
vision, embodied and simultaneously revealed an emancipatory
potential: transformations in the old order were to be paralleled -
indeed propelled - by principled aesthetic transformations in
architecture.

Modern architecture was to have been, according to the principles of
modernism, styleless - a revolt against what the founders considered
the 'hollow', the formalistic styles of academism. Thus, in 1923,

Gropius called for a new, an anti-stylistic 'approach to architecture':

> Architecture during the last few generations has become weakly
> sentimental ... Its chief concern has been with ornamentation,
> with the formalistic use of motifs, ornaments and mouldings on
> the exterior of the building ..... In this decadence ... the
> architect was engulfed in academic estheticism ... This kind
> of architecture we disown. We want to create a clear organic
> architecture ... unencumbered by lying facades and trickeries,
> we want ... an architecture where function is clearly recog-
> nizable in the relations of its forms. (Bayer et.al., 1959,
> p.27)

Paradoxically, however, yet another architectural style, a new formalism, arose from their work. The unity of form and content which the
founders attempted to realise, and which they associated with 'the new
architecture', was not to be. While the formal images of modernism –
its surface appearances – became parts of so-called International
Style, the theories – the principles – were reduced to mere techniques
for reproducing the 'modernistic' forms of that style. Forms intended
to challenge the prevailing cultural dominance became part of, were
incorporated into that dominance.

And not surprisingly – given the leading role which the pioneers
assumed for themselves and given the social circumstances in which
buildings were and continue to be produced.

The founders of modern architecture viewed themselves, and were
viewed by contemporary members of the intelligentsia, as an elite, a
vanguard – see, for example, Mies van der Rohe and Le Corbusier on
Walter Gropius. (Giedion, 1954, pp.17-19) As such, they assumed the
privilege of defining and the obligation of prescribing aesthetic
meanings for others. Thus, the utopias they envisaged were defined in
their terms and were to be conveyed via their buildings for reception,
for consumption by others. This took place in a particular social
context: one in which access to and command of resources (principally
property, finance and labour) was – and, indeed, remains – asymmetri-
cally distributed.

The new, supposedly oppositional architecture was advocated in
circumstances in which the interests of those owning buildings (and/or
controlling their usage) did not, and still do not, necessarily
coincide with the interests of the majority of people living and
working in them. Whereas the founders had anticipated that their new
architecture would be put to the service of all, in effect the style
they initiated served minority interests. And, of course, a number of
the key features of modernism appealed specifically to those with
privileged command of resources. The new architecture with the
emphasis its advocates placed on concepts such as rational planning and
organisation, mass production, economy of means, speed of contruction,
standardisation and functional utility seemed expressly relevant to the
vested interests of contemporary industrial production. Indeed,
modern architecture may be considered to have been 'successful' to the
extent that such emphases, such technical imperatives were endorsed by
its sponsors, by those who commission architectural services.

The styleless architecture that was to have challenged cultural orthodoxy, that was to have supplanted the dominant formalism of the period, became the 'international style' of dominance. Modern architecture was utilised instrumentally: its technical potential harnessed to production, its emancipatory promise discarded - its form ruptured from its content. Thus the founders' utopias became incorporated into prevailing cultural dominance: on the one hand via the stylistic reproductions of design practitioners and on the other via the technical instrumentality of those who commission their services. Impoverished in this manner, modernist aesthetics can be dismissed by such Post-Modern theorists as Venturi, as Rowe and Koetter, as Moore and Allen, as Broadbent. Denuded of content, modern architectural form can be excavated for stylistic appropriation - see, for example, Jencks (1977, pp.61, 66 and 67) on Richard Meier and Peter Eisenman.

POSTSCRIPT

> ... [I am] deeply honoured if somewhat surprised. I can't help wondering why now [1982, on being awarded the Royal Gold Medal for Architecture] when my kind of architecture is so out of fashion? To me architecture wasn't just a style, it was a fighting tool for a better society. Today architecture produces monsters, contrived, covered in hopeless frills, and in forms that have degenerated into molasses. (Berthold Lubetkin, 1982)

Aesthetic meanings, we contend, do not reside in objects: on the contrary, objects such as buildings are actively endowed with meaning and are so endowed in specific social contexts. Indeed, the active manner in which people attribute meanings to buildings may challenge or sustain existing social relationships, existing power relationships. As we have argued, in a context characterised by anticipation of social change, the meanings embodied in the aesthetic theories and principles of 'the new architecture' offered challenges to dominant cultural ideas. And in a context characterised by accommodation to an existing order, the meanings embodied in the Post-Modern stylistic repertoire reinforce and sustain dominant cultural ideas. Whereas the Moderns challenged the static formalism of academist architecture by advocating active intervention in historical processes, Post-Modernists affirm such formalism by treating 'history' as a warehouse from which styles can be selected according to individual preference. Whereas the Moderns sought to establish new principles of architectural design, Post-Modernists seize on and seek to reproduce mere images, surface duplications. Whereas the Moderns sought an end to stylistic fetishism, Post-Modernists celebrate stylistic eclecticism, the reduction of architecture to a parade of styles - from Post-Modernism to Post-Post Modernism to Free-Style Classicism to .....

BIBLIOGRAPHY

Bayer, H., Gropius, W. and Gropius, I.,(eds), (1959), Bauhaus 1919-1928, Branford, Boston.
Broadbent, G., (1977), 'A plain man's guide to the theory of signs in architecture', Architectural Design, vol.47, no.7-8, pp.474-482.
Cole, G.D.H., (ed.), (1944), William Morris; Stories in Prose -

Stories in Verse - Shorter Poems, Lectures and Essays, Nonesuch
Press, Bloomsbury.

Collins, P., (1971), Changing Ideals in Modern Architecture, Faber and
Faber, London.

Frampton, K., (1980a), 'Modern architecture', Domus, no.610, October
1980, p.26.

Frampton, K., (1980b), Modern Architecture: A Critical History,
Thames and Hudson, London.

Giedion, S., (1954), Walter Gropius, Work and Teamwork, Architectural
Press, London.

Gropius, W., (1962), Scope of Total Architecture, Collier, New York.

Jackson, A., (1970), The Politics of Architecture: A History of
Modern Architecture in Britain, Architectural Press, London.

Jencks, C., (1977), The Language of Post-Modern Architecture, Academy
Editions, London.

Le Corbusier et Jeanneret, P., (1943), Oeuvre Complète de 1910-1929,
Girsberger, Zurich.

LeCuyer, A., (1981), 'Symbols for the young', Building Design,
10th July 1981, p.2

Lubetkin, B., (1982), Sunday Times, 7th March, p.15.

Maxwell, R., (1978), in Dunster, D., (ed.), Architectural Monographs I,
Venturi and Rauch, Academy Editions, London.

Mendelsohn, E., (1944), Three Lectures on Architecture: Architecture
in a World Crisis, Architecture Today, Architecture in a Rebuilt
World, University of California Press, Berkeley.

Mills, C.W., (1978), The Sociological Imagination, Penguin,
Harmondsworth, Middlesex.

Moholy-Nagy, L., (1947), The New Vision 1928 and Abstracts of an
Artist, Wittenborn, New York.

Moore, C. and Allen, G., (1976), Dimensions: Space, Shape and Scale
in Architecture, Architectural Record Books, New York.

Pevsner, N., (1960), Pioneers of Modern Design: from William Morris
to Walter Gropius, Penguin, Harmondsworth, Middlesex.

Rowe, C. and Koetter, F., (1973), Collage City, MIT Press, Cambridge,
Mass.

Scully, V., (1979), in Venturi et.al., op.cit.

Stern, R., (1977), 'Robert Stern at the edge of Post-Modernism: some
methods, paradigms and principles for architecture at the end of the
modern movement', Architectural Design, vol.47, no.4, pp.129-130.

Stern, R., (1981), Robert Stern, Architectural Design and Academy
Editions, London.

Venturi, R., (1977), Complexity and Contradiction in Architecture,
Architectural Press, London.

Venturi, R., Scott Brown, D. and Izenour, S., (1979), Learning from
Las Vegas, MIT Press, Cambridge, Mass.

Watkin, D., (1977), Morality and Architecture: The Development of a
Theme in Architectural History and Theory from the Gothic Revival to
the Modern Movement, Clarenden Press, Oxford.

Williams, R., (1981), Politics and Letters, Interviews with New Left
Review, Verso, London.

13. Complexity, order and an architectural aesthetic

PETER SMITH

Starting from the premise that aesthetic perception represents an
extension of brain programs relating to adaptation and survival, I
relate the fundamental strategy of exacting order from complexity to
aesthetic appreciation. The proposition is tested against a variety
of architectural examples which nevertheless fall into two main
categories: boundary-dependent and linear. In the first condition
the boundary may be explicit or implicit - created in the eye of the
beholder to enable a particular assembly of buildings to stand out
from its context as harmonically rich figure against ground. In
either case the primary aesthetic condition is that unity should
outweigh particularity. This being met, the mind then seeks to
discover further levels of orderliness. The most straightforward
means of lowering complexity is to attempt to organise data into
binary sets: paired entities which have a logical connection but also
a significant level of autonomy. Binary interactions occur on two
levels: integral and discrete. The former comprises interactions
distributed within and across a building or town sequence; the latter
between discrete major architectural elements. Aesthetic reward may
follow the apprehension of orderliness within the interaction, either
equivalence or harmony. The second major category concerns the
optimum ratio of order to complexity in a linear dimension embracing
not only a building, but whole streets, neighbourhoods and
occasionally cities like Amsterdam.

There has been substantial research into aesthetic perception and the assumption is occasionally made that conclusions obtained with abstract data can be transposed to architecture and urbanism. The problem is that architectural data are usually impure in aesthetic terms. They are "adulterated" by variables such as associational symbolism or possibly fundamental symbolism. My own theoretical investigation into architectural and urban aesthetics tries to take this into account.

I still subscribe to the view that certain forms and arrangements of light and dark are attributed with common symbolic meaning. This may be the result of fuzzy brain programs or acculturation. The universality of these symbols suggests a degree of hard-wiring, but this is immaterial to the fact that, for one reason or another, people in general are emotionally moved by certain urban configurations. Why else do millions converge on historic cities where this archetypal resonance is strongest if not to experience this primordial pulse-beat?.

This responsiveness to symbols merges into the other principal source of emotional reward in cities, the aesthetic reward. At least since Aristotle, aesthetic reward has been associated with the clash between complexity and order -"similarity within dissimilars". Only since Baumgarten has the term "aesthetic" been employed. Within philosophy the term has been applied to the "detached contemplation" of phenomena: the abstract relationship between colours, tones, textures or tones and timbre in music. Cognitive meaning is said to interfere with aesthetic perception.

I have challenged this view on the grounds that the human brain is an interactive system in which parts cannot be shut-off. Cognitive meaning is bound to affect aesthetic judgement and indeed may directly contribute to it.

I have sought to widen the connotation of the term "aesthetic" on the basis that it represents a particular pattern of psychological events which occur in many situations often far removed from the rarified milieu associated with aesthetics.

What, then, is the origin of aesthetic perception?. There seems to be general agreement that it is linked with the classification facility of the brain. The survival prospects of higher animals are dependent upon their capacity to classify information correctly. This classification capability is closely associated with the exploratory drive. All higher animals have an appetite for stimulation, for the experience of surprise and novelty provided it is within tolerable limits. The obvious survival advantage of this is that it causes the animal progressively to enlarge its model of the world, thus reducing the sum total of uncertainty. The process of marrying-up each new set of experiences to the existing model or schema of the world involves a radical shake-up. Everything is altered by the experience: a measure of re-classification takes place right down the line.

There are two incentives behind the exploratory drive. The first
involves the pleasure derived from confronting novelty and surprise
and is associated with arousal and all its physiological
consequences. When the new has been grafted on to the corpus of
existing knowledge and the re-classification is complete, a second
class of pleasure comes into operation: the reward for successful
adaptation to the new information resulting in a more comprehensive
model of the world and thus less chance of being taken by surprise.
This second category of reward is connected with the lowering of
arousal; of the suppression of its physiological effects. There is a
further adaptive benefit in that this pattern of behaviour tends to
enhance the capacity to process novelty. The cycle of curiosity and
exploration leading to a higher state of orderliness is said by
Berlyne and others to be at the root of aesthetic experience.

Architecture is one of the principal sources of novelty and
surprise and occasional shock. It tends to be large in scale and is,
for the most part, unavoidable. The public appetite for new
architectural experience seems to be insatiable. Yet new buildings
have limited appeal, (though the Centre Georges Pompidou is
overwhelmed by visitors). What people take most pleasure in is more
or less familiar architecture in new combinations. This is the
appeal of historic cities; the ratio of novelty to familiarity falls
within acceptable limits. There is enough novelty to satisfy the
curiosity drive, but sufficient familiarity to prevent adaptive or
orienting overload. This is the essence of rhyme: "likeness tempered
with difference".

In its endeavour to reduce the mass of incoming data to a
manageable degree of orderliness, the mind will first compare this
data with existing models and classify accordingly. Where novelty is
identified this is assimilated into the model provided it falls
within manageable margins.

The next stage of the ordering process is to consider the
phenomenology of the data, their form and meaning; to discover if
there are further levels of orderliness lying hidden within the
complexity.

Classification is normally associated with equating sensory imput
with existing models. In terms of information this can be expressed
as encountering complexity so as to achieve a higher level of
orderliness - a richer mental model. The principles of complexity
and orderliness or redundancy can be transposed to other kinds of
informational clash apart from novelty and familiarity. The
classification routine can be adapted to judging the quality of the
relationships between phenomena and this, I believe, is where we
cross the threshold of aesthetics.

The first priority of the ordering drive on the level of
phenomenology is to discover discrete wholes in which the impression
of unity and coherence "outweighs" the assertiveness and autonomy of
the parts. Wholeness outweighs particularity. This is the first
condition of success in architecture and urbanism.

The most successful buildings are those which clearly express their
elements but which, at the same time, come across as wholes which are
much greater than the sum of their parts. This is the primary
aesthetic "dialectic" in architecture. Aesthetic success demands that
orderliness wins, but not too easily. There has to be sufficient
complexity to make the perception of unity a worthwhile mental
achievement.

A 'classic' example is the Greek temple. Its parts are clearly
expressed: columns, entablature, pediments and crepidoma, but they
are all subservient to the coherence of the whole. One might even
say the same of the Pompidou Centre in Paris which perhaps lies near
the limits of the tension between complexity and order. It has taken
time for the novelty shock to subside so that the phenomenological
clash between variety and unity can benefit from unclouded
assessment. A subjective view is that unity ultimately wins but only
after great bloodshed. Other buildings indisputably fail this
primary requirement.

In art and architecture criticism it is common to talk of the
"weight" of elements as though the mind uses the analogy of
interacting masses to work out the orderliness of a painting or
building. Information weight is made up to two components: stimulus
complexity and attributed meaning or symbolism.

Aesthetic perception is concerned with the intuitive
counter-balancing of "forces" or "weights" to produce a clear result.
It has to be said that this mental strategy of using the laws of
physics to evaluate the orderliness potential of a given network of
visual stimuli must be regarded as an enabling metaphor. After
perceiving that a given whole is greater than the autonomy of the
component parts, the mind then seeks to discover orderliness within
the constituent information. It tends to do so by organising data
into binary sets, that is, two units of information which have a
logical connection but nevertheless each possessing a significant
measure of uniqueness. This could be a two-way phenomenen since
architects frequently design buildings according to visual binary
principles, either simply or hierarchically.

To achieve this binary orderliness, information within a reasonable
band of similarity is aggregated or "chunked"; differences are
suppressed in favour of similarities. Indeed this chunking is a
mental tendency when confronted by unfamilarity. Under pressure to
achieve classification, subtle differences are ignored in favour of
the broad affinities, a tendency which, if unchecked, can
ultimately lead to psychological blindness.

Whilst binary chunking represents a dimension of orderliness
beyond schema classification, further systematising is possible on
the level of the relationships between the paired entities. This is
where the matter of aesthetic judgement comes into sharper focus.

The relationship on the binary level can achieve three conditions:

i)   balance/equivalance
ii)   harmony
iii)   ambiguity.

Balance is not to be confused with symmetry. It describes the
condition of equivalence of visual and psychological weight.
Psychological weight is the sum of visual intricacy and symbolic
meaning. Thus a relatively small object saturated with symbolism can
balance a much larger expanse of visual intricacy as proved by
Constable's paintings of Dedham Vale in which a small church tower
balances the much more extensive features of landscape and sky.

Harmony in the visual arts is epitomised by the proportions of the
golden section in which one axis outweighs the other by an amount
sufficient to eliminate uncertainty about its form but not so much as
to annihilate the subordinate axis. This principle can be translated
into much more complex informational interactions, especially in
architecture where this clash of diverse elements occurs broadly in
two ways:

i)   integral - distributed across a building
ii)   discrete - binary clash between autonomous major
                   architectural elements.

Returning to the Greek Temple, say, the Parthenon, it displays
integral clash in a variety of ways, the most obvious perhaps being
that between the vertical and horizontal axes.

Allegedly one of the main reasons for the aesthetic 'perfection' of
the Parthenon is because its front conforms overall to the
proportions of the golden section. There are other, more subtle
reasons. The Greek temple supports a much more vigorous interaction
between the vertical and horizontal principles than is represented by
the proportions of its front. The rapid rhythm of columns
accentuated by fluting makes a strong bid for "verticalness". It is
held in check by the immense combined visual weight of the
entablature and pediment and the three-stepped base or crepidoma.
Success finally goes to "horizontalness", but the relative difference
in attributed weight places this contrariety firmly within harmonic
margins.

Another binary system concerns the concepts of outside and inside.
The columniated perimeter of the temple creates a soft boundary.
"Insideness" leaks out through the space between columns. However,
the rate of intercolumnation combined with the robustness of the
columns establishes the harmonic supremacy of "boundariness".
Other visual dialogues involve the sculptured with the plain and
the round with rectangular. Of course, the ultimate aesthetic
encounter is between the Parthenon itself and other buildings of the
Acropolis, especially the entrance complex, the Propylaea. The
tangential relationship here is a magnificent piece of aesthetic
management.

Gothic architecture maximised the tension between the vertical and the horizontal with lines drawn in space. At Chartres there is harmonic stability favouring the vertical. As Gothic progressed, the vertical component increasingly got out of hand.

Renaissance churches sometimes achieved a miraculous balance of axes such as Palladio's Venetian Church facades of S.Giorgio Maggiore and II Redentore. Even Roman baroque architects like Borromini achieved equilibrium out of feverish activity as in the facade of St Agnese. Today it is the architecture of Arup Associates and Powell and Moya which sustains this axial contest, invariably expressed with great finesse.

In all these cases, to achieve an equation that is testable for aesthetic potential, the mind again indulges in "chunking". Features broadly conforming to a prototypical principle, say, verticality, are aggregated to constitute an informational "mass" which is attributed with the property of weight. This is then counterbalanced against the discrete but related partner in the binary set.

Where the outcome of the equation is either equivalence or harmony the result is aesthetic success. If there is no clear outcome to the contest, if there is ambiguity and uncertainty as to the relationship, we perceive the result as ugliness, or what Arnheim called "the clash of unco-ordinated orders". Because classification has been impossible to achieve, the mental result is aversion.

DISCRETE INTERACTION

So far this has been a description of integral binary interaction which relies on the mental capacity to aggregate and then counterbalance information. Applying the same principle, the second major binary condition measures and evaluates the ratio of discrepancy to affinity between related but clearly distinguishable units of architecture.

When the Emperor Justinian's architect placed a campanile alongside the basilican Church of St Apollinare in Classe, Ravenna, he established an architectural partnership which has endured to this day. Here are two clearly distinguishable architectural sub-wholes which are perceived to belong to the same super-ordinate whole by virtue of both symbolism and shared features such as materials and architectural forms. So the primary condition has been met: the whole is more than a mere fortuitous collision of parts.

The second problem is to discover if there is orderliness in the relationship between campanile and basilica. The tower is a universal religious symbol, which, no doubt, is why so many regard Manhatten with such reverence. So the campanile possess greater informational saturation than the basilica, which is really an all-purpose building. The early Christians very wisely chose a secular building type rather than the temple for their model. Even so, by the fourth century Bishop Eusebius was referring to the basilica as the "holy temple".

Because of this symbolic augmentation, the campanile balances the basilica in terms of attributed weight. The same is true of the superb development of this theme in Palladio's St Giorgio Maggiore.

Across the water the great campanile in the Piazza of S. Marco holds in balance an array of prestigious buildings such as the Cathedral and the Doges Palace. In the same way, the campanile of the Palazzo Pubblico in the Piazza del Campo, Siena, established a marvellous equilibration of forces with all the encompassing buildings.

To illustrate harmonic dominance within discrete entities we cannot do better than refer to English Palladianism. One of Palladio's most enduring innovations was to mark the entrance to a house with a full classical portico. He grafted the temple onto the house, a transplant which has stood the test of time. Here are two fundamentally different types of architecture, yet the combination, as seen at Prior Park, Bath, works well in that the sense that unity transcends the assertiveness of the basic parts. This being so, we can progress to evaluating the ratio of the weight of the house to that of the portico.

Once again symbolism helps to tip the scales, this time in favour of the portico. Though this feature is much smaller in visual terms, it outweighs the house by virtue of its higher rate of visual intricacy together with the symbolism of antiquity, authority and status. The contrast between light and shade in the portico supplies additional weight. The portico wins the contest by just a sufficient margin to eliminate uncertainty as to which is the dominant. This is not the case at Woburn Abbey. Here the central portico is relatively weak and fails to hold its own against the bulk of the house, supplemented by projecting wings. Where the Prior Park portico exerts sufficient gravitational "pull" to hold the building together, Woburn tends to be pulled apart by the over-assertive wings.

On a more subtle level of aesthetic discrimination Prior Park illustrates one of the reasons for the success of Georgian architecture. It concerns the ratio of window to wall. Not only are windows correctly proportioned, the aggregate of window to wall achieves just the right balance of dominant to subordinate. Georgian architecture at its best is wall-dominant within harmonic limits.

This kind of dialetic can be translated into contemporary terms. The Lloyds building in the City of London boasts an elegant stainless steel circulation tower which establishes a vigorous dialogue with the remaining "high-tech" building. In the recently completed Michael Hopkins Schlumberger Building in Cambridge, conventional glass-wall architecture is pitched against a tensile structure of Teflon-coated fabric. It is a successful partnership perhaps partly because it is a metaphor of the tent of nomadic Sahara tribesmen.

Not so successful in this discrete binary category is the Royal
Danish Embassy in London. Two slab elements are juxtaposed, one
mostly of smoked glass curtain walling, the other of stacked yellow
panels which suggest windows punched into the solid. In my view the
building falls at the first fence since it fails to achieve unity.
There is no visual logic behind the partnership; both elements could
exist independently and would be better for it.

This category of binary interaction I have termed the "diamorphic"
aesthetic in architecture, which will serve for the time being.
Following on from the analogy of diaphony, there is counterpoint, or
two or more themes expressed concurrently. This is best illustrated
by a change of key to the wider milieu of townscape.

Whilst the diamorphic principle operates extensively on the scale
of the city, it is, by definition, boundary-dependent. Much of the
appeal of historic cities lies in the quality of the 'continuo
passages'. A city like Amsterdam has few grand climaxes. The magic
of the place lies in the lineal dialogue between the dignified
vernacular domestic architecture and the canals, and the continual
tension between variety and pattern in the high-gabled facades.

In the search for order and pattern the mind picks out features
which are broadly similar and once again adopts the chunking routine.
Thus windows may be at a variety of levels and of differing size. But
they are all vertically orientated and many contain rectilinear white
painted glazing bars and nearly all have white surrounds. Gables are
all different, but nevertheless succumb to the overriding principle
of "gableness". Plot widths and building heights vary, but variety
is contained within limits which proclaim order more than anarchy.

The result is that the common factors outweight the discrepancies;
differences are contained within margins indicating pattern above
randomness. Once "pattern-ness" gets the edge over variability, then
factors which contribute to pattern are reinforced.

Amsterdam is generally regarded as a harmonious city because its
vigorous complexity is outweighed by orderliness factors.
Understanding the subtlety of these orderliness factors is an
essential component of the art of inserting new buildings into an
established setting. The overall rate of rhyme can be captured in
the new building without compromising its contemporary integrity.

Because of its affinity to contrapuntal techniques in music, it
seems appropriate to define this visual condition as the
"contramorphic" aesthetic. In architecture this may describe the
counterpoint between two architectural themes in a lineal context or
between the principles of pattern and randomness.

There is, of course, much more to the matter of architectural aesthetics, such as the positiveness of space and significance of distance, as well as the affective nature of buildings and monuments. However, these examples have been sufficient to illustrate how the primordial contest between order and complexity can be projected by architecture, and to suggest that aesthetic success has something to do with the ultimate triumph of orderliness, albeit after a struggle.

The
Parthenon

Unity defeated by particularity -
St Klemenz, Bettlach.
Switzerland

and a near thing -
The Centre Georges Pompidou,
Paris

209

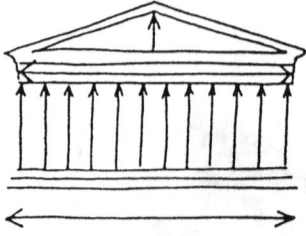

Verticalness versus
Horizontalness in
the Parthenon

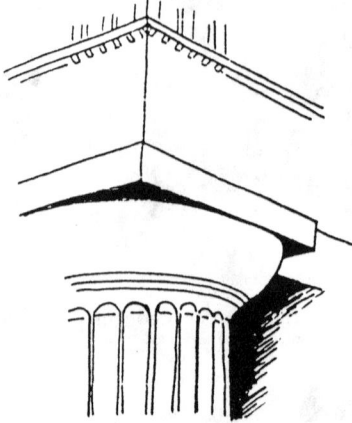

and
round versus square

Axial balance in
St Agnese, Rome

Binary balance - St Apollinare in Classe, Ravenna

and St Giorgio Maggiore, Venice

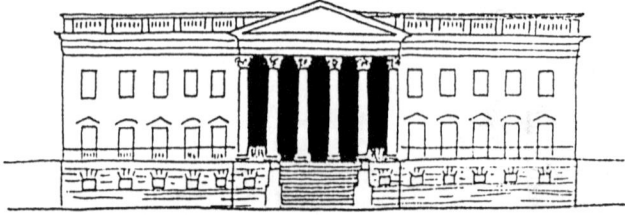

Harmonic stability - Prior Park, Bath

Instability - Woburn Abbey

Schlumberger Building, Cambridge

Royal Danish Embassy, London

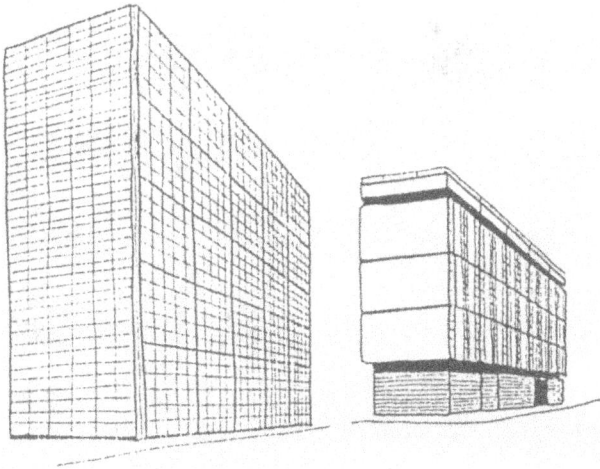

213

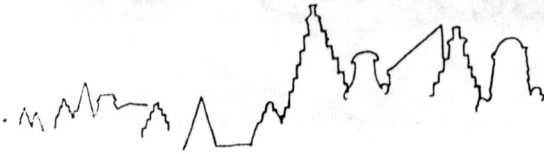

Pattern versus
complexity -
Amsterdam

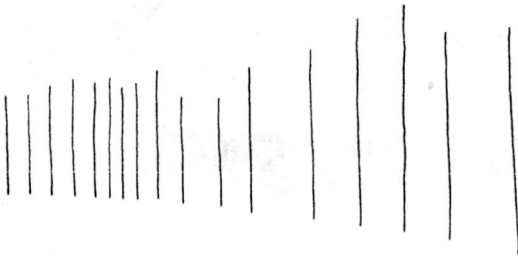

14. Contextual compatability in architecture

LINDA GROAT

The intention of this chapter is to demonstrate, through the specific example of research on contextual compatibility in architecture, how the empirical investigation of environmental meaning can be usefully informed by simultaneously drawing on both the psychological and the design literatures. The term contextual compatibility generally refers to the problem of how to relate new infill buildings to existing urban settings; as such, it represents an aspect of environmental meaning with significant implications for public policy.

The chapter lays particular emphasis on how the research objectives of this study have been informed by the combination of the psychological and design literatures. Three distinct objectives pertinent to the topic of contextual compatibility are identified. These objectives are concerned with the investigation of: 1) the meaning of contextual compatibility; 2) the preferred contextual design strategies; and 3) the key design features which affect contextual compatibility.

The subsequent development of this study is briefly summarized; and the potential significance of the findings for both the psychological and design literatures is highlighted.

PREAMBLE

Contextual fit--the problem of how to relate new infill buildings to existing urban settings--has in recent years become an important point of debate in public policy.

Consider, for example, a recent and internationally publicized example (Dunlop, 1984). The new building in question is the proposed addition to the National Gallery in Trafalgar Square, London. The winning scheme in an international competition, it was selected by a jury which included several notable architects. However, once the winning scheme was unveiled, a vigorous debate quickly ensued.

Shortly thereafter, Prince Charles exacerbated this controversy by suggesting in a speech to the Royal Institute of British Architects that the Modernist design proposal resembles "a vast municipal fire station, complete with the sort of tower that contains the siren." He then went on to characterize its effect on Trafalgar Square as "a carbuncle on the edge of a much loved and elegant friend" (Wales, 1984).

To the Prince's mind, the proposed addition represents a totally inappropriate contrast to both the original gallery and the square as a whole. Thus, he argued passionately for an addition which would "complement the elegant facade of the National Gallery" and which would continue "the concept of columns and domes."

On the other hand, supporters of the proposal have argued that the Prince's point of view is "reactionary" and "uninformed." Indeed, the architect responsible for the winning design has even suggested that to propose anything other than a "modern" design is symptomatic of a foolishly nostalgic attitude towards architecture.

CONTEXTUAL COMPATIBILITY: AN ASPECT OF ENVIRONMENTAL MEANING

This controversy over the National Gallery addition is significant in at least three respects. First, the Prince's comments exemplify, in many ways, the range of concerns that are frequently expressed in public debate over the compatibility of new infill schemes. Second, the incident also demonstrates the potential impact of this design issue in the public realm. And third, the controversy also suggests how particular aspects of the built environment may lend themselves to a wide range of interpretations. In this sense, the phenomenon of contextual compatibility clearly falls within the area of environmental psychology that is commonly labelled environmental meaning.

This area of inquiry is generally concerned with the variety of psychological processes involved in the "comprehension" (Hershberger, 1974) of the physical environment. Although there is as yet no clear consensus about how to classify the various types or levels of environmental meaning (e.g. compare Hershberger, 1974 with Dexter and Lindsey, 1976), most researchers do seem in general agreement that the comprehension of environmental meaning does entail a variety of interrelated perceptual, cognitive and affective responses to the environment (Ward and Russell, 1981). In other words, the study of environmental meaning is about how people perceive, make sense of, feel about, and, in general, interpret their environment.

216

Within the scope of this broad definitional framework, a considerable body of empirical research has emerged within the last 15-20 years. Many, perhaps even the majority, of these studies have attempted to investigate environmental meaning by adopting a relatively broad focus. In operational terms, this has typically meant that a diverse set of environmental scenes is rated according to a battery of verbal scales by a group (or groups) of respondents. The primary objective of such studies has typically been to uncover the several most salient dimensions of meaning that are common to people's experience of the environment.

While this approach has proved useful in identifying a few common aspects or dimensions of meaning, it has nevertheless been criticized for its lack of specificity regarding the particular environmental features which give rise to such meanings (e.g. Wohlwill, 1976; Canter, 1977). More specifically, Canter has observed that the actual specification of psychologically significant physical elements is a more critical issue than is commonly acknowledged in the research literature on environmental meaning.

Recently, Groat (1983) has extended this argument by suggesting that the literature on architectural criticism and theory offers an appropriate source of psychologically relevant explanations (though empirically untested) for relationships between built form and meaning. This is because many architectural practitioners and critics frequently record how they expect people to interpret or react to specific physical attributes of an environment. These design speculations thus offer the potential for forging links between the specification of environmental features and many of the psychological aspects of environmental meaning already identified in the empirical research.

The intention of this chapter then is to demonstrate, through the specific example of research on contextual compatibility, how the psychological implications of environmental meaning can be usefully investigated by simultaneously drawing on BOTH the psychological AND the architectural design literatures. In this regard, the chapter will lay particular emphasis on the formulation of the research objectives of this study and only secondarily on the actual results.

THREE RESEARCH OBJECTIVES

Because an essential goal of this research was to focus on an aspect of environmental meaning that has very clear real-world significance, it was important that the specific research objectives of the study be formulated with these real-world issues in mind. In other words, if this research was to have ecological validity, then the kind of issues raised by incidents such as the National Gallery addition had to be addressed directly.

Thus, as a result of a comprehensive review of some of the most notable public controversies, three important themes which might appropriately form a basis for empirical research were identified. Each of these themes was then analyzed within the framework of both the psychological and design literatures in order to define the specific research objectives of the study.

The following subsections of this chapter describe in detail the formulation of these three research objectives.

The meaning of contextual compatibility

Many of the public discussions about the contextual appropriateness of a given design proposal seem to hinge on rather differing interpretations of the term "compatible."

Consider, for example, the recently proposed entry pavilion for the Louvre in Paris. Designed by the world renowned architect I. M. Pei, this glass pyramid structure is to be located at the center of the grand Cour Napoleon which is embraced by the two major wings of the palace. Although the plans were announced over two years ago, the recent excavation of the site has served to embroil the proposal in a debate that "is shaking up the hearts and minds of all France" (Hoelterhoff, 1985).

Opponents of the proposal argue that the translucent glass structure constitutes an aesthetic obtrusion in the forecourt of this historic institution. Like Prince Charles, these critics are demanding that the new project embody some greater degree of continuity or consistency of form.

This viewpoint, in fact exemplifies one of the several perspectives on compatibility which is expressed in the architectural literature (Edwards, 1924; Brolin, 1980; and Zwirn, 1983). The essence of this argument is that visual continuity among ensembles of buildings is one of the most important and valued qualities of the urban streetscape. Typically, proponents of this viewpoint are prepared to endorse some degree of replication, particularly of small-scale detail and ornament, in order to achieve continuity among buildings.

On the other hand, proponents of the Pei design have argued that the proposal is not only pleasingly "insubstantial", but also appropriate in other ways. More specifically, the pyramid is viewed as an appropriate reference to the Egyptian exploits of the Emperor Napoleon, who was responsible for opening part of the Louvre as a museum. In essence, these commentators are arguing for the design on associational and symbolic grounds.

Although this viewpoint has been expressed by a number of architectural theorists, it is presented in its most radical form by Graves and Wolf (1980). For example, they suggest that one way for a building to be contextually compatible is for the new building to encourage the viewer's reinterpretation of its older neighbors. By way of example, they cite Graves' design for an addition to the Benacerraf house. According to them, the open, fragmented form of the addition creates a transition between the enclosed, self-contained house and the landscape. Their description of this design strategy is as follows: "The establishment of dependencies among existing buildings, the landscape and new structures allows one to understand all of these elements as a part of a greater, continuous organization" (Graves and Wolf, 1980, p. 70).

A second example of public debate over an infill project suggests yet another interpretation of "compatibility." In this instance, residents of a Greenwich Village (New York City) neighborhood were outraged by a proposal to replace a traditional 19th century townhouse (accidently destroyed by a Weatherman bomb in 1970) by a new design that combined traditional brick detailing with a triangular wedge projecting from the facade. Although the local residents objected (unsuccessfully) to this proposal, one notable architectural critic argued that "history's mark on that place" should not be erased. Moreover, he went on to say: "A terrible occurrence was part of the block's history, and it is right that the area acknowledge this" (Goldberger, 1980, p. 260).

Although this view of contextualism is common in contemporary architectural criticism, it is a viewpoint which can be traced to the influential 19th century theorists, John Ruskin and William Morris. Reacting to abuses in the restoration movement whereby buildings were "restored" to idealized, but historically inaccurate versions of particular styles, Ruskin began to voice strenuous objections to this practice (Overby, 1980). A few years later in 1877, William Morris echoed Ruskin's sentiment and established the Society for the Protection of Ancient Buildings. The essence of this anti-restorationist argument is that a building should be conceived of as an historic document. Thus Morris argued: "if the present treatment of (historic buildings) continued, our descendants will find them useless to study and chilling to enthusiasm" (Morris, 1966, p. 109). And further, "...every change, whatever history it destroyed, left history in the gap and was alive with the spirit of the deed done midst the fashioning" (Morris, 1966, p. 110).

The diverse range of commentary described above begins to suggest the essential flavor of one of the key issues in debates on contextual compatibility, that is the variety of ways that compatibility may actually be interpreted. Three distinct perspectives in public debate have been highlighted through the analysis of the relevant architectural literature: 1) compatibility as a function of visual continuity; 2) compatibility through deeper levels of meaning and association, and 3) compatibility as a reflection of history.

These differing interpretations of contextual compatibility can, however, be further clarified by considering them in the light of recent developments in psychology. More specifically, Crozier and Chapman (1984) suggest that in the last several years researchers working within the area of experimental aesthetics have gradually begun to attribute more importance to the role of cognitive processes in the perception of art/artforms. Thus, psychologists like Crozier and Chapman have made significant efforts to link together the two apparently disparate realms of experimental aesthetics and cognitive psychology in an effort to achieve a broader conceptual framework within which to investigate aesthetic appreciation.

One of the most significant and potentialy relevant themes in the cognitive psychology literature is that the perceptual/cognitive process is essentially an interactive and constructive one. In other words, what a person perceives and how s/he interprets it is in large measure dependent on the particular environmental features the person chooses to attend to. These choices, in turn, reflect the nature of the individual's conceptual system, the essential components of which have been variously defined in terms of schemas (e.g. Bartlett, 1932;

Neisser, 1976), constructs (e.g. Kelly 1955) and categories (Bruner et at, 1955; Smith and Medin, 1981).

Although the several models offered by these authors should by no means be considered exactly equivalent, the disparities among them seem to constitute a difference in focus rather than a difference in fundamental concept. Indeed, all of these approaches are notable for their emphasis on understanding the individual's own framework for dealing with and making sense of the world.

With reference to the topic of this research, these several approaches begin to raise the question of how contextual compatibility is most commonly conceptualized. For example, the commentary of the opponents to all three of the infill projects mentioned above suggests that some minimal level of formal similarity is a necessary prerequisite for compatibility. For these people it may be that infill buildings are seen as either fitting or not, simply based on this formal property.

Alternatively, it is possible that some of these people may conceive of a more scalar interpretation of fittingness. In other words, they might think of the various buildings as representing degrees of either more or less compatibility.

In psychological terms, both of these conceptualizations of compatibility are consistent with Kelly's definition of a construct, which he considered to be essentially bipolar (Kelly, 1955). Although Kelly defines the bipolarity of constructs as being primarily dichotomous in structure, he also acknowledges that "it is still possible to conceive of gradations...along a dimensional line" (Kelly, 1955, p. 141). Indeed, this scalar conceptualization of compatibility has already been hypothesized on an a priori basis by Wohlwill (1978) in his investigation of built structures in landscape settings.

Yet a third possible conceptualization of compatibility is suggested by the commentary of critics and theoreticians such as Morris, Goldberger, and Graves. If compatibility can be interpreted in terms of symbolic associations in one case and historic continuity in another, it may be that people can recognize several types of compatibility. Thus it could be argued that buildings are not more or less compatible, but compatible in qualitatively different ways.

Finally, it is possible that contextual compatibility may not even be a viable construct for a great proportion of people. Even though the Pei design is said to have shaken all of France, it may be that the issue was important only to a vocal minority. In other words, the silent majority may not even care or take notice.

Thus, the first research objective of this study was to explore the meaning that contextual compatibility has for people. This objective was then further elaborated in terms of the following set of questions:

Do people really construe contextual compatibility to be an important characteristic of the urban environment?
If so, how do they actual conceptualize it?
Are buildings seen as being simply compatible or not?

Or, are infill buildings evaluated in terms of representing degrees of compatibility?

Or, are buildings categorized in terms of several different types of compatibility?

How important is contextual compatibility compared to other aspects of environmental meaning?

Preferred contextual design strategies

One point of debate which frequently emerges in discussions of contextual fit is the extent to which judgments of compatibility are a matter of "taste." In other words, a common assumption is that compatibility (like beauty) is in the eyes of the beholder. Indeed, the great range of opinions expressed in public debate about infill projects suggests strongly that this may be so.

Within the design literature, at least, many authors seem implicitly to assume that compatibility must be a function of relatively idiosyncratic judgments. For example, one architectural practitioner known for his work in contextual design has argued: "It is difficult, perhaps impossible, to establish guidelines to judge what is suitable or unsuitable in historic surroundings" (Cavaglieri, 1980, p. 48). And even the author of one of the few books on contextual design has argued that preference for certain types of contextual relationships must certainly be a matter of taste (Brolin, 1982). The implication of this point of view, then, is that one would expect to find few, if any, consensual patterns of preference among any reasonably diverse set of people.

On the other hand, however, the entire concept of the design review process for historic districts is predicated on the notion that some normative standard for evaluating compatibility can be established. And indeed, hundreds of communities in the U.S. and Europe have produced rather detailed guidelines for achieving compatibility within designated districts (Lu, 1980).

Moreover, within the psychological literature, several researchers have concluded that aesthetic and environmental preferences are indeed more consensual than might be expected. For example, Kaplan (1979), who has reviewed much of the empirical research on environmental preferences, concludes that preference judgments are neither arbitrary nor idiosyncratic, but instead reveal common patterns of aesthetic values. And more specifically, with reference to architecture, Oostendorf and Berlyne (1978) argue that "individual differences in taste for architectural styles may not be as large as, especially art theorists want us to believe" (p. 146).

If it can therefore be assumed that a relatively high degree of consensus about what constitutes compatibility is possible, then the next question bécomes: what are the most commonly preferred design strategies? And what are the specific ways in which physical form is manipulated in these preferred strategies?

A number of areas of psychological research have sought to identify the salient characteristics of physical form that may substantially affect perception. For example, Gestalt psychology emphasizes the role of organizational composition (Koffka, 1935;); and Berlyne and

221

his associates, working in the realm of experimental aesthetics, have investigated the significance of various collative variables, such as complexity (Berlyne, 1971).

In recent years, various authors have attempted to apply each of these approaches to the analysis of architecture, generally, and the urban streetscape in particular (e.g. Arnheim, 1977; Jules, 1984; Prak, 1977). Unfortunately, however, neither of these models lends itself to the specification of formal variables in terms precise enough to be of use in the practical realm of contextual design. Moreover, these approaches can also be criticized for limiting their analyses simply to the perceptual and psycho-physiological aspects of psychological response to physical form.

Another approach which has been drawn upon as a basis for research on environmental preferences is Osgood et al's pioneering investigation of meaning, or "semantic space" (Osgood et al, 1957). Although the basic intention of Osgood et al's work was to identify the full range of connotative meanings, the predominant aspect of meaning which emerges from these studies is evaluative in nature. This is also largely true of the many environmental psychology studies that have employed the semantic differential/factor analytic model (See Canter, 1975). This line of research can, however, be very strongly faulted for its lack of specificity regarding the particular qualities of physical form that give rise to preferences (Wohlwill, 1976; Canter, 1977; Groat, 1983).

In fact, according to Wohlwill (1976), most research on environmental perception has managed conveniently to "sidestep" the issue by selecting sites or views without any attempt to assess them in terms of specified variables. He further argues that the very typical combination of semantic differential/factor analytic procedures yields a purely descriptive analysis. The result is that the research then reveals nothing about the role played in the respondents' judgments by any specifiable environmental characteristics.

Why should this be so? Canter suggests that the reason for such a dearth of studies with a truly environmental focus "appears to be, in part at least, the difficulty of deciding which physical attributes to study. Taken in the abstract, independently of any conceptual framework, there is an infinity of ways of dividing up and measuring physical parameters....So researchers have either selected one which caught their fancy, with disappointing results, or given up because they were spoilt for choice" (Canter, 1977, p. 159).

Given these significant criticisms of much of the previous research on environmental preferences and meaning, it seemed particularly necessary to establish a conceptual framework upon which an analysis of contextual design strategies could be appropriately based.

In this regard, one of the few relevant precedents in the environmental psychology literature is Wolwill's set of studies on the integration of built form in the landscape (e.g. Wohlwill, 1978, 1982; Wohlwill and Harris, 1980). More specifically, in a study of park settings, Wohlwill and Harris (1980) first asked a set of judges to rate the park scenes according to their degree of contrast-fittingness

222

in terms of five scales: color, texture, size, shape, and composite
fittingness. The slides of the park scenes were subsequently rated by
undergraduate students who rated them according to a set of evaluative
semantic differential scales. However, as Wohlwill (1976, p. 47)
himself implies, the most pertinent physical attributes of the natural
landscape may not be comparable to those of the urban landscape. As a
result, while the contrast-fittingness scale appears to be a potentially
useful analytic framework, the specific scales must be considered as
only crude approximations of the features most pertinent to
architectural design.

For this reason, then, the architectural and design guidelines
literatures were seen to hold significant promise-- first for
identifying key physical attributes, and secondarily for suggesting an
appropriate conceptual structure for the analysis of contextual design
strategies. With regard to the guidelines literature, most of the
guidelines documents identify various categories of features that are
seen as essential to contextual compatibility. For example, a great
many of the U.S. documents represent some variation of the doucment that
was originally adopted by Savannah in the 1960's; it identifies 16 key
design features or qualities (Lu, 1980). An important refinement of the
Savannah guidelines is exemplified by the guidelines developed for an
historic district in Dallas. In particular, the structure of the
guidelines is HIERARCHICAL, such that the 12 key design features are
identified within four categories of design characteristics: the block,
building form, building treatment, and facade accentuation (Lu, 1980).

Secondly, with regard to the architectural criticism literature, two
distinct types of contextual design analyses can be identified. The
first of these are essentially case studies, that is they present a
detailed analysis of one specific building. On the other hand, the
second approach tends to offer generalizations about the key design
features which are essential for contextual design. Among the numerous
examples of this approach are several that actually attempt to develop
TYPOLOGIES of contextual design strategies (e.g. Smith, 1977; Brolin,
1980). Thus, the architectural criticism literature begins to reveal
the same kind of hierarchical framework developed in the Dallas
guidelines document. In other words, both sets of design literatures
suggest the possibility of designating specific design features within a
set of much more general categories.

As a consequence, the conceptual framework which was eventually
developed for this research study combines the hierarchical analytic
structure evident in the design literatures with the degrees-of-
contrast scale used by Wolhwill and Harris (1980). Thus the intention
was to use this framework (Table 1) in the analysis of the various
infill designs that would be used in the study.

Another essential feature of this framework is that it distinguishes
among design attributes according to the degree of control the architect
is typically able to exercise over them. This research was, however,
concerned only with the design attributes that are under the architects
control, that is, the components of a design strategy. Thus, issues
such as the insertion of nontypical building uses or extreme contrast in
project sizes--though important--were excluded from consideration in
this study.

223

Another feature of the framework is that it defines contextual design in terms of both interior and exterior design features. This study, however, was concerned only with the impact of exterior design attributes, the most commonly considered aspect of contextual design. Thus, each of the infill scenes eventually selected for use in this study was analyzed only in terms of three components of design strategy: site organization, massing, and facade design. These general categories included, but were not limited to, the specific features listed below them in Table 1.

All three of these components are defined in terms of a 7-point scale, from contrast to replication. In effect then, each infill design strategy could be identified by a specific PROFILE SCORE consisting of these three ratings. Examples of how some of the infill schemes were eventually rated are presented on accompanying pages.

With this conceptual framework in place, it was then possible to define the second research objective of this study with appropriate clarity. In general terms, the objective was simply to identify the patterns of preference which are associated with judgments of contextual compatibility. However, this objective was then further elaborated in terms of the following set of questions.

What kind of contextual design strategies--specified in terms of profile scores--are most consistently preferred?
How similar are the preference judgments both within and between diverse groups of people?

The design features which affect contextual compatibility

Yet another important aspect of how people interpret contextual compatibility is revealed by the kind of design features that are noticed as either contributing to or detracting from a given contextual relationship.

The significance of specific design features in relating a set of buildings to their context is very poignantly revealed in the example of row housing in Philadelphia (Starr and Kasindorf, 1985). Early in 1985, a tragic fire destroyed over 60 rowhouses in a middle-class Black neighborhood after an attack on a radical political group's house accidently started a fire. The city government quickly pledged to rebuild the housing, but the initial design scheme was soundly rejected by both the local community and the local architectural critic. The reason was simply that the new design did not incorporate the front stoop, which in Philadelphia traditionally includes columns and a gabled roof. The architectural critic argued that the rowhouse design sans stoop was "decidedly un-Philadelphian." And the local city councilman declared: "You don't have that [the stoop], it's like taking everything away." As a consequence, the residents' themselves banned together with a volunteer architect who produced a new rowhouse design with a stoop, a design that the city has now pledged to build.

The significance of certain key features is also revealed in Prince Charles' commentary on the National Gallery addition. More specifically, Prince Charles argued that the columns and domes of the original National Gallery were key features that ought to be carried through in the new addition. In the framework of Prince Charles' speech, these design elements seem to embody for the Prince the essence of Renaissance-inspired architecture.

The significance of specific key features in linking new to old is a topic which figures strongly in much of the recent architectural literature. However, there is considerable controversy among the critics and practitioners as to precisely which design features are the most crucial for establishing compatibility. For example, Brolin (1980) argues strongly that small-scale details of facade design are particularly significant. On the other hand, another leading architect has recently been quoted as saying that "new designs can be made to blend in with the old simply by paying attention to scale and materials" (Johnson, 1984). And yet another architect has written that compatibility can be just as well achieved through either massing (volume and shape) or site organization (alignment, etc.) (Cavaglieri, 1980).

An important aspect of these architectural analyses is the extent to which the organization of the conceptual framework described earlier (Table 1) may be pertinent to identification of key features. For example, Brolin's argument suggests that most of the key design features would have to do with style; whereas Cavaglieri's position suggests the opposite.

With respect to psychological literature, the issue of identifying important design features that contribute to compatibility is also clearly consistent with the cognitive approach mentioned earlier. In particular, Smith and Medin (1981) have presented three alternative models of the categorization process. In their analyses of these models, they indicate the importance that recognition of specific features may play in the eventual identification of a category.

Thus, the third research objective was to identify the specific design features which most consistently and frequently contribute to contextual compatibility. This objective was then further elaborated in terms of the following set of questions:

What are the specific design features which are most consistently seen as either contributing to or detracting from contextual compatibility?
Do the majority of these key design features constitute an aspect of site organization? of massing? or style?

SUBSEQUENT DEVELOPMENT OF THE RESEARCH STUDY

The three research objectives described in the preceding sections thus formed the fundamental conceptual basis for this empirical study of contextual compatibility. Within the intentionally limited scope of this chapter, however, it is not possible to describe the full details of how these objectives were transformed into appropriate research procedures.

On the other hand, it is possible to summarize briefly a few of the essential characteristics of these procedures. More specifically, an intensisve interview procedure was developed which included the use of: the multiple sorting task (Canter, Brown, and Groat, 1985), directed sorting, rank ordering exercises, and open-ended questions.

Nearly 100 respondents-- 73 nonarchitects and 24 design review commissioners-- were asked to comment on a set of 25 infill projects that were simulated through color photographs. The data were then analyzed through a combination of: multidimensional scaling (Lingoes, 1973), inferential statistics, and content analysis.

The findings of this research are most appropriately summarized in terms of the three research objectives described earlier.

1) The Meaning of Contextual Compatibility. The construct, contextual compatibility was found to be one of the most frequently used criteria in the sorting task procedures, thus suggesting its relative importance as an aspect of environmental meaning.

Among the respondents who chose to use compatibility as a free sort criterion, the great majority construed compatibility as either a dichotomous or ordered construct. In other words, most people typically think of buildings as fitting or not fitting; or, in a scalar relationship between contrast- replication.

There was little evidence in the data that people conceptualize compatibility in terms of the qualitatively different types of compatibility suggested by architectural theorists and critics.

2) Compatibility and Preferences. The design strategies of the most preferred contextual relationships are characterized by a relatively high degree of replication, especially with respect to facade design. This tendency is consistent among the several respondent groups in the study.

3) The Design Features Affecting Compatibility. In general, facade design features were much more frequently noticed than features having to do with either site organization or massing. More specifically, the most frequently mentioned features of the buildings judged to be compatible were: materials, windows, color, apparent age, roofline, and style.

This conclusion clearly complements the findings listed in item #2 and also demonstrates the effectiveness of the conceptual framework (Table 1) in the analysis of the data.

CONCLUSIONS

The primary intention of this chapter has been to show how the phenomenon of environmental meaning can be usefully investigated by simultaneously drawing on BOTH the psychological AND the design literatures. In this regard, the preceding summary of the research findings reiterates this point by demonstrating the potential relevance of these findings to both architectural criticism and environmental psychology.

For example, the findings concerning the preferred contextual design strategies have been reported in both sets of literatures, though of course in very different presentation formats (Groat, 1984; Groat, in press). And similarly, the conceptual framework for the analysis of contextual design strategies has been presented as a tool for use in the design process (Groat, 1983b), while the discussion of people's conceptualizations of compatibility has been reported in the social science literature (Groat, 1986).

The underlying assumption of this research strategy, then, is that truly effective research on environmental meaning requires the intensive investigation not only of meaning but also the forms which embody those meanings. And more importantly, it is also being argued that achieving an adequate understanding of environmental form is something which can be usefully gained through analysis of the design literature. Without this step, empirically-based research on environmental meaning will likely provide only an incomplete understanding of the phenomenon.

REFERENCES

Arnheim, R. (1977). The Dynamics of Architectural Form. Berkeley, CA: University of California Press.
Bartlett, F. C. (1932). Remembering. Cambridge: Cambridge University Press.
Berlyne, D. (1971). Aesthetics and Psychobiology. New York: Appleton-Century-Crofts.
Biddle, J. (ed.) (1980). Old & New Architecture: Design Relationship. Washington, DC: The Preservation Press.
Brolin, B. (1980). Architecture in Context. New York: Van Nostrand Reinhold Co.
Brolin, B. (1982). Personal letter to L.N. Groat.
Bruner, J., Goodnow, J., and Austin, G., (1956). A Study of Thinking. New York: John Wiley & Sons.
Canter, D. (1977). The Psychology of Place. London: Architectural Press.
Canter, D., Brown, J. and Groat, L. (1985. "The Multiple Sorting Procedure." In Brenner, J. Brown, and D. Canter, (eds.), The Research Interview, pp. 79-114. London: Academic Press.
Cavaglieri, G. (1980). "The Harmony that Can't be Dictated." In J. Biddle (ed.), pp. 37-48.
Crozier, W. and Chapman, A. (eds.) (1984). Cognitive Processes in the Perception of Art. New York; North-Holland.
Dexter, B. and Lindsey, S. (1976). "Architectural Meaning: Is It Predictable?" Working Paper.
Dunlop, B. (1984). "Prince Charles Speaks Out Against 'Giant Glass Stumps'." The Miami Herald, June, 17, 1984.
Edwards, A.T. (1924, reprinted 1946). Good and Bad Manners in Architecture. London: John Tiranti Ltd.
Goldberger, P. (1980). "To Preserve the Visibility of Time." In Biddle (ed.), pp. 258-167.
Graves, M. and Wolf, G. (1980). "Beyond Mere Manners and Cosmetic Compatibility." In Biddle (ed.), pp. 69-78.
Groat, L. (1983). "The Past and Future of Research on Meaning in Architecture. In D. Amadeo, J. Griffin, and J. Potter (eds.), EDRA 1983. Washington DC: EDRA.
Groat, L. (1984). "Public Opinion of Contextual Fit." Architecture, the AIA Journal. November, pp. 72-75.
Groat, L. (1986). "Contextual Compatibility: A Study of Meaning in the Urban Environment." A symposium paper presented at the National Meeting of the Association of American Geographers, Minneapolis, MN.

Groat, L. (in press). "Contextual Compatibility in Architecture: An Issue of Personal Taste?" To be published in J. Nasar (ed.), The Visual Quality of the Environment: Theory, Research, and Application. Cambridge University Press.

Hershberger, R. (1974). "Predicting the Meaning of Architecture." In J. Lang (ed.) Designing for Human Behavior. pp. 147-156. Stroudsburg, PA: Dowden, Hutchinson and Ross.

Hoelterhoff, M. (1985). "Pei's Pyramid: Revolution in Napoleon's Court." The Wall Street Journal, April 23.

Johnson, S. (1984). "Architect Urges Blending of New with Old." The [Charleston, SC] News and Courier, March 20.

Jules, F. A. (1984). A Comparison of the Application to Architecture of the Ecological and Gestalt Approaches to Visual Perception. Milwaukee: Center for Architecture and Urban Planning Research.

Kaplan, S. (1979). "Perception and Landscape: Conceptions and Misconceptions." In Elsner, G. and Smardon, R. (eds.), Our National Landscape. Berkeley, CA: U.S. Forest Service, pp. 241-248.

Kelly, G. (1955). The Psychology of Personal Constructs. New York: Norton.

Koffka, K. (1935). Principles of Gestalt Psychology. New York: Harcourt Brace & Co.

Lingoes, J. (1973). The Guttman-Lingoes Nonmetric Program Series. Ann Arbor, MI: Mathesis Press.

Lu, W. (1980). "Preservation Criteria: Defining and Protecting Design Relationships." In Biddle (ed.), pp. 186-202.

Morris, W. (1966). "Manifesto of the Society for the Protection of Ancient Buildings." In M. Morris (ed.), William Morris, Artist Writer Socialist, Vol. 1, pp. 109-112. New York: Russell and Russell.

Neisser, U. (1976). Cognition and Reality: Principles and Implications of Cognitive Psychology. New York: W.H. Freeman and Co.

Oostendorp, A. and Berlyne, D. (1978). "Dimensions in the Perception of Architecture, III: Multidimensional Preference Scaling." Scandanavian Journal of Psychology, 19, pp. 145-150.

Osgood, C., Suci, G., and Tannenbaum, P. (1957). The Measurement of Meaning. Urbana: University of Illinois Press.

Overby, O. R. (1980). "Old and New Architecture: a History." In Biddle (ed.), pp. 18-36.

Prak, N. (1977). The Visual Perception of the Built Environment. Delft: Delft University Press.

Smith, E.E. and Medin, D. L. (1981). Categories and Concepts. Cambridge: MA: Harvard University Press.

Smith, P. (1977). The Syntax of Cities. London: Hutchinson.

Starr, M. and Kasindorf, M. (1985). "A House is not a Home." Newsweek, July 15.

Wales, HRH The Prince of (1984). Speech made at the Royal Institute of British Architects Gala Evening, Hampton Court.

Ward, L.M. and Russell, J.A. (1981). "The Psychological Representation of Molar Physical Environments." Journal of Experimental Psychology: General, 110 (2), pp. 121-151.

Wohlwill, J. (1976). "Environmental Aesthetics: the Environment as a Source of Affect." In I. Altman and J. Wohlwill (eds.), Human Behavior and Environment: Advances in Theory and Research, Vol. 1, pp. 37-86. New York: Plenum Press.

Wohlwill, J. (1978). "What Belong Where: Research on Fittingness of Man-Made Structures in Natural Settings." In W. Rogers and W. Ittelson (eds.) New Directions in Environmental Design Research. Washington DC: EDRA.

Wohlwill, J. (1982). "The Visual Impact of Development in Coastal
Zone Areas." Coastal Zone Management Journal, 9 (3/4), pp. 225-248.
Wohlwill, J. and Harris, G. (1980). "Response to Congruity or Contrast
for Man-Made Features in Natural Recreation Settings." Leisure
Sciences, 3 (4), pp. 349-365.
Zwirn, R. (1983). "Fit or Miss." Metropolis, Sept., 1983, pp. 22-24.

I.   GIVENS: Issues Typically Beyond the Architect's Control

   1. Site location: _____
   2. Building type: _____
   3. Size: _____

II. DESIGN PARAMETERS: Issues Partially Under the Architect's Control

   4. Prominence:
        minimum 1-----2-----3-----4---- 5-----6-----7 maximum
   5. Definition of Context:
        adjacent 1-----2-----3-----4---- 5-----6-----7 regional

III. DESIGN STRATEGY: Issues Typically Under the Architect's Control

A.   Space

   6. Exterior Site Organization:
       contrast 1---- 2-----3-----4---- 5-----6-----7 replication

       Tactics:
       _____ footprint of the building on the site
       _____ circulation: pathways, etc.
       _____ vehicular access: driveways, parking
       _____ alignment, setback distances and angles
       _____ landscaping: site demarcations
       _____ other

   7. Interior Spatial Organization:
       contrast 1-----2-----3-----4---- 5-----6-----7 replication

       Tactics:
       _____ circulation paths, hallways
       _____ room/area layouts
       _____ level changes
       _____ placements of vertical circulation
       _____ other

B.   Massing

   8. Exterior Massing
       contrast 1-----2-----3-----4---- 5-----6-----7 replication

       Tactics:
       _____ shape, complexity of overall form
       _____ articulation of base, body, top
       _____ roofline, vertical projections
       _____ other

   9. Interior Semi-Fixed Arrangements
       contrast 1-----2-----3-----4---- 5-----6-----7 replication

       Tactics:
       _____ overall configuration of partitions
       _____ arrangements of heavy furniture etc.
       _____ other

C.   Style

   10. Facade Design
       contrast 1-----2-----3-----4-----5-----6-----7 replication

       Tactics:
       _____ overall stylistic attributes
       _____ rhythm, proportion of fenestration
       _____ color
       _____ materials
       _____ degree of ornament, detail, relief
       _____ other

   11. Interior Surface Treatment
       contrast 1-----2-----3-----4-----5-----6-----7 replication

       Tactics:
       _____ overall interior style
       _____ shape, proportion of surface details
       _____ color
       _____ materials
       _____ degree of ornament, detail, relief
       _____ other

Table 1
A Conceptual Framework for Contextual Design Strategies

230

East Cambridge Savings Bank addition
East Cambridge, Mass.
Charles G. Hilgenhurst & Assoc.
photo: Particia Gill

Profile Score: 5-4-6

Enderis Hall
University of Wisconsin-Milwaukee
Milwaukee, Wis.
Plunkett Keymar Reginato
photo: Linda Groat

Profile Score: 2-1-1

Lincoln Park townhouses
Chicago, Ill.
Bauhs & Dring
photo: Linda Groat

Profile Score: 7-5-5

A Sample of the Infill Scenes Used in the Study

231

Portland Public Services Building
Portland, Or.
Michael Graves
photo: Francis Downing

Profile Score: 7-5-3

Farmers' & Merchants' Union Bank addition
Columbus, Wis.
Gornet and Shearman
photo: Valerie Johnson

Profile Score: 6-5-1

Frank-Carlsen residence
St. Paul, Minn.
Sylvia Frank/Peter Carlsen
photo: Garth Rockcastle

Profile Score: 6-4-3

A Sample of the Infill Scenes Used in the Study

232

15. Explorations in ecoanalysis

ARIE PELED

ABSTRACT

Although phenomenological studies of "Environmental" issues have become more prevalent during the last decade, they tend to stop short of a direct attempt to foster changes in the Architectural act, to bring about a therapy of places.

Ecoanalysis, the postulates of which are described in this chapter, draws on Existentialist-Phenomenological approaches to psychology to generate a dynamic process by which the person-place dialogue can be analyzed, its essences explicated and therapeutic changes initiated. Like all dynamic psychologies, Ecoanalysis addresses itself to the indivisible unity of the (I-World) dialogue and attempts to bring about changes in its relations. The world makes itself present to us always as a situation and a place. The (I-World) is experienced in its immediacy as (I-Place). While person oriented psychologies focus on the (I) pole of the (I-World) dialogue, Ecoanalysis focuses on the (World) pole, or rather on objects, people, organisms, that constitute this pole, when intended toposensually - as sensually defining places or being parts of places. Like all phenomenological enquiries, Ecoanalysis attempts to explicate the essences of our encounters with situations/places, then proceeds to explore ways by which people participating in these situations/places attempt to actualize these essences through a process of compensation/reinforcement among all their encounters in the situation/place. To illustrate the various points in the discussion, references are made to Hopper's painting: "Sunlight in a Cafeteria" and to hypothetical changes in its spatial organization.

233

1. The (I world) is an indivisible unity. The person and the world co-constitute one another. They give meaning one to the other. Being is actually "being-in-the-world".

Consciousness is "intentional". It is always a "consciousness of". It has an object: a person, a thing, an idea. It is a making present to the person of these objects. Through the existential dialogue these manifestations of The Other are invested with meanings.

2. The (I-world) relationship is a dialogue.
The person is always in a dialogue with the world as a whole and the various manifestations of The Other (people, things, space) which he or she encounter in the world. An experiencing being finds itself always in dynamic relations with the world: an acting and being acted upon, a taking, receiving, evading, penetrating. For people there is always an element of freedom − they are "condemned to choice" and an element of finality, a being limited by the conditions prevailing in the situations in which one finds (or has chosen to find) oneself. We can have only "situational" freedom.

3. The meanings of (I-world) relationships are grounded in naive, direct, immediate experience.
The Hypotheses, theories, constructs of causal thinking are derivatives of our immediate uninterpreted everyday experience of the Life-world. We experience the Life-world in its materiality and through our "embodied" existence − a being which interacts with the world through the sensory realm of his or her body.

While involved in the goal oriented activities of our daily life we tend, however, to confine ourselves to the superordinate constructs of causal thinking. We tend to take a "natural attitude" and assume that the world around us exists independently and follows certain rules.

To recapture the naivity of pre-reflective experience from which these super-ordinate constructs are derived (and prepare the ground for making possible changes in these constructs), we have to take a different attitude: a "transcedental" one.

To assume this attitude we have to attempt to suspend our preconception and presuppositions through a process of "bracketing" − making one's constructs explicit in a process (which can never be complete) or "reduction" through which the world is related to as purely a phenomenal realm.

4. The goal of existential phenomenological analysis is the making explicit of the structures or essences of phenomena.
As the meanings of a phenomenon reveal themselves through the bracketing of the life situations in which we have encountered it, some commonality among the various meanings becomes apparent. A superordinated meaning which phenomenologists define as essence or structure and for which I prefer a term used by G. Kelly (who some called a naive existentialist): core construct.

In those psychologies which attempt to facilitate changes in (I-world) relationship, in the person's relationships with his or her world, the making explicit of core constructs plays a central role. Making people aware of the core meanings of a certain phenomena is an essential

preliminary stage of any attempted change in their dialogue with the
phenomena.

In applying an existentialist-phenomenological approach to the study of
the psychological meaning of the "Physical" environment, we have first
to clarify what is the phenomena so defined. Is there a "physical" environment and if so how do we encounter it in our direct pre-reflective
experience.

Like all entities that populate our Life world, those commonly referred
to as constituting the "physical" environment are encountered in the
context of situations/places. We experience a wall, a house, a chair,
a mountain, a field as coparticipants in specific situations/places.

"Experiencing beings", writes E. Straus (1967), "while awake, always find
themselves in a situation ...   to find oneself in a situation - that
is exactly what experiencing signifies" *.

To (situation) one should add (place), since in their immediacy situations are experienced as places. (Place) is the spatial giveness of
(situation).

We always find ourselves inside a place surrounded by outside places,
which constitute that region of the world which is directly, sensorily
available to us at that moment in time.

We experience as place the immediate presence of that region of the
world in which we find ourselves.

The world does not present itself to us as an abstract entity.
The world makes itself present to us in its spatiality as a place.
The world is always encountered as a world:
a field, a room, a yard, the sea.

At every moment of our lives we find ourselves in a situation, inside a
place. We co-inhabit this place with other entities: people, things,
organisms and with those entities: walls, trees, a hill, that constitute
its boundaries:

What I call "this place", "this room", is the totality of entities made
present to me by the world in this region of space, at this time of my
life sequence.

Places are finite in the volume of space they make available and the
number of entities they accommodate.

As I move from one place to another, from one situation to the next,
they all become part of the expanding space of the world and the
continunity of my life. That space and continuity which I call: The
world, my life. But at this moment and at any moment, the world and
my life are experienced as being in this situation, in this place:
Walking in this field, Working in this yard, Sleeping in this room,
Sailing on this sea.

I can experience the wholeness of the world and the continuity of my life
only from the finite and limited context of this place and this situation

Those phenomena which "Environmental Psychology" studies, are part of situations/places: The space of a room, A window, A door, The positioning of people and furniture. These"physical"entities do not constitute the place. They join other entities: people. organisms, smells, noises, in creating that composite whole which we experience simultaneously as situation and place.

It is therefore in the context of specific situations/places and the (I-world) we enact in them, that we should carry our phenomenological reflections on the meanings invested in "environmental" phenomena.

Following is a painting by the american artist Hopper: "Sunlight in a Cafeteria". I propose that we make the place depicted in the painting the context of our enquiry and that we focus on one environmental component - the window.

The reader is asked to imagine herself/himself as sitting in the cafeteria somewhere in front of the region depicted in the painting:

You find yourself in a region of space which you share with other entities: people, objects, organisms; the man, the woman, the tables, the window, the buildings outside. You find yourself in a region of space populated by a limited number of participants, some of which: the walls, the window, the floor, constitute their boundaries and set limits to the amount of space enclosed and to the relations available with the outside.

At this particular point in your life, this region of space, this cafeteria, is all of the world that is given to you in its immediacy. If by some demonic act the regions of the world of which you are not aware while in this place, were to vanish, some time would ensue before you become aware of this change. If the unseen parts of the street or the rooms surrounding the cafeteria were to be silently demolished, it may take some time before you become aware of these changes.

This region of space , populated by entities and by the ambience of space itself; the air, the light, the noises, the*smells, is all that is given to you of the world of this moment in time .

You encounter the window, the buildings outside, the woman, the table she sits at, the chair you sit on, simultaneously as individual entities and as parts of the composite whole of the situation/place.

Your being in-Hopper's-cafeteria is composed of the multiple encounters you experience in that place. Each encounter is an (I-Other) dialogue.

Your attention can vary from one entity to another. You can glance indifferently at the buildings outside, reflect professionally on the technical details of the window, feel sexually aroused by the woman, reflect on the cheapness and vulgarity of the table, sense discomfort in sitting on the chair, etc. At the same time you may remember, reflect, visualize absent entities, whether associated or not with the cafeteria: A paragraph you are in the process of writing, a girl this woman reminds you of, a letter you forgot to post, the meaning of "bareness" which the cafeteria brings to your mind. All these encounters: Whom do you meet, what you have been thinking of, whilst in the cafeteria, join together to constitute your "being-in-this-cafeteria".

Which of the entities in the cafeteria constitute its "Physical" Environment?

Due to our Cartesian tradition we will tend to define all inanimate objects as parts of a "Physical" Environment surrounding and supporting the people that inhabit this environment.

In most situations we tend to focus on the people and to put other entities into the background. In our "natural attitude" we interpret this

(*) This overpowering totality is reflected by the Hebrew use of "The place" (HAMAKOM) as one the Deity's names.

state of affairs as indicating a dichotomy of (human) vs. (physical), of
(physical environment) vs. (activity).We than interpretate this state
of affairs as indicating a dichotomy of "human" vs. "physical". (In traditional Environmental Psychology this dichotomy has evolved into a consideration of human behavior and activities as against some surrounding
environment that provides a shell. It is this distinction between "behavior" on the one hand and "environmental shells" on the other that we
are trying to avoid.)

Reflecting on our (In the world) experience we find, however, situations
where objects were intended as focal entities and the other entities in
the place, including people, were intended as background: At an art museum, for instance, or in a supermarket. Certainly in Hopper's painting
the expressionless, static presence of the human figures makes them very
much like the objects with which they co-inhabit the cafeteria. But in
all situations/places of our Life-world we encounter all entities in
their spatiality.

The Man and the Woman in the cafeteria do not make themselves present to
you as ghosts, neither as abstract systems of constructs. They are over
there in their spatiality, defining places as much as the walls do.

And if you want to communicate with them, you have to use some "physical"
means: to talk, write, observe their behaviour, express yourself
through your body and garments.

What your direct experience reveals is not an "oyster in its shell" -
the image of humanity inhabiting a "physical" environment like
Descarte's "mind" inhabiting the body",

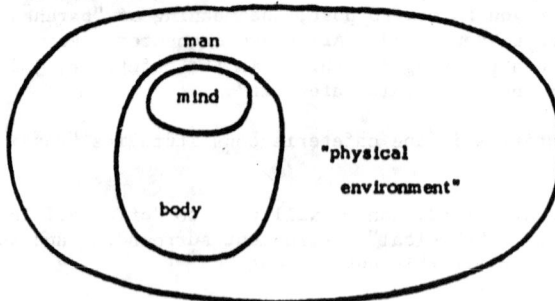

but a region of space surrounded and inhabited by entities - some of
which are inanimate, some human, some organisms. Some we tend to define
(according to criteria to be discussed further on) as "physical
environment".

The distinction between a physical and a human environment is an off-
shoot of Cartesian dualism and is not anchored in our direct pre-reflective experience. All entities present themselves to us in their spatiality: The people, the plant, the space of a room. All of them are partners in dialogues and all of them are experienced in the context of
"being-in-the-cafeteria" as a whole.

Psychological enquiries assume the existence of an environment in which
the individual acts, which he construes, reacts to, attempts to change.

Out of this environment, out of this world, some entities and relations
are picked out by the psychologist as being of special interest: the psychology of work, educational psychology; or some process in the individual or stages of development are singled out: the child, the cognitive
processes.

All these entities and relations meet the individual "out there" in the
world. They are "physical": The writing on this page, The gestures of a
speaker, A stone, A flower, A child, A glance, are all given to us in
their spatiality, out there, as part of the concrete temporality of the
world that surrounds us.

We experience and construe them. We feel, think, observe. But, in
Marleau-Ponty's terms, they are "that side of the body". Out there,
"that side of the body", everything encountered (while awake, sober and
sane) is "physical".

"Environmental" Phenomena should not therefore be studied as a special
category of entities, but as parts of the composite presence - always
spatial, of situations/places.

Cartesian dualism gives rise to a second dichotomy: (Place) vs. (Activity). When using the term "cafeteria" I may have 2 phenomena in mind:

a) My being in the Cafeteria in its wholeness, on the people, smells,
noises, that I have experienced in it. In this specific cafeteria or in
this type of situation/place which is a cafeteria.

b) The room and furniture.

There is a tendency to identify situations/places with those entities in
them which are the most enduring and stable. Since the boundaries of a
place are the first and necessary condition to its existence as an entity, they tend to be identified with it. The walls, ceiling and floor
that provide this place I am in with boundaries, is being referred to as
synonymous with the place as a whole. I refer to it as a room, although
were the walls and roof to disappear, I probably would still be able to
recognize it as a place.

I also refer to it as a "cafeteria", "the room I work in", the name of
the situation which we associate with it or which most often occurs in it.

In the first case we tend to relate to the cafeteria as a (Place), in the
second as a (Situation).

Lived, direct experience reveals a different state of affairs: the situ-
ation/place is experienced as a set of independent components which are

gathered intentionally or incidently in one region of space. <u>It does not</u> <u>have by necessity any system quality</u>. The interrelation of parts towards some central goal is created by the meanings we invest in it. Only in those cases when we intentionally structure these relations: a religious ritual, a laboratory or a pilot's cockpit, the situation/place becomes a system. Hence the fondness of the young Corbusier, for example, for places where conditions are extreme and space is at a premium as well as his fascination with ships, airplanes, motorcars, as indicated in the following illustration from Vers Une Architecture:

In them he finds the conditions of a "machine to live in".

Existentially, however, places have the quality of clothing rather than machines. When they are made into machines—goal oriented systems, they are made so intentionally.

If we were to empty the Room in Hopper's painting of all its contents we could still refer to it as the place of a (past or future) cafeteria.

Only when we are informed that it is for lease, that it will be invested with its existential presence - that of a room. A large square room, highly exposed to the outside by its window, which one enters by a rotating door. If we would then consider alterations in the window, the door, the walls, what is left as a constant participant in the place is the region of space itself, the rights of use it entitles its owner and its position in its surroundings: At the ground floor of this building, besides this street, facing these buildings.

As new entities come to inhabit it: a group of squatters, office furniture, large gaskets, new sets emerge. In each of which the room plays its part of making available a limited amount of space and structuring the relations of the room with the surrounding outside.

The distinction between "Situation" and "Place" is, however, part of our "natural attitude" which tends to view short term situations/places of loose boundaries in which the most prominent and active participants are people - situations, as being different in kind from long term situa - tions/places in which stable inert things play a central role - places. Phenomenological reflection reveals, however, that both are situations/ places, that situation is but a place within a place, and that place is an active encounter, a situation.

What we are dealing with here is a spatial hierarchy of situations/ places. At a spatially super-ordinated level we have the stable bounda- ries of the place - the walls, floor, ceiling of a room, a courtyard, a street, as well as the space enclosed by these boundaries, defined as place.

At a spatially sub-ordinated level we have the entities inhabiting the region of space which when temporary and mobile are defined as activity and when stable and inert as internal places.

There are acts being performed inside places. Some participants are more active than others: A gust of wind, A passing car, The fire in the stove. Human participants bring to the place intentional, autonomous action. Activity, however, belongs to Cartesian dualism: an active content in a static container.

The phenomena defined as a "physical environment" are, in fact, space and entities intended by us in a certain mode - a <u>toposensual</u> mode.

The term "toposensual" refers to our tendency to define as part of the "physical environment" any entity - a person, a wall, an apple, that defines a place or is related in the context of a place by its ability to enclose, obstruct and support through its texture, shape, ambience, and the consistency of its body. We do relate to it neither as a means of <u>production</u>, nor as a substance to be <u>incorporated</u>, nor as a sign <u>representing</u> other entities.

At one extreme, the room which on the face of it is a pure "environmental' entity, can be intended as a tool - for example, if it is going to be demolished and its materials are going to be used for other purposes.

In fantasies it can even become, as in the story of Hansel & Gretel, food - an object to be incorporated.

At the other extreme, the man and the woman, in so far as they obstruct my view of the region behind them, and participate in defining the place of the table or in constituting the ambience of the room - being part of the diffuse activity: the coming and going, sounds, colours, movement, that we experience as filling the place, they, the man and the woman, can also be defined as toposensual entities.

In between, we find objects commonly intended as food and as tools: the cup of coffee, the bottles, encountering us toposensually: as defining a place on the table, as being part of the table place, as taking part, through the sensuality of their presence, (their shape, colour, consistency), in creating the ambience of the room.

Some of the participants which share the situation/place with me are inanimate, some of them have a specific role in the situation, a role, which stemming from their toposensual aspects, one can define as supportive, intermediating. The toposensuality of entities allows them to be experienced in a certain role in one situation, and in a different role in another situation.

All artifacts in the painting which I do not relate to as food or signs or tools, and thus relate to toposensualy, are the subject matter of environmental psychology. All artifacts which in this situation, this context, are experienced not as substances to be incorporated, nor as signs nor as means of production, but as objects in their own right which encounter me in a supportive, enriching, toposensual role - The chair I sit on, the table I lean on and whose texture I feel, the walls which surround me, enclosing, protecting; the plant which is there for my vicarious satisfaction rather then to yield fruit. All these artifacts and objects which I encounter in a situation/place in a toposensual mode are the subject matter of "environmental" psychology and are eventually defined as parts of the physical environment - the "Um-Welt". These entities, however, do not comprise a separate system of their own. Whilst in the cafeteria I do not experience them as a separate system, but are rather parts, individual parts, in the <u>composite identity and presence</u> of the place.

Objects are related in a situational context rather than through some arbitraty category such as: Chairs, Tables, Objects, Furniture, which in fact constitute later attempts to classify.

In its immediacy the chair encounters me as a toposensual entity: to be touched, to be reflected on, to be looked upon, to be sat on, and as part of the situation/place of the table, as well as part of the wider situation/place of the cafeteria.

One is aware that the cafeteria becomes differentiated into internal sub-places; the region of tables 16, of table 12, the region of the window, the region near the door, the outer walls, the region near table 5, the passage 24. All the entities which are part of these regions, these pla-ces, are experienced in their context, rather than as parts of the cate-gories into which they can be classified.

Looking at chair 19 I relate it to the table, and chair 15 and table 16 to the region of space in which they are located and to the bottles on the table.

We encounter the various entities in the situation/place as participants in a composite super-ordinated entity which we call the situation/place.

I have so far refrained, not unintentionally, from referring to archi-tecture.

By its very definition, architecture confines itself to a specific kind of entities: objects purposefully produced for their toposensual quali-ties and intended to be parts of one predominant type of place: the house. I feel that to address ourselves to the "architectural act" rather than architecture would broaden our universe of discourse in a way conduceive to growth and change.

By the "architectural act", I mean that active intervention in the world by which we intend entities and space toposensually.

The subject matter of any experientially oriented psychological research is the (I-World) dialogue. Although phenomenologically the (I-World) is

an indivisible unity, not to be separated into its component poles, psychology tends traditionally to focus on the (I) pole. The (World) pole
is treated as background, as a repertoire of situations, through the
interpretation of which the life plan of the individual can be analyzed.

The making explicit of the psychological meaning of the toposensual object demands however, a shift of focus. While keeping the (I-World) relation and the (I-Place) and (I-Other) as the relationship we study, we
should shift our focus towards the (World) pole or rather to the toposensually intended objects which are part of the (World) pole.

If the (I-World) unity is what we should reflect upon when studying the
toposensual object, then the existential meaning invested in social relations and people's life plans, should be relevant to our enquiry.

In our encounter with the window in Hopper's Cafeteria, as with all windows, such a general existential meaning becomes evident: Choice.

As a place comes into being and the world is redivided anew into inside
and outside, we encounter the birth of a Holon.

In "The Ghost in the Machine", Koestler defines each component in a system as: "... a Holon, a Janus-faced entity who, looking inward, sees
himself as a self-contained unique whole, looking outward as a dependant
part, His self-assertive tendency is the dynamic manifestation of his
unique wholeness, his autonomy and independance as a holon. Its equally
universal antagonist, the integrative tendency, expresses his dependance
on the larger whole to which he belongs: his 'part-ness' ... the self-
assertive tendency is the dynamic expression of the holon's wholeness,
the integrative tendency, the dynamic expression of its partness".

Each place is a Holon, keeping its identity by simultaneously integrating its components and being self-assertive towards its outside,kee-
ping its identity and its boundaries. As we enter a place and become
part of it, we experience, in our turn, the conflicting forces of being
Integrated in the place and keeping our independence, our Self-
Assertiveness.

One way of reinforcing this Self-Assertiveness is by circumventing the
intermediacy and integrativeness of the place through direct access to
the surrounding outside. Access to the outside of a place becomes a
means of enhancing one's experience of freedom in a situation/place.

The boundaries of a place are experienced as part of the limits of one's
"situational freedom".

In the context of this drama, the window (and door), makes available to
us conditions of Choice. The ability to choose between being part of a
place and relating to its outside. The active opting out provided by
the door and the vicarious opting out made present by the window.

The ability of the window to enable one to detach oneself from the intermediacy of the place, or rather, a hierarchy of places one is in,
from their integrativeness, is poetically expressed in Crivelli's "An-
nunciation". We find here the virgin, in her moment of grace, being
approached by a ray of light which cuts through all intermediacies: The
city, the street, the people outside, the house, the room- relating her

244

directly to God. In the midst of this rich, full scene, she is obli-
vious to all. Her entire being surrenders to this beam of light.

In Crivelli's painting the quest for grace, for transcendence is answered,
visibly answered, by the celestial beam of light which cuts through the
thick body of the city to bring to the praying girl the divine message.
In Hopper's cafeteria, as in all places he paints, secularized people
face towards an empty space, a cold sun, blind walls, in an unacknowledged
search for grace. Nothing stands between them and the outside, the sky,
light. Unlike Crivelly's city, all here is transparent, effortlessly
transparent and open. There is no struggle, no obstacles. Unlike the
praying girl, they do not look inwards, nor kneel in prayer, but boldly
direct themselves towards outside, the sun, the sky, space. But their
unstated quest remains unanswered. The large windows in his paintings
open up to empty skies, a harsh light, walls in which blind windows are
carved in like scars.

The extreme conditions of detachment from the place they are in, the
almost unlimited spatial situational freedom at their disposal makes
available to them a barren world. Freedom and Bareness. Freedom to

<u>detach</u> oneself from the cafeteria situation/place combined with the <u>ste-rile</u> presence of the street and houses outside and of the window itself.

The same detachment and bareness is made present by other participants in the situation/place.

The plant, table 16, the man, the space of the room. In each of them I experience a variation on the same meaning dimensions of intimacy/detachment and liveliness/bareness.

But let's imagine that the plant is substituted by a large bouquet of flowers,
that the table is loaded with food,
that the man is a lively character or somebody I know well,
And that the room has been redecorated and the walls provided with warm colours and soft textures:

Each change has brought about a reduction of detachment and bareness in the entities which underwent those changes. Altogether the composite detachment and bareness of the place has been reduced.

We may find then that some of the participants who remain unchanged are "out of place". That they do not fit the intimacy and liveliness which are now endowing the Gestalt of the place/situation as a whole.

At this stage, I would like to draw attention to 3 important points:

1. The meanings we invest in the window will join in any variation in the composite presence of the place. If, for example, the cafeteria would be transformed into an office situation, the unanswered quest made present by the window will become part of it. Following below is a juxtaposition of the Cafeteria painting with another one: Hopper's "Conference at night".

There is nothing out of place here.

The notion of an appropriate fit between (activity) and (place) is part of the Universe of Discourse described in Foucault's books, which since the 18th century generated various sytems of control, regimentation, classification.

Organizing the boundaries and furniture in a place so that they can be parts of only one type of situation limits our situational freedom. In certain situations: religious ritual, scientific experiments, living in extremely hostile environments - a space ship, a submarine, in all these situations a "tight fit" may be suitable, since we give up in advance much of our freedom under extreme, adverse conditions or for the sake of metaphysical or operative goals. In most situations of our Life World no such extreme conditions prevail. To narrow our options in these situations becomes an overt act of renunciation of freedom, of obsession and ritualization of relationships which could have been richer and freer.

In the composite presence of the place, walls, windows, people meet us each in its turn in an independent dialogue.

All dialogues become part of the composite dialogue with the situation/place as a whole.

2. The emergence of a Gestalt of intimacy and liveliness is made possible by all encounters sharing this common dimension of meaning (among other meanings we invest in them).

3. The emergence of the Gestalt is a gradual process: For example, if only the plant is changed, it will still be experienced as "out of place" or "an enlivening object" in the context of a situation/place still experienced as essentially barren and detached. It is only at a certain stage in the accumulating changes in the system that it is encountered as predominantly lively and intimate.

This third point brings me to the issues of compensation and reinforcement among the meanings of various encounters in the situation/place and of my intentions towards the situation/place as a whole.

When, as described above, the situation/place slowly changes its meaning, we experience the new intimacy and liveliness of each additional entity as reinforcing those already intimate and lively and compensating or detracting from the bareness and detachment of the others.

What we encounter here is a change in the composite whole of the situation. The exposure and bareness of the "Cafeteria" window combines with the intimacy and bareness of the people and the furniture around them to create a situation in which, paradoxically, we experience both a conflict between the exposure to outside and the intimacy of the group (maybe curtains should be drawn or their postures become more formal), and at the same time less frustrating in the context of their goal oriented business meeting than in the more sensual, passive situation of the cafeteria where an atmosphere of "waiting for" is prevalent.

The meaning invested in the window and the meanings invested in the group are not in causal relationships but in positional ones. In both encounters I experience some common meanings and therefore they can reinforce and compensate one another:

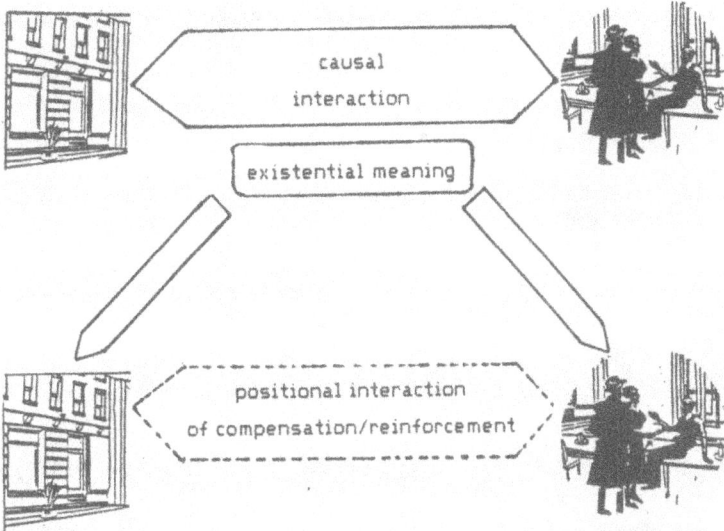

if something would change in the social climate of the cafeteria itself, the impact of the window would still be positional and not causal. Let's assume that the cafeteria is being taken over by a group of "punks", or that I spot a friend I have not seen for years or that the entire place is being reorganized and made into a self-service. Insofar as there is in any of these relations, as in all relations, an inherent tension of integration and self-assertiveness and of liveliness/bareness, the window will play a part in them.

Depending upon my construing of these events, it may add to the sterility of punk culture, add to the sense of sadness of the chance reunion with an old friend and reinforce the detachment and sterility of a self-service establishment.

My own relations to the emerging balances of bareness/liveliness, detachment/intimacy, my tendency to attempt and change them, will depend on my construing of (being in a cafeteria) as a whole.

Why did I come there in the first place? Which of the meanings I invest in (Being in a Cafeteria) brought about my decision of engaging in the situation/place? What meanings did I try to actualize in engaging in the situation? Or in accepting someone's proposal to join him/her in the situation/place?

Let us assume either of the 4 possibilities:

1. That I was hungry and this happened to be the first place I came upon.

2. That I came there to find intimacy, with my thoughts, or with another person.

3. That I came there as an art connoisseur to be in the presence of the Cafeteria that Hopper painted (let us assume that the painting depicted an actual place and the place has not been demolished).

249

4. That I had a quarrel, am fed up with the demands of personal relationships and want to feel anonymous, just a customer. Not a father, a
husband, an employee, but just someone who is drinking his coffee in
peace.

In each case, my focus of experience will tend to be slightly different:

In the first, it may be initially exclusively on the food on my plate,
then, my hunger appeased, I may ease myself in my chair and look around.

On the second occasion, I may confine myself intentionally to the region
of my table. Occasional glances or diffused staring at the surroundings
may provide, however, relief from over-intimacy.

The third will induce me to focus intensely on the room, its decor and
ambience and I may look for consistencies and changes since painted by
Hopper.

On the fourth occasion, on the other hand, I may find the entire scene,
especially its active aspects, of interest.

From past experience, I have built some expectations about (being in a
Cafeteria) situation. In Kellian terms I employ a construction subsystem to anticipate the (being in the cafeteria) event. The immediate
goals I mentioned above may lie inside the range of convenience of this
subsystem or may come about by broadening the system.

I propose that in each situation/place we will attempt to enact through
the composite unity of all our relationships - with people, things,
places - the meanings we invest in the situation/place as a whole - the
superordinated construct we employ in the situation.

Imagining myself again in Hopper's Cafeteria, I may find that I am able
to experience attractiveness and repulsion, intimacy and detachment,
dominance and submission in all my encounters in the cafeteria.

I may find the   /flower   \   /attractive   \
                 |building | |threatening |
                 \woman/man /   \uninteresting/

I may feel   /powerless\   /to change the ambience of the room.\
                 \confident / |to flirt with the woman or man. |
                                      \to pay for the coffee I drink.   /

I may   /focus on   \/the entrance door.   \
                 |not pay attention |the woman/man at the next table. |
                 \   to   /\the whole of the cafeteria.   /

I propose that we will tend to relate all these relationships to the
super-ordinated constructs of our (being-in-the-cafeteria). The meanings
of the situation/place as a whole.

We have been witnessing an underlying process of reinforcement and compensation among the situation as a whole and the dialogues of which it
is composed and the dialogues made available by the outside.

This process is made possible by all my dialogues in the situation sharing the same existential meaning. We invest the same meanings in people, things, organizms, places. As a result, our relationships with them are cumulative, interchangeable, compensatory. The universe of discourse and techniques of enquiry of an authentic psychology of the person and a psychology of place are the same. There is no "Environmental" psychology. The definition in itself is alienating. To label a branch of psychology as having a focus on the environment is to imply a separation that alienates people from their environment.

My argument has come by now full circle to the (I-world) unity and the psychology of the toposensual experience of entities demanding a shift of focus rather than a separate discipline of its own.

- - - - - - - - - -

We come now to the last, focal aspect of the existential-phenomenological analysis of the toposensual - the question of their therapeutic change.

During the last decade, through Ecoanalytic workshops, I have attempted to initiate such changes in a variety of situations/places focusing mainly on the division of space - the location, segregation and orientation of places.

Each workshop of 10-25 participants starts by making explicit their constructs of the situation/place as a whole (through repertory grids, free association, open inverviews), after which the participants proceed to deal projectively with the spatial organization of the situation/ place through cognitive maps, location tasks, design exercises. The core constructs of each individual are then analyzed and the group engages in a process of defining ways by which the dialogues with the toposensual components of the situations/places analyzed can play an existentially enriching part. Returning to the 4 scenarios described above in the first and second you may find the composite intimate and lively (but not over-intimate and lively), situation/place as validating your expectations otherwise you may leave or (if you have been told that you are going to spend this hour in another type of place, or you are being kept there by some persistent and insensitive partner) you may feel cheated and even violent.

Such would be the case also when you come looking for detachment. I propose that you will look for a balance slightly tilted in the direction you are looking for:

Slightly towards intimacy/liveliness or slightly towards detachment/ bareness.

This holds true for most situations in our Life-world. We engage in dialogues in which (if they are going to facilitate our well-being and growth) a balanced degree of mutuality and change has to be kept: of stability and ability of change, of involvement and detachment, of reception and production, of dominance and submission, as if distributed on a Gauss curve.
Most of the situations of our life world fall somewhere at the centre of the graph. Only few situations fall at the two extreme poles of focused and ecstatic situations:

```
Praying                         Performing a
---------------        /\       scientific experiment
getting drunk         /  \      -----------------------
---------------       \  /      flying a jet on
dancing                \/       combat mission
```

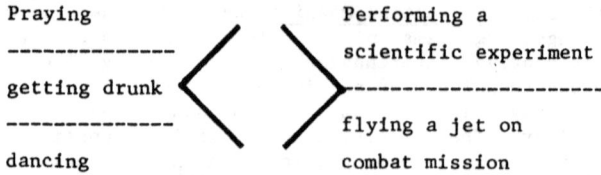

An excessive dichotomisation of situations/places alienates our Life-World. The same holds good about the toposensually-intended entities that take part in the composite presence of these situations/place .

The I - other dialogue is a demanding encounter and we tend to evade the commitment of the(I-Thou) by intending the situation as a cool, objectified (I-it).

From experiencing the Other as a self sufficient, whole, rich and complex, to relating to the Other as an object of our observation and uncommitted action.

The Other in its manifestation: human, inanimate, plant, including the toposensual other such as a door or a window.

In the architectural tradition, the escape to the(I-It):turning the other into an estranged entity - an object of manipulation and observation, finds expression in two major trends: one views the architectural act as a functional or rational process, the second sees architecture as art, media, a system of signs.

Whoever defines a window or a door as suited for a specific, specialized purpose only: to enable entry/to block entry; To let light, sun, and fresh air through; To block light, sun and fresh air; without considering or being aware of the relationships mediated by the door and window, whoever acts in this way, impoverishes the ability of the toposensual Other to encounter us in a rich dialogue. As a direct consequence, our existence is impoverished.

Moreover, by setting himself limited goals, the designer uncritically creates relationships, which had he been aware of, he might have wanted to alter.

Despite all this we have to keep in mind that the meaning matrix generated by the door and window is rooted in the function of opening/closing.

The second escape route from the immediate, expressive presence of the toposensual Other, is more subtle.

It begins by extracting the architectural object from the life world and placing it in the conceptual world of art, symbols and signs.

The difference between a cathedral and a Rembrandt painting, for example, is in the mode of our involvement with them:

Rembrandt's "The Sacrifice of Isaac" can arouse my compassion but I will never be able to change anything in the tragic scene taking place time and again before my eyes.

I am an outside observer. I am uncommitted.

A cathedral, on the other hand, exists here and now in my Life world.
When in it, I am committed, I am here.
Every change in it is a change (minor or major) in my here and now, in
my existence, and as a being responsible for its acts and evasions.

The toposensual other shares the Life-World with me, the world into
which and from which all symbols emerge.

Functionalism does not attempt to deal at all with the question of meaning. The existential meaning remains subconscious.

It brings about changes in the world without any attempt on the part of
their perpetrator to predict their outcome and control their meaning.

Either that, or it is an act which hides its value positions:
Bringing about changes in the world, to which the public in whose name
one acts, remain unconscious to one's motives.

Aestheticism does try to deal with the problem of meaning, but it does
so by transferring the entity from the immediate world it co-inhabits
with us, a world of responsibility and commitment, to another world. A
world which is the subject of contemplation . Invulnerable and
uncommitted.

Every design decision - the form, the size, depth, and location of a
window or door, the shape and the materials it is made of, is a value
decision.

It creates for us partners for dialogues: Entities, which can be rich
and growth oriented or dull and stultifying.

Understanding the existential meaning of window and door enables us to
comprehend the possibilities of dialogue inherent in their identity
and presence.

As we can discern in the life plan, in the intentions, of a man the
ability and will to choose, to preserve, to open up to possibilities, to
look back longingly; so can we discern in the limits of place/world and
the openings set in them, different degrees of choice, actualization
and possibility.

And as the ability of every man and woman to grow, to become, depends
on his or her ability to preserve a balance between the opposing polls,
between the actualized and the unactualized, and on his or her ability
to choose one's way independently,so is the ability of a place to be
partner in a balanced dialogue, dependent on its ability to present us
with entities and relationships which incorporate a balance between the
actualized and the unactualized. It depends on the dialogue occuring
from positions of freedom of choice and not under coercion/obedience.

One of the ways by which the world/place presents us with balances of
actualization and open possibilities of choice and coercion, is by means
of the setting of limits and the location of openings in them.

Among the imagined scenarios in Hopper's cafeteria, it is only when you engage in the situation/place as an observer - you relate to it as a relic, that its intimacy or detachment, its liveliness or bareness will be of no concern for you, as long as it is still intact as when Hopper painted it.

The place/situation on all its participants is transformed then into an aesthetic object. It is no part of the continuum of commitments, desires, fears of your life/world.

In Hopper's "Cafeteria' - the room, the furniture, space itself is detached, arid, rejecting - in short - alienated. Can this be changed? Should it be changed? Can we approach place therapeutically as we would approach a person or a group who feel that their (I/we-world) dialogue is alienated, narrow, sterile, stagnant.

Let me state right away that I can not find any ontological reason for therapy. There is an inherent growth oriented position in any therapy. But a person or a group are free to choose stagnation and death. The same applies to places. Alienated places reduce the lifeness of our world. They are riding, over-detached or over-intimate. Specialized, unresponsive.

Once however we have made a choice and decided on growth as our core construct, the answer to the first question as to the ability of a therapy of places, is positive.

Here, as with the individual we have to consider, the situational freedom of a place - what is open to change and what has to be accepted by the changer, owner, designer, user.

The situational freedom of a place is determined by two factors:
1) the _resources_ available for its creation space, materials and manpower.

2) the _surroundings_ out of which its region of space has been carved. If, for example, instead of the dead street, the surroundings would have been taken from another Hopper painting: "The Camel's Hump".

The scene of bareness would have been reduced. The horizons widened.

The surroundings made present in the "Cafeteria" painting are the street and its blind buildings. We can assume that the "Cafeteria" itself is on the ground level of a similar type of building.

Let's imagine that you have just purchased the ground floor and intend to build a cafeteria there or that you are an architect who has got the job of producing the design of the cafeteria; the first conflict you will face, consciously or subconsciously, is between the freedom inherent in "being in the street" - relative to "being in the cafeteria" (due to its being a public domain and its exposure to the elements) and the bleakness of the street and its surrounding houses.

If I open up the cafeteria, like in Hopper's painting, to the empty street, the blind houses and the harsh light, I create a situation in which I pay for my experience of an enhanced freedom by being exposed to the presence of these sterile entities. Freedom and bareness are added to the composite meaning of the being -in-the-cafeteria situation.

On the other hand if, as many designers and owners do, I were to completely cut the cafeteria off from the outside, I would create a place which does not provide any relief from its intimacy, and the presence of which excludes all possible relations with the outside Ecodrama of sky, earth, sun, atmosphere and public domain.

I experience a loss of freedom in part of my existential horizon.

I experience an overwhelming predominance of actualized possibilities.

If, in addition to the lack of windows, we encounter low lights, warm textures, an abundance of small niches, the over-intimacy and the presence of the actualized in the place is further reinforced.

In such a situation, when the outside has nothing to offer, it is the presence of choice itself which should be elaborated. It is the availability of options for detaching oneself from the inside which must be stressed, rather than entities and places out there, in the presence of which one would vicariously like to be.

It is therefore the window as place, as a situation in itself, which needs elaborating, while its size is minimized and the regions of the outside it makes visible are dispersed and disconnected from each other.

As to its presence and the light it casts into the room: a warm light of an intricate pattern may reinforce the intimacy and liveliness of the situation/place, while a cool, restrained presence and cold light of neutral patterns may reinforce its detachment and bareness.

Both the over-exposure of Hopper's cafeteria and the over-intimacy of closed, artificially illuminated places, attempt to relate to windows at the level of immediate dialogue. There are, however, other occasions on which the window is approached as a symbolic object, or as a mechanism, without any attempt to integrate it in the "here and now" continuum of the situation/place.

During a seminar in which I worked with students of architecture on the meanings of windows and their design implications I asked them to make changes in the window of Hopper's Cafeteria. They attempted to achieve a cafeteria space that will keep its liberating quality (in the sense that it enables one to be in contact with the street) while reducing the impact of its bareness. As a result of the in-the-world mode which prevailed in our dealing with the situation/place and the window during the seminar, the windows seem to have been intended situationally, nor as signs neither as mechanisms. The following 3 examples are by (in order of presentation) Yael Barhana, Samuel Comforti and Elazar Malichi. The changes made in the outer walls of the cafeteria will, from now on, be part of the composite whole of any future situation that will occur in this region of space.

In all future situations, the meaning of (detachment) & (bareness) will be reduced and the (being part of) and (substantial) increased.

This at the topological level - the sheer positioning, screening, and opening up. These outer walls however, are entities in their own right- on their own identity and presence. They may, for example, be made of thin, Spartan components or heavy, opulent ones.

In each case, their spareness or richness will join the composite dialogue of each situation/place and add their specific meaning to the composite of (being-in-this-place).

— — — — — — — — ——— — — — — — —

Any therapy is essentially a change in the existential structures, essences of the phenomenon and its meaning.

Ecoanalysis attempts to make explicit the core constructs of the meaning we invest in toposensual space and objects, so as to facilitate a process by which the alienation and growth potential of place become part of the design decisions.

Architecture, redefined in the light of Ecoanalysis, becomes that human act which defines the boundaries of situations/places in ways that add to the whole of the composite potential for growth they make available to us.

We have now come full circle with our reflections on the context in which the meanings of the "physical environment" should be looked for. During the last decade through Ecoanalytic workshops and related research, I have attempted to apply this model to a variety of groups and issues: Passengers in Air Terminals, Laymen, Architects, Psychologists on their Home and the Surroundings of Home, Teachers and Pupils at Schools, Staff Members of industry on their work place. Students, on their Faculty and Dormitories. Kibbutz Members on the design of their Community. For each group and issue, the context was different, and so were the spatial components analyzed. The analysis of the situation/ place, however, evolved around the reoccuring dynamic structure put forward in this paper and had the therapeutic change of the spatiality of places as its goal.

257

The relevance of phenomenological approaches to the study of "Environmental" issues, has been proposed by several authors in the course of the last decade. Buttimer has argued that understanding the particular life spaces of people in cities is essential if we are to understand how the planning and development of those cities should proceed. Researchers with a more general value orientation towards the creation of more authentic and more meaningful places, such as Relph (1981), have argued that phenomenology provides a basis for radically new departures in considering the implications of the "Physical" surroundings. Various other authors have shown how this approach may be applied to specific types of places, such as Korosec-Serfaty's (1984) study of the cellar and the attic. However, no one seems to aim to employ this approach as a basis for changing the discourse about the architectural act, for a new way of reaching design decisions about the spatiality of places. In particular the debate on the phenomenological framework has been rather confused as to the nature of phenomenology. Sixsmith (1983) has pointed out, for example, that Relph (1976) and Seamon (1979) fall back into an essentially dualistic framework in which there is a real world and a subjective world and the phenomenologist can give more emphasis to the subjective world. It is one of the tenets of the present discussion that by taking a more existentialist orientation towards phenomenology, some of these confusions and weaknesses in the literature can be handled.

That emphasis should be put on the unity of the (I-World) and on choice and action as fundamental human conditions.

While existential theories like those of Biswanger, Frankel and May draw on the insights provided by this approach in fostering changes in the lives of individuals and groups, no such attempt has heretofare been made in dealing with those phenomena in that realm of our lives which is defined (wrongly, as I hope to prove) as the "physical environment".

Ecoanalysis - the postulates of which are described in this chapter, consists of such an attempt to actively and therapeutically draw on the insights of Existential - Phenomenological psychologies to bring about changes in the design of the spatiality of places. These insights can be regarded as having therapeutic implications because they are always concerned with healing the potential rift between the individual and the situation/place in which he or she find themselves.

While Psychoanalysis, as in all dynamic approaches to the (I-World), focuses on the experiencing (I), Ecoanalysis, while also addressing itself to the unity of the (I-World), focuses on the (World) pole, or rather on the Spatiality of the world which we encounter as place.

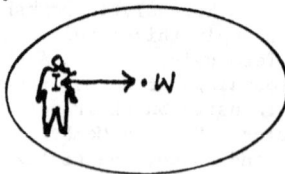

Existentialist-phenomenological enquiries are based on the following fundamental assumptions about a person's relations with his or her world:

BIBLIOGRAPHY

Buttimer, A., (1976) "Grasping the Dynamism of the Lifeworld", Annuals Association of American Geographers, 66, pp. 277-92.

Korosec-Serfaty, P., (1984) "The Home from Attic to Cellar", Journal of Environmental Psychology, 4, pp. 303-321.

Relph, E., (1976) Place and Placelessness. Pion, London.

Relph, E., (1981) Rational Landscapes and Humanistic Geography. Croom Helm, London.

Seamon, D., (1979) A Geography of the Lifeworld: Movement, Rest and Encounter. Croom Helm, London.

Sixsmith, J.A., (1983) Comment on the Phenomenological Contribution to Environmental Psychology Journal of Environmental Psychology, 3, pp. 109-111.

Straus, E. (1967) Phenomenological Psychology. Tavistock, London.

16. The significance of imagination and its place in architectonic creation

KLAUS PETER WALCHER

The aim of this contribution is to bring out a fundamental facet of the relationship of man to the environment he is projecting, constructing and living in. The basic layer of the creative process that preceeds concrete action and reaches at the same time beyond the momentary possibilities of creative realization, is investigated. In this layer different motivational impulses are transformed and concentrated into an imaginative "pre-Gestalt". This sublime but forceful psychic reality plays an important role in the individual and society.

BRIEF SYNOPSIS

The relationship between man and his environment at the level at which this relationship is immediately presented to his consciousness and becomes the object of his attention is in urgent need of study in the field of the natural, social and cultural environment. Such studies will reveal new aspects, borne jointly by various disciplines.

THE "HOME DREAMER"

As a starting point we choose the work by Bachelard (1975) in which space, the essential medium of architecture, is subjected to a radical phenomenal analysis. His "Poetics of Space" attempts to make us aware of a primary layer of experience in which the latent images of the origin of the dwelling function rest, where "the house is one of the greatest powers of integration for thought, memories, and dreams of man" (Bachelard 1975, 38). Even the "smallest home" with the "illusion of being cared for lovingly" is linked with "anthropocosmic ties". The

260

psychologist comes least close to this when he describes houses in terms of their comforts. It is rather the psychoanalyst who understands the concealed contents of "below" and "above", "light" and "dark", the "heroism of the staircases" and the "intimate values of verticalism". It is the phenomenologist, however, who first arrives at an "extreme meaning of the images", for he is searching for the "roots of the dwelling function". He finds them in "reverie", the power of imagination as the link between memory and dream. Through the memories of all the houses where we have found refuge, in all the houses in which we have dreamed of living, an intimate and concrete being can be recognized which would be a justification of the unique value of all our images of protected inwardness. That is where the main problem lies" (Bachelard 1975, 35).

In order to solve this problem, Bachelard prefers to gather the roots from poetic information, in no way, however, but a mere literary replacement of signs or metaphors. By means of the "language of image" for which he has been searching, he tries to find a description of the immanent meaning of lived-experience that is as precise as possible without recourse to historical meaning. From the indefinitenesss of this immanent meaning in the current act of cognition a peculiar sort of objectivity arises, a "subjective meaningfulness". Bachelard's "home dreamer" lives from this indefiniteness, "those mental fields in which so to speak an innate devotion to the original function of dwelling is expressed" (Bachelard 1975, 36). The fundamental-sensual experience reveals the spatial, symbolic images of fantasy while "daydreaming". Moreover, the striving for creative development is embedded into cosmological forces as well as kept on a human plane. Any objectifying attitude is bound to miss this direction that is rather similar to the alchemistic process of sublimation, as a commentator of Bachelard points out: "The treatment of space in mathematical terms or even in terms of descriptive metaphor leads to the loss of the 'tonalization of being', generating much of our contemporary art and architecture with its large-scale coldness while meeting all the criteria of function, utility, and efficency. Architects, who would work from the images of their souls, would create only those spaces which invite caresses" (Denton 1974, p.19).

This existential phenomenology is committed to upgrading the activities of fantasy with the aim of removing the ties of mental habits and setting on one hand the imaginative, dynamic attitude against, on the other a scientific attitude based on intersubjective disagreement and conceptual definition. It would be inaccurate to think that this imaginative attitude is only a plea for the abolition of deterministic images. The intention is rather to point out that imagination forms an origin of meaning upon which the foundation of concrete ideas is based.

In order to understand this statement clearly it is essential to recognize that the indefiniteness of the imaginative dynamic is a positive and fundamental phenomenon. Relevant to this is the work of Marleau-Ponty (1966).

261

PHENOMENOLOGICAL EXCURSION

In his phenomenology perception means original cognition, namely
"presence of an atmosphere, of a horizon or, if you like, of a
"structure" which assigns its current situation to the consciousness.
Perception is not the experiencing of manifold impressions which have
suitable memories to supplement them, but the experience of the emerging
of an immanent meaning from a constellation of conditions without which
a reference to memories would not be possible" (Marleau-Ponty 1966, p.42).

This expressionless depth of consciousness is the origin of every
creative performance. In various descriptions of consciousness this is
as a primary, "autistic", (day-)dreaming, contextual state
differentiated from a secondary, reality orientated, centralistic one
(Freud 1900, Bleuler 1911, Gurwitsch 1955, McKellar 1957).
Imagination, then, is an expression of consciousness which, in its
intentional directedness is virtually effective through these layers of
consciousness. Brentano (1874) and James (1890) carried out the first
step in the direction of modern psychological-phenomenological analysis
of consciousness by way of conceiving the actual nature of
consciousness as a process. This reaches beyond the hierarchical
elaborations of higher mental processes (Eysenck 1984) and supplements
the structuralistic definitions of the genetic theory of knowledge
(Piaget and Inhelder 1973).

THE INTELLECTUAL FORCE FIELD

How can what has been said so far be evaluated in the light of the
interpretation of the natural, social, and cultural environment? In
his review Rapoport (1977) states that perceptual environmental
evaluation is the most simple case of "creative imagination" which "is
more a matter of overall affective response than of a detailed analysis
of specific aspects, it is more a matter of latent function, and it is
largely affected by images and ideals" (Rapoport 1977, p.60).
Especially with reference to the built environment, Rapoport
demonstrates with empirical evidence that environmental meaning is not
based, in the first place, on the eyecatching characteristics of style,
spatial geometry, decoration, and colour. These are specific foci for
establishing the coherence of meaning. Rather, meaning is based on the
variability of a complex field of perception, i.e. on the subtle
differences in style, proportion, colour and, furthermore, on the
relations between light and shadow, sounds, smells, temperatures. In
their unique combination they constitute a number of associative
relations which in their entirety form a unified context for meaning.

What has been ascertained with regard to perception applies in the
same way to the orientation of action. "There is an important more
general and theoretical argument that also stresses the importance of
meaning - this has to do with the distinction already introduced
between manifest and latent functions and, more specifically, the
distinctions between activities, how an activity is done, what are
associated activities, and the meaning of a given activity. It appears
that the meaning of activities is their most important characteristic,
corresponding to the finding that symbolic aspects are the most

important in the sequence of "concrete object, use object, value object, symbolic object". (Rapoport 1982, 32-33).

The hierarchy of meaning of objects is embedded into the force field of practical living. Symbolic objects are no dreamlike past-oriented images, but aspects of the environment which is itself a system of all the cultural conditions. This fusion of the individual and socio-cultural aspects has been clearly described by Bourdieu (1974): "The intellectual force field is more than just an aggregate of isolated forces, a juxtaposition of elements simply strung together. Rather, like a magnetic field it forms a system of force lines: the powers at work in it or their effects may be described as just as many forces that give the field ... its specific structure. On the other hand each of these forces determines the affiliation to this field: each one owes to the particular position it holds in this field, the characteristics of the position which cannot be derived from its purely immanent composition, and a particular role which determines the kind of connection with the cultural force field" (Bourdieu 1974, 76). One can say that, at the level of control, the imaginative forces have not lost their impact, being pragmatically tied-up has rather changed their function.

A VESSEL FOR EMOTION

It will now be shown, how this line of reasoning can be given further shape within the context of architectural design. This is relatively easy since we have a convincing forethinker in Giedion (1956). His starting point is a cultural criticism which he derives from the loss of the understanding of the essence of technology. This loss is in no way caused by the existence of the technocivilized world per se but by the inadequate power of integration resulting from the fact that the structures of thought and emotion increasingly drift apart. "These correlations between reality and its symbols of emotion are just as unresolved as the functioning of the consciousness and its influence on our actions. But at the moment when they are disturbed, responsibility expires." (Giedion 1956, p.14).

It is the loss of balance of the inner forces which furthers the growing incapability of ordering and controlling the progressive mechanization of life. As early as 1938 he said "Production as an end in itself and, in emotional matters, flight into romanticism, go side by side these days." (Giedion 1956, p.16). In the end everyone becomes brutalized because of the machinery that has been made. He recognizes the constructive power of imagination as it is expressed most clearly in art, as a means of regaining the inner equilibrium and the personal capability to develop. "There is no development that could live without that formation soprano voice which is called art. Art? Emotion? It needs expressions which seemingly serve no other purpose than to be a vessel for emotion." (Giedion 1956, p.12). Without possessing operational criteria about what qualifies as art, a generally valid qualitative criterion will be found for it in truthfulness. Put more precisely it concerns a seismographic ability to locate its problematic constellation in the cultural force field which one comprehends intellectually, absorbs emotionally and would like to express from an internalized point of view. In contrast to that, official art may, of course, achieve quite the opposite effect, namely, that of not being aesthetic.

The inferences are obvious. Art is a medium which creates its means of expression from the available anonymous forces of time. As it has a relatively "free hand" it is most likely to be in a postion to announce future things in a code. Imagination becomes a detector which is able to register tensions and, simultaneously, prophetic force which anticipates new equilibria in an exemplary way.

Imagination as a means for creating a future-oriented image, does not overstep any boundaries in the artistic area towards evasions of fantasy but rather in the social area towards "tended living". The classic functions of living, working, associating, and recreating can be integrated if a will of expression succeeds in asserting itself, a will emanating from the interplay of the social forces aiming at this integration. Indeed, any technical solution is proceeded by a moral, social and aesthetic one.

The fact that this thought is utopian in essence cannot be denied, for the isolated arts would have to expand to an overall work of art, the concern for the necessities of life would have to become a community concern. It is the spirit of the 'Bauhaus' which made the most convincing attempt at such an integration in this century. "Let us all together desire, devise, create the new construction of the future which will be all in one form: architecture, plastic art and painting, and which will, in days to come, rise to the sky from millions of hands of craftsmen as a crystal symbol of the new coming faith." (Gropius 1979, 165). Obviously, the gathering of forces can find its clearest expression in the symbolic; and it has long since exceeded the strength of a single individual. Thus, the practical relevance of the 'Bauhaus' is confined to giving strong impulses which germinate afresh again and again. However, the "New Monumentality" (Giedion 1956, 27 and following pages) which was to create a "vessel for emotion" has remained a desideratum until today. Thus, it has not yet been decided whether by means of the praised and cursed beginnings of the new way of building from the "Congresses Internationaux d'Architecture Moderne" in 1928 or today's Urban Design Research, steps have indeed been taken towards a new unified plurality, or whether everything remains a mere symptom of confusion.

AN EXEMPLARY LIFE

Moholy-Nagy, a visionary of modernism, lived in a world of imagination. His comments on this are amazingly well in agreement with those mentioned in this study:

"It is the artist's duty today to pentrate yet-unseen ranges of the biological functions, to search the new dimensions of the industrial society and to translate new findings with an emotional orientation. The artist unconsciously disentangles the most essential strands of existence from the contorted and chaotic complexities of actuality, and weaves them into an emotional fabric of compelling validity, characteristic of himself as well as of his epoch. This ability to

264

select is an outstanding gift based upon intuitive power and insight, upon judgement and knowledge, and upon inner responsibility to fundamental biological and social laws which provoke a reinterpretation in every civilization. This intuitive power is present in other creative workers, too, in philosophers, poets, scientists, technologists. They pursue the same hopes, seek the same meanings, and - although the content of their work appears to be different - the trends of their approach and the background of their activity are identical. They all must draw from the same source, which is life in a certain society, in a certain civilization" (Moholy-Nagy 1947, 11).

Deeply inspired by a light-vision experienced in early life, a personal task arises ("Recognize the light-pattern of your life") that leads in the end to an objectified and hither-to unknown restructuring of space. Space in its relationship to time, that is comprehended in its motion, is only the most consequent expression of emancipation from material gravity, of which light, being the "most emancipated" medium, serves as a model.

Out of this view emerges a program that makes equal use of art, science, and technology in order to shape the environment. "The more people understand and master this type of thinking in relationships the easier it will be to realize social planning and a better living. Vision in motion is a tool to render the complexity of these processes as simply as the economist attempts in his field when he speaks about all this as a matter of man hours, that is, operations measured by time.

"We are heading toward a kinetic, time-spatial existence; toward an awareness of the forces plus their relationships which define all life and of which we had no previous knowledge and for which we have as yet no exact terminology. The affirmation of all these space-time forces involves a reorientation of all our faculties.

Space-time stands for many things: relativity of motion and its measurement, integration, simultaneous grasp of the inside and outside, revelation of the structure instead of the facade. It also stands for a new vision concerning materials, energies, tensions, and their social implications.

This conception is still unpredictable in its consequences for the improvement of the affairs of mankind, though the artist as well as the designer already experiment with it at a new level of consciousness. The designer has to think in terms of integrated processes of materials and production, sales, distribution, financing and advertising; the contemporary artist consciously or intuitively tries to express the substance of his specialized field as the result of forces in space and time and to integrate it with social reality. He prepares a new and creative vision for the masses, and with it a new orientation for a healthier life plan. But in order to benefit society, the artist's work must penetrate everyone's daily existence" (Moholy-Nagy 1947, 268-269).

The mental existence of Moholy-Nagy can be pursued on two levels of generalization. The first is concerned with his individual life style.

The urge to resolve static forms reveals itself as a leitmotif in all stages of his life. The motif is in accordance with an assumption of the humanistic in the psychology of human motivation which recognizes the principle of actualization of individual potential.

"There is an internal, biological pressure to develop fully the capacities and the talents that have been inherited; the central motivation of the individual is to grow and to enhance the basic self.

The acceptance of an actualization tendency is an axiom of humanistic psychology - it is not subject to proof or disproof" (Weiner 1985, 409).

Maslow (1954), the prominent representative of this movement, describes a multitude of need systems which he puts into a hierarchy with the categories physiological, safety, love, esteem, and self-actualization. He characterizes the lower needs by deficit (D) values (e.g. lack of proper shelter) of which the attainment must be ensured if the being (B) values (e.g. absence of meaning of life), which are related to the higher needs, are to gain thematical relevance.

Assuming such a regular dependence of being values on deficiency motives could not remain without reply since it is contrary to many experiences (Inglehart 1977; cf. also Fietkau 1984). This has been impressively documented by the work of Frankl (1946), but it could be substantiated with Moholy-Nagy's life itself (Moholy-Nagy 1950). Nonetheless, it is valuable to point to Maslow's central message:

"All human concerns, all human institutions, and all human cultures rest on human nature. Since we know little about human nature, theories (usually incorrect ones) about human nature have served in lieu of organized and valid facts and substantiated laws. Such theories, whether valid or not, have always been at the roots of the various theologies, political and economic philosophies, and social beliefs by which mankind has lived.

I am convinced that the failure of the various value systems that have been tried in the past (power politics, war, religion, nationalism, the various economic systems, the rationalistic as well as the romantic philosophies, technology and engineering, mechanistic science) has been due largely to their being founded on erroneous conceptions of human nature and of society. And however paradoxical this may sound. I am afraid that a number of psychologists are also working with erroneous preconceptions and unconscious assumptions about human nature (and about society) which, because they are implicit and unconscious, can maintain and perpetuate themselves beyond the reach of testing for a considerable time to come" (Maslow 1954, 353).

This touches the second level of generalization indicating the transition from individual life style to that of society. Correspondingly imagination reaches an additional degree of transformation. Here, the unifying tendency of the individual consciousness has ceased and, all the more, the transcending overtones of individual imagination have vanished. Nevertheless its

uncontrollable and unpredictable impulses influence the intellectual
force field of society. It can be shown with reference to Moholy-Nagy
and as well as to the history of the Bauhaus.

NEW CONCEPTUAL HORIZONS

The impulses of individual imagination, operating within a socially
based intellectual force field, poses particular problems when
considering the functions of architecture. For instance, although it
is quite evident that architecture is a created space system, this
statement appears to be somewhat problematical:

> "We see on the one hand, how architecture depends on the space
> concept, and on the other hand how easily spaces, Space, 'extension
> and spatiality', in opposition to 'time', tend to constitute a
> confused conglomerate, especially in works about the 'esthetics of
> architectural forms'." (Ankerl 1981, 16).

As a result, the concept of multi-functionality holds a central
position in the present argument. It was introduced by the
Czechoslovakian philosopher Mukarovsky (1983). For him architecture is
a:

> "typical case of poly-functional production; it is justified that
> modern theorists of architecture regard the building as a place for
> an ensemble of life processes. The architectural configuration
> differs from all other human artefacts – even such complicated
> products as machines – because it is not committed to the execution
> of one particular activity, but furnishes the spacial environment for
> various human activities" (Mukarovsky 1983, 220).

In particular Mukarovsky differentiates between the functional levels
of current purpose, that which has genetically and historically
developed over the years and the aesthetical-symbolic functions.
Especially "with the complicated and delicate problem of the aesthetic
function in architecture", we have to proceed from the fact

> "that whatever it may arise, it represents the dialectual negation of
> functionality itself. Each function with the exception of the
> aesthetic one can ultimately find a manifestation in the appropriate
> utilization of an object alone. Whenever the aesthetic function
> comes to the fore, it will be the more intense, the more an object
> exists for its own sake" (Mukarovsky 1983, 223).

Here the transcending quality of consciousness is fully confirmed,
for it is the imagination that is able "to build a link in evolutionary
transfers between past and future stratifications of functions; it then
... serves as a factor of development and indicator of change"
(Mukarovsky 1983, 224). The uniting of the aesthetic with the other
functions results in a multi-functionality which exactly summarizes the
different levels of generalization mentioned above. This extensive
functional network and its pattern of invariance has until now remained
undiscussed.

The perpectives we are concerned with here can not yet be elucidated
by a generative design-technique. It someone can say: "Whereas
'Vitruvian' research is done by lone scholars working in museums and
libraries, 'post-Vitruvian' is done by research teams working in what
the Americans call 'systems laboratories'" (March 1976, XII), this
optimism is only understandable in the narrow context of product-
Gestalt. But what is the good of the highly praised city of Brazilia,
if it will only too son be contradicated by reality?

"Brasilia has, far from becoming the egalitarian city it was supposed
to be, given form to social differentiation. Primary and secondary
functions in which the planners and architects had every confidence
have been transformed or replaced. The ideology of a community of
equals, which was to have become visible in the urban structure and
the imagery of the buildings, has given way to other visions of life
in society. And this has happened without there having been any
gross mistakes in design on the part of the architects, given the
'programme' they accepted. The mistake was in accepting that
programme, with the social systems identified or implied in it, as
definitive and timeless, and in assuming that having been designed
for that program, the architecture would see it realized ...

So while the architects took a position of passive service with
respect to the exigencies set out in the preliminary study they were
given, undertaking to invent forms that would answer to these, they
might better have oriented their passivity toward the fact that, no
matter how valid the programme and no matter how well designed the
forms, no forms created by an architect are going to prevent events
from taking an autonomous course around them" (Eco 1980, 60-61).

As a consequence, in contrast to this a full format is required, as has
been pre-detined by Mukarovsky and later introduced by Preziosi:

"Human built environments are subject to change and transformation
over space and time - a characteristic not demonstrated for the
architectonic environments of other species; this property is itself
a manifestation of the fact that the code is fundamentally a system
of relationship rather than a system of forms" (Preziosi 1979, 16).

Within such a broad interpretation of the spatiotemporal system,
imagination is one focus in the organization of built environment.
Precisely this has been recognized by Moholy-Nagy with intuitive
certainty. Beyond that Preziosi makes transparent an essential
principle, contingent on his holistic and genetic orientation, which
has been formulated by Krampen (1979) in terms of a socio-theoretical
allusion:

"Ultimately, the potential for change of human activity is rooted in
the concrete history of men who perform meaningful activities. In
each 'act' on the 'stage' on which this history unfolds, certain
social classes are posed in opposition of interest to other classes.
Instruments and signs are the props of these protagonists,
differentiated by their different roles in the class conflict which
is evolving with a dialectical rhythm" (Krampen 1979, 315).

The developmental principle effective here is philosophically rooted in the "transactional" paradigm of pragmatism (Dewey and Bentley 1949). At the same time it incorporates a scientific program, even a moral dimension. This principle determines the "epigenetic landscape of human society" (Waddington 1977) in a central point. Any progressive and relatively stablized social system is based upon a positive relationship towards the dialectics of an open development.

Bibliography

Ankerl, G. (1981) Experimental sociology of architecture. A Guide to theory, research, and literature. Mouton, The Hague.

Bachelard, G. (1975) Poetik des Raumes. Wien: Ullstein, Frankfurt, Berlin.

Bleuler, E. (1911) "Dementia praecox oder Gruppe der Schizophrenien" in Handbuch der Psychiatrie, IV. Abt. 1. Wien: Deuticke.

Bourdieu, P. (1974) Zur Soziologie der symbolischen Formen. Suhrkamp, Frankfurt.

Brentano, F. (1874) Psychologie vom empirischen Standpunkt. 1. Band. Neu hrsg. von O. Kraus, Hamburg: Meiner 1955.

Denton, D.E. (1974) "The Image. Gaston Bachelards language of space in International Journal of Symbology 5, 14-21.

Dewey, J. and Bentley, A.F. (1949) Knowing and the known. Beacon Press, Boston.

Eco, U. (1980) "Function and Sign: the semiotics of architecture in Broadbent, G., Bunt, R. and Jencks, Ch. eds. Signs, symbols, and architect Wiley & Sons, New York, 11-69.

Eysenck, M.W. (1984) A handbook of cognitive psychology. Lawrence Erlbaum Assoc., Hillsdale, N.J.

Fietkau, H.-J. (1984) Bedingungen ökologischen Handelns. Gesellschaftliche Aufgaben der Umweltpsychologie. Weinheim, Basel: Beltz.

Frankl, V.E. (1946) Ein Psycholog erlebt das Konzentrationslager. Wien: Verlag fur Jugend und Volk.

Freud, S. (1900) Die Traumdeutung. Uber den Traum. In: Gesammelte Werke, Band II/III. Imago Publishing & Co, London.

Giedion, S. (1956) Architektur und Gemeinschaft. Tagebuch einer Entwicklung. Rowohlt, Hamburg.

Gropius, W. (1979) Das Endziel aller bildnerischen Tatigkeit ist der
Bau! In: Schneede, U.M. (Hrsg.) Die zwanziger Jahre. Manifeste und
Dokumente deutscher Künstler. Köln: Du Mont.

Gurwitsch, A. (1955) The phenomenological and the psychological
approach to consciousness. Phil. Phenommenol. Res. 15.

Inglehart, R. (1977) The silent revolution: Changing values and
political styles in western publics. Princeton University Press,
Princeton.

James, W. (1890) Principles of psychology, Vol 1. Holt & Co, New York.

Krampen, M. (1979) Meaning in the urban environment. Pion, London.

March, L. ed. (1976) The architecture of form. Cambridge University
Press, Cambridge, Mass.

Maslow, A.H. (1954) Motivation and personality. Harper, New York.

McKellar, P. (1957) Imagination and thinking. Cohen and West, London.

Merleau-Ponty, M. (1966) Phanomenologie der Wahrnehmung. Walter de
Gruyter & Co, Berlin.

Moholy-Nagy, L. (1947) Vision in motion. Paul Theobald, Chicago.

Moholy-Nagy, S. (1950) Moholy-Nagy. Experiment in totality. M.I.T.
Press, Cambridge, Mass.

Mukarovsky, J. (1983 (1937)) Zum Problem der Funktionen in der
Architektur. Zeitschrift fur Semiotik 5, 217-228.

Piaget, J. and Inhelder, B. (1973) Memory and intelligence. Basic
Book, New York.

Preziosi, D. (1979) Architecture, language, and meaning. The origins
of the built world and its semiotic organization. Mounton, The
Hague, Paris, New York.

Rapoport, A. (1977) Human aspects of urban form. Pergamon, Oxford.

Waddington, C.H. (1977) Tools for thought. How to understand and apply
the latest scientific techniques of problem solving. Basic Books,
New York.

Weiner, B. (1985) Human motivation. Springer, New York, Berlin,
Heidelberg, Tokyo.

Brief biographies of
contributors

FLORA AMONI received her degree in Philosophy from the University of Rome. She taught Anthropology at the University of Viterbo for six years. Since 1981 she has been participating in the research project on People and Environment at the Istituto di Psicologia of the C.N.R. (National Research Council) in Rome.

GILLES BARBEY was educated as an architect and practised in England, the United States and Switzerland for many years. While designing domestic environments, he became interested not only in the architectural aspects of housing but also in the life experience of the inhabitants. His concern for the relations between the physical environment and human behaviour was initiated in the late 1960's and gradually developed into a historical perspective. He has written a book and several articles on the history of mass housing. His involvement with the domestic environment and especially with the interior of the home is based on a triangular perspective which combines spatial, historical and social considerations. Barbey is also an active consultant in the historical conservation of buildings. He is the chief editor of a series of publications on Swiss architectural heritage. He is also the chairman of IAPS, the International Association for the Study of People and their Physical Surroundings.

YVONNE BERNARD is head of the team of researchers on Culture and Environment in the Institut d'Esthetique et des Sciences de l'Art of the C.N.R.S. (National Council for Scientific Research) in Paris. In 1984 she was awarded the title of Doctor in Human Sciences by the University of Paris X-Nanterre. Her research interests include the psychology of art and environmental psychology.

MIRILIA BONNES is research scientist in the Istituto di Psicologia of the C.N.R. (National Research Council) in Rome and Professor in Social Psychology at the University of Rome. She has been publishing on environmental psychology since 1970. Her work has focused mainly on environmental cognition and perception. She is presently co-ordinator of the Environmental Perception Group of the MAB (Man and Biosphere) UNESCO research Programme n.11 on the city of Rome.

DAVID CANTER is Professor of Applied Psychology at the University of Surrey where he also directs the postgraduate programme in Environmental Psychology. He started his research career in the School of Architecture at the University of Strathclyde, in Glasgow, after completing a Ph.D. in Psychology at Liverpool University. Since then he has published 10 books and over 100 papers on various aspects of the interplay between people and their physical surroundings. These publications have benefited considerably from collaboration with dozens of students and colleagues who are now professionally active throughout the world and from lectures and extended visits he has been able to make throughout Europe, Asia, North and South America. He is managing editor of the <u>Journal of Environmental Psychology</u> and appears fom time to time on British TV and radio discussing environmental matters.

He has a particular interest in the development of richer theories of action/place studies that utilise the insights of social and phenomenological approaches in combination with the scientific advantages of facet meta-theory and has published widely on these themes. He sees this as the most powerful theoretical basis for a discipline that can be effectively applied. In 1978 he established the environmental and behavioural design consultants, Interlogos Ltd that has worked for a number of major organisations including British Leyland and United Biscuits as well as for British government departments. He currently is funded by a number of international companies to develop his work on human behaviour in emergencies to examine safety motivation in industry.

BOYOWA ANTHONY CHOKOR is a Lecturer in the Department of Geography and Regional Planning, University of Benin, Nigeria, where he teaches Environmental Cognition, Urban Geography and Planning at both undergraduate and postgraduate M.Sc. and Ph.D. levels. Previously, he taught at the University of Calabar, Nigeria before obtaining his Ph.D. at University College, London (University of London), specialising in Environmental Perception, Planning and Landscape Evaluation. He has recently published a number of papers on the theme of Environment - behaviour - design and has been at the forefront in advocating a more critical humanistic geographical orientation for developing countries. His current research aims to clarify the cultural, social meanings and symbolic qualities of houses and neighbourhoods in the African urban context for planning and re-development purposes.

M. VITTORIA GIULIANI is research scientist in the Istituto di Psicologia of the C.N.R. (National Research Council). She holds a degree in Philosophy from the University of Rome. As a research assistant in the Centro di Cibernetica e di Attivita Linguistiche in the University of Milan she carried out studies in semantics and psycholinguistics. In 1973 she joined the Istituto di Psicologia where she began her research in environmental psychology. Her interests are focused mainly on affects and values associated with environmental representations.

LINDA N GROAT is Assistant Professor in the Department of Architecture, University of Wisconsin-Milwaukee where she teaches environment-behavior studies, design theory, and studio courses. She received her MFA in design from California Institute of Arts and her M.Sc. and Ph.D. in Environmental Psychology from the University of Surrey.

She has worked for architecture firms in the San Francisco Bay Area, both as a designer and as a design research consultant. Her design work has received recognition in the form of design awards and publications in the architectural press.

Since joining the faculty at UWM, the primary focus of her work has been the investigation of meaning in contemporary architecture through the use of empirical methodologies. In addition to the study of contextual compatibility which is reported in this book, her other recent research includes a study of the perceived meanings in Modern and Post-Modern architecture. Both of these empirically-based studies have been reported in the professional architectural journals. She has also written a variety of theoretically-based articles on the relationship between architectural theory and environmental psychology.

PAUL HARRIES and STEPHEN PURDEN are architectural practitioners; each of them has carried out postgraduate work in the fields of the professional ideology of architects and of space usage.

ANTHONY KING: studied history, education and sociology at the Universities of Sheffield, Manchester, S. Carolina, Washington and London. Lived and worked for five years in India as Visiting Professor, Department of Humanities and Social Sciences, Indian Institute of Technology, Delhi. Research and teaching over the last few years (in departments of history, sociology, building, planning, architecture, urban design) has principally been concerned with understanding the way in which, on one hand, built environments are socially produced and, on the other, the influence they have on the societies which produced them. Currently teaching at the Development Planning Unit, Bartlett School of Architecture and Planning, University College, London; the Architectural Association, London, and Brunel, the University of West London where he is Associate Senior Research Fellow.

PERLA KOROSEC-SERFATY is Associate Professor of Psychology at the Universite Louis Pasteur, Strasbourg, France. She holds academic degrees in both Philosophy and psychology and her second Doctorate (Doctorat d'Etat) is in Sociology from the Sorbonne-Rene Descartes University. Her main interests and publications concern the social use of space, the contemporary modes of appropriation of public spaces, the social historical approach of public life and sociability and the phenomenology of dwelling.

KLAUS LANDWEHR, Dipl.-Psych., received his degrees in psychology from the University of Bonn and is currently teaching at the University of Bielefeld (F.R.G.). He read papers at the most recent IAPS and EDRA meetings, at the International Congress of Psychology 1984, at various meetings of experimental psychologists, and also at the International Wittgenstein Symposia of philosophers. This reflects well his interest in both applied research as well as in theoretical and methodological issues. Klaus Landwehr is a proponent of the ecological approach to the study of perception and action in the sense of the late James J Gibson. Current research is on conditions of visually perceiving specifics of surface quality of different materials, on the coordination of locomotion with respect to specifics of ground surface layout, and on the prediction of aesthetic preference in terms of objective attributes of the "ambient optic array".

ALAN LIPMAN holds the Personal Chair in the Welsh School of Architecture, University of Wales Institute of Science and Technology. HOWARD HARRIS is Senior Lecturer in the School of History and Theory of Art and Design, South Glamorgan Institute of Higher Education.

They have jointly written some two dozen papers; in the main, these comprise polemical discussion of theory and method in social studies and in architecture. Direction: socialist humanism. Philosophy: historical materialism.

CATHERINE MOUGENOT. Sociologist (Catholic University of Louvain - 1973), Doctor of Environmental Sciences (Fondation Universitaire Luxembourgeoise, Arlon - 1981); researcher and lecturer in 'social environmental studies' at the Fondation Universitaire Luxembourgeoise, Arlon, Belgium.

At present, she is involved in research into the development of state housing policy and its impact on rural areas in Belgium. The basis for this research is to analyse the relationship between on the one hand concrete achievements and their spatial distribution, and on the other, the changing ways in which institutions think and act.

ARISTIE PAPADOPOULOU. Architect, Dipl. Ing, since 1975 from Aristotle University of Thessaloniki. Research and teaching collaborator in the Laboratory of Design and Industrial Aesthetics from 1976, and recently in the Department of Architectural Design and Architectural Technology, School of Architecture, Faculty of Technology, of the same university. DEA of philosophy from University of Paris I (Sorbonne) 1980.

She is interested in the theory of architecture, and architectural design. In particular, her theoretical research refers to the process of production of architectural form, and her speculations are in the same direction with current formulations and philosophy and criticisms of scientific, aesthetic, and architectural theories. The intention is to apply theoretical results in design, and particularly in small scale projects where intervention aims at the renovation of the city image. These projects are carried out preferably in the academic framework and with the co-operation of students of architecture.

RENA PAPAGEORGIOU-SEFERTZI. Architect, Dipl. Ing. since 1970 from Aristotle University of Thessaloniki. Research and teaching collaborator in the Laboratory of Design and Industrial Aesthetics of the same university from 1971. 1978-1980, postgraduate student at the University of Surrey, M.Sc. degree in Environmental Psychology, 1980. Currently, permanent lecturer in the Department of Architectural Design and Architectural Technology, School of Architecture, Faculty of Technology of Aristotle University of Thessaloniki.

Architectural design and theory of architecture have been and remain persistent research interests during all these years though their perspective varies. (aesthetic, design methods, environmental psychological approach, epistemological approach). Most previous studies refer to educational environments and their users and are empirical in approach. Recent work stands criticial towards empiricism and its theoretical presupositions and applies a marxist perspective. The objective is on the one hand to overcome difficulties which arise because of the general, holistic character of this perspective by specifying research on the production of the architectural form, and on the other to apply theoretical findings in architectural design.

ARIE PELED is a practicing architect and holds a Ph.D. in Environmental Psychology. At the Ecoanalysis Laboratory, which he founded a decade ago at the Faculty of Architecture, Israel Institute of Technology, individuals and groups are provided with a variety of techniques such as: Repertory Grids, Location Tasks and Design Exercises, for exploring and analysing their experience of situations/places. Teachers, office workers, residents and others, explore their experience of schools, office spaces, homes, - analysing the essences of their relations and the part played by spatial aspects in generating these essences.

His theoretical interests lay in expanding psychological existential/phenomenological approaches to the analysis of the experience of the spatiality of places. Ecoanalytic research and workshops, focus on the part played by the spatial in generating the creative quality, the alienation and possible enrichment of the person/place dialogue.

PETER F SMITH. Since 1961 Peter Smith has been developing theories concerned with human reactions to various types of architecture and urbanism. The progress of the research is mapped by four books: Third Millennium Churches, The Dynamics of Urbanism, The Syntax of Cities and Architecture and the Human Dimension. The present paper is a condensed portion of a recently completed book The Dynamics of Harmony.

He is Head of Architecture and Landscape at Leeds Polytechnic and principal of the architectural and town planning practice of Ferguson Smith and Associates.

ROSS THORNE was trained as an architect, and after a few years in practice was invited to join the staff of the Department of Architecture, University of Sydney. He became interested in building evaluation in 1969, working on a cross-cultural research project with David Canter in 1970. Together with three psychologists he formed the Architectural Psychology Research Unit at the University of Sydney, then was appointed in 1976 to the Directorship of the small, independently funded Ian Buchan Fell Research Centre within the Faculty of Architecture. The field of research which concerns the Centre is housing, and since his taking up this last position the direction has been towards assessing attitudes to different types of housing, housing preference and evaluation of the elderly in high-rise purpose-built housing. Associate Professor Thorne is currently chairman of the association for People and Physical Environment Research (PAPER).

KLAUS PETER WALCHER is Associate Professor of Psychology at the University of Oldenburg (FRG), where he joined the Institute for Research on Man-Environment Relations in 1984. He holds academic degrees in psychology, physiology and zoology. His main interest is focused on the analysis of consciousness. Starting from experimental studies on problem solving and visualisation, this approach has been extended into the study of environmental cognition.

Index

For Product Safety Concerns and Information please contact our EU
representative GPSR@taylorandfrancis.com
Taylor & Francis Verlag GmbH, Kaufingerstraße 24, 80331 München, Germany

www.ingramcontent.com/pod-product-compliance
Lightning Source LLC
Chambersburg PA
CBHW070557270326
41926CB00013B/2341

9 781032 816227